murach's
React

Mary Delamater
Scott McCoy

MIKE MURACH & ASSOCIATES, INC.

3730 W Swift Ave. • Fresno, CA 93722
www.murach.com • murachbooks@murach.com

Editorial team

Authors: Mary Delamater
                    Scott McCoy

Editor: Joel Murach

Production: Juliette Baylon

Murach also has books on these subjects:

AI-assisted programming

AI-Assisted Programming with Copilot

Web development

HTML/CSS
JavaScript
JavaScript and jQuery
PHP and MySQL
ASP.NET Core MVC

Programming languages

Python
Java
C#
C++

Databases

MySQL
SQL Server
Oracle

Data science

Python for Data Science
R for Data Analysis

For more on Murach books, please visit us at www.murach.com

10 9 8 7 6 5 4 3 2 1
ISBN: 978-1-943873-25-8

Contents

Contents

Expanded contents

Section 1 Get started fast

Introduction

React was released by Facebook in May 2013. Although initial adoption
was slow, React became one of the most popular libraries for front-end web
development by 2018. Today, React continues to be one of the most popular
front-end development libraries, especially for large apps with complex user
interfaces. These days, a quick search of job postings shows that it's currently
one of the most in-demand skills for web developers.

Who this book is for

This book is for anyone who wants to learn how to use React to develop user
interfaces for web apps. That includes anyone who wants to use React to
develop a single-page app (SPA) or an app that gets its data from a web API.

Developing a React app requires writing HTML, CSS, and JavaScript. Because
of that, the prerequisites for this book are a basic understanding of these
subjects. So, if you're a student who has taken a course in HTML/CSS and a
course in JavaScript, you have the prerequisite skills for this book.

In case your JavaScript skills are rusty, this book reviews some JavaScript
skills and expands on others. For example, chapter 2 explains how functional
programming works in JavaScript and how it's typically used in React apps.
Similarly, chapter 12 shows how to add static typing to a React app by using a
superset of JavaScript known as TypeScript.

Recommended software

To work with React, we recommend installing VS Code (Visual Studio Code)
and using it as your integrated development environment (IDE) as shown in
this book. In addition, you need to install Node.js and use it as shown in this
book.

Once you install VS Code and Node.js, we recommend getting started with
React apps by using Vite. That's because Vite provides a fast and modern build
toolchain and development server. Later, if you want your production apps to
use server-side rendering (SSR), you can convert them to Next.js as shown by
the last chapter in this book.

The downloadable files

You can download all the files for this book from our website as described in chapter 1. These files include the code for the apps presented throughout this book. This makes it easy for you to review this code, to run it, and to experiment with it.

In addition, the download includes the starting points for the exercises at the end of each chapter as well as the solutions to those exercises. That way, you can do the exercises on your own. Then, you can use the exercise solutions to check your work. Or, if you get stuck, you can use the exercise solutions to overcome any learning roadblocks.

Please send us your thoughts

When we started this book, our goal was to make it as easy as possible for you to get started with React. Now, we hope we have succeeded, and we wish you all the best with developing React apps. If you have any comments, we would love to hear from you. We're always interested in what you have to say about our books, and we always do our best to use your feedback to improve future editions.

Thanks!

Joel Murach

Joel Murach
Editor

Section 1

Get started fast

React is a JavaScript library that focuses on building the user interface (UI) of web-based applications. React helps you build highly responsive web applications that can feel as seamless as desktop applications.

This section gets you off to a fast start with React. Since the chapters in this section build on each other, you should read them in sequence. When you finish these chapters, you should have the basic skills you need to develop and debug realistic React apps. After that, you can skip to any of the chapters in section 2.

Chapter 1

Create your first React app

React is a JavaScript library that developers at Meta (formerly Facebook) created internally in 2011 to address problems they encountered when using plain JavaScript to build and maintain a large, dynamic web application. In 2013, they released React to the public.

This chapter starts by explaining how a React app is different than a plain JavaScript app. Then, it shows how to set up your computer for this book and how to create a new React app. After that, this chapter finishes by presenting a simple but realistic React app. When you complete this chapter, you'll be able to create simple React apps of your own!

React compared to JavaScript

This section explains the differences between a React app and a plain JavaScript app (sometimes called a *vanilla JavaScript app*). This explanation should help you understand some of the problems that React is designed to solve.

In this chapter, the text shows where CSS files are typically located. However, it doesn't show the CSS that's stored in these files because it's just simple CSS that you might see in any web app. If you want to view this CSS, all of these CSS files are available in the download for this book.

The Hello app

To compare plain JavaScript with React, this chapter presents two versions of the Hello app, one written in plain JavaScript and the other created with React. To keep things simple, this app consists of just one input field, one button, and a <p> element that displays a message. This isn't a dynamic, UI-rich web app that React works best for, but it works well for demonstration purposes.

The Hello app accepts a name from the user in the input field. Then, when the user clicks the button, it displays a "Hello!" message for that name in the <p> element. The following screen shows how it looks when displayed in a browser.

The Hello app in a browser

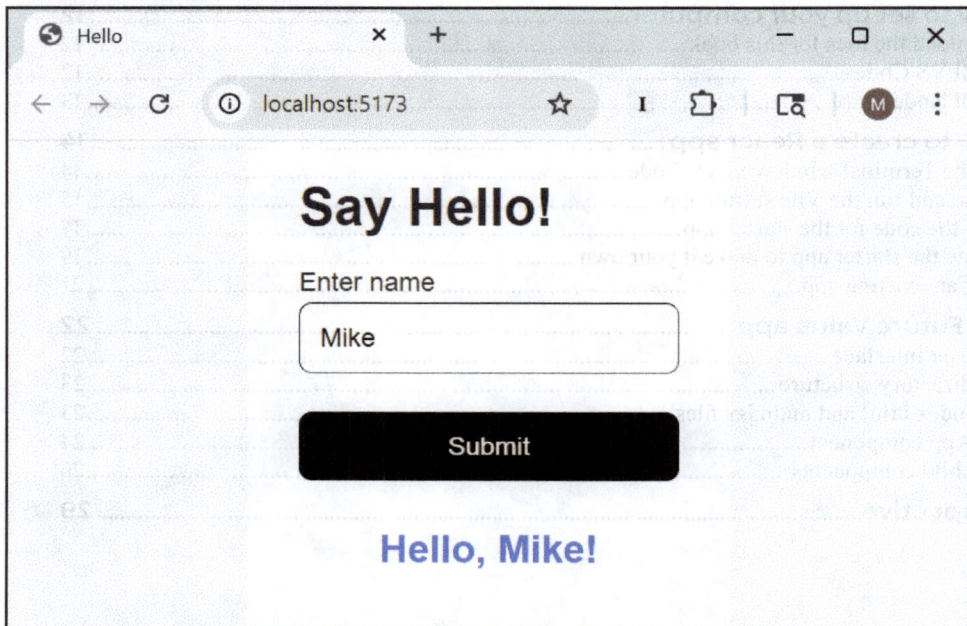

A JavaScript app is organized by file

A plain JavaScript app is usually organized by file. For example, the plain JavaScript version of the Hello app uses the following directory structure.

The directory structure of the plain JavaScript app

```
hello-plain/
├── index.html
├── scripts/
│   └── scripts.js
└── styles/
    ├── main.css
    └── form.css
```

One benefit of this structure is that it provides for a *separation of concerns*. For example, web designers can work on the HTML and CSS files while programmers work on the JavaScript files.

One drawback of this structure is that you might have to edit files in three different places to make a single change to the UI. Another drawback is that developers working on different parts of the UI might try to access the same file simultaneously.

A React app is organized by component

A React app, by contrast, separates concerns by component instead of by file. In React, a *component* contains the HTML (sort of – more on that in a minute), CSS, and JavaScript for a part of the UI. For example, the React version of the Hello app uses the following directory structure.

The directory structure of the React app

```
hello-react
├── index.html
└── src
    ├── App.css
    ├── App.jsx
    ├── index.css
    ├── main.jsx
    └── components
        ├── HelloDisplay.css
        ├── HelloDisplay.jsx
        ├── HelloForm.css
        └── HelloForm.jsx
```

The index.html file is in the root directory, but everything else is in the src (short for "source") directory. The files with .jsx extensions are React components.

The main component sets up the website to use React, while the App component builds the React app.

The index.css file stores the CSS that applies to the website as a whole, such as theme and global styles. This CSS file is co-located with the main component.

Similarly, the App.css file stores the CSS that applies to the React app itself. This CSS file is co-located with the App component. Co-locating the CSS with the components they style is a React pattern. It keeps the HTML, CSS, and JavaScript for a component in one place, which makes the component easier to maintain.

The components subdirectory in the src directory is organized similarly. It has two components that contain the main functionality of the app. The HelloForm component displays the input field and the button, while the HelloDisplay component displays a message in a <p> element.

As before, the CSS files that style the two components are co-located with them. Again, this keeps the HTML, CSS, and JavaScript for each component in one place, which makes them easier to maintain.

The App component uses the HelloForm and HelloDisplay components to build, or compose, the React app. It also coordinates the state of these components.

Organizing an App by component makes it easy to modify a component. For example, if you decide that the HelloDisplay component isn't working the way you want, you can modify that component by editing its JSX and CSS files. When you're working on a large app, that makes it easy to work on a specific part of an app.

JavaScript code is imperative

The code in a plain JavaScript file is *imperative*, which means that it gives step-by-step instructions to the browser, telling it how to interact with the HTML elements in the DOM (Document Object Model).

The index.html file in the plain JavaScript version of the Hello app contains the following HTML.

The index.html file of the plain JavaScript app

```
<!DOCTYPE html>
<html lang="en">
<head>
    <meta charset="UTF-8">
    <meta name="viewport" content="width=device-width, initial-scale=1.0">
    <link rel="stylesheet" href="styles/main.css">
    <link rel="stylesheet" href="styles/form.css">
    <title>Hello</title>
</head>
<body>
    <div class="app">
        <h1>Say Hello!</h1>
        <form>
```

```
        <div>
            <label for="name">Enter name</label>
            <input type="text" id="name" name="name" autofocus />
        </div>

        <div>
            <button type="submit">Submit</button>
        </div>
    </form>

    <div class="hello-display">
        <p id="msg"></p>
    </div>
</div>
<script src="scripts/scripts.js"></script>
</body>
</html>
```

This HTML defines the elements of the app including a <form> element that includes a label, text field, and button. It also defines a <div> element that's used to display the message.

The script.js file in the plain JavaScript version of the Hello app contains the following code.

The script.js file of the plain JavaScript app

```
document.addEventListener("DOMContentLoaded", () => {

    // get the DOM node for the form
    const form = document.querySelector('form');

    // add an event listener for the submit event of the form
    form.addEventListener('submit', (e) => {
        // prevent default form submission
        e.preventDefault();

        // get the element to display the message
        const msg = document.querySelector('#msg');

        // retrieve and validate user input
        const name = document.querySelector('#name').value;
        if (name === "") {
            // display the error message
            msg.classList.add('error');
            msg.textContent = "Please enter a name";
        } else {
            // display the message
            msg.classList.remove('error');
            msg.textContent = `Hello, ${name}!`;
        }
    });
});
```

This JavaScript provides instructions to the browser on how to interact with the HTML elements. To start, it tells the browser to attach an event listener for the

DOMContentLoaded event. Within that event listener, it tells the browser to get the <form> element and attach an event listener for the submit event of the form.

Within the submit event listener, the JavaScript tells the browser to prevent the form submission, get the element with an id of "msg", and get the value of the element with the id "name". Finally, it tells the browser to set the text of the msg element to either an error message or a welcome message, depending on the value of name.

React code is declarative

In a React app, by contrast, you *declare* what you want the state of the app to be under certain conditions and what the UI should look like based on that state. This is known as writing *declarative code*. Then, React determines how best to do it, and issues the imperative instructions to the browser behind the scenes.

The index.html file for the React app contains the following HTML.

The index.html file of the React app

```
<!doctype html>
<html lang="en">
    <head>
        <meta charset="UTF-8" />
        <meta name="viewport" content="width=device-width, initial-scale=1.0" />
        <title>Hello</title>
    </head>
    <body>
        <div id="root"></div>
        <script type="module" src="/src/main.jsx"></script>
    </body>
</html>
```

This file doesn't contain any of the HTML for the React app. Instead, it only contains a <div> element with an id of "root". This is where React renders the App component stored in the App.jsx file shown next.

The App.jsx file

```
import { useState } from 'react';

import HelloForm from './components/HelloForm';
import HelloDisplay from './components/HelloDisplay';
import './App.css';

const App = () => {
    // state variables and setter functions
    const [name, setName] = useState('');
    const [msg, setMsg] = useState('');
    const [errorMsg, setErrorMsg] = useState('');
```

```
    // event handler for form submission
    const handleSubmit = () => {
        // clear previous messages
        setMsg('');
        setErrorMsg('');

        // validate input and set messages accordingly
        if (name === "") {
            setErrorMsg("Please enter a name");
        } else {
            setMsg(`Hello, ${name}!`);
        }
    };

    // event handler for input field change
    const handleNameChange = (e) => setName(e.target.value);

    return (
        <div class="container">
            <h1>Say Hello!</h1>
            <HelloForm
              name={name}
              onNameChange={handleNameChange}
              onSubmit={handleSubmit}
            />
            <HelloDisplay
              msg={msg}
              errorMsg={errorMsg}
            />
        </div>
    )
};

export default App;
```

The code in the App.jsx file is a JavaScript module that exports a function named App that defines a React component.

The App component includes both the JavaScript and what appears to be the HTML for the React app. Actually, though, it's all JavaScript. The code in the return statement that looks like HTML is *JSX*, which is a *JavaScript syntax extension*. JSX lets you write JavaScript that looks like HTML. You use JSX to make declarations about what React should do. Then, when React builds the app, it converts the JSX to JavaScript instructions that update the DOM.

The App component defines state variables and setter functions by calling the useState() function. This function returns an array with two elements: a variable and a setter function that updates that variable.

After defining the state for the app, the component defines event handler functions for events that fire when the form submits and when the text in the input field changes. These event handlers don't issue instructions to the browser. Instead, they use the setter functions to update the state of the component. Then, when the state changes, React sends instructions to update the browser.

In the JSX, the App component declares how React should use the state and event handlers it defined. To do that, it uses *JSX component syntax* to create *JSX elements* (also known as *JSX component tags*), and it passes state variables and event handlers to the attributes of those elements.

Specifically, the JSX tells React to use the HelloForm component to show the input field for the name and to call the handleSubmit and handleNameChange event handlers when needed. And it tells React to use the HelloDisplay component to display the message or error message. But it doesn't tell the browser how to do this, and neither do the components it uses. React handles that. In other words, you tell React *what* to do, and it figures out *how* to do it.

The code for the HelloForm component is stored in the following JSX file.

The HelloForm.jsx file

```jsx
import './HelloForm.css';

const HelloForm = ({name, onNameChange, onSubmit}) => {
    const handleSubmit = (e) => {
        e.preventDefault();    // prevent default form submission
        onSubmit();            // call the function passed by the parent
    };

    return (
        <form onSubmit={handleSubmit}>
            <div>
                <label htmlFor="name">Enter name</label>
                <input type="text" id="name" name="name"
                    value={name}
                    onChange={onNameChange}
                    autoFocus
                />
            </div>
            <div>
                <button type="submit">Submit</button>
            </div>
        </form>
    );
};

export default HelloForm;
```

This code begins by defining an event handler that prevents the default form submission and calls the function passed to the onSubmit prop. Then, it uses JSX to define the elements of the form.

The code for the HelloDisplay component is stored in the following JSX file.

The HelloDisplay.jsx file

```jsx
import './HelloDisplay.css';

const HelloDisplay = ({msg, errorMsg}) => (
    <div className="hello-display">
        <p className={errorMsg ? 'error' : ''}>
            {errorMsg ? errorMsg : msg}
        </p>
    </div>
);

export default HelloDisplay;
```

If the errorMsg variable contains text, this code adds the error class to the <p> element and displays the error message. Otherwise, it removes the error class from the <p> element and displays the welcome message.

React code does not access the DOM directly

As described earlier, React interacts with the DOM for you. When working on an app, you define the state and what the UI should look like based on that state, and React handles the details. For example, you declare what function should run when a button is clicked, and React attaches that function as an event handler. Or, you declare a state variable and connect it to a field via JSX, and React updates the state when the field changes and re-renders that part of the UI when needed.

This helps you avoid writing boilerplate DOM manipulation code, which is nice. However, the real power of React lies in *how* it interacts with the DOM.

When your app initially renders, React builds a *virtual DOM*. This is a lightweight, in-memory representation of the actual DOM. Then, when a change in the app's state triggers a re-render, React builds a new virtual DOM that reflects the updated UI. Next, React runs a *diffing algorithm* that compares the new virtual DOM to the old one to figure out what changed. Finally, it updates only the changed parts of the real DOM. If nothing changed, it makes no updates at all. The following list summarizes these steps.

How React uses a virtual DOM to update the DOM

1. React creates a virtual DOM.
2. A change in the app's state triggers a re-render.
3. React creates a new virtual DOM.
4. React compares the old and new virtual DOMs to determine what has changed.
5. React updates what has changed in the browser's DOM.

You might think that all this work could slow your app down, but it actually makes it faster. That's because code that manipulates the actual DOM is significantly slower than code that manipulates an in-memory virtual DOM. In a web app with lots of DOM interaction, this can make a big difference in performance.

How to set up your computer

Now that you know some important terms and concepts about React, you're ready to set up your computer for this book so you can start creating some React apps. That includes installing Visual Studio Code (VS Code), an IDE that's optimal for working with React. In addition, it includes installing Node.js and its package manager, npm.

Download the files for this book

The download for this book includes files for the apps the book presents as well as for the exercises at the end of each chapter. As a result, if you want to view or run these apps or do the exercises, you should download these files as shown next.

How to download the files for this book

1. Go to www.murach.com and find the page for this book.
2. Scroll down to the "FREE downloads" tab and click it.
3. Click the Download Now button for the zip file. This should download a zip file.
4. Double-click the zip file. This should create a folder named react.
5. Move the react folder to the correct folder. We recommend putting it in a folder named murach within your Documents folder, but you can put it wherever you like.

Install VS Code

To work with React, you can use a text editor or an IDE (Integrated Development Environment). There are many options available to you, but this book shows how to use VS Code. As a result, if you want to follow along with this book, you can install VS Code as described next.

How to install VS Code

1. Download the installer file from https://code.visualstudio.com/download.
2. Double-click the installer file. This should run the installer program.
3. Respond to the resulting dialogs. You can accept the default options.

VS Code can be used to write code in most languages including HTML, CSS, and JavaScript. In addition, it includes an integrated terminal that allows you to access the command line on your operating system. As a result, it's a great IDE for developing React apps.

Install Node.js

Node.js is an open-source, cross-platform, runtime environment that executes JavaScript code outside a web browser. When you install it, it includes *npm (Node Package Manager)*, a package manager for the JavaScript programming language that's commonly used when working with React. Since Node.js may already be installed on your system, you can start by checking whether it's already installed as shown next.

How to check whether Node.js is installed

1. Start VS Code.
2. Display the Terminal window by selecting View ▶ Terminal or by pressing Ctrl+` or Cmd+`.
3. Type "node -v" at the end of the command line and press Enter.

A node command that checks whether Node.js is installed

```
>node -v
v22.15.0
```

If this node command displays a version number as shown here, Node.js is already installed. If it doesn't, you can install Node.js as shown next.

How to install Node.js

1. Go to the download page for Node.js. One way to find this page is to search the internet for "node.js download".
2. Click the button for the installer file for the most current LTS (Long Term Support) release and respond to the resulting dialogs.
3. If you get any warning dialogs, choose to continue with the installation. This should download the installer file to your computer.
4. Double-click the installer file to start the installer.
5. Respond to the resulting dialogs by accepting the default options.

After installing Node.js, you can run the "node -v" command again to make sure Node.js installed correctly.

How to create a React app

Now that you have your computer set up, you're ready to develop your first React app. To start, this section reviews some skills for using the Terminal window in VS Code when working with React apps.

Use the Terminal window in VS Code

To work with Node.js and npm, you need to enter commands in a *command-line interface (CLI)*. To do that, you could use the Command Prompt in Windows or Terminal in macOS. However, if you're using VS Code, it's usually easier to use the integrated Terminal window, which works equally well for both Windows and macOS.

Once you've started VS Code, you can use either of the following techniques to open the Terminal window.

Two ways to open the Terminal window

- Select View→Terminal from the menus
- Press Ctrl+` (backtick) or Cmd+` (backtick)

When you first open the Terminal window, it displays a Terminal session that displays the current directory followed by a > symbol. To change the directory, you can use VS Code to open a different folder. Or, you can enter a cd (change directory) command after the > symbol followed by the path of the directory as shown next.

Change the directory

```
>cd /murach/react
```

Since this command starts with a front slash, it navigates to the root directory for the current drive. This allows you to specify the complete path for any directory on the current drive.

If you want to navigate relative to the current directory, you can do that too. For example, to navigate down one level, you can enter the cd command followed by the name of the directory.

Navigate down one level

```
>cd apps
```

Or, to navigate up one level, you can enter the cd command followed by two dots.

Navigate up one level

```
>cd ..
```

If any directory in the path has spaces or other forbidden characters in its name, you can enclose the path in double quotes.

Navigate to a directory that has spaces in its name

```
>cd "apps/my first react app"
```

Once you navigate to the directory you want, you can run npm commands by typing npm followed by the command. For example, the following npm command lists all the installed packages in the current project.

An npm command to list installed packages

```
>npm list
```

When you're done with the Terminal window, you can close it. If you want to preserve your session, click the Hide button (X icon) in the upper right corner of the Terminal window. This hides the window but doesn't end the terminal session. Then, you can use the View→Terminal menu item or shortcut key to redisplay the terminal session in the Terminal window.

If you want to close the Terminal window and also end the terminal session, click the Kill button (trash can icon) to the left of the X icon.

Create and run the Vite starter app

Node Package Manager (npm) allows you to install and manage JavaScript packages in your project. This includes packages that are tools to create, or *scaffold*, React starter apps.

Node Package Manager provides two React scaffolding tools: *Create React App (CRA)* and *Vite* (pronounced "veet"). CRA was developed by the React team and was the standard for many years. Because of that, you'll often see it in online examples.

Recently, though, Vite has become the standard because it's faster than CRA and also easier to customize. As a result, this book shows how to use Vite.

To create a new React app using Vite, start VS Code and open the folder that you want to create the app in. Then, open a Terminal window and enter the following command.

Create the project in the current directory

```
>npm create vite@latest my-app
```

This uses the latest version of Vite to create a project in a subdirectory named my-app, but you can change my-app to any name that you want.

When you run this command, it asks a series of questions. To create a React app that uses JavaScript (not TypeScript), you can use the arrow keys to select the following answers.

The options for the create Vite command

```
◇   Select a framework: React
◇   Select a variant: JavaScript
◇   Use rolldown-vite (Experimental)?: No
◇   Install with npm and start now? No
```

To switch to the subdirectory for the project, you can use the following cd command to change the current directory to the project directory.

Navigate to the project directory

```
>cd my-app
```

After the current directory has been set correctly, you can use the following npm command to install all libraries that the project depends on, which are known as *dependencies*.

Install the dependencies

```
>npm install
```

This creates a subfolder in your project named node_modules to store the dependencies.

Once you install the dependencies, you can use the following npm command to start a development web server.

Start the development web server

```
>npm run dev
```

This runs the app on a development web server and displays a message in the Terminal window that includes the URL of the development web server.

The Terminal window with the URL of the development server

```
PROBLEMS    OUTPUT    DEBUG CONSOLE    TERMINAL    PORTS


  VITE v6.3.5  ready in 281 ms

  →  Local:   http://localhost:5173/
  →  Network: use --host to expose
  →  press h + enter to show help
▌
```

By default, Vite uses port 5173, but if for some reason that port isn't available, it tries the next available port. To run the web app, open a browser and navigate to the displayed URL. An easy way to do that is to hold down the Ctrl key and click on the URL. Then, your default web browser should display the Vite starter app shown next.

The Vite starter app displayed in a browser

To stop the development web server, click in the Terminal window and press Ctrl+C. To start the server again, enter the "npm run dev" command in the Terminal window. One easy way to do that is to press the up arrow key until the Terminal window displays the "npm run dev" command. Then, press Enter to run that command again.

View the code for the starter app

To get a better understanding of how React works, you can view the starting folders and files for the Vite starter app. In particular, you might want to take a closer look at the highlighted files shown next.

The starting folders and files

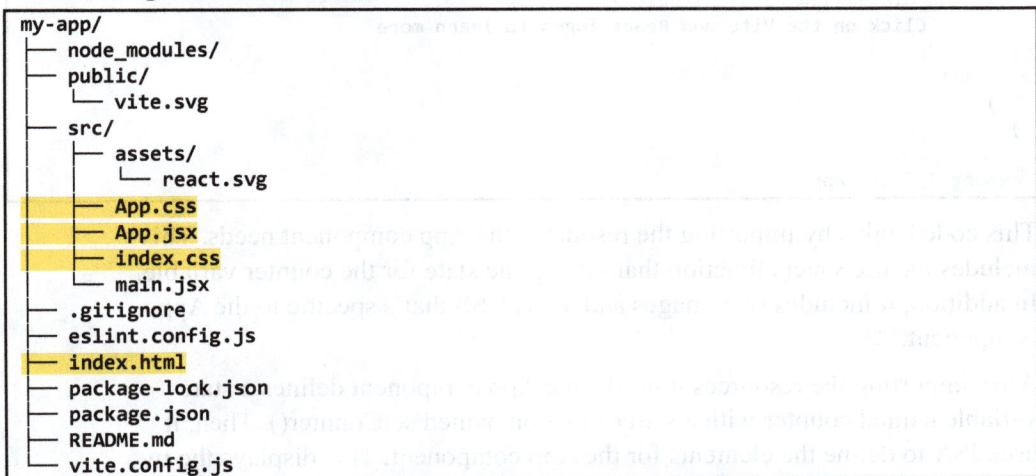

```
my-app/
├── node_modules/
├── public/
│   └── vite.svg
├── src/
│   ├── assets/
│   │   └── react.svg
│   ├── App.css
│   ├── App.jsx
│   ├── index.css
│   └── main.jsx
├── .gitignore
├── eslint.config.js
├── index.html
├── package-lock.json
├── package.json
├── README.md
└── vite.config.js
```

Of these files, the index.html contains the <title> element for the app, and the index.css file contains the CSS for the app. So, these files define a starting point for the app.

Then, the App.jsx and App.css files define and format the App component that contains most of the functionality for this app. To start, the App.jsx file contains the following code.

The App.jsx file

```jsx
import { useState } from 'react'
import reactLogo from './assets/react.svg'
import viteLogo from '/vite.svg'
import './App.css'

function App() {
  const [count, setCount] = useState(0)

  return (
    <>
      <div>
        <a href="https://vite.dev" target="_blank">
          <img src={viteLogo} className="logo" alt="Vite logo" />
        </a>
        <a href="https://react.dev" target="_blank">
          <img src={reactLogo} className="logo react" alt="React logo" />
        </a>
      </div>
      <h1>Vite + React</h1>
      <div className="card">
        <button onClick={() => setCount((count) => count + 1)}>
          count is {count}
        </button>
        <p>
          Edit <code>src/App.jsx</code> and save to test HMR
        </p>
      </div>
      <p className="read-the-docs">
        Click on the Vite and React logos to learn more
      </p>
    </>
  )
}

export default App
```

This code begins by importing the resources the App component needs. This includes the useState() function that sets up the state for the counter variable. In addition, it includes two images and some CSS that's specific to the App component.

After importing the resources it needs, the App component defines a state variable named counter with a setter function named setCounter(). Then, it uses JSX to define the elements for the App component. This displays the two images, a heading, a Counter button, and so on. For now, you don't need to understand the details of how this code works, but you should have a general idea of how it works.

As you review this code, you may notice that it doesn't include semicolons after its statements. Instead, it relies on *automatic semicolon insertion (ASI)*. In React apps (and JavaScript in general), it's more common to include semicolons after statements. That's because most popular style guides recommend using semicolons for clarity and to avoid potential issues with ASI. As a result, most of the code presented in this book includes semicolons after JavaScript statements.

Update the starter app to make it your own

Now that you have run the starter app and reviewed its code, you can change it to make it your own. For example, you can modify the index.html to set an appropriate title for your app, and you can modify the index.css file so it contains the starting CSS you want.

More importantly, you can modify the App component to compose and coordinate other components. To do that, you can add a components directory to hold your components and their CSS files. For example, to add two simple components that display a hello message and the current date, you can create a components directory and add files for two components as shown next.

A components directory with files for two components

```
my-app/
├── components/
│   ├── Hello.css
│   ├── Hello.jsx
│   ├── CurrentDate.css
│   └── CurrentDate.jsx
```

Both components include a CSS file located in the same directory.

The Hello component shown next displays a hello message.

The Hello component

```jsx
import './Hello.css';

const Hello = () => {
    return (
        <div className="hello">
            <h2>Hello, World!</h2>
            <p>Welcome to my React application!</p>
        </div>
    );
};

export default Hello;
```

To start, this code imports the CSS file for the component. Then, it defines an arrow function named Hello() that returns a <div> element, and it exports that function so it can be imported by other components.

The CurrentDate component shown next displays the current date.

The CurrentDate component

```
import './CurrentDate.css';

const CurrentDate = () => {
    const today = new Date();
    const formattedDate = today.toLocaleDateString();

    return (
        <div className="current-date">
            Today's Date: {formattedDate}
        </div>
    );
};

export default CurrentDate;
```

To start, this code imports the CSS file for the component. Then, it defines an arrow function named CurrentDate(), and it exports that function so it can be imported by other components. Within the function, the code uses JavaScript to get the current date. Then, it uses braces to embed the current date within the <div> element that the component returns.

After defining the Hello and CurrentDate components, you can update the App component to import and use those components as shown next.

The updated App component

```
import Hello from './components/Hello';
import CurrentDate from './components/CurrentDate';
import './App.css';

const App = () => {
    return (
        <>
            <h1>My React App</h1>
            <Hello />
            <CurrentDate />
        </>
    )
};

export default App;
```

To keep things simple, this App component doesn't define any state or event handlers. It just imports the components and uses them to build the UI.

As you make these changes to the app, the browser should automatically display them. When you're done, the browser should display the following app.

The updated app displayed in a browser

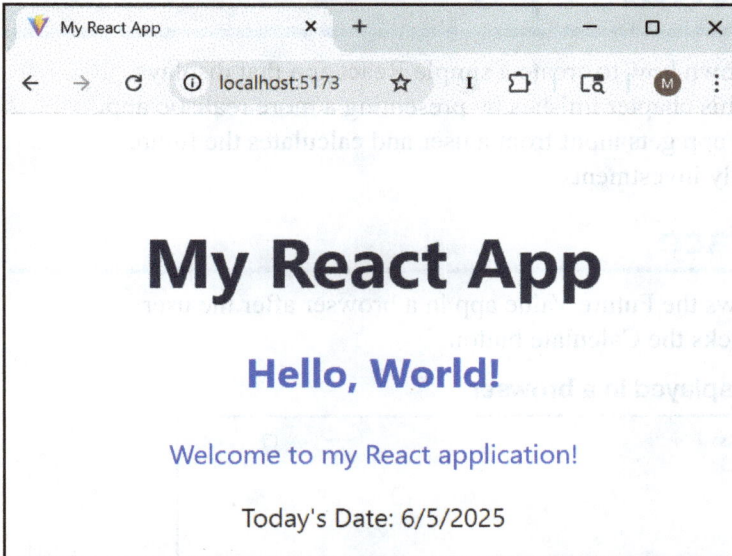

At this point, if you're not going to use the images for React and Vite that are in the public and assets directories, you can delete them.

Copy an existing app

Although it's easy to use a Vite template to create a new app, you can also use an existing app as your starting point. To do that, you can make a copy of an existing app as shown next.

How to copy and run a React app

1. In File Explorer (Windows) or Finder (macOS), copy the folder that contains the React app and paste it where you want it. This may take a while, especially if the dependencies for the app have been installed.
2. Rename the new folder to an appropriate name for the app.
3. Use VS Code to open the new folder. This should set the new folder as the current directory.
4. Open the Terminal window to display the command line.
5. Enter the "npm install" command to install the dependencies.
6. Enter the "npm run dev" command to run the development server.
7. Use a web browser to navigate to the URL for the development server.

By the way, you can use steps 3-7 to run the apps available from the download for this book. That is, you can use VS Code to open the app, you can enter the commands to install the dependencies and start the development server, and you can use a browser to navigate to the URL for the development server.

The Future Value app

So far, this chapter has shown how to create a simple React app that displays some information. Now, this chapter finishes by presenting a more realistic app named Future Value. This app gets input from a user and calculates the future value of a series of monthly investments.

The user interface

The following screen shows the Future Value app in a browser after the user enters valid values and clicks the Calculate button.

The Future Value app displayed in a browser

The UI consists of a <header> element and a <main> element. The <main> element contains text fields for a monthly investment, a number of years, and an interest rate. In addition, it includes a Calculate button and a <p> element that displays the result of the calculation below the button. Or, if the user enters invalid values, the app displays an error message in the <p> element.

The directory structure

The Future Value app uses the following directory structure.

The directory structure of the Future Value app

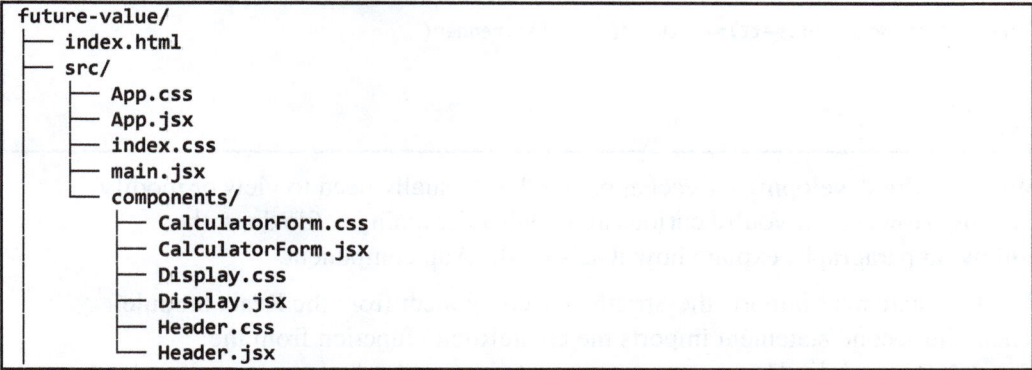

```
future-value/
├── index.html
├── src/
│      ├── App.css
│      ├── App.jsx
│      ├── index.css
│      ├── main.jsx
│      └── components/
│             ├── CalculatorForm.css
│             ├── CalculatorForm.jsx
│             ├── Display.css
│             ├── Display.jsx
│             ├── Header.css
│             └── Header.jsx
```

Here, the root directory contains the index.html file. Then, the src directory contains the main.jsx and index.css files as well as both files for the App component. Finally, the src/components directory contains three components that the App component uses.

The index.html and main.jsx files

The index.html file contains the <title> element that specifies the text to display in the browser tab. In addition, it contains a <div> element with an id of "root", which is where React renders the app.

The index.html file

```html
<!doctype html>
<html lang="en">
    <head>
        <meta charset="UTF-8" />
        <meta name="viewport" content="width=device-width, initial-scale=1.0" />
        <title>Future Value Calculator</title>
    </head>
    <body>
        <div id="root"></div>
        <script type="module" src="/src/main.jsx"></script>
    </body>
</html>
```

The index.html file also contains a <script> element that imports the main.jsx file.

The main.jsx file

```
import { StrictMode } from 'react';
import { createRoot } from 'react-dom/client';
import App from './App.jsx';
import './index.css';

createRoot(document.getElementById('root')).render(
    <StrictMode>
        <App />
    </StrictMode>
);
```

When you're developing a React app, you don't usually need to view or modify this file. However, if you're curious about what the main.jsx file does, the following paragraphs explain how it sets up the App component.

The first statement imports the StrictMode component from the React module. Then, the second statement imports the createRoot() function from the ReactDOM module. The next two statements import the App component and index.css files.

The StrictMode component only runs in development. It doesn't add anything to the display of the app, but it issues warnings if your React code does things it shouldn't.

The createRoot() function tells React where to display the app on the page. In this case, it tells React to display the app within the <div> element that has the id of "root". This returns the root object that React needs to render the app and track its state.

When you call the createRoot() function, it returns a root object. To start the app, this code calls the render() function from the root object and passes it the component to render. Here, the code passes the StrictMode component, which contains the App component. This tells React to render the App component in the "root" element, in strict mode.

The App component

The App.jsx file contains the App component. This component composes the app by rendering other components. In addition, it sets up and manages the state that's shared by the components that it renders.

The App component

```
import { useState } from 'react';

import Header from './components/Header';
import CalculatorForm from './components/CalculatorForm';
import Display from './components/Display';
import './App.css';
```

```
// helper function to calculate the future value
const calcFutureValue = (monthlyAmount, years, interestRate) => {
    let futureValue = 0;
    const months = years * 12;
    const monthlyRate = interestRate / 12 / 100;

    for (let i = 0; i < months; i++) {
        futureValue = (futureValue + monthlyAmount) * (1 + monthlyRate);
    }
    return futureValue;
};

const App = () => {
    // state variables to hold error message and future value
    const [errorMsg, setErrorMsg] = useState('');
    const [futureValue, setFutureValue] = useState(null);

    // event handler for form submission
    const handleSubmit = (numAmount, numYears, numRate) => {
        if (
            isNaN(numAmount) || isNaN(numYears) || isNaN(numRate) ||
            numAmount < 0 || numYears < 0 || numRate < 0
        ) {
            setErrorMsg("Please enter valid non-negative numbers.");
        } else {
            const fv = calcFutureValue(numAmount, numYears, numRate);
            setFutureValue(fv);
            setErrorMsg('');
        }
    };

    return (
        <>
            <Header />
            <main className="container">
                <CalculatorForm onSubmit={handleSubmit} />
                <Display value={futureValue} errorMsg={errorMsg} />
            </main>
        </>
    );
};

export default App;
```

To start, the App component imports the functions and components that it
needs. After that, it defines a helper function that calculates the future value.
Since this helper function doesn't interact with the UI, it makes sense to store it
outside of the function that defines the App component.

The function that defines the App component begins by setting up the state it
needs to manage, which is the state that's shared by the two components. This
consists of the future value that's calculated by the app and the error message.

After setting up state, the App component defines the event handler that's called
when the user submits the form. This event handler specifies three parameters

for the data entered by the user, which is provided by the CalculatorForm component. Then, the event handler validates the data it receives.

If any of the parameters aren't numbers or are less than zero, the data is invalid. In that case, the event handler sets the state variable for the error message. Otherwise, the code calculates the future value, sets the state variable for the future value, and sets the state variable for the error message to an empty string.

After defining the event handler, the App component returns the JSX that defines the UI for component. It starts with a React fragment, which is the <></> element. This is necessary because a React component must return a single element or a React fragment.

Within the React fragment, the JSX specifies the Header component, the <main> element, the CalculatorForm component, and the Display component. When it does this, it uses braces to assign the event handler to the onSubmit attribute of the CalculatorForm and to assign the two state variables to the value and errorMsg attributes of the Display component.

In the JSX, the <main> element contains the CalculatorForm and Display components. However, the <main> element isn't actually HTML. It's JSX, which is JavaScript code. That's why the <main> element uses the className attribute instead of the class attribute. This is necessary because class is a reserved word in JavaScript. As a result, JSX uses the className attribute, not the class attribute, to specify CSS classes.

The child components

The Future Value app uses three child components named Header, CalculatorForm, and Display. All three components have CSS files of the same name that they import. The CSS files are co-located in the components directory.

The Header component is the simplest of the three components.

The Header component

```
import './Header.css';

const Header = () => {
    return (
        <header className="header">
            <h1>Future Value Calculator</h1>
        </header>
    );
};

export default Header;
```

This component starts by importing its CSS file. Then, it exports some JSX that React uses to render a <header> element. This is a common way to handle headers, footers, sidebars, and so on.

The CalculatorForm component provides the text fields and the Calculate button of the Future Value app.

The CalculatorForm component

```
import { useState } from 'react';
import './CalculatorForm.css';

const CalculatorForm = ({ onSubmit }) => {
    // state variables for input fields
    const [amount, setAmount] = useState('');
    const [years, setYears] = useState('');
    const [rate, setRate] = useState('');

    // event handler for form submission
    const handleSubmit = (e) => {
        // prevent default form submission
        e.preventDefault();

        // convert input values from strings to numbers
        const numAmount = Number(amount);
        const numYears = Number(years);
        const numRate = Number(rate);

        // call the function sent from the parent
        onSubmit(numAmount, numYears, numRate);
    };

    return (
        <>
            <form onSubmit={handleSubmit}>
                <div>
                    <label htmlFor="amount">Monthly amount</label>
                    <input type="number" id="amount" name="amount"
                        value={amount}
                        onChange={(e) => setAmount(e.target.value)}
                        required autoFocus />
                </div>

                <div>
                    <label htmlFor="years">Number of years</label>
                    <input type="number" id="years" name="years"
                        value={years}
                        onChange={(e) => setYears(e.target.value)}
                        required />
                </div>

                <div>
                    <label htmlFor="rate">Interest rate</label>
                    <input type="number" id="rate" name="rate"
                        value={rate}
                        onChange={(e) => setRate(e.target.value)}
                        required />
```

```
                    </div>
                <div>
                    <button type="submit">Calculate</button>
                </div>
            </form>
        </>
    );
};

export default CalculatorForm;
```

The function that defines this component defines a parameter for a property, or *prop*, that's passed to it. This prop is named onSubmit, and it corresponds to the onSubmit attribute that's set in the JSX element in the parent component, the App component. This makes it possible for the App component to pass an event handler to the CalculatorForm component.

After defining its prop, this function defines the state for its three text fields. Then, it defines an event handler for the form submission. This event handler begins by preventing the default behavior of the form submission, which is to post to the server. This is necessary because this app is designed to process the data on the client, not to post the data to the server.

After cancelling the default behavior, the event handler continues by converting the three state variables for the user input from strings to numbers. Then, it calls the event handler in the onSubmit prop and passes the three numbers to that event handler.

After the event handler, this component returns JSX that specifies the text fields and button of the calculator form. For each field, it sets the value attribute to the state variable, and it sets the onChange attribute to a setter function that changes the state variable to the current value for the field. After that, React takes care of the rest.

This component codes the event handlers for the onChange attributes as inline functions. This is a common React pattern.

Once again, it's important to note that these components specify JSX, not HTML. That's why the <label> elements use the htmlFor attribute that's used by JSX, not the for attribute that's used by HTML. This is necessary because JavaScript reserves the for keyword for coding loops.

If the user enters valid data in the CalculateForm component, the Display component displays the result of the future value calculation. Otherwise, it displays an error message.

The Display component

```
import './Display.css';

// Helper function for currency formatting
const formatToCurrency = (value) => {
    return value.toLocaleString('en-US', {
        style: 'currency',
        currency: 'USD'
    });
}

const Display = ({ value, errorMsg }) => (
    <div className="display">
        {errorMsg && <div className="error">{errorMsg}</div>}
        {!errorMsg && value != null &&
            <div>Future Value: {formatToCurrency(value)}</div>}
    </div>
);

export default Display;
```

The Display component starts by defining a helper function that formats the future value as currency. Since this helper function doesn't interact with the UI, it's coded outside the Display component.

After the helper function, the Display component defines two props that correspond with two attributes set in the JSX element in the parent, the App component. Then, it returns its JSX.

Within the JSX, the code uses conditional statements to display the correct elements. If an error message exists, it returns a <div> element that displays the error message with a CSS class of error. If the error message doesn't exist but a future value does, it returns a <div> element that displays the future value. And if there's no error message or future value, such as when the app initially loads, it doesn't display anything.

Perspective

This chapter has presented the concepts and skills that you need to get started with creating React apps. At this point, you should be able to create some simple React apps of your own, even ones that process input from a user such as the Future Value app that's presented at the end of the chapter.

However, this chapter has moved fast. Because of that, you might not completely understand how to develop apps of your own. Also, there's a lot more to learn! That's why the rest of the chapters in this section review some of the skills presented here and expand on them.

Terms

vanilla JavaScript app

separation of concerns

React component

imperative code

declarative code

JSX (JavaScript syntax extension)

JSX component syntax

JSX elements

virtual DOM

diffing algorithm

Node.js

npm (Node Package Manager)

command-line interface (CLI)

scaffold

Create React App (CRA)

Vite

dependencies

automatic semicolon insertion (ASI)

prop

Exercise 1-1: Create and adjust a starter app

Create a Vite starter app

1. Start VS Code and open the ex_starts/ch01 folder.
2. Open a Terminal window and enter the command to Create a Vite app named my-vite-app.
3. Use the cd command to change the current directory to the my-vite-app directory.
4. Enter the commands to install the dependencies and start the development web server. Note the URL for the development web server.
5. Open a browser and navigate to the development web server.
6. Click the Counter button a few times to see how the app works.

Modify the code for the starter app

7. Open the index.html file and change the <title> element so it includes your name such as "Jake's React app".

8. Save your changes and switch to the browser to view the new title in the browser tab.

9. Open the App.jsx file in the src directory. Delete the imports for the Vite and React logos, the <div> that displays the logos, and the <p> elements that display the "Edit" and "click to learn more" messages.

10. Change the <h1> element to match the title that you entered earlier.

11. Save your changes and switch to the browser to view them.

Add a CountDisplay component

12. Add a components directory to src and add two files to it: CountDisplay.jsx and CountDisplay.css.

13. In CountDisplay.jsx, import CountDisplay.css.

14. Add an arrow function that defines the CountDisplay component like the one shown next.

```
const CountDisplay = ({ count }) => {
    return (
        <p>Current count: {count}</p>
    );
};
```

15. Add a className attribute (not a class attribute) to the <p> element so you can use a CSS class to style this <p> element.

16. In CountDisplay.css, add a style rule for that CSS class and use that rule to style the <p> element.

17. In CountDisplay.jsx, export the CountDisplay function as the default export.

18. In App, import CountDisplay and render it after the button. Then, assign the count state variable to the count attribute of CountDisplay.

19. Change the text of the button to no longer display the count state variable.

20. Save your changes and switch to the browser to view them.

Exercise 1-2: Refactor the Future Value app

Start from an existing app

1. Copy the future-value folder from the apps/ch01 folder to the ex_starts/ch01 folder.

2. Use VS Code to open the future-value folder that's in the ex_starts/ch01 folder.

3. Open a Terminal window. Note that it displays the future-value folder as the current directory.

4. Enter the commands to install the dependencies and start the development web server.

5. Use a browser to view the app.

6.   Enter valid data in the text fields and calculate a future value.

Add a Footer component

7.   Add Footer.jsx and Footer.css files to the components directory. You can use the Header.jsx and Header.css files as a guide.

8.   In Footer.jsx, add JavaScript that gets the current year. Since this doesn't affect the UI, place the code outside the component function.

9.   In the JSX for the Footer component, return a <footer> element that contains a <small> element. The text of the <small> element should be a copyright symbol (©), the current year, and the name of the app.

10. Modify the App.jsx file to import the Footer component and render it after the <main> element.

11. Save your changes and switch to the browser to view them.

Update the Header and Footer components to accept props

12. Modify the component functions for Header and Footer so they each accept a prop named appName.

13. Modify Header so it uses the appName prop for the text of the <h1> element.

14. Modify Footer so it uses the appName prop in the <small> element.

15. Modify App so it defines a variable named appName and passes it to both Header and Footer.

16. Save your changes and switch to the browser to view them. The app should look the same as before, but now it's easier to change the app name since it's only stored in one place.

Chapter 2

Master JavaScript for React

If you have a strong foundation in JavaScript and functional programming, you can probably skip or skim this chapter. Otherwise, you can use this chapter to master some JavaScript skills that are commonly used when working with React. In particular, most React apps makes extensive use of functional programming. In addition, they often make extensive use of the spread operator and ES6 modules.

An introduction to functional programming

Functional programming is a style of programming that evolved from the ideas introduced by lambda calculus in the 1930s. Today, functional programming is supported by many modern programming languages including JavaScript.

A review of arrow functions

When working with functional programming in React, it's common to use arrow functions. As a result, if you aren't already comfortable with arrow functions, you should take a moment to review how they work.

The following example illustrates a few key points about arrow functions. It shows three ways to code a simple arrow function that defines one parameter named prevCount and returns one value.

The same arrow function coded three ways

```
// Two statements
(prevCount) => {
    const newCount = prevCount + 1;
    return newCount;
}

// One statement - long format
(prevCount) => {
    return prevCount + 1;
}

// One statement - concise format
(prevCount) => prevCount + 1
```

Here, the first function uses two statements to increment the prevCount parameter by 1 and return the new value for the count. To do that, it uses braces around both statements, a return keyword, and semicolons at the end of each statement.

The second function uses a single statement to perform the same task. To do that, it doesn't define a constant named newCount. Instead, it codes the expression that updates the prevCount parameter as part of the return statement.

The third function removes the braces, the return keyword, and the semicolon and codes the entire function on one line. This is possible because braces and the return keyword aren't required when a function only contains one statement. In addition, when a function only contains one statement, it's a common practice to remove the semicolon that ends the statement. The following figure summarizes these rules and conventions.

If an arrow function only has a single return statement, you can…

- Omit the braces around the statement.
- Omit the return keyword that starts the statement.
- Omit the semicolon that ends the statement.

If an arrow function only has one parameter, the parentheses around the parameter are optional. However, this book usually includes parentheses around parameters, even when there's only one parameter. This maintains a consistent approach for all parameters and makes it easier to visually identify parameters when reading code.

How functional programming works

Although JavaScript works as a procedural language and an object-oriented language, it also supports functional programming. It does that by treating functions as first-class citizens. A function is a *first-class citizen* when you can use it anywhere you would use any other value in the programming language.

For example, you can assign a function to a constant as shown next.

Assign a function to a constant

```
const incrementCount = (prevCount) => prevCount + 1;
```

This example assigns an arrow function to a constant named incrementCount. This is a common pattern in React. However, it's also possible to use the let keyword to assign an arrow function to a variable.

In addition, you can pass a function to another function as shown next.

Pass a function to another function

```
setCount(incrementCount);
```

This code passes the function that's assigned to the incrementCount constant to the setCount() function that sets the count variable. As a result, the setCount() function increments the count variable by 1.

If you want, you can set a function as an event handler as shown next.

Set a function as an event handler

```
<button onClick={() => setCount(incrementCount)}>
```

This code assigns an arrow function to the onClick event of a button. This arrow function doesn't define any parameters and passes the incrementCount() function to the setCount() function. As a result, when the user clicks the button, React calls the arrow function. This is a common pattern in React.

If you want to code this event handler without using the incrementCount constant, you can code the function that increments the count variable within the setCount() function as shown next.

Set a function as an event handler without using a constant

```
<button onClick={() => setCount((prevCount) => prevCount + 1)}>
```

Now that you've seen some examples of how JavaScript treats functions as first-class citizens, here's a summary of how you can use JavaScript to work with functions.

In JavaScript, you can...

- Assign a function to a constant or a variable.
- Pass a function to another function as an argument.
- Return a function from another function.
- Assign a function to a data structure such as an array or object.

This chapter doesn't show how to return a function from another function or how to store a function in a data structure. However, these are common techniques, and you'll see some examples of them later in this book.

How pure functions work

When working with functional programming, it's a best practice to use pure functions. A *pure function* takes some input, processes it, and returns a result without causing a *side effect*, which is an operation that changes something outside of the function. Because of that, pure functions provide the following benefits.

Benefits of pure functions

- Easier to test and debug
- Easier to understand

Pure functions are easier to test and debug because they always return the same result given the same input without any side effects. Because of that, you know exactly what they do.

Pure functions are easier to understand because you only need to understand the code within the function and don't need to keep track of any side effects. If you're used to procedural programming or object-oriented programming, pure functions might seem more complicated at first. However, once you get used to functional programming, you should start to appreciate how easy pure functions are to understand.

To understand pure functions, you can start by looking at a function that's not pure as shown next.

Not pure – Changes something outside the function

```
let count = 0;
const incrementCount = (by = 1) => {
  count = count + by;              // Changes something outside the function
  return count;
};
```

Example usage

```
console.log("Count: " + count);            // Count: 0
console.log("Count: " + incrementCount()); // Count: 1
console.log("Count: " + incrementCount(2)); // Count: 3
```

This code begins by defining a variable named count outside of a function named incrementCount(). The function increments the count variable by a default value of 1 or by the specified amount. This function works correctly, but it's a little tricky to test. That's because you need to know the value of the variable that's defined outside the function to be able to make sure the function is working correctly.

To convert this function to a pure function, you can add a parameter for the count variable as shown next. That way, you don't need to define the count variable outside of the function.

Pure – Doesn't change anything outside the function

```
const incrementCount = (prevCount, by = 1) => {
  const newCount = prevCount + by;
  return newCount;
};
```

Example usage

```
console.log("Count: " + incrementCount(0));    // Count: 1
console.log("Count: " + incrementCount(1, 2)); // Count: 3
```

Within the function, the first statement defines a constant named newCount and assigns it the value that's created by incrementing the prevCount variable by a default value of 1 or by the specified amount. Since this function is pure, the statements that use it are easy to test since they don't use anything outside of the function.

To code this pure function more concisely, you could rewrite it as shown next.

A more concise way to code the incrementCount() function

```
const incrementCount = (prevCount, by = 1) => prevCount + by;
```

When you use React to set state, you should always use pure functions. To do that, you should not access state within a call that sets state as shown next.

Bad practice – State may be stale

```
const Counter = () => {
  const [count, setCount] = useState(0);

  // Accesses state directly
  const handleClick = () => setCount(count + 1);

  return (<button onClick={handleClick}>Count: {count}</button>);
};
```

That's because React uses asynchronous calls to set state. As a result, if you access state within a function that's setting state, the state may be stale. For instance, in the previous example, the count variable might be set by another user after React gets the value of the count variable but before it sets the new count. This would cause the counter to display an inaccurate count.

To prevent stale state, you should use a pure function as shown next.

Good practice – Prevents stale state

```
const Counter = () => {
  const [count, setCount] = useState(0);

  // Uses a pure function to change state
  const handleClick = () => setCount((prev) => prev + 1);

  return (<button onClick={handleClick}>Count: {count}</button>);
};
```

When you pass a pure function to a setter function, React calls the passed function with the current state value. Since this code passes a pure function to the setCount() function, React can always update the count correctly.

To summarize, a pure function obeys the following rules.

A pure function…

- Defines at least one parameter.
- Doesn't change anything outside of the function such as state or global variables.
- Returns a value or another function.
- Treats all parameters as immutable.

So far, this chapter has shown how to code functions that follow the first three rules. Next, this chapter shows how to code functions that follow the fourth rule.

How to treat parameters as immutable

In JavaScript, most data structures such as objects and arrays are *reference types*, not value types. That means that if you pass an object or an array as a parameter, the function gets a reference to the original object or array, not a copy of its data. As a result, the code within the function can change, or *mutate*, the original data structure. Because of that, a parameter that's a reference type is known as a *mutable parameter*.

If a function changes a mutable parameter, the data structure is changed both inside and outside the function, which violates the rules of creating a pure function. As a result, to create a pure function, you must treat mutable parameters as *immutable*. This means that you should not change, or mutate, the parameter. If the function needs to return a modified version of the parameter, you can make a copy of the parameter, make the changes to it, and return the copy.

Update an object

To illustrate how you can treat an object parameter as immutable, this chapter uses movie objects like the one defined next.

A movie object with three properties

```
const movie = { id: 1, name: "Wizard of Oz", year: 1939 }
```

This object defines three properties (id, name, and year). To use a function to update an object like this one, you can use a function like the one shown next. This function defines three parameters: a movie object, a name, and a year.

The spread operator copies the object parameter

```
const updateMovieObj = (movie, name, year) => {
    return {
        ...movie,    // use spread operator to copy movie object
        name,        // update name property with name value
        year: +year // use + to convert year to a number
    };
}
```

To treat the movie parameter as immutable, the updateMovieObj() function returns a new object that's defined by the curly braces. Within these braces, the code begins by using the spread operator (...) to copy the movie parameter and all of its properties. Then, it updates the name property by setting it to the name parameter, and it updates the year property by setting it to the year parameter. This maintains immutability by not modifying the movie parameter directly, which is a best practice in React state management.

To update the name, this code just specifies the name of the parameter. This works because the name of the parameter is the same as the name of the object property. If it wasn't the same, you could use object notation to specify the property to update. For example, if you wanted to update a property named title with a value named newTitle, you could use the following notation.

The syntax for when the names of the property and value are different

```
propertyName: valueName
```

To update the year, this code uses the + operator to convert the year argument from a string (which is common when reading input values in React forms) to a number. This stores the year property as a numeric value in the returned object.

In JavaScript, when using an arrow function with a concise body (without curly braces), you can return an object literal directly. However, you must wrap it in parentheses as follows.

A more concise way to code the updateMovieObj() function

```
const updateMovieObj = (movie, name, year) =>
    ({ ...movie, name, year: +year });        // enclose object in parentheses
```

The parentheses tell JavaScript to treat what's inside as an expression (the object), not a block of code (multiple statements). Without the parentheses, the function would return undefined. This is a common mistake and leads to unexpected results or syntax errors.

To test this function, you can use a statement like the one shown next.

Test the updateMovieObj() function

```
const movie = { id: 1, name: "Wizard of Oz", year: 1939 }
updatedMovie = updateMovieObj(movie, "The Wiz", "1978");
```

This creates a movie object like the one that follows.

The updatedMovie object

```
{ id: 1, name: "The Wiz", year: 1978 }
```

This changes the name and year properties for the object, but it leaves the id property set to its original value. And it leaves the original movie object unchanged as shown next.

The movie object

```
{ id: 1, name: "Wizard of Oz", year: 1939 }
```

The following figure summarizes a best practice for working with object parameters in React.

When working with an object parameter...

- Don't directly modify the object by setting one of its properties.
- Do use the spread operator to copy the object before modifying its properties.

Add an item to an array

Similarly, if you're working with a function that defines a parameter that's an array, it's a bad practice to directly modify the parameter. For example, you might have an array of movie objects like the one that follows.

An array of movies

```
const movies = [
    { id: 1, name: "Wizard of Oz", year: 1939 },
    { id: 2, name: "The Matrix", year: 1999 }
];
```

If you want to add another movie object to this array, you could define a function called addMovie like the one shown next.

The spread operator copies the array parameter

```
const addMovie = (movieList, movie) => [...movieList, movie];
```

This function defines two parameters: movieList and movie. The movieList parameter defines an array of movie objects, and the movie parameter defines the movie object to be added. To treat the array parameter as immutable, the addMovie() function uses the spread operator (...) to create a new array that includes all elements from the movieList array, and it add the new movie to the end of the new array.

By returning a new array, the addMovie() function supports the immutable data pattern, which is a best practice in a React app. This makes it easier to track changes, debug, and optimize performance.

To test this function, you could use the following code.

Test the addMovie() function

```
const movie = { id: 3, name: "Superbad", year: 2007 }
const newMovies = addMovie(movies, movie);
console.log(movies);         // the original array
console.log(newMovies);      // the new array
```

Here, the first statement creates a movie object, the second statement uses the addMovie() function to add the movie to the list of movies, the third statement prints the original array to the console, and the fourth statement prints the new array to the console.

If you view the console, it displays the original array that's stored in the movies variable as follows.

The movies array

```
[{ id: 1, name: "Wizard of Oz", year: 1939 },
 { id: 2, name: "The Matrix", year: 1999 }]
```

And it shows the new array that's stored in the newMovies constant as follows.

The newMovies array

```
[{ id: 1, name: "Wizard of Oz", year: 1939 },
 { id: 2, name: "The Matrix", year: 1999 },
 { id: 3, name: "Superbad", year: 2007 }]
```

This works correctly because the spread operator (…) makes a copy of the original array before adding an item to the array. It's a common mistake to use the push() method of the original array to add an item. This modifies the original array, not a copy of the array.

When you view the console, you're probably going to see each array displayed twice. That's because you're probably running the development server in strict mode. When you do that, React renders each component twice to make sure it renders the same both times. This helps React make sure the function that creates the component is pure.

The following figure summarizes a best practice for working with array parameters in React.

When working with an array parameter…

- Don't directly modify an array parameter by calling its push() method to add items.
- Do use the spread operator to copy the array parameter before adding items.

How to transform arrays

When you work with an array, you often need to transform it by displaying it, updating its items, removing items from it, or summarizing its data. To do that, it's common to use the three immutable methods of an array shown next.

Three immutable methods commonly used with React

Method	Description
map(function)	Executes the specified callback function once for each element and returns a new array that contains the results.
filter(function)	Returns a new array containing all the elements that meet the condition of the specified callback function.
reduce(function, init)	Executes the specified callback function that returns all the elements reduced to one value, processed in ascending sequence. The optional second parameter sets an initial value for the eventual return value.

These methods are known as *immutable methods* because they don't modify the original array. Instead, they return a new array.

Map an array to display it

To display an array, you typically use the map() method to map some or all of the items in the array to HTML elements. For example, the MovieList component that follows maps an array of movies to <ul> and <li> elements.

A component that displays an array by mapping its items

```
const MovieList = ({ movies }) => (
  <ul className="movie-list">
    {movies.map((movie) => (
      <li key={movie.id}>{movie.name} ({movie.year})</li>
    ))}
  </ul>
);
```

As a result, after CSS is applied, a browser might display the component as shown next.

The array displayed by a browser

Wizard of Oz (1939)

The Matrix (1999)

Map an array to update it

It's also common to use the map() method of an array to update an item in an array. To do that, you can code a pure function like the updateMovie() function that follows.

A pure function that updates an array

```
const updateMovie = (movieList, updatedMovie) =>
    movieList.map(
        (movie) => movie.id === updatedMovie.id ? updatedMovie : movie
    );
```

Here, the first parameter is the array of movies, and the second parameter is the movie that you want to update. Within the function, the single statement calls the map() method from the array of movies and passes it a callback function that specifies how to update the array.

The callback function defines a movie object as a parameter. Then, it checks whether the id of each movie object matches the id of the updatedMovie parameter. If the id matches, the function swaps the updated movie for the original movie. Otherwise, it keeps the original movie.

When the updateMovie() function finishes executing, it returns the array that's returned by the map() method. This works because the map() method returns a copy of the movieList array, not a reference to the original movieList array.

To test this function, you can use the following code.

Test the updateMovie() function

```
const movieToUpdate = { id: 1, name: "The Wiz", year: 1978 };
const updatedMovies = updateMovie(movies, movieToUpdate);
console.log(updatedMovies);       // display the updatedMovies array
```

Here, the first statement creates a movie object with an id of 1, the second statement uses the updateMovie() function to update the array of movies, and the third statement prints the updated array to the console. If you view the updated movies in the console, it appears as follows.

The updatedMovies array

```
[{ id: 1, name: "The Wiz", year: 1978 },
 { id: 2, name: "The Matrix", year: 1999 },
 { id: 3, name: "Superbad", year: 2007 }]
```

Here, the movie with an id of 1 has been updated, but the other two movies are copies of the movies in the original array.

Filter an array to delete items

To delete an item from an array parameter, it's a common pattern to use the filter() method as shown in the next example.

A pure function that deletes a movie by filtering an array

```
const deleteMovie = (movieList, id) =>
    movieList.filter(
        (movie) => movie.id !== id
    );
```

Here, the deleteMovie() function defines two parameters: an array of movies and the id of the movie to delete. Within the function, the code calls the filter() method of the array and passes it a callback function that checks whether the movie's id is different than the id of the movie to delete. This returns a copy of the array that keeps all movies except any movie that has an id that matches the id of the movie to delete.

To test this function, you can use the following code.

Test the deleteMovie() function

```
const deletedMovies = deleteMovie(movies, '1');
console.log(deletedMovies);       // display deletedMovies array
```

Here, the first statement deletes the movie with the id of 1. Then, the second statement prints the array that's returned to the console.

The deletedMovies array

```
[{ id: 2, name: "The Matrix", year: 1999 },
 { id: 3, name: "Superbad", year: 2007 }]
```

This shows that the deletedMovies array no longer includes the movie with the id of 1.

Reduce an array to summarize it

To summarize the data in an array parameter, it's a common pattern to use the reduce() method as shown in the next example.

A pure function that reduces an array of objects to an array of values

```
const getYears = (movieList) =>
  movieList.reduce(
    (yearsList, movie) => [...yearsList, movie.year],    // callback
    []                                                    // initial value
  );
```

Here, the function named getYears() accepts an array of movie objects. Within the function, the code calls the reduce() method of the array and passes it a callback function and an initial value of an empty array. As a result, the initial value of the eventual return value is an empty array.

The callback function accepts two parameters. The first is the current state of the eventual return value, called an *accumulator*. And the second is the current element in the array. Here, for each movie object in the array of movies, the callback adds the integer value for the movie year to the accumulator. To do that, it uses the spread operator to copy the accumulator and add the current year to the array of years.

To test the getYears() function, you can call it as shown next.

Test the getYears() function

```
console.log(getYears(movies));    // result is [1999, 2007]
```

This passes the movies array to the getYears() function and prints the resulting array to the console, which displays all of the years in the array. In other words, this reduces an array of objects to an array of values.

You can also use the reduce() method of an array to reduce an array of objects to a single value. For example, the getMaxYear() function shown next gets the maximum year from the movies in the array.

A pure function that reduces an array of objects to a single value

```
const getMaxYear = (movieList) =>
  movieList.reduce(
    (max, movie) => (movie.year > max) ? movie.year : max,    // callback
    0                                                          // initial value
  );
```

This code begins by calling the reduce() function from the array and passing it a callback function and an initial value of 0. The callback function defines two parameters: a maximum value and a movie object. Then, it checks whether the movie year is greater than the maximum value. If so, it sets the movie year as the maximum value. Otherwise, it keeps the previous maximum value.

To test this code, you can call the getMaxYear() function as shown next.

Test the getMaxYear() function

```
console.log(getMaxYear(movies));     // result is 2007
```

This code begins by passing the movies array to the getMaxYear() function. Then, it prints the value for the maximum year to the console. In other words, it reduces an array of objects to a single value.

Other important JS skills for React

Now that you know how to use pure functions to work with objects and arrays in React, you're ready to learn a couple more JS skills that are commonly used in React apps.

Destructure an object

If the JSX for a component contains attributes, React passes an object to the component. When it does this, it passes an object that contains properties that correspond to each attribute. In React, these properties are called *props*.

For example, the Future Value app described in the previous chapter defines a component named Display that has props named errorMsg and value. To display such a component, you can code JSX for the component with errorMsg and value attributes as shown next.

JSX for the Display component

```
<Display value="12345.67" errorMsg="Please enter a valid number." />
```

Under the hood, React creates an object that has errorMsg and value properties like the one shown next.

The object that React passes to the Display component

```
{
    errorMsg: "Please enter a valid number.",
    value: "12345.67"
}
```

React continues by passing that object to the function that defines the Display component. As a result, the Display component can access the properties of the object by defining a parameter.

A Display component that uses the object to access props

```
const Display = (props) => (
    <div className="display">
        <div className="error">{props.errorMsg}</div>
        <div>Future Value: {props.value}</div>
    </div>
);
```

In this case, the code uses a common naming convention by specifying a name of props for the object parameter. Then, it uses the errorMsg and value properties to display the error message and value that are stored in the props object within appropriate <div> elements.

To make it easier to access the properties of an object, it's a common React pattern to use braces ({}) to destructure the object as shown next.

A Display component that uses destructuring to access props

```
const Display = ({ value, errorMsg }) => (
    <div className="display">
        <div className="error">{errorMsg}</div>
        <div>Future Value: {value}</div>
    </div>
);
```

Instead of specifying a name for the object parameter, this code specifies a set of braces to extract the properties from the object. Within these braces, the code specifies the names of the properties, separating each property with a comma. This extracts the values of the properties into variables of the same name that the rest of the function can access.

Import and export modules

Although JavaScript provides several ways to implement modules, React uses *ES6 modules* (*ECMAScript modules*). ES6 modules are the standard way to implement modules in modern JavaScript. For example, the following code implements a module that exports the Header component.

A component that imports a CSS file and exports itself

```
import './Header.css';

const Header = () => (
    <header className="header">
        <h1>Future Value Calculator</h1>
    </header>
);

export default Header;
```

To start, the import statement imports a file named Header.css that's stored in the same directory as the Header component. Then, the export statement exports the Header component to make it available for import in other files.

By using the default keyword, the export statement allows other modules to import this component without needing to use curly braces or match the exact name of the component, though it's common practice to keep the name the same for consistency. This is a standard way to share React components across different parts of a project, and it promotes modularity and code reuse.

For example, the App component could import the Header component with the following statement.

Import a component from a JSX file

```
import Header from './components/Header';
```

This imports the Header component that's stored in the Header.jsx file in the components folder.

If you need to import one or more functions from a library such as React, you can do that as shown in the following examples.

Import a single function from the React library

```
import { useState } from "react";
```

Import multiple functions from the React library

```
import { useState, useEffect } from 'react'
```

If you need to export a single function, you can code the export keyword in front of the function declaration as shown next.

Export a single custom function

```
export function getNextNumber() {
    return ++count;
}
```

Then, you can import that function using an import statement like the one shown next.

Import a single custom function

```
import { getNextNumber } from '../../utils/NumberUtils';
```

This statement imports the getNextNumber() function that's stored in the NumberUtils.js file in the utils directory. Because the export statement didn't use the default keyword to identify that function as the default export for the NumberUtils file, the import statement needs to include braces around getNextNumber, and it needs to use the exact name of the function.

The Movie List app

To show how all of these JavaScript skills can work together within a React app, this chapter finishes by presenting a simple Movie List app.

The user interface

When you run this app for the first time, the browser should display a user interface like the one that follows.

The Movie List UI

This app displays a list of movies with a Delete button to the right of each movie. If you click a Delete button, the app deletes the corresponding movie.

This app also displays an Add Movie button below the list of movies. If you click the Add Movie button, it adds a movie to the list.

The App component

Most of the code for this app is stored in the App component that follows. If you read through this code and its comments, you can probably understand most of it.

The App.jsx file

```
import { useState } from "react";
import MovieList from "./components/MovieList";
import "./App.css";

// pure function to add a new movie
const addMovie = (movieList, movie) => [...movieList, movie];

// pure function to delete a movie
```

```
const deleteMovie = (movieList, id) =>
  movieList.filter((movie) => movie.id !== id);

// define an array of initial movies
const initialMovies = [
  { id: 1, name: "Wizard of Oz", year: 1939 },
  { id: 2, name: "The Matrix", year: 1999 },
];

const App = () => {
  // state variable, setter, and initial value for movies
  const [movies, setMovies] = useState(initialMovies);

  // event handler that uses a pure function to add a movie
  const handleAddMovie = () =>
    setMovies(
      addMovie(movies, { id: 3, name: "Inception", year: 2010 })
    );

  // event handler that uses a pure function to delete a movie
  const handleDeleteMovie = (id) =>
    setMovies(deleteMovie(movies, id));

  // return JSX for the App component
  return (
    <div className="container">
      <header className="header">
          <h1>My Movies</h1>
      </header>
      <main className="main-content">
        <MovieList
          movies={movies}
          onAdd={handleAddMovie}
          onDelete={handleDeleteMovie}
        />
      </main>
      <footer className="footer">
          <p>© My Movies. All rights reserved.</p>
      </footer>
    </div>
  );
};

export default App;
```

To start, the App component imports the useState() function from the React
library, the MovieList component described later in this chapter, and a CSS file
that provides the formatting for the app.

After importing the needed files, the code defines one pure function for adding
a movie and another pure function for deleting a movie. These functions are
coded before the function that defines the App component because they are
pure functions that don't interact with the UI. As a result, they don't need to be
coded within the App component.

After defining the pure functions, the code defines an initial array that stores two movie objects. Although this array supplies some starting data for the app, it doesn't interact with the UI. As a result, it's also coded before the function that defines the App component.

The function for the App component begins with a statement that stores the initial movies array in a state variable named movies. Then, the code defines one event handler that uses a pure function to add a movie and another event handler that uses a pure function to delete a movie. The pure functions are necessary because the calls to the setMovies() function are asynchronous. As a result, passing a pure function to them is a best practice that prevents the stale state problem.

After defining the event handlers for the Add and Delete buttons, the code displays the elements for the page. Of these elements, the MovieList component displays all movies in the list and attaches the event handlers for the component. To make this work, the App component passes the movies array and the event handlers to the MovieList component.

As you review the code, note that the event handler for the Add button adds a hard-coded movie named Inception that was released in 2010. As a result, it doesn't define any parameters. However, the event handler for the Delete button defines a parameter for the id of the movie to be deleted.

The MovieList component

The MovieList component displays the list of movies as well as the Delete and Add Movie buttons. In addition, it attaches the event handlers for the two buttons. To do that, it uses the following code.

The MovieList.jsx file

```jsx
import "./MovieList.css";

const MovieList = ({ movies, onAdd, onDelete }) => {
  return (
    <div className="movie-list">
      <ul>
        {movies.map((movie) => (
          <li key={movie.id}>
            {movie.name} ({movie.year})
            <button onClick={() => onDelete(movie.id)}>Delete</button>
          </li>
        ))}
      </ul>
      <button onClick={() => onAdd()}>Add Movie</button>
    </ div>
  );
};

export default MovieList;
```

To start, this code imports the CSS that's specific to this component. Then, it uses destructuring to extract the movies array and the event handlers from the object that's passed to it.

After extracting the properties, it uses JSX to display the list of movies within a <ul> element. To do that, it uses the map() method of the array to display each movie and its Delete button within an <li> element. As it does that, it uniquely identifies each <li> element by specifying the movie id as the key for the element. In addition, it sets the onClick property for each Delete button to the event handler that deletes the movie. To make this work, the code passes the id for the movie to the event handler. As a result, clicking the Delete button deletes the corresponding movie.

After displaying the list of movies, this code adds a <button> element to define the Add Movie button. Then, it sets the onClick property of the Add Movie button to the event handler that adds a movie to the list. As a result, clicking the Add Movie button adds a movie.

Perspective

This chapter presents some JavaScript skills and concepts that are commonly used with React. Along the way, it also introduces some skills for working with components in React. However, the next chapter expands on the skills you need to use React to develop components.

Terms

first-class citizen

pure function

side effect

reference type

mutable parameter

immutable parameter

immutable method

accumulator

ES6 module

ECMAScript module

Exercise 2-1: Refactor the Counter app

Review the starting code

1. Open the counter project in the ex_starts/ch02 folder.
2. Run the app to make sure it works correctly.

Use destructuring instead of the props object

3. Modify the parameter list of the Counter component so it extracts the value of the text property of the props object.
4. Modify the body of the Counter function to use the extracted value rather than the props object.
5. Save your changes and test the app to make sure it still works correctly.

Rewrite the incrementCount() function

6. In App, code the incrementCount() arrow function so it's a single statement in long format. Save your changes and run the app to make sure it still works correctly.
7. Code the incrementCount() arrow function so it's a single statement in concise format.
8. Save your changes and test the app to make sure it still works correctly.

Use an inline event handler function

9. Comment out the incrementCount() and handleClick() functions.
10. Code an inline event handler for the onClick attribute of the button that passes a pure function to setCount() that increments the count by one. You can use the commented out functions as a guide.
11. Save your changes and test the app to make sure it still works correctly.

Exercise 2-2: Refactor the Movie List app

Review the starting code

1. Open the movie-list project in the ex_starts/ch02 folder.
2. Run the app to make sure it works correctly.

Use destructuring instead of the props object

3. Modify the parameter list of the MovieList component so it extracts the movies array and the onAdd and onDelete event handlers.
4. Modify the body of the function to use the extracted values.
5. Save your changes and test the app to make sure it still works correctly.

Rewrite the functions

6. In the App component, comment out the addMovie() and deleteMovie() functions.

7. Update the event handers so they use inline arrow functions. You can use the commented out functions as a guide.

8. Save your changes and test the app to make sure it still works correctly.

Write a new function

9. In the browser, open the developer tools and display the console. Then, click the Add Movie button more than once, and note the error message(s) in the console. The issue is the code that adds a movie uses the same key for every new movie.

10. Write a function that reduces the movies array to the max id value.

11. Change the event handler that adds a movie so it uses the new function to set the id to the max id plus 1.

12. Save your changes and test the app. Now, you should be able to add more than one movie with no errors.

Chapter 3

Develop components with JSX and props

Components are the building blocks to create a dynamic UI with React. This chapter reviews some skills that were presented in the previous chapters, and it presents new skills like conditionally rendering JSX and working with props.

An introduction to React components

These days, a React component is usually a JavaScript function that describes a portion of the UI. Components let you break your UI into small, reusable pieces. To describe the UI, a React component uses *JSX*, a JavaScript syntax extension that provides a way for you write JavaScript that looks like HTML.

It's possible for a React component to be a class instead of a function. However, in modern React, function components are preferred, so that's the technique used throughout this book. If you need to work with class components, you can find many examples online.

Create a component

Since a React component is typically a JavaScript function, writing one is fairly straightforward. To illustrate, the following example shows a simple React component that defines a header.

A component that returns a header

```
const Header = () => (
    <header>
        <h1>Welcome to My React App!</h1>
    </header>
);

export default Header;
```

Since this component is named Header, it should be stored within a file named Header.jsx. The function for this component doesn't define any parameters. Instead, it just uses JSX to return a <header> element that contains an <h1> element. Since the JSX returns a single element that wraps other elements, this code doesn't need to use a React fragment.

However, if you need to create a component that returns multiple elements, you can use a *React fragment* to wrap the other elements. The most common way to create a React fragment is to use the shortcut syntax (<> and </>) as shown next.

A component that wraps multiple elements in a React fragment

```
const Hello = () => (
    <>
        <h2>Hello, World!</h2>
        <p>Welcome to my React application!</p>
    </>
);

export default Hello;
```

Use a component

Once you've created a custom component like one of the two components shown previously, you can use it in another component. To do that, you start by importing the component. Then, you include it in your JSX by writing a *JSX element*, or *JSX component tag*. For example, the following App component imports and uses the two components shown earlier.

An App component that imports and renders two other components

```
import Header from './components/Header';
import Hello from './components/Hello';
import './App.css';

const App = () => (
    <div className="container">
        <Header />
        <main>
            <Hello />
        </main>
    </div>
);

export default App;
```

The code for the App component begins by importing the Header and Hello components from a directory named components. Since each component is the default export of the file that contains it, these import statements don't need braces. Then, the code continues by importing the CSS for the App component.

After the imports, the App component uses JSX to render some HTML elements as well as some React components. To do that, it uses lowercase for the HTML elements, and it capitalizes the React components. For example, the JSX for the Header component is <Header />, not <header />. This is important because React treats lowercase elements as standard HTML.

In addition, this code uses self-closing tags like <Header /> for the React components. It's also possible to code an explicit closing tag like <Header></Header>. However, for components like these, it's more common to use the self-closing tags since they're more concise.

When to break a component into smaller components

In general, it's a good practice to break your components into smaller components when you can. This leads to the following benefits.

Some of the benefits of breaking components into smaller components

- Smaller components are easier to reuse.

- Smaller components are easier to test.
- Smaller components are easier to refactor.
- Multiple small components generally makes your JSX cleaner.
- You can encapsulate behavior and styles.

To illustrate, the following App component could be broken down into smaller components.

A component that could be split into smaller components

```
import Hello from './components/Hello';
import './App.css';

const App = () => (
    <div className="container">
        <header className="header">
            <h1>My React App</h1>
        </header>
        <main>
            <Hello />
        </main>
        <footer className="footer">
            <p>My React App. All rights reserved.</p>
        </footer>
    </div>
);

export default App;
```

Here, both the header and the footer could be separate components. Then, they could be reused by any component that needs the header and footer. This is illustrated by the following App component.

The same component after it has been split into smaller components

```
import Header from './components/Header';
import Hello from './components/Hello';
import Footer from './components/Footer';
import './App.css';

const App = () => (
    <div className="container">
        <Header />
        <main>
            <Hello />
        </main>
        <Footer />
    </div>
);

export default App;
```

This cleans up the JSX in the App component. In addition, any CSS that's specific to the header and footer can be encapsulated in those components. For example, you can code a Header.css file that contains any CSS that's specific to the Header component.

In summary, breaking a component down into smaller components is often a good practice. However, it's possible to go too far.

Possible downsides of breaking components into smaller components

- Your project can become too complex and hard to follow.
- If the component is simple and there's no duplication, it's not necessary.
- If you break a component into smaller components because you think you *might* reuse it, but then you never do, you've wasted time and effort.

Basically, you should make sure you really need to break a component into small components before you do it. This is sometimes called the *YAGNI (You Aren't Going to Need It)* principle. For example, make sure you are really going to reuse a Header and Footer component before you break them out.

Best practices for React components

Now that you have a basic idea of how React components work, you're ready to learn about some of the best practices for creating React components. If some of these best practices don't make complete sense to you now, don't worry. They should become clearer as you progress through this book.

Best practices for React components

- **One component per file.** This makes your code easier to organize.
- **One responsibility per component.** This keeps your component small and focused, which makes it easier to test, reuse, and maintain.
- **Use Pascal case for component names.** For example, CalculatorForm and MovieList use Pascal case, so they follow this convention.
- **Export the component as part of a module.** It's possible to define an inline component as part of another component, but this is considered a bad practice because it violates the one-component-per-file rule and limits reuse.
- **Make the component the default export.** This makes it easier to import the component and helps enforce the one-component-per-file rule.
- **Return a single element.** To return multiple elements, wrap them in an HTML element like <div> or a React fragment (<>). If you use an HTML element, React adds that element to the DOM. By contrast, React doesn't add a fragment to the DOM. Instead, it only adds the elements within the fragment.
- **Enclose JSX that spans multiple lines in parentheses.** This isn't a React requirement, but it helps avoid issues with JavaScript's automatic semicolon insertion.
- **Use arrow functions.** A component can be a regular function or an arrow

function, but arrow functions are the most common style in modern React.

- **Write components as pure functions.** This means they should have no side effects during rendering.

How to work with JSX

JSX is a JavaScript syntax extension that lets you write JavaScript that looks like HTML. Learning how to work with JSX is a critical skill for creating React apps.

Attributes that differ in JSX and HTML

Since JSX looks like HTML, you already know how to write JSX if you know how to write HTML. However, there are a few exceptions. For example, JSX uses the className and htmlFor attributes to avoid the class and for keywords that are used by JavaScript.

In addition, multi-word attributes that are all lowercase in HTML are camel case in JSX. For example, the HTML attributes named autofocus and tabindex become the autoFocus and tabIndex attributes in JSX. That's because JSX follows the JavaScript convention of using camel case for attribute names.

When React renders the JSX to the browser, it converts all of these attributes to the standard HTML attributes. For instance, it converts className to class and autoFocus to autofocus. The following table shows some important attributes that differ between HTML and JSX.

Attributes that differ in JSX and HTML

HTML attribute	JSX attribute	
class	className	
for	htmlFor	
autofocus	autoFocus	
autocomplete	autoComplete	
tabindex	tabIndex	
onclick	onClick	
readonly	readOnly	
maxlength	maxLength	
colspan	colSpan	
accesskey	accessKey	
enctype	encType	
novalidate	noValidate	
formnovalidate	formNoValidate	
accept-charset	acceptCharset	(dash removed)
xlink:href	xlinkHref	(colon removed)

In this table, the last two attributes with dashes and colons convert to camel case only. That's because dashes and colons aren't allowed in JSX.

The exception to this is data-*, aria-*, and custom attributes. For those, React allows dashes and passes the attributes straight to the DOM without any changes. For instance, if you add attributes like data-id, aria-label, or murach-data, React renders them to the browser as-is.

The following React component uses some of these attributes.

A component with JSX for a button

```
const EditButton = () => (
    <button
        className="btn"
        type="submit"
        aria-label="Edit"
        title="Edit"
        accessKey="e"
        my-custom-attribute="this is rendered as-is">
        <i className="fa fa-pencil" aria-hidden="true"></i>
    </button>
);

export default EditButton;
```

For this component, React renders the following HTML to the browser.

The HTML that React renders to the browser

```
<button
    class="btn"
    type="submit"
    aria-label="Edit"
    title="Edit"
    accesskey="e"
    my-custom-attribute="this is rendered as-is" >
    <i class="fa fa-pencil" aria-hidden="true"></i>
</button>
```

This shows that React renders the className attributes as class, and it renders accessKey as accesskey. However, it doesn't change the aria-* and custom attributes.

Finally, you should know how the style attribute differs between HTML and JSX. In HTML, the value of a style attribute is a CSS string as shown next.

The style attribute in HTML

```
<div style="color:red; font-size: 12px">...</div>
```

However, in JSX, the value of the style attribute is a JavaScript object as shown later in this chapter.

Embed JavaScript in JSX

When working with JSX, you often need to include a JavaScript constant, variable, or expression. To do that, you enclose the value within braces as shown next.

A component that embeds a value in the JSX

```
const CurrentDate = () => {
    const today = new Date();
    const formattedDate = today.toLocaleDateString();

    return (
        <div className="current-date">
            Today's Date: {formattedDate}
        </div>
    );
};

export default CurrentDate;
```

This component begins with two JavaScript statements that define constants. Then, it returns some JSX where the value of the second constant is embedded in the JSX. To do that, this code uses braces within the JSX.

If you don't need to code JavaScript statements before the JSX, you can use a similar technique to embed a JavaScript expression in the JSX as shown next.

A component that embeds an expression in the JSX

```
const Footer = () => (
    <footer className="footer">
        <p>© {new Date().getFullYear()} My React App. All rights reserved.</p>
    </footer>
);

export default Footer;
```

And if you want to use JSX to change the style attribute, you can pass a JavaScript object to the style attribute as shown next.

A component that embeds a JavaScript object in the style attribute

```
const Header = () => (
    <header style={{color: 'red', fontSize: '12px'}}>
        <h1>My React App</h1>
    </header>
);

export default Header;
```

For this to work, the JavaScript object needs to follow the rules shown next.

Rules for embedding a JavaScript object in the style attribute

- Use two sets of braces.

- Property names must be camel case (fontSize, not font-size).
- Property values that are strings must be in quotes.
- Numeric values are considered strings if they contain units (px, em, etc).

Of these rules, the trickiest one is that you must code two sets of braces. This is necessary because the outer set of braces indicates that you're embedding JavaScript within JSX, and the inner set of braces defines the JavaScript object.

Conditionally render JSX

You can't embed if statements in JSX. However, there are several techniques to embed conditional expressions in JSX. One is to embed a ternary expression as shown next.

Embed a ternary expression in the JSX

```
const Hello = () => {
    const hour = new Date().getHours();
    const isMorning = hour >= 0 && hour < 12;

    return (
        <>
            <h2>
                {isMorning ? "Good Morning, World!" : "Hello, World!"}
            </h2>
            <p>Welcome to my React application!</p>
        </>
    );
};

export default Hello;
```

Another technique is to embed a *short-circuit expression*. This is a common React pattern that uses the JavaScript AND logical operator (&&) to return the JSX after the operator only if the expression before the operator evaluates to true. For example, the following component returns the JSX only if the isNewYear expression evaluates to true.

Embed a short-circuit expression in the JSX

```
const Hello = () => {
    const today = new Date();
    const isNewYear = today.getMonth() === 0 && today.getDate() === 1;

    return (
        <>
            <h2>Hello, World!</h2>
            <p>Welcome to my React application!</p>
            {isNewYear && <h3>Happy New Year!</h3>}
        </>
    );
};

export default Hello;
```

In general, it makes sense to use short-circuit expressions when you don't have an else case, and the ternary operator when you do.

If the JSX after the short-circuit operator contains multiple elements, you must wrap them in an HTML parent element or a React fragment. And if the expression spans multiple lines, you should code it within parentheses. For example, the following component returns JSX that contains two elements only if the isNewYear expression evaluates to true.

A short-circuit expression that uses a React fragment

```
const Hello = () => {
    const today = new Date();
    const isNewYear = today.getMonth() === 0 && today.getDate() === 1;

    return (
        <>
            <h2>Hello, World!</h2>
            <p>Welcome to my React application!</p>
            {isNewYear && (
                <>
                    <h3>Happy New Year!</h3>
                    <p>Wishing you a year filled with joy and success!</p>
                </>
            )}
        </>
    );
};

export default Hello;
```

If the conditional logic you need in your component is more complex than these examples, it's usually best to put the logic in a function and then call the function in your JSX as shown next.

Embed a function call in the JSX

```
const Hello = () => {

    const getGreeting = () => {
        const hour = new Date().getHours();
        if (hour >= 0 && hour < 12) {
            return "Good morning";
        } else if (hour >= 12 && hour < 18) {
            return "Good afternoon";
        } else {
            return "Good evening";
        }
    };

    return (
        <>
            <h2>{getGreeting()}, World!</h2>
            <p>Welcome to my React application!</p>
```

```
        </>
    );
};

export default Hello;
```

This code begins by defining a function named getGreeting() that uses an if/else statement to get the correct greeting based on the hour. Then, the JSX in the Hello component calls the getGreeting() function to display the correct greeting.

How to work with props

So far, the components you've seen in this chapter are stand-alone components. That is, they don't need any additional data to do their work.

Often, though, you need to pass some data to a component to make it useful. For example, a Header component is more reusable if you pass it the text to display within the <h1> element. Then, you can use it in any web app.

Since a React component is a JavaScript function, it can receive data via parameters. However, when coding parameters for a React component, you should follow the conventions described next.

Create a component with props

When React renders your custom component, it calls the function you exported in your component file. When it does that, it automatically passes an object as an argument to your function. This object contains properties that correspond to the attributes specified in the JSX for the component.

To access these properties, called *props* in React, you can use object destructuring to extract the properties you want to use as shown next.

A Header component that uses object destructuring

```
const Header = ({text}) => (
    <header>
        <h1>{text}</h1>
    </header>
);

export default Header;
```

Here, the destructuring pattern extracts the text property from the props object and assigns it to a variable named text. Then, the component uses that variable in the JSX. This is a common React pattern.

This Header component uses the text property of the props object to set the content of the <h1> element. For this to work, the JSX that uses the component must include an attribute named text as shown next.

The JSX for the Header component with a text attribute

```
<Header text="My React App" />
```

When you use object destructuring, you can assign a default value to make a property optional as shown next.

A Header component with an optional property

```
const Header = ({text, subtitle = "Welcome!"}) => (
    <header>
        <h1>{text}</h1>
        <h2>{subtitle}</h2>
    </header>
);

export default Header;
```

You can also use an optional Boolean property to conditionally render JSX as shown next.

A Header component with an optional Boolean property

```
const Header = ({text, showLogo = false}) => (
    <header>
        {showLogo && <img src="/my-logo.png" alt="Logo" />}
        <h1>{text}</h1>
    </header>
);

export default Header;
```

Here, the default value is false, so the logo only shows if you specifically set the showLogo property to true. To do that, you only need to code the name of the Boolean property. For example, the following JSX sets the showLogo property to true and causes React to display the logo.

JSX that sets a Boolean property to true

```
<Header text="My React App" showLogo />
```

Create a component with children

This is all great, but what if you want your component to contain other elements within its opening and closing tags? For instance, what if you'd like your Header component to work like the following component?

The JSX for a Header component that contains a child element

```
<Header text="My React App">
    <p>Welcome to my app!</p>
</Header>
```

To make this possible, React automatically includes a prop named children in the props object. This prop contains the content between the opening and closing tags of the component. For example, the following code defines a Header component that renders any content between its tags.

A Header component that uses the children prop

```
const Header = ({text, children}) => (
    <header>
        <h1>{text}</h1>
        {children}
    </header>
);

export default Header;
```

This version of the Header component adds the children prop to the destructuring pattern. Then, it uses that prop to display the inner content of the component between the <header> tags. It still uses the text prop to set the text of the <h1> element, but it also uses the children prop to display the content coded within the <Header> tags.

The children prop can contain any content that can be rendered by React such as HTML elements, React components, strings, and arrays. You can also conditionally render the children prop as shown next.

A Header component that conditionally renders children

```
const Header = ({text, children}) => (
    <header>
        <h1>{text}</h1>
        {children && <div>{children}</div>}
    </header>
);

export default Header;
```

This is useful for components that might sometimes be used without children.

Code open-ended props

When you have a component that wraps an HTML element, it's common to want to be able to use all of the attributes of the wrapped element without having to explicitly write props for each one. To make this possible, you use the JavaScript rest (...) and spread (...) operators to create components that accept an open-ended set of props. For example, the following code defines a component that wraps an <a> element that's configured to open in a new tab.

The NewTabLink component

```
const NewTabLink = ({ children, ...props }) => (
    <a
        className="new-tab-link"
        target="_blank"
        rel="noopener noreferrer"
```

```
        {...props}
    >
        {children}
    </a>
);

export default NewTabLink;
```

Here, the destructuring pattern extracts the children prop and uses the rest operator to collect the rest of the props in an object named props. Then, the JSX explicitly sets the className, target, and rel attributes of the <a> element. Next, the spread operator spreads the props as attributes of the <a> element. Finally, the JSX inserts the children prop as the content of the <a> element.

To create a NewTabLink component, you can specify a single attribute.

A NewTabLink component with a single attribute

```
<NewTabLink href="https://google.com">Google</NewTabLink>
```

Or, you can specify multiple attributes.

A NewTabLink component with multiple attributes

```
<NewTabLink href="https://reactjs.org"
    accessKey="R"
    title="(Alt + R) to open React website"
    aria-label="Learn more about React"
    className="strong-link">React</NewTabLink>
```

In other words, you can work with the NewTabLink component just like you would a standard HTML <a> element.

The second NewTabLink passes a className property to the component. However, the NewTabLink component specifies a default value for className. So, which one takes effect? That depends on where you place the code that spreads the props.

How to override props

To override the...	Place the code that spreads props...
Default value	After the default value
Passed in prop	Before the default value

The NewTabLink component places the code that spreads the props after the default values. As a result, the JSX that passes a className prop overrides the default value of the className prop.

If you want to merge values rather than override them, you can use object destructuring to extract the prop and then append it to the default as shown next.

The NewTabLink component with merged className attribute

```
const NewTabLink = ({ children, className = '', ...props }) => (
    <a
        className={`new-tab-link${className ? ' ' + className : ''}`}
        target="_blank"
        rel="noopener noreferrer"
        {...props}
    >
        {children}
    </a>
);

export default NewTabLink;
```

This version of the NewTabLink component uses JavaScript string interpolation to append any className prop to the default value (new-tab-link) for the className attribute. If there's a className prop, it appends a space followed by the class name. Otherwise, it appends an empty string.

Work with keys

When working in React, you often need to display the elements in an array as an unordered list. To do that, it's common to use the map() method of the array. When you do, you must assign a unique key to each item in the list as shown next.

A component that renders an unordered list with keys for the items

```
const items = [
    { id: 1, value: 'Item 1' },
    { id: 2, value: 'Item 2' },
    { id: 3, value: 'Item 3' }
];

const List = () => {
    return (
        <ul>
            {items.map((item) => (
                <li key={item.id}>{item.value}</li>
            ))}
        </ul>
    )
};

export default List;
```

This allows React to use the key to track the state of each item and only re-render items that have changed. If you omit the key, React displays a warning in the browser's console.

If you're rendering a list of components, the key goes where you use the map() method, not within the component itself. For example, the following ListItem component displays the value for the item but doesn't provide a key.

A ListItem component that doesn't provide a key

```
const ListItem = ({value}) => (
    <li>{value}</li>
);

export default ListItem;
```

However, the List component that uses the item object specifies the key for the ListItem component and passes the value to it as shown next.

A List component that adds a key to each ListItem component

```
import ListItem from './ListItem';

const List = ({items}) => {
    return (
        <ul>
            {items.map((item) => (
                <ListItem key={item.id} value={item.value} />
            ))}
        </ul>
    )
};

export default List;
```

In summary, the <li> element inside the ListItem component doesn't need a key. Rather, the ListItem component itself needs the key so React can track the ListItem components rendered by List. In fact, ListItem doesn't even have access to the key because it's only used internally by React.

When you need a key for an item in an array, you may be tempted to use the array index as the key. However, that's not a good practice in most cases. That's because the array index isn't associated with the data in the element, just with the element's position in the array. So, if you move or delete elements, the indexes associated with the elements change. This makes it hard for React to accurately track the items in a list.

In general, it's a good practice to use one of the following values as the key for an item.

Common values that are used as keys

- **The database id.** If the items are retrieved from a database, you can use the database id as the key.

- **A unique string.** If the items are strings and you're sure there can't be duplicates, you can use the item string as a key.

- **A generated unique identifier.** If there aren't any unique keys in the data for the items, you can generate a *unique identifier (UID)* for each item in your React code. To do that, you can use the uuid (universally unique identifer) npm package.

In summary, when displaying a list of items, you should use the following guidelines for the keys.

Guidelines for keys

- Each item in the list must have a unique key attribute.
- The key should be directly associated with the data in the item.

Work with keys in fragments

When you need to wrap multiple elements in a single element, but you don't want that single element to be added to the DOM, you can use a React fragment. Most of the time, you can use the shortcut syntax (<></>) for this. However, if you need to add a key to the fragment, you must import and use the Fragment element from the React module as shown next.

A component that uses keys with the React Fragment element

```jsx
import { Fragment } from "react";

const terms = [
  { term: "React", description: "A JavaScript library for building UI." },
  { term: "JSX", description: "A syntax extension for JavaScript that ..." },
  { term: "props", description: "Inputs to components that allow data ..." },
];

const ReactTerms = () => (
    <dl>
    {terms.map((item) => (
        <Fragment key={item.term}>
            <dt>{item.term}</dt>
            <dd>{item.description}</dd>
        </Fragment>
    ))}
    </dl>
);

export default ReactTerms;
```

Because each term in the list is unique, this component can use the term property as the key for each item.

The Movie List app

This chapter ends by presenting the Movie List app. This app uses components to display a list of movies. To keep things simple, this version of the app is static. That is, it only displays the movies. Then, the next chapter presents a version of this app that adds, edits, and deletes movies.

To save space, this chapter doesn't present the CSS files for the app. These files contain basic CSS, and you can view them in the download for this book, if you want.

The user interface

The Movie List app displays a header, a list of movies, and a footer as shown next.

The user interface for the Movie List app

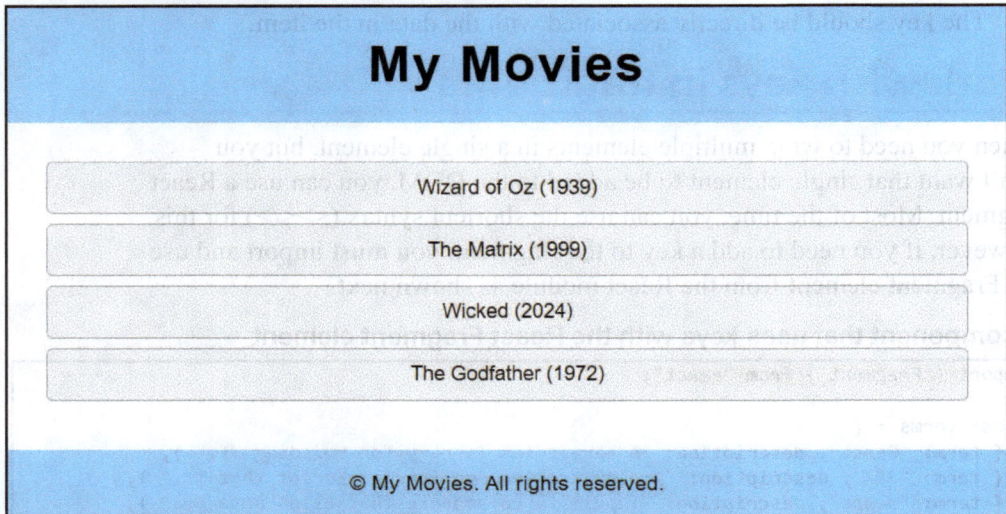

My Movies

Wizard of Oz (1939)

The Matrix (1999)

Wicked (2024)

The Godfather (1972)

© My Movies. All rights reserved.

The list item for each movie displays the movie's name and year. If there are no movies, a single list item displays a message that there are no movies.

The components directory

With the exception of the App component, all of the components for the Movie List app are stored in the components directory shown next.

The directories and files for the components

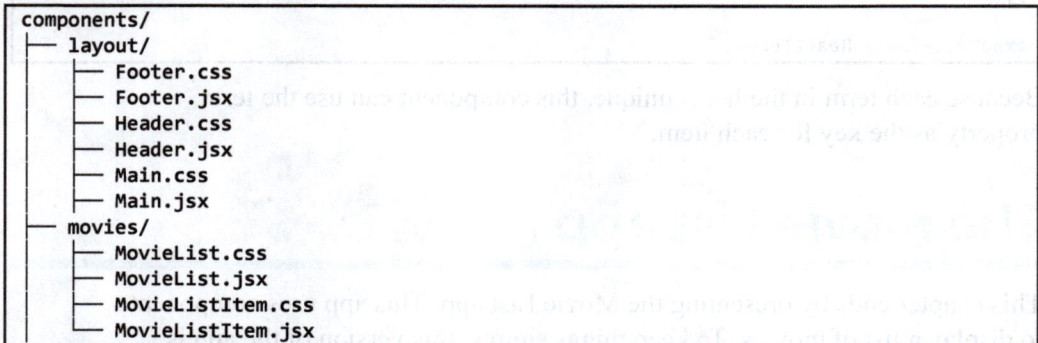

```
components/
├── layout/
│   ├── Footer.css
│   ├── Footer.jsx
│   ├── Header.css
│   ├── Header.jsx
│   ├── Main.css
│   └── Main.jsx
├── movies/
│   ├── MovieList.css
│   ├── MovieList.jsx
│   ├── MovieListItem.css
│   └── MovieListItem.jsx
```

These components are organized into two subdirectories. The layout directory contains general-purpose components for the layout of the app that you could reuse in other web apps. By contrast, the movies directory contains components that are specific to the movie list.

When an app has a lot of components, organizing them into subdirectories can make it easier to find the component you want. This makes the components easier to maintain.

The App component

In the src directory for the app, the App.jsx file defines the main container component, the App component. This component creates the Movie List app by rendering other components.

To help you understand how the App component works, the following code contains more comments than you would typically find in production code.

The App component

```
// import the components for the page layout
import Header from './components/layout/Header';
import Main from './components/layout/Main';
import Footer from './components/layout/Footer';

// import the component for the movie list
import MovieList from './components/movies/MovieList';

// import the CSS for the App component
import './App.css';

// app name to display in the header and footer
const appName = 'My Movies';

// array of movies to display in the movie list
const movies = [
    { id: 1, name: "Wizard of Oz", year: 1939 },
    { id: 2, name: "The Matrix", year: 1999 },
    { id: 3, name: "Wicked", year: 2024 },
    { id: 4, name: "The Godfather", year: 1972 }
];

const App = () => {
    // JSX for the App component
    return (
        <div className="container">
            <Header text={appName} />
            <Main>
                <MovieList movies={movies} />
            </Main>
            <Footer text={appName} />
        </div>
    );
};

export default App;
```

The App component starts by importing the child components that it needs. In addition, it imports the CSS file that's co-located with it.

After importing what it needs, App defines constants for the name of the app and the initial movie objects for the list. These constants are declared outside the function that defines the App component. That way, they aren't re-created on each render, possibly causing re-renders.

After defining the constants, the function for the App component returns some JSX. This JSX starts with a <div> element that's assigned to the CSS class named container.

Within the <div> element, the JSX renders the Header and Footer components by passing them the constant that contains the name of the app. Then, within the Main component, the JSX renders the MovieList component by passing it the array of movies to display.

The layout components

The layout components are Header, Main, and Footer. They are general-purpose components that wrap semantic HTML elements typically used for layout. They accept props to determine what they display.

The Header component accepts a prop named text and displays that prop within an <h1> element in the <header> element.

The Header component

```
import './Header.css';

const Header = ({ text }) => (
    <header className="header">
        <h1>{text}</h1>
    </header>
);

export default Header;
```

The Footer component also accepts a prop named text, but it displays that prop within a <p> element in the <footer> element.

The Footer component

```
import './Footer.css';

const Footer = ({ text }) => (
    <footer className="footer">
        <p>© {text}. All rights reserved.</p>
    </footer>
);

export default Footer;
```

The Main component extracts the children prop that's automatically provided by React and displays it between its opening and closing tags.

The Main component

```
import './Main.css';

const Main = ({ children }) => (
    <main className="main-content">
        {children}
    </main>
);

export default Main;
```

This allows the Main component to contain other HTML elements or React components.

The movie components

The movies directory contains the MovieList and MovieListItem components. Both are specific to the Movie List app.

The MovieList component contains the code for displaying a list of movies.

The MovieList component

```
import MovieListItem from "./MovieListItem";
import "./MovieList.css";

const MovieList = ({ movies }) => (
    <ul className="movie-list">
        {movies.length === 0 ? (
            <MovieListItem movie={null} />
        ) : (
            movies.map((movie) =>
                <MovieListItem
                    key={movie.id}
                    movie={movie}
                />
            )
        )}
    </ul>
);

export default MovieList;
```

The MovieList component begins by importing the MovieListItem component as well as the CSS that's specific to the movie list. Then, it defines a movies prop that contains the list of movies to display. Next, the code checks the movies prop to conditionally render JSX.

If the prop doesn't contain any movies, the code renders a MovieListItem component, but it passes a value of null for the movie attribute. Otherwise, the code maps each movie to a MovieListItem component. To do that, it sets the key for the movie to the movie's id and it sets the movie attribute to the movie object.

The MovieListItem component contains code for displaying the movie.

The MovieListItem component

```
import "./MovieListItem.css";

const MovieListItem = ({ movie }) => (
    movie ? (
        <li className="movie-list-item">
            {movie.name} ({movie.year})
        </li>
    ) : (
        <li className="movie-list-empty">
            There are no movies in this list!
        </li>
    )
);

export default MovieListItem;
```

This component begins by importing its CSS. Then, it defines a prop for the movie object. Next, the code checks the movie prop to conditionally render JSX.

If the movie prop contains data, MovieListItem displays an <li> element with the movie name and year. Otherwise, it displays an <li> element with a message that there are no movies. The CSS class it assigns the <li> to also depends on whether there's movie data.

Perspective

This chapter has presented two of the most important skills for developing React components, working with JSX and working with props. If you understand the Movie List app that's presented at the end of this chapter, you are well on your way to mastering React. However, to create a realistic React app, you need to add state to the app as shown in the next chapter.

Terms

React fragment

JSX

JSX element

JSX component tag

short-circuit expression

props

unique identifier (UID)

YAGNI (You Aren't Going to Need It)

Exercise 3-1: Refactor the My Playlist app

This exercise shows how to refactor the My Playlist app shown next to fix an issue with keys, make it more modular, and add some conditional JSX.

Review the starting code

1. Open the my-playlist project in the ex_starts/ch03 folder. Note that all the code for the app is in the App component.
2. Run the app to see how it works.
3. In the browser, open the developer tools and view the console. It should display an error message about keys.

Fix the keys issue

4. Find the code that displays the songs in an unordered list. Add a unique key for each list item.
5. Save your changes and refresh the browser to view the playlist again. The console should no longer display the error message.

Create Header and Footer components

6. Add a components directory to the src directory.
7. Add Header.jsx and Footer.jsx files to the components directory.
8. Move the <header> and <footer> elements from the App component to the Header and Footer components. Add a prop to each component for the app name.

9. Add Header.css and Footer.css files to the components directory. Move the CSS in App.css that styles the <header> and <footer> elements to the CSS files for Header and Footer.

10. Add import statements to the JSX files for Header and Footer so they import their CSS files.

11. Update App to import and render Header and Footer.

12. Save your changes and view them in the browser. The app should look the same as before, but now the code is more modular, and you have Header and Footer components that you can re-use.

Create a Playlist component

13. Add Playlist.jsx and Playlist.css files to the components directory, move the unordered list to the Playlist component, and co-locate the CSS that styles the list. Pass the songs to Playlist in a prop.

14. Update App to import and render Playlist.

15. Save your changes and view them in the browser. The app should look the same as before.

Conditionally display a star

16. In App, add a property named fave to one or more of the song objects in the array and set its value to true.

17. In Playlist, add code that conditionally displays the following span element if fave is true.

```
<span>&#9733;</span>
```

18. Save your changes and switch to the browser to view them. Any song with the fave property should display a star to its right.

Update Header to allow child elements between its tags

19. In Header, change the code to display the children prop between the tags of the <header> element, after the <h1> element.

20. In App, add a <p> element to Header that says, "Favorite songs marked with a star".

21. Save your changes and switch to the browser to view them.

Chapter 4

Add state to components

Most React apps use state to provide the dynamic data for a component. As a result, to create dynamic React apps, you need to learn how to work with state. To start, this chapter presents some concepts and skills for working with state. Then, it adds state to the Movie List app presented in the previous chapter.

How to work with state

In a React app, *state* refers to the data that a component needs to track. For example, state can be user input, such as a username or password in a login form. But it can also be internal variables like counters or data retrieved from a web API.

To work with state, React provides a function named useState(). This function is known as a *hook* because it lets you "hook into" the lifecycle of a React component. So, the useState hook lets you use React to work with state in your components.

Before showing how to work with state, this chapter shows how to define event handlers in React. That's because you typically use event handlers to work with state.

Create an event handler

To create an event handler in React, you assign a function to an event raised by an element or component. For example, the following code assigns a function to the click event of a button.

A component with an event handler for the click event of a button

```
const Goodbye = ({text, children}) => {
    // define a function to handle the click event
    const handleClick = () => {
        console.log(`Goodbye! ${text}`);
    };

    // assign the function to the button's click event
    return (
        <button onClick={handleClick}>
            {children}
        </button>
    );
};

export default Goodbye;
```

In this example, the component begins by defining a function to handle an event. Then, it assigns that function to the onClick attribute of an HTML element. To do that, this code just provides the function name without any parentheses. That's because this code is passing the function as a reference, not calling it. The function is called later when the event specified by the attribute occurs.

In React, you can access all standard DOM events by coding lowercase "on" followed by the capitalized event name. For instance, you can code an attribute named onClick to access the click event, onChange to access the change event, and so on.

To call the event handler, you can use JSX to create a button as shown next.

JSX that uses the component

```
<Goodbye text="See you later!">
    Sign Off
</Goodbye>
```

Then, if you display this button and click on it twice, it should print two messages to the browser console as shown next.

The browser console after a user clicks the button twice

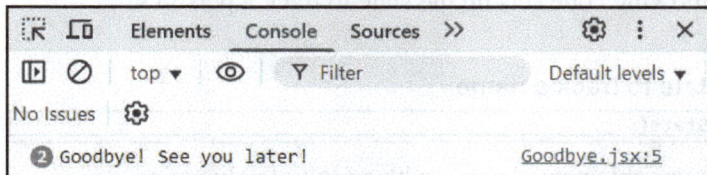

R Lo	Elements	Console	Sources	>>		⚙ ⋮ ✕

```
▯ ⊘    top ▾    ◉    ▼ Filter              Default levels ▾
No Issues  ⚙
  ❷ Goodbye! See you later!              Goodbye.jsx:5
```

A common React pattern for short event handlers is to code them inline, rather than defining a separate function. For example, you could code the Goodbye component with an inline event handler for the click event of the button as shown next.

An inline event handler

```
const Goodbye = ({text, children}) => (
    <button onClick={() => console.log(`Goodbye! ${text}`)}>
        {children}
    </button>
);

export default Goodbye;
```

At this point, you may be thinking that this event handler doesn't seem very useful. And you'd be correct! In a real-world web app, an event handler would do something more useful like accepting input from the user and dynamically changing the app based on that input. That's where state comes in.

Define state

When you use a function to define a React component, you can set the state for a component with the useState hook. To use this hook, you begin by importing it from the React module. Since this hook isn't the default export, you must use braces in the import statement as shown next.

An import statement for the useState hook

```
import { useState } from 'react';
```

The following table summarizes how the useState hook works.

The useState hook

Function	Description
useState(init)	Returns an array with two elements: a state variable and a function that sets the state variable. In addition, you can specify an initial value for the state variable.

After you import the useState() function, you can call it to set up state for a variable. For example, the following code sets up the state to track a person's name.

A statement that creates state to track a name

```
const [name, setName] = useState('');
```

This statement creates a state variable named name with an initial value of an empty string and a setter function named setName(). It uses array destructuring to extract the state variable and its setter function from the array that the useState() function returns. You can name the variable and setter whatever you want, but *variableName* and *setVariableName* is a common React pattern.

One typical use of state is to track the data a user enters into an <input> element. To do that, you can code JSX that uses the state variable and setter function as shown next.

The JSX for an <input> element where user can enter a name

```
<label htmlFor="name">Enter your name:</label>
<input
    type="text"
    id="name"
    value={name}
    onChange={(e) => setName(e.target.value)}
/>
```

Here, the JSX sets the name variable as the value of the <input> element, and it sets the inline event handler function for the change event to the setName() function. Within the setName() function, this code uses the event object that JavaScript passes to every event handler to get the current value of the <input> element.

When you assign the state variable to the value attribute like this, React manages the state of the form control. This is called a *controlled component*, and it means the value "lives" in React state, not in the browser's DOM as it does in plain JavaScript. Then, React uses that state to decide when to update the DOM with the current value.

To update the state variable, you call the state setter function, often in the event handler for the change event. As the user types, React updates the state and re-renders the component to reflect the new value.

Co-locate state

In most cases, you want state to be as local to the component that uses it as possible. This is sometimes called *co-locating state*. For example, here's a Hello component that uses state to get a name from the user and display that name in a greeting.

The Hello component

```
import { useState } from 'react';

const Hello = () => {
    const [name, setName] = useState('');
    const [greeting, setGreeting] = useState('Hello, World!');

    // event handler for the submit event of the form
    const handleSubmit = (e) => {
        e.preventDefault(); // prevent the page from reloading
        setGreeting(name ? `Hello, ${name.trim()}!` : 'Hello, World!');
    };

    return (
        <>
            <div>
                <h2>{greeting}</h2>
                <p>Welcome to my React application!</p>
            </div>
            <form onSubmit={handleSubmit}>
                <label htmlFor="name">Enter your name:</label>
                <input
                    type="text"
                    id="name"
                    value={name}
                    onChange={(e) => setName(e.target.value)}
                />
                <button type="submit">Submit</button>
            </form>
        </>
    );
};

export default Hello;
```

Here, the Hello component defines a state variable named name that has an initial value of an empty string and a setter function. It uses this state to make the <input> element that gets the name from the user a controlled component. As a result, when the user enters a name, React updates the state and re-renders as needed.

Hello also defines a state variable named greeting with an initial value of "Hello World!" and a setter function. It uses this state to create and display a greeting based on the name entered by the user. To do that, it defines an event handler for the submit event of the form. In the event handler, it uses the current value of the name variable to create a greeting, which it passes to the setGreeting() function. The submit event of the form occurs when the user clicks the Submit button or presses Enter in the input field.

As you review this code, you might wonder why it handles the submit event of the form instead of the click event of the button. After all, if this code handled the click event, it wouldn't need to prevent the default action of the form, which would simplify the code. However, it's a common React pattern to write event handlers for the submit event of the form because using the submit event provides several accessibility benefits. These benefits make your app easier to use, and they make it more accessible for users with disabilities.

Accessibility benefits of using the submit event of a form

- A user can submit the form by pressing Enter.
- It's more clear to assistive technologies that this is a form.
- It handles keyboard and screen reader interactions better.

To use this Hello component, you can code it within an App component.

An App component that uses the Hello component

```
import Hello from './components/Hello';

const App = () => (
    <div className="container">
        <Hello />
    </div>
);

export default App;
```

Since the state that Hello needs is co-located, App doesn't need to know anything about it. It can just use the component.

This looks pretty clean! However, there's a problem. Hello follows the rule of co-locating state, but it doesn't follow the rule of one responsibility per component. Hello has two responsibilities: it gets the name from the user, and it displays the greeting.

Lift state

To fix this, you can split Hello into two components, HelloForm and HelloDisplay. However, since the two new components share some state, you need to *lift* that state into the closest parent, which is App. Then, the parent manages the state, and passes it down to the child components as needed.

In Hello, which state is shared? The state of the name is only used by the form. In other words, it isn't shared with the display. As a result, it can be co-located with HelloForm. The state of the greeting, by contrast, is used by both the form and the display. So, it needs to be lifted to the parent component, App.

For example, the following HelloDisplay component doesn't have any internal state of its own.

The HelloDisplay component

```
const HelloDisplay = ({greeting}) => (
    <div>
        <h2>{greeting}</h2>
        <p>Welcome to my React application!</p>
    </div>
);

export default HelloDisplay;
```

This component receives a greeting prop and embeds it in the JSX.

The following HelloForm component still manages the state for the name, but it doesn't manage state for the greeting.

The HelloForm component

```
import { useState } from 'react';

const HelloForm = ({onSubmit}) => {
    const [name, setName] = useState('');

    // event handler for the submit event of the form
    const handleSubmit = (e) => {
        e.preventDefault();  // prevent the page from reloading
        onSubmit(name);      // call the onSubmit function passed by the parent
    };

    return (
        <form onSubmit={handleSubmit}>
            <label htmlFor="name">Enter your name:</label>
            <input
                type="text"
                id="name"
                value={name}
                onChange={(e) => setName(e.target.value)}
            />
            <button type="submit">Submit</button>
        </form>
    );
};

export default HelloForm;
```

This component receives a prop named onSubmit, which is an event handler. This follows a React convention of naming props that are event handlers on*EventName* as in onSubmit or onChange.

The first statement in HelloForm defines the state to track the name entered by the user.

The second statement defines an event handler for the submit event of the form. Within this event handler, the first statement prevents the default behavior of the form, which prevents the page from reloading when the user clicks on the Submit button. Then, the second statement calls the onSubmit event handler it receives from App and passes the name variable to that function.

It's a good practice for HelloForm to include an event handler that prevents the default behavior of the form for two reasons. First, this contains the behavior of the form within the form, which makes it easier for other developers to use. Second, it makes sure that the form never reloads the page, regardless of how the parent handles submission.

To use these HelloDisplay and HelloForm components, you can use the following App component.

An App component that uses HelloDisplay and HelloForm

```
import { useState } from 'react';
import HelloForm from './components/HelloForm'
import HelloDisplay from './components/HelloDisplay'

const App = () => {
    const [greeting, setGreeting] = useState('Hello, World!');

    // event handler for the submit event of the form
    const handleSubmit = (name) => {
        setGreeting(name.trim() ? `Hello, ${name}!` : 'Hello, World!');
    };

    return (
        <div className="container">
            <HelloDisplay greeting={greeting} />
            <HelloForm onSubmit={handleSubmit} />
        </div>
    );
}

export default App;
```

This App component starts by defining the greeting state that's shared between HelloDisplay and HelloForm. Then, it defines an event handler for the submit event that calls the setGreeting() function. That's how App manages the state, even though this function is actually called by HelloForm.

After defining the event handler, App renders the JSX for the app. To do that, it passes the greeting state variable to HelloDisplay, and it passes the handleSubmit() function to HelloForm.

Since greeting state is defined in the App component, App owns that state and is responsible for updating it. In other words, HelloForm doesn't manage the greeting state directly. Instead, it notifies App when an update is needed by calling the function it receives from App. Then, App updates the state and passes the updated value to HelloDisplay, which re-renders automatically when its prop changes.

Types of components for working with state

When working with state, it's often helpful to think of components as being in one of the following categories.

Types of components for working with state

Component type	Description
Presentational	Receives state and callback functions from its parent via props rather than managing its own state. Typically focuses only on rendering UI.
Hybrid	Manages some of its own state and also receives callback functions from its parent via props. Typically manages its own UI state.
Container	Manages state and app logic and passes state and callback functions down to other (often presentational or hybrid) components. Typically focuses on app logic and structure.

In the preceding examples, HelloDisplay is a *presentational component*. It has no internal state of its own. Instead, it receives the greeting prop from its parent and displays it.

HelloForm is a *hybrid component*. It manages the UI state for the name field, but it also receives the callback function for the form submit event from its parent.

And App is a *container component*. It manages the greeting state, defines a callback function for updating it, passes the state variable to HelloDisplay, and passes the callback function to HelloForm.

Use single state object

So far, this chapter has presented examples that create separate state variables.

Separate state variables

```
const [firstName, setFirstName] = useState('');
const [lastName, setLastName] = useState('');
```

This is clear and straightforward. In addition, each setter function updates only one value, so you never have to worry about overriding any other state values. Using separate state variables is often the easiest and safest option, especially for small forms or unrelated values.

However, if you have a large number of state variables, or if the state variables are closely related, it can make sense to use a single state object instead.

A single state object

```
const [name, setName] = useState({ firstName: '', lastName: '' });
```

This is less repetitive and easier to pass to a child component. However, calling the state setter function for a state object can lead to the following problems.

Two common problems when setting a state object

- **Overwriting other properties.** Setter functions replace the entire object. As a result, if you pass an object with just the changed property to the setter function, all other properties are lost.
- **Using stale state.** Since state setter functions are asynchronous, you might get an outdate value if you read the state object from within the setter function.

To avoid these problems, you can pass an *updater function* to the setter function.

An updater function for a state object that avoids both problems

```
setName((prev) => ({ ...prev, firstName: 'Mary' }));
```

The updater function must be a pure function. When you pass it to the setter function, React queues the updater function and calls it after it processes all other pending updates. This makes sure that when your update executes, it's working with the latest state.

In addition, React automatically provides the latest state as the prev argument to the updater function. As a result, in the body of the function, you can create a new object that merges the previous state with the new property values you specify. To do that, you create a new object by coding an object literal ({}). However, to make sure JavaScript knows it's an object literal and not a code block, you enclose it within parentheses.

Within the object literal, you start by use the spread operator (...) to copy all the properties of the previous state to the new object. Then, you code values for any of the object properties that you want to update. If a property already exists in the values you copied from state, it's overwritten. Otherwise, it's added. This makes sure that all previous values are preserved and only the specified ones are updated or added.

You can run into similar problems with arrays, and also with primitive values that use the previous state value to update state, such as incrementing a counter. In those cases, too, the solution is to use an updater function as shown next.

An updater function that adds an element to an array

```
setMovies((prev) => [...prev, movie]);
```

This setter function returns a new array. Within the array literal, the spread operator adds all the elements of the current state array to the new array. Then, the new element is appended.

An updater function that increments a counter

```
setCount((prev) => prev + 1);
```

This setter function returns the current state value incremented by 1.

Prefill a form

React components should be pure functions. This means they return the same output for the same input, and they don't cause side effects while the component renders. A *side effect* is anything that affects something outside the component's rendering process. The following are examples of side effects.

Side effect examples

- Changing the DOM.
- Fetching data from an API.
- Setting timers.
- Writing to local storage.
- Manually updating state in response to props.

Side effects may make a component less predictable and may even interfere in React's rendering process.

However, sometimes a component needs to perform a side effect. For example, if you want to pre-fill an edit form with the current values of the data being edited, that causes a side effect.

You might think you could prefill a form by passing the current values to the state setters. However, if you call the setters from the component, you update the state while the component is rendering. This triggers a re-render, which calls the setters again, which sets off an infinite render loop.

To avoid this, you can use the useEffect hook. This hook specifies a function that runs after the component has rendered, or mounted. This lets you update state without triggering re-renders.

The useEffect hook

Function	Description
`useEffect(func, depArr)`	Accepts a function and a dependency array. React calls the function after the component mounts, and after any value in the dependency array changes. If you only want the function to run once after the component mounts, pass an empty array ([]) as the dependency array.

Like the useState hook, you import the useEffect hook from the React module. Then, you call the useEffect() function as shown next.

A component that uses the useEffect hook to fill a form

```
import { useState, useEffect } from 'react';

const EditProfileForm = ({ user, onSubmit }) => {
    const [firstName, setFirstName] = useState('');
    const [lastName, setLastName] = useState('');

    useEffect(() => {
        if (user) {
            setFirstName(user.firstName);
            setLastName(user.lastName);
        }
    }, [user]); // Run when the user prop changes

    const handleSubmit = (e) => {
        e.preventDefault();
        onSubmit(firstName, lastName);
    };

    return (
      <form onSubmit={handleSubmit}>
          <label>
              First Name:
              <input
                  type="text"
                  value={firstName}
                  onChange={(e) => setFirstName(e.target.value)}
              />
          </label>
          <label>
              Last Name:
              <input
                  type="text"
                  value={lastName}
                  onChange={(e) => setLastName(e.target.value)}
              />
          </label>
          <button type="submit">Save</button>
      </form>
  );
};

export default EditProfileForm;
```

The first argument to the useEffect() function is an anonymous function that begins by checking that the user prop exists. If it does, the function calls the state setter functions with values from user. Since the <input> elements are controlled components (their values are tied to state), React automatically displays these updated state values in the form fields.

The second argument to the useEffect() function is the dependency array with one element, the user prop. This tells React to run the function in the first argument once when the component mounts and again anytime the user prop changes.

The Movie List app

This chapter ends by presenting the Movie List app. This app displays a list of movies and allows users to add, edit, and delete movies. To do that, it adds state to the Movie List app presented in the previous chapter.

The user interface

When the Movie List app starts, it displays two initial movies in the list.

The Movie List app with two initial movies

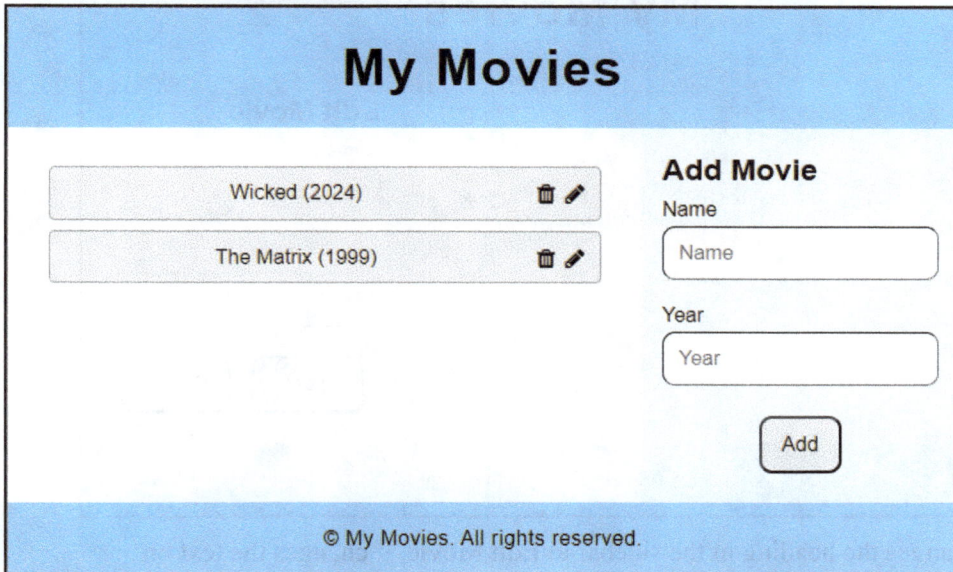

In addition, it provides a form in the sidebar that provides a way for the user to add a movie. If the user enters a name and year in the form and clicks Add, the app immediately displays the movie in the list.

In the list of movies, the app displays the name and year of each movie as well as a delete icon (trash can) and an edit icon (pencil) for each movie. To display the delete and edit icons, this app uses the Font Awesome CSS library.

To make the Font Awesome icons available, the index.html file for the app includes the following <link> element.

A <link> element that makes the Font Awesome icons available

```
<link rel="stylesheet" href="https://cdnjs.cloudflare.com/ajax/libs/font-awesome/6.4.0/css/all.min.css"/>
```

This approach imports the Font Awesome library from a CDN (content delivery network). Because of that, you don't have to install the library for your app.

However, if don't want to rely on a third-party CDN, you can use the npm command to install this library for your app. For more information about installing and using this library, you can search the internet or ask AI.

When the user clicks either icon, the form in the sidebar changes to confirm the edit or delete operation for the selected movie. For example, if the user clicks the edit icon for a movie, the app selects the movie and displays it in the form as shown next.

The Movie List app after a movie is selected for editing

My Movies

		Edit Movie
Wicked (2024)	🗑 ✏	**Name**
The Matrix (1999)	🗑 ✏	The Matrix
		Year
		1999
		[Update] [Cancel]

This changes the heading in the sidebar to Edit Movie, it changes the text on the button to Update, and it displays a Cancel button.

If the user updates the data for a movie and clicks Update, the movie list immediately displays the changes. In addition, the sidebar changes the heading back to Add Movie, it changes the text on the button to Add, and it hides the Cancel button.

The delete icon works similarly. However, when the user clicks on the delete icon for a movie, the sidebar displays the values for the movie in read-only fields. As a result, it isn't possible to modify the values. Instead, the user must click the Delete button to confirm the deletion or the Cancel button to cancel the deletion.

The App component

The src directory for the app contains the App component. This component creates the Movie List app by rendering other components. In addition, it sets up and manages the state shared by the components that it renders.

To help you understand how the App component works, the following code contains more comments than you would typically find in production code. In addition, since this code is long, this chapter splits it into multiple parts with a brief discussion of the most important points after each part.

The App component (part 1)

```
// import the useState hook from the React module
import { useState } from 'react'

// import the components for the page layout
import Header from './components/layout/Header';
import Main from './components/layout/Main';
import Sidebar from './components/layout/Sidebar';
import Footer from './components/layout/Footer';

// import the components for displaying the movie list and form
import MovieList from './components/movies/MovieList';
import MovieForm from './components/movies/MovieForm';

// app name to display in the header and footer
const appName = 'My Movies';

// sample movies to populate app on load
const initialMovies = [
    { id: 1, name: "Wicked", year: 2024 },
    { id: 2, name: "The Matrix", year: 1999 },
];
```

This code imports all of the items that the App component needs, including the useState hook. In addition, it defines two constants that don't interact with the user interface.

Within the function that defines the App component, the code sets up the state variables and the event handlers.

The App component (part 2)

```
const App = () => {
    // set up two state variables, their setter functions, and initial values
    const [movies, setMovies] = useState(initialMovies);
    const [selectedMovie, setSelectedMovie] = useState(null);

    /*********************************************/
    /* event handlers for MovieList and MovieForm */
    /*********************************************/

    // add a new movie
    const handleAdd = (newMovie) => {
        setMovies((prev) => [...prev, newMovie]);    // updates MovieList
    };

    // select a movie and specify the mode (edit or delete)
    const handleSelect = (movie, mode) => {
        setSelectedMovie({...movie, mode});          // updates MovieForm
    };
```

```
// edit a movie
const handleEdit = (updatedMovie) => {
    setMovies((prev) =>                 // updates MovieList
        prev.map((movie) =>
            movie.id === updatedMovie.id ? updatedMovie : movie
        )
    );
    setSelectedMovie(null);        // updates MovieForm to add mode
};

// delete a movie
const handleDelete = (id) => {
    setMovies((prev) =>                 // updates MovieList
        prev.filter((movie) =>
            movie.id !== id
        )
    );
    setSelectedMovie(null);        // updates MovieForm to add mode
};

// cancel edit or delete
const handleCancel = () => {
    setSelectedMovie(null);        // updates MovieForm to add mode
};
```

Here, the state consists of an array to hold the movies and a variable to hold the selected movie. After defining its state, the App component defines the event handlers that it needs to pass to the MovieList and MovieForm components. None of these event handlers specify how to update the display for MovieList or MovieForm. Instead, these event handlers just update the state that App manages, and React automatically updates the display based on how the child components use this state.

For example, the handleAdd event handler uses the setMovies() function to update the state that's used by the MovieList component. This causes React to automatically update the display for the movie list.

Similarly, the handleSelect event handler uses the setSelectedMovie() function to update the state that's used by the MovieForm component. This causes React to automatically update the display for the form.

The App component finishes by returning its JSX.

The App component (part 3)

```
return (
    <div className="container">
        <Header text={appName} />
        <Main>
            <MovieList
                movies={movies}
                onSelect={handleSelect}
            />
        </Main>
        <Sidebar>
```

```
                <MovieForm
                    selectedMovie={selectedMovie}
                    onAdd={handleAdd}
                    onEdit={handleEdit}
                    onDelete={handleDelete}
                    onCancel={handleCancel}
                />
            </Sidebar>
            <Footer text={appName} />
        </div>
    )
}

export default App;
```

This JSX starts with a <div> element that's assigned to the CSS class named container.

After the <div> element, the JSX renders the Header component by passing it the text to display. It renders the Main component and the Sidebar components, which embed the MovieList and MovieForm components, respectively, between their opening and closing tags. And it renders the Footer component by passing it the text to display.

This JSX passes the state that the App component manages to the MovieList and MovieForm components. Specifically, it passes the movies array to MovieList, and it passes the selectedMovie object to MovieForm. Because of that, React can automatically update each of these components when their state changes.

In addition, this JSX passes the event handlers that work with the state to the MovieList and MovieForm components. To do that, the JSX specifies an attribute name such as onAdd or onSelect and passes the corresponding event handler to that attribute.

The components directory

With the exception of the App component, all of the components for the Movie List app are stored in the components directory shown next.

The components directory

```
components/
├── common/
│   ├── FormButtons.css
│   ├── FormButtons.jsx
│   ├── FormInput.css
│   ├── FormInput.jsx
│   ├── Icon.css
│   └── Icon.jsx
├── layout/
│   ├── Footer.css
│   ├── Footer.jsx
│   ├── Header.css
│   ├── Header.jsx
│   ├── Main.css
```

```
        ├──  Main.jsx
        ├──  Sidebar.css
        └──  Sidebar.jsx
├──  movies/
        ├──  MovieForm.css
        ├──  MovieForm.jsx
        ├──  MovieList.css
        ├──  MovieList.jsx
        ├──  MovieListItem.css
        └──  MovieListItem.jsx
```

These components are organized into three subdirectories. The common directory contains general-purpose components that you can reuse in other web apps. The layout directory contains components for page layout like the ones described in the previous chapter. And the movies directory contains components that are specific to the movie list.

The layout components

The four layout components are Header, Main, Sidebar, and Footer. Since these components work the same as the layout components presented in the previous chapter, this chapter doesn't present their code.

The common components

The common directory contains the FormInput, FormButtons, and Icon components. These components are general-purpose components that are presentational. In other words, they work with the state they receive via props, rather than declaring and managing their own state.

The FormInput component shown next makes it easier to display the <label> and <input> elements that are commonly needed on a form.

The FormInput component

```jsx
import './FormInput.css';

const FormInput = ({ label, name, value, onChange, ...props }) => (
    <>
        <label className="form-label" htmlFor={name}>{label}</label>
        <input
            className="form-input"
            type="text"
            id={name}
            name={name}
            value={value}
            onChange={onChange}
            {...props}  // Spread operator to include any additional props
        />
    </>
);

export default FormInput;
```

This component begins by extracting the label, name, value, and onChange props from the props object. Then, it uses the rest operator to collect the rest of the props in a variable named props.

The JSX for this component returns a <label> element and its associated <input> element. To do that, this code wraps these elements in a React fragment.

The <label> element displays the text in the label prop. In addition, it uses the htmlFor attribute to associate the label with the input field.

The <input> element begins by setting default values for the className and type attributes. Since it does this before it spreads the props variable, these values can be overwritten by values in props. Then, it sets the value and onChange attributes to the value and onChange props. As a result, if the parent component passes a state value and setter to these props, FormInput is a controlled component.

The FormButtons component shown next adds the Add, Edit, Delete, and Cancel buttons to a form.

The FormButtons component

```
import './FormButtons.css';

const FormButtons = ({ isEditing, isDeleting, onCancel }) => (
    <>
        <button type="submit" className="btn">
            {isDeleting ? 'Delete' : isEditing ? 'Update' : 'Add'}
        </button>
        {(isDeleting || isEditing) && (
            <button type="button" className="btn" onClick={onCancel}>
                Cancel
            </button>
        )}
    </>
);

export default FormButtons;
```

This component starts by accepting props for Boolean values that indicate whether the form is in edit or delete mode and by accepting a prop for an event handler named onCancel.

The JSX can return two <button> elements, so it wraps them in a React fragment.

The first button is an Add, Edit, or Delete button that submits the form. As a result, its type is set to "submit". The text for this button depends on the value of the isDeleting and isEditing props.

By contrast, the second button is a Cancel button that only displays if isEditing or isDeleting is true. Since this button shouldn't submit the form, this code sets its type attribute to "button". Similarly, it assigns the onCancel event handler to its onClick attribute. As a result, that event handler runs when the Cancel button is clicked.

The Icon component shown next adds an icon that you can click like a button.

The Icon component

```
import './Icon.css';

const Icon = ({ title, className, onClick, ...props }) => {
    if (onClick) {
        return (    // Render as clickable icon
            <button
                title={title}
                aria-label={title}
                onClick={onClick}
                className="icon-button"
                {...props}
            >
                <i className={className} aria-hidden="true"></i>
            </button>
        );
    }
    else {
        return (    // Render as decorative icon
            <i
                title={title}
                aria-label={title}
                className={className}
                {...props}
            />
        );
    }
};

export default Icon;
```

This component uses the onClick prop to determine whether the icon is clickable. If so, the component returns a <button> element that contains an <i> element, and it sets the onClick attribute of the <button> element to the event handler in the onClick prop. Otherwise, this component returns an <i> element for a decorative icon.

Either way, this component uses the title prop to set the title and aria-label attributes for the icon. However, the clickable icon sets aria-label on the <button> element and hides it on the <i> element.

In this chapter, the Movie List app uses the Icon component to create the clickable Edit and Delete icons needed by each movie in the list. In the next chapter, the Movie List app uses this component to add a decorative icon before each movie in the list.

The movie components

The movies directory contains the MovieList, MovieListItem, and MovieForm components. They are all specific to the Movie List app.

The MovieList component shown next is a presentational component that gets state from its parent, App.

The MovieList component

```
import MovieListItem from "./MovieListItem";
import "./MovieList.css";

const MovieList = ({ movies, onSelect }) => (
    <ul className="movie-list">
        {movies.length === 0 ? (
            <MovieListItem movie={null} />
        ) : (
            movies.map((movie) =>
            <MovieListItem
                key={movie.id}
                movie={movie}
                onSelect={onSelect}
            />
            )
        )}
    </ul>
);

export default MovieList;
```

This component begins by importing the MovieListItem component, which is also a presentational component. Then, the MovieList component accepts a movies prop that contains the list of movies to display and an event handler prop to select a movie for editing or deletion.

The JSX begins by checking the movies prop to see if it contains any movies. If it doesn't, the code passes a null value to the MovieListItem component to indicate that no movies are available from state.

However, if the movies prop contains movies, the code maps each movie to a MovieListItem component. To do that, it sets the key for the movie to the movie's id, it sets the movie attribute to the movie object, and it sets the onSelect attribute to the onSelect event handler.

This code doesn't call the onSelect event handler. Instead, it passes that prop down to MovieListItem. This is known as *prop drilling*. Extensive prop drilling can clutter your code and make it hard to understand and refactor. However, for this app, the prop drilling is easy enough to understand.

The MovieListItem component shown next displays the data for a movie, and it uses the Icon component to also display the Edit and Delete icons for that movie.

The MovieListItem component

```
import Icon from "../common/Icon";
import "./MovieListItem.css";

const MovieListItem = ({ movie, onSelect }) => (
    movie? (
        <li className="movie-list-item">
            {movie.name} ({movie.year})
            <Icon
                title="Edit"
                className="icon fa fa-pencil"
                onClick={() => onSelect(movie, 'edit')}
            />
            <Icon
                title="Delete"
                className="icon fa fa-trash"
                onClick={() => onSelect(movie, 'delete')}
            />
        </li>
    ) : (
        <li className="movie-list-empty">
            No movies yet. Add your first one!
        </li>
    )
);

export default MovieListItem;
```

This component begins by accepting props that contain the movie data and an event handler function to select a movie for editing or deletion. If the movie exists, it uses the movie prop to display the movie's name and year. Then, it uses the Icon component to display the icons for the Edit and Delete icons.

To display the Edit icon, this code sets the title attribute to "Edit", and it sets the className attribute to "icon fa fa-pencil" to display a Font Awesome icon that looks like a pencil. In addition, it sets the onClick attribute to an inline event handler that calls the onSelect prop and passes it the movie and a string of "edit" for the selection mode.

The code for displaying the Delete icon works similarly. However, it passes different values to the attributes of the Icon component. For example, it passes "icon fa fa-trash" to the className attribute to display a Font Awesome icon that looks like a trash can.

Either way, the event handlers originally defined in App pass through MovieList and MovieListItem to Icon. When the Edit or Delete icon is clicked, its handler calls back up to App, notifying it that the state has changed. The intermediate components just pass data and event handlers along, and the App component manages the state.

The MovieForm component shown next is a hybrid component that gets some state from its parent, App, and also manages some internal UI state. As the name implies, this component displays a form to work with a movie. This provides a way to add and delete movies. Since this component contains many lines of code, this chapter presents it in multiple parts.

The MovieForm component (part 1)

```
// import functions
import { useState, useEffect } from 'react'
import { v4 as getUniqueID } from 'uuid';

// import components and CSS
import FormInput from '../common/FormInput';
import FormButtons from '../common/FormButtons';
import './MovieForm.css';
```

Here, the code imports the useState and useEffect hooks from the React module. Then, it imports a function named v4 from the uuid module and gives it an alias of getUniqueID.

The uuid module isn't part of React, but it is an npm package that you can install to generate a *UUID (universally unique identifier)*. To install this package, run the following command in the terminal.

The command for installing the uuid package

```
npm install uuid
```

After importing the uuid module, the MovieForm component imports the FormInput and FormButtons components. Then, it uses a function to define the MovieForm component as shown next.

The MovieForm component (part 2)

```
const MovieForm = ({ selectedMovie, onAdd, onEdit, onDelete, onCancel }) => {
    // state variables
    const [name, setName] = useState('');
    const [year, setYear] = useState('');

    // effect to prefill the form. this effect runs when
    // the component mounts and when selectedMovie changes
    useEffect(() => {
        if (selectedMovie) {
            setName(selectedMovie.name);
            setYear(selectedMovie.year.toString()); // convert year to string
        } else {
            setName('');
            setYear('');
        }
    }, [selectedMovie]);  // dependency array
```

This function accepts props for the selected movie as well as event handlers to add, edit, delete, and cancel the edit or deletion of a movie. Then, it defines state variables and setters for the name and year of a movie.

After defining its state, MovieForm uses the useEffect hook to prefill data in the form. To do that, it passes a function to the useEffect() function that checks the selectedMovie prop. If it has a value, it passes the name and year properties of the selected movie to the setName() and setYear() setters. Otherwise, it resets the form by passing empty strings to the setName() and setYear() setters. In addition, it passes the selectedMovie prop as the dependency array. This tells React to run the function when MovieForm mounts and when the value of selectedMovie changes.

The MovieForm component (part 3)

```
// determine whether movie is being added, edited, or deleted
const isEditing = selectedMovie?.mode === 'edit';
const isDeleting = selectedMovie?.mode === 'delete';
const isAdding = !selectedMovie;

// event handler for the submit event of the form
const handleSubmit = (e) => {
    // prevent default form submission behavior
    e.preventDefault();

    // add, edit, or delete movie
    if (isAdding) {
        onAdd({ id: getUniqueID(), name, year: +year }); // year to number
    } else if (isEditing) {
        onEdit({ ...selectedMovie, name, year: +year }); // year to number
    } else if (isDeleting) {
        onDelete(selectedMovie.id);
    }
};
```

After prefilling the form, MovieForm defines Boolean flags that indicate whether a movie is being added, edited, or deleted. To do that, it checks the mode property of the selectedMovie object. If its value is 'edit', the code sets isEditing to true. If its value is 'delete', the code sets isDeleting to true. And if the object is null, the code sets isAdding to true.

After setting the Boolean flags, MovieForm defines an event handler named handleSubmit that's called when the form submits. This handler begins by cancelling the default form submission. Then, it checks the Boolean flags.

If isAdding is true, the code adds a new movie to the list. To do that, it calls the onAdd prop and passes it a new object with id, name, and year properties. It calls the getUniqueID() function to generate the id value, and it uses the (+) operator to convert the year from a string to a number.

If isEditing is true, the code updates the movie's data. To do that, it calls the onEdit prop and passes it a copy of selectedMovie merged with the name and year stored in state. This overwrites the name and year properties in selectedMovie while preserving the id property. Once again, it uses the (+) operator to convert the year value to a number.

If isDeleting is true, the code deletes the selected movie. To do that, it calls the onDelete prop and passes it the id of the selected Movie.

Finally, the MovieForm component returns its JSX as shown next.

The MovieForm component (part 4)

```jsx
    return (
        <form onSubmit={handleSubmit}>
            <div className="movie">
                <h2>
                    {isAdding && "Add Movie"}
                    {isEditing && "Edit Movie"}
                    {isDeleting && "Confirm Delete"}
                </h2>
                <FormInput
                    label="Name"
                    name="name"
                    value={name}                          // state variable
                    onChange={(e) => setName(e.target.value)} // state setter
                    placeholder="Name"
                    disabled={isDeleting}  // make read-only if deleting
                    required
                />
                <FormInput
                    label="Year"
                    type="number"
                    name="year"
                    value={year}                          // state variable
                    onChange={(e) => setYear(e.target.value)} // state setter
                    placeholder="Year"
                    disabled={isDeleting}  // make read-only if deleting
                    required
                />
            </div>
            <FormButtons
                isEditing={isEditing}
                isDeleting={isDeleting}
                onCancel={onCancel}
            />
        </form>
    )
}

export default MovieForm;
```

This JSX defines a form and assigns the handleSubmit event handler to the onSubmit attribute. Within the form, it uses the Boolean flags to determine whether the heading should be "Add Movie", "Edit Movie" or "Confirm Delete".

After displaying the correct heading, it uses FormInput to display the labels and text fields for the name and year. Because it passes the state value and setter to the value and onChange attributes, these FormInput components are controlled components. Also, since the second FormInput passes a type prop of "number", this overrides the default value of "text".

The JSX uses FormButtons to display the Add/Edit/Delete button and the Cancel button on the form. To do that, it passes the isEditing flag to the isEditing attribute and the isDeleting flag to the isDeleting attribute.

In addition, it passes the onCancel event handler it receives from its parent to the onCancel attribute. By contrast, no event handler is passed for the Add/Edit/Delete button. That's because that button is a submit button. As a result, clicking it triggers the submit event of the form that contains it.

MovieForm is a hybrid component because it receives some state from its parent, App. However, it also manages its own UI state, including defining event handlers, managing side effects, and passing state to child components.

Perspective

This chapter presented the most important skills for working with state in React components. To do that, this chapter introduced you to two hooks, useState and useEffect. The next chapter presents more information about using these two hooks, and it presents the most important skills for working with other hooks.

Terms

state

hook

controlled component

co-locating state

lifting state

presentational component

hybrid component

container component

side effect

prop drilling

universally unique identifier (UUID)

Exercise 4-1: Refactor the My Playlist app

This exercise shows how to refactor the My Playlist app shown next to add state and event handlers for the buttons on the form.

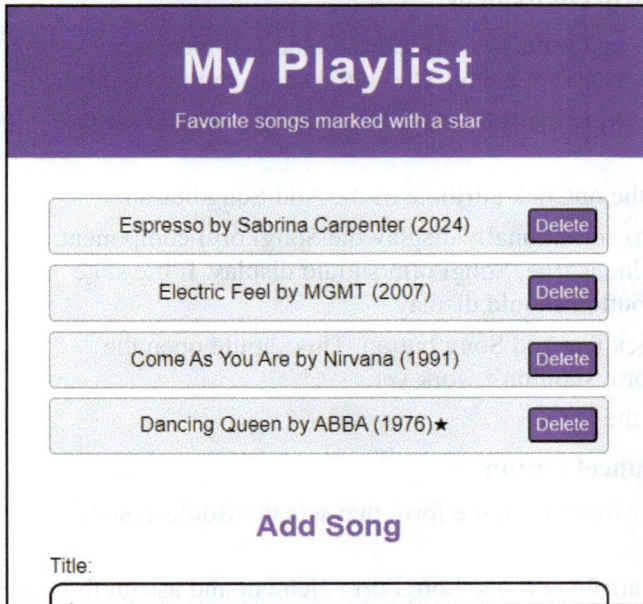

Review the starting code

1. Open the my-playlist project in the ex_starts/ch04 folder.

2. Open the components in the components directory and review them.

   - Header and Footer are the same as the previous chapter.

   - Input is new, but you don't need to change it. It uses open-ended props so you can override or add to the default attributes.

   - SongForm is new and uses Input to create a form to add a song. SongForm accepts two event handlers as props.

   - Playlist accepts an event handler as a prop and has a Delete button.

   - App imports SongForm and has comments that indicate the state and event handlers it should have.

3. Run the app and click on some of the buttons. They shouldn't do anything yet.

Add state for the list of songs

4. In App, import the useState hook and create a state variable and setter for an array of songs. You can use the existing songs array as the initial value. To make your code more readable, you can change the name of the existing array to initialSongs if you want.

5. Update the JSX for the Playlist component to assign the state variable to the songs attribute.

6. Switch to the browser and make sure the app still works the same.

Add state to display the SongForm component

7. In App, create a state variable and setter for a Boolean value that indicates whether to display the SongForm component. The initial value should be false.

8. Code an event handler for showing the form. This event handler should set the Boolean state value to true.

9. Assign this event handler to the onClick attribute of the Add Song button.

10. Use the Boolean state value to conditionally display the SongForm component below Playlist. If the state value is true, SongForm should display. If the state value is false, the Add Song button should display.

11. Switch to the browser and click the Add Song button. This should open the form to add a song, but the form shouldn't work yet.

12. Refresh the browser to close the form.

Add an event handler for the Cancel button

13. In App, code an event handler for closing the form that sets the Boolean state variable to false.

14. In the JSX, add an onCancel attribute to the SongForm element and assign this event handler to it.

15. In SongForm, assign the onCancel prop to the onClick attribute of the Cancel button.

16. Switch to the browser, click on the Add Song button to open the form, and click on the Cancel button to close the form.

Add an event handler for the Add button

17. In App, code an event handler that accepts a song object and adds it to the array of songs in state.

    This handler should add a unique id value to the object before adding it to state. To do that, you can use the uuid package as shown in the chapter. Or, you can use the reduce() method of the array to get the max id value of the songs in state and add 1 to that for the new id.

    This handler should also set the Boolean state variable to false so the form closes after adding a song.

18. In the JSX, add an onAdd attribute to the SongForm element and assign this event handler to it.

19. In SongForm, import the useState hook and add state variables for the title, artist, year, and favorite fields in the form.

20. In the JSX, review the Input elements. Note that year and favorite override the default type value of 'text'.

21. For the text fields, add value and onChange attributes that use the state variables and setters to the Input elements for the text fields.

22. For the checkbox, add checked and onChange attributes that use the state variables and setters. In the onChange attribute, use the e.target.checked property to get the current value of the checkbox.

23. Code an event handler for the submit event of the form that calls the onAdd prop and passes the local state data to it as an object. Make sure the submit button doesn't submit the form to the server.

24. In the JSX, assign this event handler to the onSubmit attribute of the form.

25. Switch to the browser, click Add Song, enter valid values, and click Add. This should close the form and display the song in the list.

Add an event handler for the Delete buttons

26. In App, code a handler that accepts the id value of a song and uses it to remove the song from the array of songs in state.

27. In the JSX, add an onDelete attribute to the Playlist component and assign this event handler to it.

28. In Playlist, code an inline event handler for the onClick attribute of the Delete button that calls the onDelete prop and passes it the id of the selected song.

29. Switch to the browser and click Delete on one or more songs. This should remove the songs from the list.

Chapter 5

Enhance components with hooks

In React, components are the building blocks that describe the UI. Hooks, by contrast, define the logic that brings the UI to life. This chapter shows how to use hooks to "hook into" the React component lifecycle. It expands your knowledge of the hooks presented in the previous chapter, shows how to use some other hooks available from React, and shows how to write custom hooks to encapsulate and reuse logic across components.

An introduction to hooks

In React, each component has a lifecycle, and you often need to run code at specific points in that lifecycle. When you use functions to define components, as shown in this book, you can use *hooks* to "hook into" the lifecycle of a component. This allows you to work with state, side effects, and other React features.

The React component lifecycle

To understand hooks, it helps to understand the React component lifecycle. A React component goes through three main lifecycle phases.

The three phases of the component lifecycle

1. **Mount (initial render).** React creates the component and adds it to the DOM.
2. **Update (re-render).** When a change is made to a component's props or state, React runs the component function again. Then, it updates the DOM as needed.
3. **Unmount.** React removes the component from the DOM.

Within these phases of the lifecycle, there's an internal rendering cycle.

The internal rendering cycle

* **Render.** React calls the component function, translates the JSX to a virtual DOM, and compares it to the previous virtual DOM (if any).
* **Commit.** React applies any needed changes to the actual DOM.
* **Effects.** React runs any side effects. This step also runs any cleanup functions from previous effects as described later in this chapter.

The following diagram shows the component lifecycle.

The component lifecycle with the rendering cycle

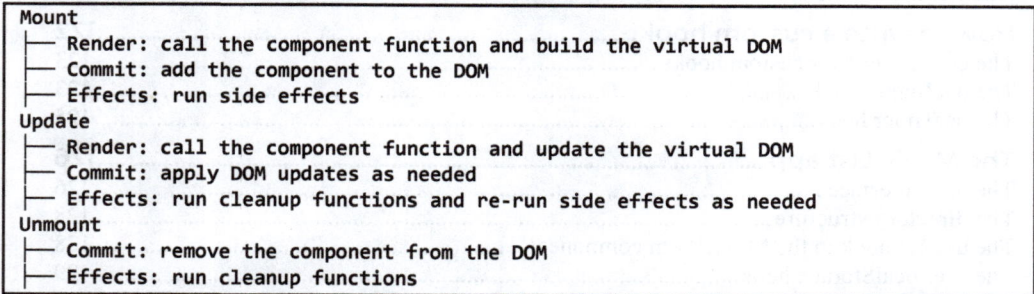

```
Mount
├── Render: call the component function and build the virtual DOM
├── Commit: add the component to the DOM
├── Effects: run side effects
Update
├── Render: call the component function and update the virtual DOM
├── Commit: apply DOM updates as needed
├── Effects: run cleanup functions and re-run side effects as needed
Unmount
├── Commit: remove the component from the DOM
├── Effects: run cleanup functions
```

The Render step doesn't occur in the Unmount phase because React is removing the component from the DOM in that phase.

Where hooks fit in the component lifecycle

The following tables describe when some common built-in hooks run in the component lifecycle. These tables should enhance your understanding of the useState and useEffect hooks described in the previous chapters.

These tables also describe two other hooks (useRef and useLayoutEffect). For now, don't worry if you don't understand them! Later, this chapter shows how to use them.

React built-in hooks in the component lifecycle

Mount	Description
Render	useState creates and initializes a state value
	useRef creates and initializes a stable reference object
Commit	React updates the DOM
	React assigns a DOM node to the reference object
Effect	useEffect and useLayoutEffect run side effects

Update	Description
Render	useState returns the current stored state value
	useRef returns the same reference object as before
Commit	React updates the DOM
	React updates the DOM node in the reference object as needed
Effect	useEffect and useLayoutEffect run cleanup functions and re-run side effects only if dependencies change

Unmount	Description
Commit	React removes component from the DOM
Effect	useEffect and useLayoutEffect run all cleanup functions

The Rules of Hooks

Now that you understand the React component lifecycle and where hooks fit into it, it's helpful to understand how React calls the hooks in a function component.

During the mount (initial render) phase, React calls all the hooks in a function component in order. This might seem confusing, since you just learned that the side effects in useEffect run after render and commit, during the effects step. That's because React calls useEffect() during render, but it doesn't call its callback function at that time. Instead, it schedules the callback to run after commit.

During the update (re-render) phase, React checks the useEffect() dependency array for changes from the previous render. If there are any, it schedules the callback to run after commit. And if there's a cleanup function like one of the cleanup functions presented later in this chapter, React schedules it to run before the callback.

To make this work, React tracks the hooks by their position in the function component. For example, consider the following code.

The start of a component that uses hooks

```
const MovieForm = ({ selectedMovie, onAdd, onEdit, onDelete, onCancel }) => {
    const [name, setName] = useState(''); // hook #1
    const [year, setYear] = useState(''); // hook #2

    useEffect(() => {                      // hook #3
        if (selectedMovie) {
            setName(selectedMovie.name);
            setYear(selectedMovie.year.toString());
        }
    }, [selectedMovie]);
```

When React mounts this component, it moves from top to bottom and calls the hooks in order. The first call to useState() is hook #1, the second call to useState() is hook #2, and the call to useEffect() is hook #3. React associates the name state with hook #1, the year state with hook #2, and the side effect callback and the values in the dependency array with hook #3. Then, when React re-runs this component during update, it calls the hooks in order again and retrieves the state, dependency arrays, and other data associated with each position.

Because React calls all the hooks in order and expects them to be in the same position each time, there are some limits to how you can use hooks. The React team calls these the *Rules of Hooks*.

The Rules of Hooks

- **Only call a hook at the top level.** You can't call a hook in a conditional statement, loop, or nested function.
- **Only call a hook from a function component or another hook.** You can't call a hook from a regular function, a class component, or outside a function component.

The first rule is necessary because React can't track the hooks if the order of the hooks changes between renders. For example, suppose that the second call to useState() in the previous example is coded within a conditional statement. When the condition is false and useState() isn't called, the useEffect() call becomes hook #2 and React tries to associate the year state with it. This can lead to errors.

The second rule is necessary because hooks rely on React's rendering process, which only happens inside function components or custom hooks. So, if you code a hook in a regular function or class, React won't track it and the hook won't work as expected.

There's a plugin called eslint-plugin-react-hooks that helps enforce the Rules of Hooks. To get this plugin to work in VS Code, you can use VS Code to install the ESLint plugin, run "npm install eslint-plugin-react-hooks" to install the React hooks plugin, and configure that plugin in your project. This chapter doesn't show how to work with this plugin, but you can find information about it online.

More skills to work with state

The previous chapter showed how to use the useState hook in components. Now, this chapter reviews some of that material and presents some additional skills for working with state.

The useState hook

The useState hook allows your component to "remember" a value between renders and to update that value. When you update the value, it triggers a re-render of the component. To use the useState hook, you begin by importing it from the React module as shown next.

Import the useState() function

```
import { useState } from 'react';
```

Then, you call the useState() function with an optional initial value as shown next.

Call the useState() function

```
const [name, setName] = useState('');
```

The useState() function returns an array with the current state value and a setter function to update that value. Because the setter triggers a re-render of the component, you can't call it directly during rendering. If you do, you start an infinite render loop. Instead, you can call the setter in an event handler or in a useEffect() callback.

When you call a state setter to update an object or array based on the previous state, you should pass a function to the setter. React automatically passes the previous state to this function, and the function should return a new copy of the object or array with changes, as shown next.

A state setter with a function

```
setMovies((prev) => [...prev, newMovie]);
```

This makes sure you don't lose data, since React replaces the entire object or array when you call the setter. It also avoids issues with stale data that can happen because React updates state asynchronously.

How React stores state values

When React calls useState() on mount (initial render), it stores the initial value internally. In other words, the value that useState() returns lets you access the state value, but that's not where React stores it between renders.

When you call the setter function returned by useState(), React updates its internal value and schedules a re-render of the component. On update (re-render), React runs the component function again and the call to useState() returns the updated internal value.

In other words, your component doesn't hold onto the state value. React does. On each render, React gives your component a fresh copy of the current state.

How the initial value works

The initial value that you pass to useState() is optional. That is, you can call useState() with no argument as shown next.

Bad practice - Call the useState() function with no initial value

```
const [name, setName] = useState();
```

When you omit the initial value, React assigns undefined to its internal state on mount. For instance, in the previous example, the initial value of name is undefined.

However, in almost all cases it's better to explicitly set an initial value. If you want your initial value to be empty, you can pass null as shown next.

Set the initial state value to null

```
const [name, setName] = useState(null);
```

And if you want to clear a state value you can pass null again as shown next.

Clear the state value by resetting it to null

```
setName(null);
```

Passing null indicates that the value is intentionally set to empty, perhaps to indicate that no value is selected or the value has been cleared. Undefined, by contrast, typically indicates a missing or uninitialized value.

React only uses the initial value on mount. On every re-render, React ignores the initial value and returns the state value it stores internally.

How and when to use an initializer function

As you just learned, React only uses the initial value passed to useState() on mount. When the initial value is a variable or literal value, that's no problem.

However, when it's an expression or a function call, that can cause unnecessary work. Consider the following example.

The initial value is a function call

```
const [today, setToday] = useState(new Date());
```

Here, the function call that creates the date object runs on every render of the component, even though React only uses the value it returns on mount. In other words, a new Date object is created on every render but React ignores it after the initial render. This is called *eager initialization*.

For functions that run fast, like Date(), this usually isn't a problem. Even though it might seem wasteful to create and discard Date objects, in most cases it won't affect the performance of your component.

However, for more expensive operations, this can slow your component. In those cases, you can pass a function that returns a value instead. This function is called a *function initializer.*

The initial value is a function initializer

```
const [name, setName] = useState(() => localStorage.getItem("name") || "friend");
```

Here, since useState() receives a function definition, React knows to call that function only once, on mount. This is called *lazy initialization.*

Most of the time, eager initialization is fine. But if the initial value requires expensive computations or involves side effects (such as reading from local storage or parsing a query string), it's often best to use a function initializer.

More skills to work with side effects

In the previous chapters, you learned that a React component should be a *pure function*. That means it always returns the same JSX given the same props and state, and it doesn't cause any side effects during rendering.

In React, a *side effect* is an action that goes beyond rendering a component. Common examples include fetching data, setting timers, updating the document title, reading/writing local storage, and attaching event listeners.

In addition, any action that isn't safe to perform during render because it isn't pure can be considered a side effect. For example, you shouldn't call a state setter function directly during render.

Sometimes, of course, you want your component to take one of these actions. For example, the previous chapter shows how to use the useEffect hook to set state.

The useEffect hook

The useEffect hook lets you schedule a side effect to run after your component renders and React commits any changes to the DOM. To use this hook, you begin by importing it from the React module as shown next.

Import the useEffect() function

```
import { useEffect } from 'react';
```

Then, you call the useEffect() function, passing it two arguments as shown next.

Call the useEffect() function to set the document title

```
useEffect(() => {
    const hour = new Date().getHours();
    document.title =
        hour < 12 ? 'Good morning!' :
        hour < 18 ? 'Good afternoon!' :
        'Good evening!';
}, []);
```

In the useEffect() function, the first argument specifies a callback function that React runs after the component renders and commits. In this example, the callback creates a new Date object and uses it to set the title property of the document object. This sets the text that displays on the tab in the browser.

The second argument specifies a *dependency array* that tells React whether to re-run the callback on update. If any of the values in the array change between renders, React re-runs the callback. If the array is empty, React runs the effect only once, on mount. Here, the empty dependency array means the title property is set once, after the component renders for the first time.

Use the dependency array

The dependency array you pass to useEffect() should contain all the values used in the effect that come from the component's scope. This includes props passed to the component and state defined in the component. If you don't include these values, your effect may run with stale values.

However, you don't need to include values that are stable. If you know a value isn't going to change between renders, it doesn't need to be in the array. The most common example of a stable value is a state setter function. React guarantees that these don't change, so you don't need to include them in the dependency array.

Finally, you should know that the dependency array is actually optional. If you omit it, React runs the side effect after every render. For instance, the following code logs a message to the console on every render.

Log a message to the console on every render

```
useEffect(() => {
    console.log('Run on every render');
}); // no dependency array
```

Usually, this isn't what you want. Most of the time, you want to make sure the effect only runs under certain conditions. However, running an effect on every render can be useful in rare circumstances. The most common circumstance is when you want to log something on every render of the component as shown in the previous example.

Return a cleanup function

Often, React doesn't automatically manage side effects, so you need to clean them up manually. To do that, make sure the callback function you pass to useEffect() returns a *cleanup function*.

For instance, React doesn't automatically wire window events like it does component events. So, if you want to work with window events, such as resize or scroll, you need to add and remove those events handlers yourself.

Consider the following example.

Add and remove an event listener

```
// state to manage window size
const [size, setSize] = useState({
    width: window.innerWidth,
    height: window.innerHeight,
});

// effect to add event handler for window resize events
useEffect(() => {
    const handleResize = () => {
        setSize({ // don't need function updater bc the entire state is replaced
            width: window.innerWidth,
            height: window.innerHeight,
        });
    };

    // add event listener to the window object
    window.addEventListener('resize', handleResize);

    // return cleanup function to remove the event listener
    return () => window.removeEventListener('resize', handleResize);
}, []); // empty array: run once on mount
```

In this example, the callback adds an event listener for the resize event of the window object. Then, the callback returns a cleanup function that removes that event listener.

In addition, the value passed to setSize() is an object rather than an updater function. In this case, you don't need to use an updater function to prevent lost or stale data because this code replaces the entire state object with a new one.

Another common use case for cleanup functions is asynchronous tasks like timers or fetch requests. If these tasks are still running when the effect re-runs or the component unmounts, it can lead to memory leaks or bugs such as trying to update state on an unmounted component. Returning a cleanup function helps avoid these problems.

In the following example, the callback starts a timer to count elapsed seconds. Then, the callback returns a cleanup function that stops the timer on unmount.

Set up and clear a timer

```
// state to track elapsed seconds
const [seconds, setSeconds] = useState(0);

// effect to start a timer that updates count every second
useEffect(() => {
    // setInterval returns an ID we can use to clear the timer later
    const intervalId = setInterval(() => {
        setSeconds(prev => prev + 1); // use function updater to set state
    }, 1000);

    // cleanup function clears the timer when component unmounts
    return () => clearInterval(intervalId);
}, []); // empty array: run once on mount
```

When you return a cleanup function in the callback sent to useEffect(), here's how React uses it.

How React uses a cleanup function returned by useEffect()

Lifecycle phase	Description
Mount	React saves the cleanup function but doesn't run it.
Update	If any dependencies have changed, React runs the saved cleanup function, calls the effect again, and saves the new cleanup function.
Unmount	React runs the last saved cleanup function.

During update, React only runs the cleanup function if any value in the dependency array has changed. Otherwise, it doesn't run the cleanup function or re-run the effect.

During unmount, by contrast, React runs the cleanup function whether or not any dependencies have changed. That's to make sure that all resources are cleaned up before it removes the component from the DOM.

When to use the useLayoutEffect hook

React has another hook to run side effects named useLayoutEffect. You use this hook to avoid visual flickers and glitches when your side effect measures or mutates the DOM. Since that rarely happens, you typically don't need to use useLayoutEffect.

Like the useEffect() function, the useLayoutEffect() function accepts a callback function and a dependency array. And, the callback runs after the component renders and changes are committed to the DOM.

However, while the useEffect() callback runs asynchronously after the browser paints the DOM, the useLayoutEffect() callback runs synchronously after commit but before the paint phase. As a result, useLayoutEffect() blocks the painting of the DOM until the effect completes, which can cause performance issues. So, you should only use useLayoutEffect() if useEffect() causes UI flickers or glitches.

Common use cases for the useLayoutEffect hook

- Measure and adjust layout
- Synchronize animations and transitions
- Manually scroll or resize elements
- Third-party libraries that expect to be rendered synchronously before paint

At this point, you may be wondering, why would I measure or mutate the DOM anyway? Isn't React designed to keep me from working directly with the DOM? Yes, it is. However, you may occasionally need to mutate the DOM as described in the next section.

How to write imperative code

In some cases, you need to interact directly with the DOM. For example, if you need to set focus on an element or control an audio or video element, you need to interact directly with the DOM. To do that, you can use the useRef hook to write imperative code.

The useRef hook

The useRef hook lets you create an object that refers to a DOM element. Then, you can write code that works with that reference.

To use the useRef hook, you begin by importing it from the React module as shown next.

Import the useRef() function

```
import { useRef } from 'react';
```

Then, you call the useRef() function with an optional initial value.

Call the useRef() function

```
const nameRef = useRef(null);
```

The useRef() function creates an internal object with a property named current, assigns the initial value to the current property, and returns a reference to the object. Like useState(), the initial value is only used on mount and is ignored on subsequent re-renders. However, unlike useState(), useRef() doesn't support lazy initialization with an initializer function. If you pass a function as an initial value, React assigns the function itself to current, not the value the function returns.

At this point, you have a reference object, but it doesn't refer to a DOM element yet. To make that reference, you modify your JSX to add a ref attribute to a DOM element and assign the reference object to it as shown next.

Add a ref attribute in the JSX for the name field

```
<input
    id="user-name"
    name="user-name"
    type="text"
    ref={nameRef}
    value={name}
    onChange={(e) => setName(e.target.value)}
/>
```

The ref attribute tells React you want a reference to this DOM element. In other words, it tells React to let your code interact with this element directly.

React calls the useRef() function during render and creates the reference object at that time. However, React doesn't assign the DOM element to the current property of that object until commit. Specifically, it assigns it after the DOM is updated but before the browser paints the DOM. This means you need to wait until after commit to work with a reference object that contains a DOM node.

For example, the following code shows how to set the focus on the name field after the component renders and is committed to the DOM.

Set focus on the name field

```
useEffect(() => {
    nameRef.current.focus();
}, []);
```

Pass refs to a component

With React 19 and later, you can use reference objects, also known as refs, with custom components. To do that, you pass a ref object to the component's ref attribute. Then, React includes that ref as a prop. Within your custom component, you pass the ref to the DOM element you want to expose.

The following example shows an Input component that receives a ref as a prop and passes it to its <input> element.

An Input component that receives a ref

```
const Input = ({ref, ...props}) => {
    return <input ref={ref} {...props} />;
};
```

Here, the code passes the ref prop of the Input component to the ref attribute of the <input> element. Because of this, you can use Input in a parent component and pass a ref to it, just like you would with a built-in DOM element.

The following example shows a parent component that passes a ref to Input.

A parent component that uses the Input component

```
import { useRef, useEffect } from 'react';
import Input from './components/Input';

const App = () => {
    const inputRef = useRef(null);

    useEffect(() => {
        inputRef.current.focus();
    }, []);

    return <Input ref={inputRef} />;
};
```

Here, App creates a reference object with useRef() and passes it to Input in the JSX. Then, Input passes the ref to a DOM element. So, the ref created in App points to the DOM element specified by Input. This lets App set the focus on the <input> element within Input.

Prior to React 19, you couldn't pass a ref as a regular prop. Instead, you needed to import the forwardRef() function from React and use it to wrap your component. Although this book doesn't present the forwardRef() function, you can find good documentation about it online if you need to support it.

Another use for the useRef hook

The useRef hook is designed to allow developers to access the DOM and write imperative code. However, developers soon discovered another "off label" use, which is to store a value between renders.

Of course, you can already use state to store a value between renders. But, when you update a state value, you trigger a re-render of the component. If the value you're storing doesn't affect the UI, you might not want to re-render. So, developers began to use the reference object returned by useRef() to store values like timer ids, previous state values, previous prop values, or cached data.

The following example presents a component that uses a reference object to store a previous prop value between renders.

The HighScoreDisplay component

```
import { useRef } from "react";
import './HighScoreDisplay.css';

const HighScoreDisplay = ( {newHighScore} ) => {
    // ref to store high score - set to 0 on mount
    const highScore = useRef(0);

    // update high score if new high score is greater
    if (newHighScore > highScore.current) {
        highScore.current = newHighScore;
    }

    return (
        <div className="high-score-display">
            <h3>High score: {highScore.current}</h3>
            <h4>Latest high score: {newHighScore}</h4>
        </div>
    );
};

export default HighScoreDisplay;
```

Here, the HighScoreDisplay component creates a reference object named highScore and assigns an initial value of zero to its current property. This initial value is only assigned on mount. After that, React ignores it and returns the same reference object with the latest value of current on every render.

After setting the initial value, HighScoreDisplay compares the prop value to the stored value. If the prop value is greater, it replaces the stored value. This code doesn't need to use useEffect() to update the current property because you can read from or write to a reference object that stores a non-DOM value at any time.

With React 19 and later, you can use cleanup functions with refs when the component unmounts. For scenarios such as the ones presented in this chapter, that's unnecessary because React already clears refs automatically on unmount. For more details, you can view the React documentation online.

How to write a custom hook

So far, this chapter has shown you how to use some of the built-in hooks that React provides. However, you can also define your own custom hooks. A custom hook lets you encapsulate logic and reuse it across components.

A custom hook can use built-in hooks like useState or useEffect. It can also use other custom hooks.

A custom hook doesn't have to interact deeply with the React component lifecycle to be useful. If it makes your app more modular and readable, encapsulating logic that uses state can be reason enough for a custom hook.

The conventions for custom hooks

A custom hook in React is a regular JavaScript function. You don't need to do anything special to create one. However, there are some conventions you need to follow for your hook to work properly.

Conventions for a custom hook

- **Start its name with 'use'.** This notifies React that your function is a hook so it knows to track it and enforce the Rules of Hooks.
- **Only call other hooks.** A custom hook can call built-in hooks or other custom hooks but shouldn't call React components or regular functions, even if those functions contain hooks.
- **Use parameters or hooks to receive outside data.** This keeps a custom hook reuseable and independent from the components that use it.
- **Return a value that a component can use.** This is how a custom hook shares logic across components. The return value can be a single value, an object, an array, or a function.
- **Don't use any JSX.** A custom hook shouldn't work with or return JSX.
- **Use the .js file extension**. Since a custom hook should only contain JavaScript, not JSX, a file that contains a custom hook should use the .js extension, not the .jsx extension.

Technically, you can define a custom hook that follows these conventions even if it doesn't call built-in hooks like useState or useRef. That's because the main purpose of a custom hook is to encapsulate reusable logic. However, if your custom hook doesn't call any hooks, it's probably better to write it as a regular utility function instead. That way, React doesn't spend resources tracking it or enforcing the Rules of Hooks.

The useToggle hook

To give you an idea of how a hook can be used, the following code creates a hook that encapsulates functionality for toggling a Boolean value on or off.

The useToggle hook

```
import { useState } from 'react';

export const useToggle = (initialValue = false) => {
    // state to keep track of the toggle value
    const [value, setValue] = useState(initialValue);

    // function to toggle the value
    const onToggle = () => setValue(prev => !prev);

    // return an array with the current value and the toggle function
    return [value, onToggle];
};
```

Here, the useToggle hook starts by using state to keep track of whether the toggle value is true or false. Then, it defines a function that calls the state setter to update the state to the opposite value. Finally, it returns an array with two values: the current toggle value and the function to change the toggle value.

You can use the useToggle hook in a toggle button like the one shown next.

The UI for a toggle button

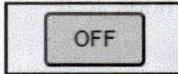

```
OFF
```

To create a button like this, you can define a ToggleButton component that uses the useToggle hook as shown next.

A component that uses the useToggle hook

```jsx
import { useToggle } from '../hooks/useToggle';

const ToggleButton = () => {
    // use the custom hook to set up the toggle state and function
    const [isToggled, toggle] = useToggle();

    return (
        <button onClick={toggle}>
            {isToggled ? "ON" : "OFF"}
        </button>
    );
};

export default ToggleButton;
```

Here, the ToggleButton component begins by importing the custom useToggle hook. Like the built-in hooks, this import statement uses braces. That's because useToggle() is a named export of the useToggle.js file, not the default export. This matches the style of built-in hooks.

In the body of the function, ToggleButton calls useToggle() and extracts the toggle variable and function. This works much like calling useState() in that it returns a variable and a function that changes the variable. Then, the code returns JSX that defines a button. This button uses the toggle() function as its click event handler, and it uses the toggle value to determine the text that's displayed on the button.

Although this example is easy to follow, it's not very useful. All this component does is toggle the button text between ON and OFF. Still, it shows a simple example of encapsulating logic in a hook, and the rest of this chapter presents some more complex examples.

The useTimer hook

The custom useTimer hook shown next encapsulates the logic to start a timer when a component mounts. In addition, it stops the timer when the component unmounts. This is general-purpose logic that you can use in web apps for clocks, slideshows, and so on.

The useTimer hook

```
import { useEffect, useRef } from 'react';

export const useTimer = (onTick, tickInterval) => {
    // use a ref to store the latest version of the onTick function
    const onTickRef = useRef(onTick);

    // update the ref whenever onTick changes
    useEffect(() => {
        onTickRef.current = onTick;
    }, [onTick]);

    // start the timer on mount or whenever tickInterval changes
    useEffect(() => {
        // do nothing if tickInterval is not provided
        if (tickInterval == null) return;

        // start the timer and store its id
        const id = setInterval(() => onTickRef.current(), tickInterval);

        // stop the timer on unmount or whenever tickInterval changes
        return () => clearInterval(id);
    }, [tickInterval]);
};
```

The hook starts by creating a ref for the onTick prop. Then, it uses an effect to run some code on mount or whenever the onTick prop changes. This makes sure that the timer always calls the latest version of the onTick() function, which helps to avoid issues when the onTick() function depends on state or props that may change over time.

The hook continues by using an effect to run some code on mount or whenever the tickInterval prop changes. If a tick interval exists, this code starts the timer and runs the latest version of the onTick() function once every tick interval. In addition, it returns a cleanup function that stops the timer when the component unmounts or whenever the tickInterval prop changes.

You can use the useTimer hook in a Clock component like the one shown next.

The UI for a Clock component

```
1:38:57 PM
```

The code for this Clock component is shown next.

A Clock component that uses the useTimer hook

```
import { useState } from 'react';
import { useTimer } from '../hooks/useTimer';
import './Clock.css';

const Clock = () => {
    // local state to hold the current time
    const [now, setNow] = useState(new Date());

    // function and interval to pass to the timer hook
    const onTick = () => setNow(new Date());
    const interval = 1000;   // 1000 ms = 1 second

    // pass function and interval to the timer hook
    useTimer(onTick, interval);

    return (
        <div className="current-time">
            {now.toLocaleTimeString()}
        </div>
    );
};

export default Clock;
```

The Clock component begins by using state to store the current time. Then, it defines an onTick() function that sets the current time in state. In addition, it defines an interval of 1000ms (1 second). Next, it calls the useTimer() function and passes the onTick() function and the interval. This runs the onTick() function once every second until the component unmounts or the interval changes. The JSX for the Clock component just uses a <div> component to display a string for the current time that's stored in state.

The Movie List app

This chapter ends by presenting an enhanced version of the Movie List app from chapter 4. This version automatically moves the focus to the name field in the form, allows users to drag and drop the movies in the list to change their order, and stores the movies in local storage so they persist. To provide this functionality, the Movie List app uses built-in and custom hooks.

The user interface

The following screen capture shows how the Movie List app looks after displaying some movies.

The Movie List app with some movies

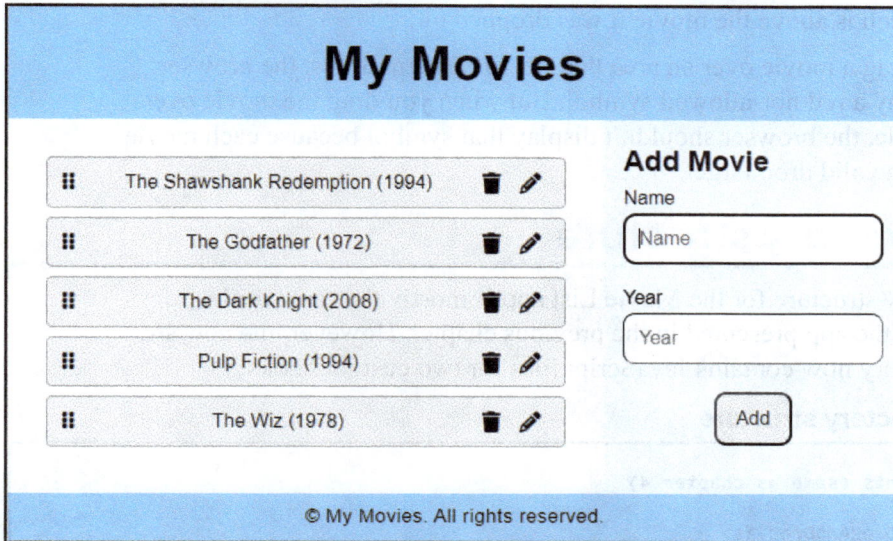

When this app loads, it moves the focus to the name field in the form. In addition, each movie in the list has a 'grip' icon to the left of the name that indicates the movie is draggable.

The following screen capture shows how the Movie List app looks when a movie is being dragged to a new position in the list.

The Movie List app while a movie is being dragged to a new position

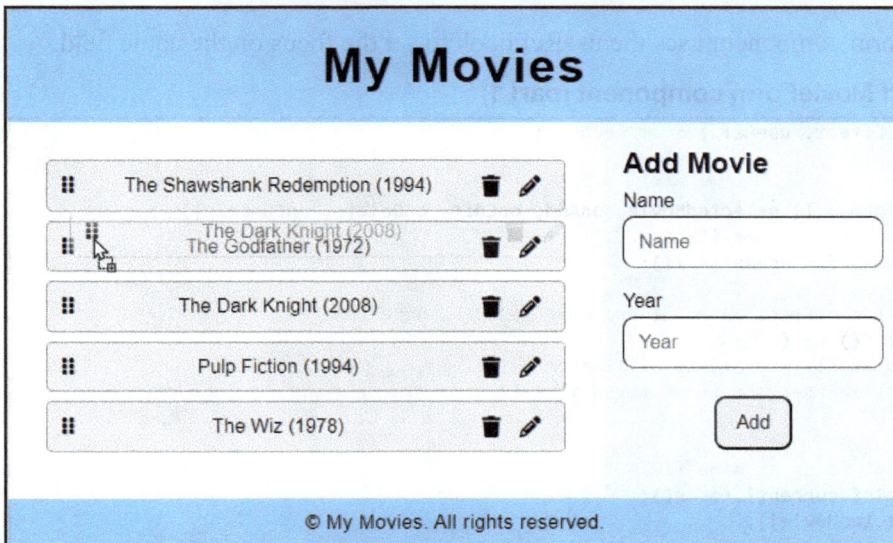

Here, one movie is being dragged over the movie above it. While it's being dragged, the browser displays the movie in light transparent text as it moves with the mouse. Once it's dropped, the browser displays the movie in its new position, which is above the movie it was dropped on.

When you drag a movie over an area that doesn't accept drops, the browser should display a red not-allowed symbol. But when you drag the movie over another movie, the browser shouldn't display that symbol because each movie in the list is a valid drop target.

The directory structure

The directory structure for the Movie List app is mostly the same as the structure for the app presented in the previous chapter. However, the new src/hooks directory now contains JavaScript files for two custom hooks.

The src directory structure

```
src
├── components (same as chapter 4)
├── hooks
│   ├── useDragAndDrop.js
│   └── useLocalStorage.js
└── (same as chapter 4)
```

This chapter describes both of the custom hooks a little later. But first, it describes how the Movie List app uses the built-in useRef hook.

The useRef hook in the MovieForm component

The MovieForm component uses the useRef hook to set the focus on the name field.

The updated MovieForm component (part 1)

```
import { useEffect, useRef } from 'react';
...

const MovieForm = ({ selectedMovie, onAdd, onEdit, onDelete, onCancel }) => {
    // define ref to name field
    const nameRef = useRef(null);

    // run side effects on mount and when selectedMovie changes
    useEffect(() => {
        // prefill the form if editing or deleting,
        // clear the form if no movie is selected
        ...

        // set focus on name field
        nameRef.current?.focus();
    }, [selectedMovie]);

    const handleSubmit = (e) => {
        // prevent default form submission behavior
        // add, edit, or delete the movie
```

```
        // set focus on name field after form submission
        nameRef.current?.focus();
};
```

To start, the MovieForm component imports the useRef hook. Then, it creates a reference to an object called nameRef and assigns a null value to it.

Within the effect that runs when the component mounts or the selected movie changes, this code uses the focus() method to move the focus to the object that the nameRef variable refers to. Similarly, in the submit event handler, this code moves the focus to the object that nameRef refers to. Both statements that move the focus use the optional chaining operator (?.) to make sure the object exists before calling the focus() method.

For this to work, the JSX for the component passes the nameRef variable to the ref attribute of the FormInput component as shown next.

The updated MovieForm component (part 2)

```
<FormInput
    ref={nameRef}          // assign this component to nameRef
    label="Name"
    name="name"
...
```

This assigns the ref for the name field to the ref attribute of the FormInput component for the name field.

For this to work, FormInput needs to assign the ref to one of its DOM elements as shown next.

The updated FormInput component

```
...
const FormInput = ( {ref, label, name, value, onChange, ...props} ) => (
    <>
        <label className="form-label" htmlFor={name}>{label}</label>
        <input
            ref={ref}  // assign this element to ref
            className="form-input"
            type="text"
...
```

Here, the FormInput component passes the ref prop to the ref attribute of the <input> element in the JSX. This allows any component that uses FormInput to pass a reference to its <input> element. This provides a way for the MovieForm component to set the focus on one of its FormInput components.

The useLocalStorage hook

The useLocalStorage hook encapsulates the functionality of reading from and writing to the browser's local storage.

The useLocalStorage.js file

```javascript
import { useState, useEffect } from 'react'

const useLocalStorage = (key, initialValue) => {
    // local state to manage the value in local storage; function initializer
    // that reads from local storage only runs once on mount
    const [value, setValue] = useState(() => {
        try {
            const stored = localStorage.getItem(key);
            return stored !== null ? JSON.parse(stored) : initialValue;
        } catch (error) {
            console.error(`Error reading localStorage key "${key}":`, error);
            return initialValue;
        }
    });

    // update local storage whenever the state value changes
    useEffect(() => {
        try {
            localStorage.setItem(key, JSON.stringify(value));
        } catch (error) {
            console.error(`Error writing localStorage key "${key}":`, error);
        }
    }, [key, value]);

    return [value, setValue];
};

export default useLocalStorage;
```

The useLocalStorage() function accepts a key and an initial value and uses them to create local state that tracks a value in local storage. The hook passes a function initializer to useState() so the code that reads local storage for the initial value only executes once, on mount.

After creating local state, the code uses an effect to update local storage whenever the local state value changes. Then, it returns the state value and setter in an array. That way, the calling code can call the setter to update local storage.

This hook uses error handling when it reads and writes from local storage because working with local storage can throw errors. For instance, local storage throws errors if cookies are blocked. Similarly, JSON.parse() throws errors if the JSON is malformed.

The App component uses the useLocalStorage hook to store movies in the browser's local storage.

The App component

```javascript
import { useState } from 'react'
import { useLocalStorage } from './hooks/useLocalStorage';
...

const App = () => {
```

```
// use custom hook to manage local storage for movies
const [movies, setMovies] = useLocalStorage('movies', []);
...
```

This call to the useLocalStorage() function reads the movies from local storage into the state variable named movies. In addition, this call returns a setMovies() function that the rest of the code in the App component can use to write the movies to local storage.

The useDragAndDrop hook

The useDragAndDrop hook contains the code that enables drag and drop functionality.

The useDragAndDrop.js file (part 1)

```
import { useRef } from "react";

export const useDragAndDrop = (onDrop) => {
    // Ref to store the item being dragged
    const dragItem = useRef(null);

    // Ref to store the item currently being hovered over
    const dragOverItem = useRef(null);
```

The useDragAndDrop() function accepts the onDrop prop, which is a function that contains the logic to run when an item is dropped. Then, this code creates refs to store the item being dragged and the item being hovered over.

The useDragAndDrop.js file (part 2)

```
    // called when dragging starts; records the item being dragged
    const handleDragStart = (item) => dragItem.current = item;

    // called when a dragged item enters another item's space;
    // records the item currently being hovered over
    const handleDragEnter = (item) => dragOverItem.current = item;

    // called when a dragged item is over a valid drop target;
    // required to allow drop (browser prevents drop by default)
    const handleDragOver = (e) => e.preventDefault();

    // called when dragging ends (drop or cancel)
    const handleDragEnd = () => {
        // get the current items from the refs
        const from = dragItem.current;        // source item
        const to = dragOverItem.current;      // target item

        // if both refs are set and point to different items,
        // call onDrop with source and target items
        if (from !== null && to !== null && from !== to) {
            onDrop(from, to);
        }

        // reset for next drag
```

```
            dragItem.current = null;
            dragOverItem.current = null;
    };
```

After defining the two references, the code defines four functions. These functions handle the events that occur when the drag starts, enters an item, is over an item, and ends.

To start, the handleDragStart() function stores the item being dragged, and the handleDragEnter() function stores the item being hovered over.

Then, the handleDragOver() function prevents the browser's default behavior. This is necessary because a browser doesn't accept a drop by default. As a result, to make the element being hovered over a valid drop target, you need to prevent the default action.

Finally, the handleDragEnd() function calls the onDrop() function if both refs have an item that aren't the same. Either way, it clears both refs for the next drag.

The useDragAndDrop.js file (part 3)

```
    // Return the drag event handlers
    return {
        handleDragStart,
        handleDragOver,
        handleDragEnter,
        handleDragEnd
    };
};
```

This hook returns the drag event handlers as methods of an object. This provides drag-and-drop functionality to consumers of this hook.

For this chapter, the App component has been updated to pass a function that handles the reordering of the movies to MovieList as shown next.

The App component

```
...
const App = () => {
    ...
    // reorder movies after drag and drop
    const handleReorder = (fromMovie, toMovie) => {
        // don't do anything if no movies or same movie
        if (!fromMovie || !toMovie || fromMovie.id === toMovie.id) return;

        // update the movies state
        setMovies(prev => {
            // get the indexes of the movies
            const fromIndex = prev.findIndex(m => m.id === fromMovie.id);
            const toIndex = prev.findIndex(m => m.id === toMovie.id);

            // if neither index is found, return previous state
            if (fromIndex === -1 || toIndex === -1) return prev;
```

```
                // copy previous state
                const updated = [...prev];

                // reorder the movies
                const [moved] = updated.splice(fromIndex, 1);
                updated.splice(toIndex, 0, moved);
                return updated;
        });
    };

    ...
    return (
            ...
            <MovieList
                movies={movies}
                onSelect={handleSelect}
                onReorder={handleReorder}
            />
            ...
```

Similarly, this chapter updates the Movie List component to pass the handleReorder function to the useDragAndDrop hook as shown next.

The MovieList component

```
import { useDragAndDrop } from '../../hooks/useDragAndDrop';
import MovieListItem from './MovieListItem';
import './MovieList.css';

const MovieList = ({ movies, onSelect, onReorder }) => {
    // pass onReorder to the useDragAndDrop hook and get the object it returns
    const dnd = useDragAndDrop(onReorder);

    return (
        <ul className="movie-list">
            {movies.length === 0 ? (
                <MovieListItem movie={null} />
            ) : (
                movies.map((movie) =>
                    <MovieListItem
                        key={movie.id}
                        movie={movie}
                        onSelect={onSelect}
                        onDragStart={() => dnd.handleDragStart(movie)}
                        onDragEnter={() => dnd.handleDragEnter(movie)}
                        onDragOver={dnd.handleDragOver}
                        onDragEnd={dnd.handleDragEnd}
                    />
                )
            )}
        </ul>
    );
};

export default MovieList;
```

After passing the function it receives from App to the useDragAndDrop hook, this code assigns the object the hook returns to a variable named dnd. You could use destructuring here to extract the individual functions from this object. However, since there are several functions, it's cleaner to use a single variable like this. When you do, it's best to use a short name that works like an alias.

The JSX for MovieList assigns the functions returned by the hook to the component's attributes. It assigns handleDragOver() and handleDragEnd() directly to the onDragOver and onDragEnd attributes. By contrast, it assigns inline functions to the onDragStart and onDragEnter attributes. These inline functions call handleDragStart() and handleDragEnter() respectively, passing them the current movie.

For this to work, this chapter also updates the MovieListItem component so it sets its draggable attribute to true and accepts and uses these drag and drop event handlers as shown next.

The MovieListItem component

```
import Icon from '../common/Icon';
import './MovieListItem.css';

const MovieListItem = ({ movie, onSelect, onDragStart, onDragOver,
    onDragEnter, onDragEnd }) => (
    movie? (
        <li
            className="movie-list-item"
            draggable="true"
            onDragStart={onDragStart}
            onDragOver={onDragOver}
            onDragEnter={onDragEnter}
            onDragEnd={onDragEnd}
            <Icon className="fa fa-grip-vertical" title="Reorder" />
            {movie.name} ({movie.year})
...
```

This code assigns new event handlers to the associated events of the <li> element in the JSX. It also uses an Icon component to display a grip icon to the left of the movie name.

Perspective

This chapter presented the most important skills for using hooks. To do that, it reviewed two built-in hooks (useState and useEffect), it presented another built-in hook (useRef), and it showed how to create custom hooks. The next chapter shows how to fetch data from a web API, including how to use a hook to do that. Later in this book, chapter 11 shows how to use two more hooks (useMemo and useCallback) to improve performance.

Terms

hook
Rules of Hooks
eager initialization
function initializer
lazy initialization
pure function
side effect
dependency array
cleanup function

Exercise 5-1: Refactor the Playlist app

This exercise shows how to refactor the Playlist app to use a modal dialog like
the one shown next to add or delete songs.

Review the starting code

1. Open the my-playlist project in the ex_starts/ch05 folder.
2. Review the code in the App.jsx file. Notice that it codes SongForm within an
   HTML <dialog> element and the Add Song button after that.

3. Review the CSS in App.css to see that it contains some styles for the <dialog> element. The positioning styles center the dialog in the screen.

4. Run the app to see that the Add Song button displays but SongForm doesn't. That's because the <dialog> element that contains SongForm is hidden by default.

Use imperative code to show and hide the dialog

To show a <dialog> element, you call its showModal() or show() method. And to hide it, you call its close() method. In other words, you need to use imperative code.

5. In App, import the useRef hook and create a ref to access the <dialog> element. Set the initial value of the ref to null.

6. Update the event handler that shows the form. Use the ref to call the showModal() function of the <dialog> element.

7. Update the event handler that hides the form. Use the ref to call the close() function of the <dialog> element.

8. Update the event handler that adds a song. Use the ref to call the close() function of the <dialog> element after adding the song.

9. In the JSX, assign the ref you created in step 5 to the ref attribute of the <dialog> element.

10. Switch back to the browser and click the Add Song button. It should open the Add Song form in a modal dialog. Make sure the Add and Cancel buttons work as expected.

11. After adding a song, click Add Song again. You should see the song you just added still in the form. That's because the code doesn't remove SongForm from the DOM.

12. Update SongForm to clear the fields after adding a song. To do that, set the state to empty strings for title, artist, and year, and false for favorite.

Create and use a custom useDialog hook

13. Add a hooks directory to src with a useDialog.js file.

14. Code a useDialog hook that imports the useRef hook and creates a ref for a dialog.

15. Define functions that use the ref to open and close the dialog. You can use the code you just added to App as a guide.

16. Code the return value of the hook as an object that contains the ref, the open function, and the close function.

17. In App, import the useDialog hook. Then, call useDialog() and extract the ref, the function that opens the dialog, and the function that closes it.

18. Delete the old code that creates the ref and the event handlers, and use the ref and functions from the useDialog hook instead.

19. Switch to the browser and make sure the app still works correctly.

Create a confirmation dialog for deleting a song

20. Open the Playlist.jsx file. Note that the JSX contains a <dialog> element with a "Delete?" message and Confirm and Cancel buttons, and the code contains comments and stubs for what's needed.

21. Import the useState hook and create a state variable for the song that's selected for deletion.

22. Import the custom useDialog hook and call it to get the ref and functions for the dialog.

23. Update the event handler for the Delete button. Pass the song the handler receives to the state setter, and open the dialog.

24. Update the event handler for the confirm button. Use the id of the song in state to call the onDelete prop, and close the dialog.

25. Update the event handler for the Cancel button. Set the song in state to null and close the dialog.

26. In the JSX, assign the ref from useDialog to the ref attribute of the <dialog> element.

27. Update the "Delete?" message in the dialog to display the song title and artist. Make sure there's a song in state before using the properties.

28. Switch back to the browser and delete a song. It should open a modal dialog with a confirmation message. Make sure the Confirm and Cancel buttons work as expected.

Create and use a custom useLocalStorage hook

29. Add a useLocalStorage.js file to the hooks directory.

30. Code a useLocalStorage hook that accepts a key and an initial value and returns a current value and a setter function in an array. You can use the example in the chapter as a guide.

31. In App, import the useLocalStorage hook and use it to replace the state variable for the array of songs. Use "songs" as the key and the existing songs array as the initial value.

32. When you're done, delete the code that imports useState since App no longer needs it.

33. Switch to the browser and add and delete some songs. Then, refresh the browser to make sure the app retrieves your current songs from local storage rather than reverting to the initial songs in App.

Chapter 6

Use a web API to work with data

Most React apps use an API (Application Programming Interface) that's running on a web server to store their data. That way, the data can be stored on a web server, and the React app can run in a browser on the client.

This chapter begins by presenting some basic skills for using JavaScript to work with a web API that's running on a server, including how to use the Fetch API. Then, it shows how to run an API using your own computer as the server, and it shows how to use a React app to use that API to work with data.

An introduction to web APIs

This chapter starts by presenting a public *Application Programming Interface (API)* that's running on a web server. Then, it summarizes four HTTP methods that you can use to work with data that's available from a web server.

The JSON Placeholder API

The JSON Placeholder API is a public web API that provides sample data in JSON format. This API returns data that mimics the kind of data that's typically returned by real web APIs. Using an API like this one allows you to practice making API calls without having to set up an account with a service or worry about other implementation details.

The JSON Placeholder API follows the principles of *REST* (*Representational State Transfer*), an architectural style for designing web services. As a result, the JSON Placeholder API can be called a *RESTful API*. In a RESTful API, there's clear separation between client and server where the server handles data storage and the client handles user interface.

The JSON Placeholder API is available from the following URL.

The base URL for the JSON Placeholder API

```
https://jsonplaceholder.typicode.com
```

Typically, the *base URL* of an API returns some documentation about the API. For the JSON Placeholder API, the base URL returns a landing page with information about the API and how to use it.

To access the data that the API serves, you can use the URL for an *endpoint* like the one shown next.

The URL for an endpoint that returns data for all users

```
https://jsonplaceholder.typicode.com/users
```

For example, if you enter this endpoint in your browser, it displays the JSON that it returns as shown next.

Some of the JSON that's returned by the endpoint URL

```
[
  {
    "id": 1,
    "name": "Leanne Graham",
    "username": "Bret",
    "email": "Sincere@april.biz",
    ...
  },
  ...
  {
```

```
      "id": 10,
      "name": "Clementina DuBuque",
      "username": "Moriah.Stanton",
      "email": "Rey.Padberg@karina.biz",
      ...
   }
]
```

Four common HTTP methods

You typically use the default HTTP method, the GET method, to retrieve data from a web API. However, you can use three other HTTP request methods to add, update, and delete data. In summary, to work with a web API, you typically use one of the following HTTP methods.

Four common HTTP methods

Method	Typical use
GET	Gets data. Stores the data to be returned in the body of the response. Often uses the URL to identify the data to be retrieved.
POST	Adds data. Stores the data to be added in the body of the request.
PUT	Updates data. Stores the data to be updated in the body of the request and often uses the URL to identify the data to be updated.
DELETE	Deletes data. Often uses the URL to identify the data to be deleted.

When you use these methods, HTTP sometimes transfers data by storing it in the body of the request or response, and it sometimes uses the URL of the request to pass a parameter that identifies the data to update or delete.

How to use the Fetch API

To use JavaScript to work with a web API, you typically use an asynchronous function to make the request. That way, the user interface can stay responsive while the web server processes the request and returns a response. To make an asynchronous request with JavaScript, you typically use the Fetch API.

Introduction to the Fetch API

The Fetch API provides objects and methods for making *asynchronous requests*. To start, you can use the fetch() method shown next to make an asynchronous request.

The fetch() method

Method	Description
fetch(url, options)	Makes an asynchronous request to the specified URL. If no options are included, this method makes a GET request.

Calling the fetch() method returns a Promise object that eventually returns a Response object. A Promise object has the following three states.

Three states of a Promise object

- **Pending:** After a promise has been created but before the request returns a value
- **Fulfilled:** When the request is successfully resolved
- **Rejected:** If an error occurs during the request

When a Promise object is first created, it starts in the pending state. From there, a promise can move to either the fulfilled state or the rejected state. A promise is fulfilled if the API request successfully returns a value, but it is rejected if an error occurs during the request.

Make a GET request

The chapter has already shown how to make a GET request to the JSON Placeholder API by entering the URL in a browser. This works because a browser uses the HTTP GET method by default.

However, if you want to use JavaScript code to make a GET request, you can use the fetch() method as shown next.

A function that gets data

```
// URL to get users from a public API
const usersURL = "https://jsonplaceholder.typicode.com/users";

// An async function to get users from an API
const getUsers = async () => {
    const response = await fetch(usersURL);   // defaults to GET
    if (!response.ok) {
        throw new Error("Network response was not ok");
    }
    const json = await response.json();
    console.log("Users retrieved", json);
    return json;
};
```

This code starts by defining a constant that contains the URL for a public web API. Then, it defines an asynchronous function named getUsers().

Within the getUsers() function, the first statement calls the fetch() method, passes it the URL, and awaits the response. Since this code doesn't specify an HTTP method, the fetch() method uses the default GET HTTP method to send the request.

Once the promise resolves, an if statement checks whether the response is OK. If it isn't OK, it throws an error that can help you troubleshoot the problem. Otherwise, it continues by calling the json() method of the response and waiting for its promise to resolve. Once it does, it logs the JavaScript object to the console and also returns it to the calling code.

If you run this code from a React app, you can use the browser console to view the array of users that's returned. In this case, the browser console should show an array like this:

The array that's logged to the browser console

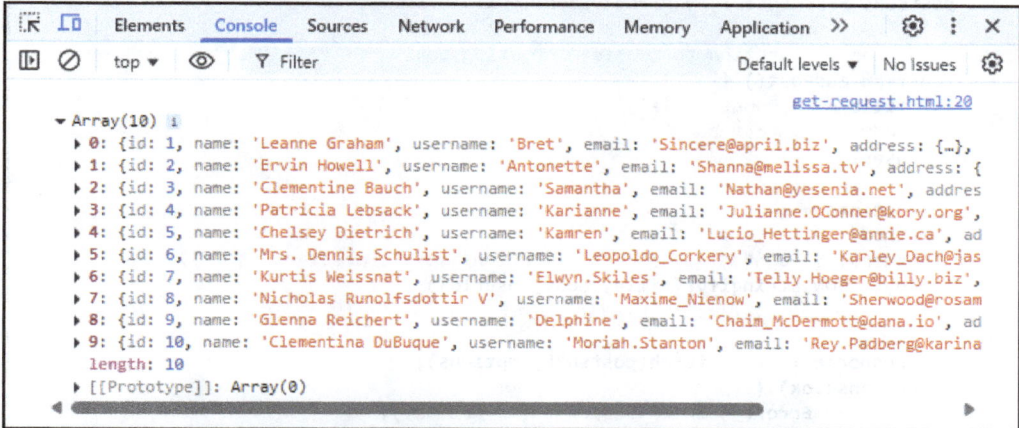

In a React app, you need to control when you run methods that use the Fetch API. One way to do that is to put them within a useEffect() function as shown next.

Code that calls a function when the component mounts

```
// load users when component mounts
useEffect(() => {
    getUsers();
}, []);
```

That way, the getUsers() function only runs once when your React component mounts. Here, the empty dependency array means this function is called only after the first render, not on updates. Without the useEffect hook, the getUsers() function would run on every render, which is inefficient and could cause bugs.

When you view the console, you may notice that it displays two arrays, even though it seems like it should only display one. If so, that's because you are using the "npm run dev" command to run the app on a development server. On a development server, React uses strict mode by default, which intentionally calls some functions twice to help you detect side effects and see how your components handle being mounted and unmounted. If you want to display each array only once, you can use the "npm run preview" command to run the app in preview mode.

Make a POST request

Making a POST request requires you to provide some additional options when calling the fetch() method.

A function that adds data

```
// URL to work with blog posts from a public API
const postsURL = "https://jsonplaceholder.typicode.com/posts";

// An asynchronous function to create a new blog post
async function addPost() {
    const title = 'My post title';
    const body = 'My post body';
    const userId = 1;

    const options = {
        method: 'POST',
        headers: { 'Content-type': 'application/json; charset=UTF-8', },
        body: JSON.stringify({title, body, userId})
    };

    const response = await fetch(postsURL, options);
    if (!response.ok) {
        throw new Error("Network response was not ok");
    }
    const json = await response.json();
    console.log("Post added", json);
    return json;
}
```

This code example uses the /posts endpoint of the JSON Placeholder API instead of the /users endpoint. Since this is a POST request, the request creates a new blog post via the API.

To create the blog post, the code starts by declaring title, body, and userID variables that make up the content of the blog post. Then, the code declares a JSON object named options that contains the HTTP method (POST), the HTTP headers, and the data that the API should use to create the blog post. Next, it sends the request to the API via the fetch() method.

When the request completes, the JSON response is logged to the console as shown next.

The object that's logged to the console

```
 top ▼  ◉   ▽ Filter                                    Default levels ▼   No Issues  ⚙
                                                                    post-request.html:30
▼ Object i
    body: "My post body"
    id: 101
    title: "My post title"
    userId: 1
  ▶ [[Prototype]]: Object
```

This response includes an id value for the newly created blog post, which is how APIs typically work. However, since JSON Placeholder only provides sample data, it just simulates creating a new blog post but doesn't actually do it. As a result, if you run this request again, you'll get the same id value.

Make a DELETE request

Like GET requests, DELETE requests typically don't need additional parameters beyond the HTTP method. That's because the URL typically includes a value that identifies the data to delete. For example, rather than passing the id of the post that you want to delete in the request body, you typically send a DELETE request to a URL that includes that id as shown next.

A function that deletes a post

```
const deletePost = async () => {
    const postId = 1;
    const url = postsURL + "/" + postId;
    const response = await fetch(url, {method: 'DELETE'});
    if (!response.ok) {
        throw new Error("Network response was not ok");
    }
    const json = await response.json();
    console.log("Post deleted", json);
    return json;
}
```

This code makes a DELETE request to a URL that ends with "posts/1". As a result, it deletes the blog post with an id of 1. Again, since the JSONPlaceholder API is for testing only, this just simulates deleting the blog post with an id of 1 but doesn't actually do it.

Make a PUT request

Making a PUT request works much like a POST request combined with a DELETE request. PUT requests typically update data. In particular, you store the new data for the updated object in the body of the request, and you use the URL to identify the existing object that you want to update. As you might expect, you set the method of the request to PUT as shown next.

A function that updates data

```
const updatePost = async () => {
    const postId = 1;
    const url = postsURL + "/" + postId;

    const title = 'New title';
    const body = 'New body';
    const userId = 1;

    const options = {
```

```
    method: 'PUT',
    headers: { 'Content-type': 'application/json; charset=UTF-8', },
    body: JSON.stringify({postId, title, body, userId})
};

const response = await fetch(url, options);
if (!response.ok) {
    throw new Error("Network response was not ok");
}
const json = await response.json();
console.log("Post updated", json);
return json;
}
```

This function updates existing data with a PUT request. It starts by building the URL for a specific post by appending a post id of 1 to the URL. Then, the function defines the new data that replaces the existing post: a new title, body, and user id.

If you're using the JSON Placeholder API to test this code, keep in mind that posts/1 is the only endpoint that's configured to work with PUT requests. In addition, sending a PUT request to this endpoint doesn't actually change the data. Instead, it sends a simulated response as if the data had changed.

Similar to the code for the POST request, this code includes an options object for the HTTP method, the HTTP headers, and the body content of the request. Then, the function follows similar logic for fetching, error checking, and returning the response.

An introduction to the Movies API

The Movies API provides a way to store data about movies on a server. This API could be run on a web server, but this book shows how to run it on your own computer so you can use it to simulate a web API.

Start the API on your computer

For development purposes, it's often helpful to use your local computer as the server for an API rather than use one available from the web. That way, you can make sure your code for adding, updating, and deleting data is working correctly before you upload it to the web.

To run the Movies API on your computer, you can use the following procedure.

How to start the server for the Movies API

1. Use VS Code to open the apps/ch06/movies-api folder.
2. Open the Terminal window. The movies-api folder should be the current folder.
3. Run the following node app.mjs command to start the server.

The node command that starts the Movies API

```
react/apps/ch06/movies-api> node app.mjs
API listening on port 2000
```

Here, the message that's displayed after you run the command shows that the API is listening on port 2000. As a result, you can test the API by starting a browser and entering the following URL.

The URL for the local Movies API server

```
http://localhost:2000
```

Browsing to this URL should display the documentation for the API. This documentation includes information about the API as shown next.

A Chrome browser displaying the base URL for the Movies API

Here, the Pretty-print option is selected. As a result, the browser displays the JSON that's returned by the API in a format that's easy for a human to read.

To run a React app that accesses this API, you can open a second instance of VS Code. To do that, you can select the New Window menu item or press the shortcut key as shown next.

How to open a second instance of VS Code

- Select File ▶ New Window from the menus
- Press Ctrl+Shift+N

Review the documentation

API documentation should help developers understand how to interact with an API effectively. It should include the base URL, available endpoints, required parameters, request/response formats, and example usage.

To keep it simple, the documentation of the Movies API only provides some basic information about the data model and its endpoints. For example, the basic data model info shows the five properties stored for each movie. This shows that the id property is generated automatically by the API, the name and year properties are required, and the stars and order properties are optional with default values of 0.

The documentation for the data model

```
...
    dataModel: {
      movie: {
        id: "integer (auto-generated)",
        name: "string (required)",
        year: "integer (required, 1888 - current year + 5)",
        stars: "integer (0-5, defaults to 0)",
        order: "integer (0 or greater, defaults to 0)"
      }
    },
...
```

The documentation also provides some basic information about each endpoint that's summarized in the following table.

The endpoints for the Movies API

Method	URL	Description
GET	/movies	Gets all movies.
GET	/movies/:id	Gets the movie specified by the id.
POST	/movies	Adds the movie data in the request to the list of movies.
PUT	/movies/:id	Updates the movie specified by the id with the data in the request.
DELETE	/movies/:id	Deletes the movie specified by the id.

However, the documentation could provide more info about each endpoint such as the request body structure, expected response format, sample usage, and so on.

Use a browser to make a GET request

If you want to test the GET requests available from this API with your browser, you can enter the appropriate URL in the browser. For example, to access the data for all movies, you use the /movies endpoint. This returns the JSON for all movies stored in the API as shown next.

A browser that displays the JSON for all movies

```
←  →  C      ⓘ  localhost:2000/movies          ☆  ⬠  ⬡    ● ⋮

Pretty-print ☑

[
  {
    "id": 1,
    "name": "The Shawshank Redemption",
    "year": 1994,
    "stars": 0,
    "order": 0
  },
  {
    "id": 2,
    "name": "The Godfather",
    "year": 1972,
    "stars": 0,
    "order": 0
  },
  {
    "id": 3,
    "name": "The Dark Knight",
    "year": 2008,
    "stars": 0,
    "order": 0
  },
```

To access the data for a specific movie, you add the id for the movie that you
want to access to the URL path. So, to get the data for the movie with an id of
1, you add 1 to the end of the /movies endpoint in the browser as shown next.

A browser that displays the JSON for a single movie

```
←  →  C      ⓘ  localhost:2000/movies/1        ☆  ⬠  ⬡    ● ⋮

Pretty-print ☑

{
  "id": 1,
  "name": "The Shawshank Redemption",
  "year": 1994,
  "stars": 0,
  "order": 0
}
```

Using a browser to make a GET request is a good way to test an API to make
sure it's running. However, React apps typically use the Fetch API to send
requests to an API as illustrated by the following Movie List app.

The Movie List app

The Movie List app for this chapter uses the locally hosted Movies API to store
the data for the movies in its list. In addition, it uses a local JSON file to store
some famous movie quotes.

The UI

The user interface for the Movie List app should be familiar to you by now. However, this version shows all of the movies available from the Movies API when it loads. In addition, it displays famous movie quotes in the footer.

The UI for the Movie List app

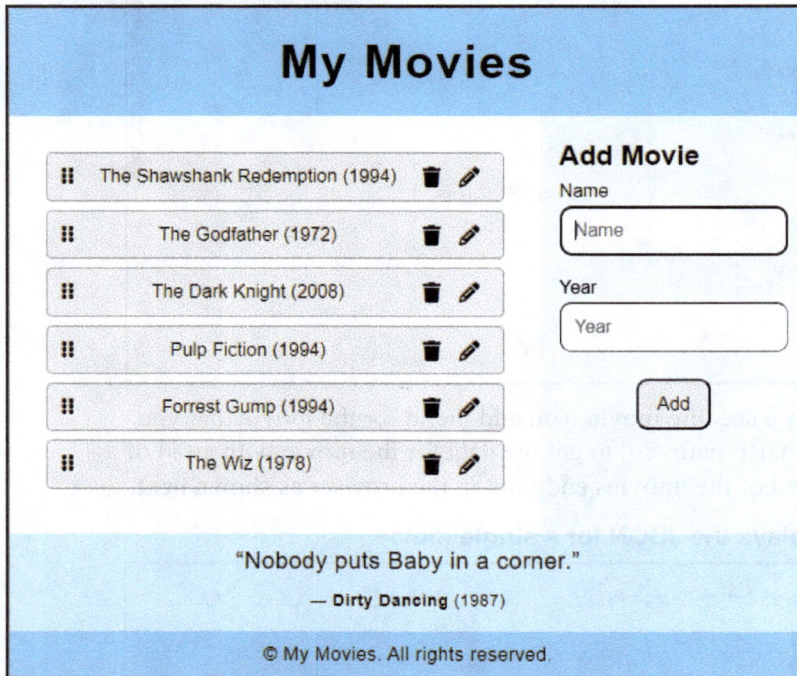

My Movies

The Shawshank Redemption (1994)	🗑 ✏
The Godfather (1972)	🗑 ✏
The Dark Knight (2008)	🗑 ✏
Pulp Fiction (1994)	🗑 ✏
Forrest Gump (1994)	🗑 ✏
The Wiz (1978)	🗑 ✏

Add Movie

Name

> Name

Year

> Year

[Add]

"Nobody puts Baby in a corner."

— **Dirty Dancing** (1987)

The directory structure

The directory structure for the Movie List app is mostly the same as the structure for the app presented in the previous chapter. However, there are two significant differences as shown next.

The src directory structure

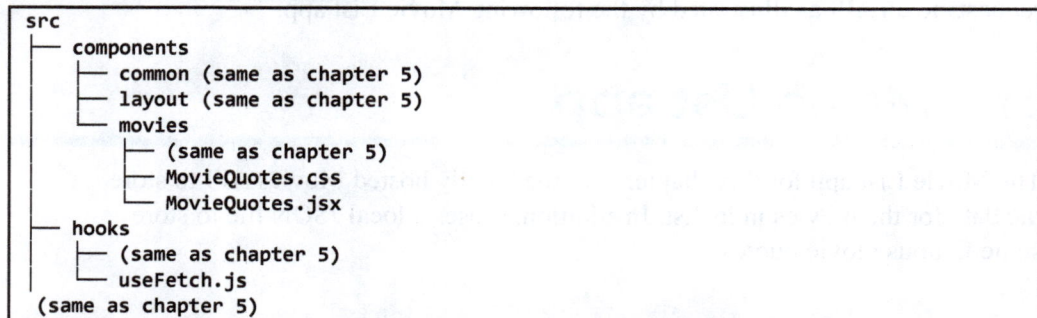

```
src
├── components
│   ├── common (same as chapter 5)
│   ├── layout (same as chapter 5)
│   └── movies
│       ├── (same as chapter 5)
│       ├── MovieQuotes.css
│       └── MovieQuotes.jsx
├── hooks
│   ├── (same as chapter 5)
│   └── useFetch.js
(same as chapter 5)
```

First, the components/movies directory contains the JSX and CSS files for a new MovieQuotes component. Second, the hooks directory contains the JavaScript file for a new custom hook named useFetch.

The useFetch hook

The useFetch hook shown next encapsulates some of the functionality of the Fetch API. You can use this hook to work with data from a web API like the Movies API, and you can also use it with a local text file as illustrated by the MovieQuotes component shown later in this chapter.

The useFetch.js file

```javascript
import { useState } from "react";

export const useFetch = () => {
    // state to manage loading status and errors
    const [loading, setLoading] = useState(true);
    const [error, setError] = useState(null);

    // function to perform the fetch
    const fetchData = async (url, options = {method: 'GET'}) => {
        setLoading(true);
        setError(null);
        try {
            const response = await fetch(url, options);
            if (!response.ok) {
                const errorData = await response.json();
                throw new Error(errorData.error ||
                    `Fetch failed with status: ${response.status}`);
            }
            const data = await response.json();
            return data;              // success - return data object
        }
        catch (err) {
            setError(err.message);    // save error message
            return null;              // failure - return null
        }
        finally {
            setLoading(false);        // set loading to false either way
        }
    };

    // function to create an options object for fetch calls
    const createOptions = (method, body = null) => {
        const options = { method };
        if (body) {
            options.headers = { 'Content-Type': 'application/json' };
            options.body = JSON.stringify(body);
        }
        return options;
    };

    // return the functions and the loading and error state
    return { fetchData, createOptions, loading, error };
};
```

The useFetch hook starts by defining local state to track loading status and any errors. Then it defines an asynchronous fetchData() function that accepts a URL and an options object for a request. Because of the default value of the options object, this parameter is optional for GET requests.

The fetchData() function initially sets the loading state to true and the error state to null. That way, components that call fetchData() can use these values to display appropriate loading and error messages.

Then, the function uses a try-catch statement to call the fetch() function. If there's a network error, the catch block executes. If there's not, but the response is not OK, the code builds an appropriate error and throws it, which also causes the catch block to execute. If the response is OK, the function returns the data from the response.

The catch block updates the error state with the error message and then returns null. This allows the calling code to check the response for null to see if the call succeeded. You could also just re-throw the error here, and then the calling code can use a try-catch statement to check for success. Which you choose is mostly a matter of personal preference.

The finally block runs on success and on failure. It sets the loading state to false, so a component that calls fetchData() can update its loading message.

Next, the useFetch hook defines a createOptions() function that automates the creation of an options object for the fetch() function. Finally, the hook returns an object that contains both functions, the loading state, and the error state.

The updated App component

The App component is updated to work with the Movies API as well as local state. To do that, it imports the useFetch hook, gets the functions and state it returns, and codes a constant with the base URL of the API, as shown next.

Import and call the useFetch hook

```
import { useState, useEffect } from 'react';
import { useFetch } from './hooks/useFetch';
...
const API_URL = 'https://localhost:2000';
...
const App = () => {
    const [movies, setMovies] = useState([]);
    const [selectedMovie, setSelectedMovie] = useState(null);

    // get fetch functions and loading/error state from custom hook
    const { fetchData, createOptions, loading, error } = useFetch();
    ...
```

Now App can use the URL constant, the createOptions() function, and the fetchData() function to make API calls. And, it can use the loading and error state values to conditionally render appropriate messages in JSX when the data is loading or when an API call returns an error.

Providing loading and error messages is a common React development pattern for two reasons. First, code that interacts with APIs often takes a few seconds to complete, so it's a good practice to display a loading message during this time. Second, whenever code accesses an API, there's a possibility of an error, so you need to be able to display an error message.

Next, App loads the movies from the Movies API when the component mounts.

Load the movies

```
// load movies from API on mount
useEffect(() => {
    loadMovies();
}, []);

const loadMovies = async () => {
    const movies = await fetchData(`${API_URL}/movies`);
    if (movies) {
        setMovies(movies);
    }
};
```

This code begins by calling useEffect(). The dependency array is empty so the effect only runs once, when the component first renders. The body of useEffect() contains a single statement that calls the loadMovies() function.

The loadMovies() function is coded separately for two reasons. First, you can't code an asynchronous callback within useEffect, so if you want to run an asynchronous callback, you have to code it separately and then call it within useEffect. Second, the JSX needs a function to call to re-load the movies if there's an error.

The loadMovies() function appends the /movies endpoint to the base URL and passes it to the fetchData() function returned by the useFetch hook. Then, it checks whether fetchData() returned a value. If so, it passes the movies returned from the API to the movies state setter.

The loadMovies() function doesn't need to address anything else because fetchData() does. Remember, fetchData() starts by setting the loading state to true and the error state to null. On error, it sets an appropriate error message in the error state, and when the API call is done, it sets the loading state to false. This pattern is the same for all the event handlers that work with the API. Because of this, App can use the loading and error values from the hook to display loading and error messages in the JSX.

The App component also updates the handleAdd() function as shown next.

Updated event handler for adding a movie

```
const handleAdd = async (movieToAdd) => {
    // add to API on server
    const options = createOptions('POST', movieToAdd);
    const response = await fetchData(`${API_URL}/movies`, options);

    // add to local state on client if successful
    if (response) {
        setMovies((prev) => [...prev, response.movie]);
    }
};
```

The handleAdd() function starts by creating an options object that contains the data needed to create a new movie. To do that, it calls the createOptions() function from the useFetch hook and passes it the POST HTTP method and the movie object it received. After that, it appends the /movies endpoint to the base URL and passes the URL and the options to the fetchData() function.

Like loadMovies(), this function checks whether fetchData() returns a value. If so, it adds the movie returned from the API to the movies state. This is important, because the movie from the API contains the id value created on the server.

The updated handleDelete() function works similarly to handleAdd().

Updated event handler for deleting a movie

```
const handleDelete = async (id) => {
    // delete from API on server
    const options = createOptions('DELETE');
    const response = await fetchData(`${API_URL}/movies/${id}`, options);

    // delete from local state on client if successful
    if (response) {
        setMovies((prev) => prev.filter((movie) => movie.id !== id));
        setSelectedMovie(null);
    }
};
```

It starts by calling createOptions() to create an options object for deleting a movie. Then, it passes the appropriate URL and the options to the fetchData() function. Note that it appends the /movies endpoint and the id it receives to the base URL.

Finally, if the API returns a value, the function removes the movie with the specified id from the movies state and clears the selected movie state. To remove the movie, it just uses the value in the id parameter. That's because updating the API didn't change the id. The response object returned by the API contains a deletedMovie object, so you could use its id property instead. However, there isn't a good reason to do that, since it's the same as the value in the id parameter.

The updated code for the handleEdit() function works similarly to handleAdd() and handleDelete().

Updated event handler for editing a movie

```
const handleEdit = async (movieToUpdate) => {
    // update in API on server
    const options = createOptions('PUT', movieToUpdate);
    const response =
        await fetchData(`${API_URL}/movies/${movieToUpdate.id}`, options);

    // update in local state on client if successful
    if (response) {
        setMovies((prev) =>
            prev.map((movie) =>
                movie.id === movieToUpdate.id ? movieToUpdate : movie
            )
        );
        setSelectedMovie(null);
    }
};
```

It starts by calling createOptions() to create an options object with the data to update a movie. Then, it passes the appropriate URL and options to the fetchData() function. Finally, if the API returns a value, the function updates the selected movie in the movies state and clears the selected movie state.

After updating the event handlers to use the Movies API, App updates its JSX to conditionally render messages based on the loading and error states from the useFetch hook. In addition, it displays the new MovieQuotes component.

Updated JSX for the App component

```
<Main>
    {loading && <p>Loading movies...</p>}
    {error && (
        <div className="error-message">
            {error} <button onClick={loadMovies}>Reload</button>
        </div>
    )}
    {!loading && !error &&
        <MovieList
            movies={movies}
            onSelect={handleSelect}
            onReorder={handleReorder}
        />
    }
</Main>
...
<Footer text={appName} >
    <MovieQuotes />
</Footer>
```

Here, the JSX in the Main component displays a message that says, "Loading movies…" if the loading state is true. Then, it conditionally renders an error message if the error state is not null. This also displays a Reload button that provides a way for the user to call the loadMovies() function again when an error occurs, which is convenient if there is a temporary problem with the API and you want to try loading the movies again. Finally, if the loading value is false and the error value is null, it displays the list of movies.

The JSX in the Footer component displays the new MovieQuotes component. This works because Footer can include children above the copyright notice as shown next.

Updated JSX for the Footer component

```
const Footer = ({ text, children }) => (
    <footer className="footer">
        { children }
        <p>© {text}. All rights reserved.</p>
    </footer>
);
```

The MovieQuotes component

The MovieQuotes component uses the useFetch hook to retrieve and display movie quotes. The data for these movie quotes is stored in a file that's in the public directory and stores JSON for movie quotes as shown next.

The movie_quotes.json file

```
[
    {
        "quote": "Nobody puts Baby in a corner.",
        "movie": "Dirty Dancing",
        "year": 1987
    },
    ...
    {
        "quote": "I see dead people.",
        "movie": "The Sixth Sense",
        "year": 1999
    }
]
```

The following MovieQuotes component gets and displays the data from this file.

The MovieQuotes component

```
import { useState, useEffect } from 'react';
import { useTimer } from '../../hooks/useTimer';
import { useFetch } from '../../hooks/useFetch';
import './MovieQuotes.css';

const MovieQuotes = () => {
    // state to hold quotes and index of current quote; initalize index to 0
    // to show first quote on load
    const [quotes, setQuotes] = useState([]);
    const [index, setIndex] = useState(0);

    // get fetch function and loading/error state from custom hook
```

```
    const { fetchData, loading, error } = useFetch();

    // Fetch movie quotes on mount from local JSON file
    useEffect(() => {
        loadQuotes();
    }, []);

    const loadQuotes = async () => {
        // public folder is root for static assets in React
        // so don't need to specify in the path
        const quotes = await fetchData("/movie_quotes.json");
        setQuotes(quotes);
    };

    // Advance the quote index every 5 seconds
    useTimer(() => {
        if (quotes && quotes.length > 0) {
            setIndex((prevIndex) => (prevIndex + 1) % quotes.length);
        }
    }, 5000);

    // Handle loading and error states
    if (loading) return <p>Loading quotes...</p>;
    if (error) return <p>Unable to load quotes</p>;
    if (!quotes || quotes.length === 0) return <p>No quotes available.</p>;

    // Get the current quote based on the index
    const current = quotes[index];

    return (
        <div className="movie-quotes">
            <blockquote>
                "{current.quote}"
            </blockquote>
            <p>
                — <strong>{current.movie}</strong> ({current.year})
            </p>
        </div>
    );
};

export default MovieQuotes;
```

This component imports the useTimer and useFetch hooks. Within the component's function, the code defines local state to hold the quotes and the index of the current quote. Then, it calls useFetch() and uses the fetchData() function it returns to get the data for the quotes from the movie_quotes.json file.

Next, it calls useTimer() to advance to the next index every 5 seconds. In this code, the modulus operator (%) makes sure the index re-starts at zero when it reaches the last quote in the data.

The JSX uses the loading and error values from the useFetch hook to provide appropriate loading and error messages as needed. When loading is complete and there are no errors, it displays the current quote.

Perspective

This chapter presented the most important skills for using a web API to get the data for your React apps. To do that, it reviewed some skills for using JavaScript's Fetch API, it showed how to run the Movies API on your computer, and it showed how to modify the Movie List app to use the Movies API. This included how to use a custom hook named useFetch to get data from a web server.

Terms

Application Programming Interface (API)

REST (Representational State Transfer)

RESTful API

base URL

endpoint

asynchronous request

Exercise 6-1: Add a concurrency check

This exercise shows how to improve the Movie List app by checking whether a record has changed since it was selected for editing. If it has, the app allows the user to overwrite the data on the server or cancel the edit by displaying a dialog like the one shown next.

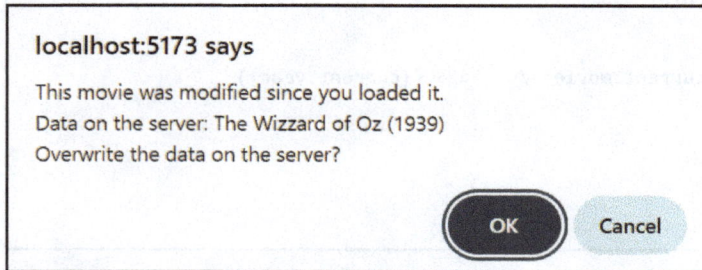

localhost:5173 says

This movie was modified since you loaded it.
Data on the server: The Wizzard of Oz (1939)
Overwrite the data on the server?

OK   Cancel

Start the Movies API and the Movie List app

1. Use VS Code to open the movies-api project in the apps/ch06 folder.
2. Open the Terminal and enter "node app.mjs" to start the Movies API.
3. Start a browser and navigate to localhost at the port displayed in the Terminal. That should display the JSON that documents the API.
4. Start a second instance of VS Code.
5. Open the movie-list project in the ex_starts/ch06 folder.
6. Open the Terminal and start the development server.

7. Use a browser to view the Movie List app.

8. Test the app by adding, editing, and deleting a movie.

Add a concurrency check

9. In the App component, import the useRef hook and create a ref for a movie object. Then, update the handleSelect() function to store a copy of the selected movie in the ref.

10. Review the handleEdit() function. Note that it starts by calling the confirmConcurrency() function and updates if it returns true.

11. In the confirmConcurrency() function, comment out the statement that returns true. Then use the fetchData() function from the useFetch hook to get a single movie from the API by id. If the call to fetchData() returns null, return false.

12. If the call to fetchData() returns true, get the movie stored in the ref and compare it to the movie returned from the API. If the name or year haven't changed, return true. Otherwise, use the window.confirm() method to display a dialog like the one shown at the beginning of this exercise.

13. Return the return value of window.confirm(). This value will be true if the user wants to overwrite and false if they don't. Although calling window.confirm() is a side effect, you don't need the useEffect hook because you're calling confirmConcurrency() in an event handler.

Test the concurrency check

14. Switch to the browser running the app and select a movie for editing, but don't click Update yet.

15. Switch to the instance of VS Code that's open to the movies-api project. Open the movies.json file and make a change to the name or year of the movie you selected for editing, and save this change.

16. Switch back to the browser running the app and click Update. It should display the dialog like the one shown at the beginning of this exercise.

17. Click OK to overwrite the data on the server. Then, switch back to the movies.json file. The edit you made in the app should have overwritten the edit you made manually.

Exercise 6-2: Save the sort order to the server

This exercise shows how to improve the Movie List app to save the sort order to the server. This is possible because the data model stored in the API includes an optional order property. As a result, you can use that property to sort the movies and save the sort order.

Sort movies by order and include an order value on add

1. If necessary, follow steps 1 through 8 of exercise 6-1 to start the Movies API and the Movie List app.

2. In the App component, update the loadMovies() function to sort the movies returned from the API by order before passing them to state.

3. Update the handleAdd() function to add an order value to the movie before saving it. To do that, use the reduce() method to get the highest order value in the movies array, then add 1 to it.

Test your changes

4. Switch to the browser running the app and add a new movie.

5. Switch to the instance of VS Code that's open to the movies-api project. Open the movies.json file to view the new movie. It should have an order of 1 because the other movies have the default order value of 0.

6. In movies.json, change the order value of another movie to 2 and save that change.

7. Switch back to the browser running the app and refresh the page. The movie that you changed in the last step should now be at the bottom.

Update the reorder code to save the new order values to state

8. Update the handleReorder() function so it's asynchronous.

9. Add code that creates an ordered movie array from the movie array. To do that, you can use the map() method and its optional index parameter to set the order property of the current movie to the current index.

10. Add code that creates an array that contains all of the movies that have changed order. To do that, compare the ordered movie array to the movies array by using the filter() method of the ordered movie array to filter by the order property. Then, you can use the find() method of the movies array to compare the current order value to the original order value.

11. Update the state setter so it saves the ordered movie array.

12. If there are movies in the filtered array, save them to the server. To do that, loop through the movies and make a PUT request for each one.

Test the reorder code

13. Switch to the browser running the app and reorder the movies.

14. Switch to the movies.json file and review the movies. They should all have an order value that reflects the order that you chose.

Add code to handle errors on reorder

The error handling in the useFetch hook may not work the way you want with this reorder code. That's because an update that succeeds might overwrite an earlier update that failed. Or, you might not get an error message that makes sense. One way to address that is to set your own error.

15. In the useFetch hook, add the setError() function to the return object.

16. In App, get the setError() function from the useFetch hook.

17. In handleReorder(), add a Boolean flag named isResponseOK to track API errors. Add it before the loop that updates the server and initialize it to true.

18. Within the loop, add code that checks whether the response from the PUT request is null. If it is, set the flag to false.

19. After the loop, add code that checks the flag. If it's false, use the setError() function from useFetch to set an appropriate error message.

Test the error handling

20. In the movies.json file, change the id of one of the movies. Make sure it doesn't match the id of any other movie.

21. Switch to the browser running the movie and reorder the last movie so it's in first position. This causes all movies get a new order value, and it should display the error message you just added.

22. In the movies.json file, fix the id of the movie you just changed.

Chapter 7

Debug a React app

So far, this book has already presented many techniques that you can use to debug a React app. Most of these skills are the same skills you can use to debug a traditional JavaScript app. For example, you can log data to the console and use your browser's development tools to view that data. Now, this book shows some additional skills that you can use to debug React apps.

Similarly, this book has already presented many issues that developers often encounter when debugging React apps. For example, you can avoid stale state and avoid overwriting state variables by following the practices described in chapter 4. Now, this book reviews some of these issues and presents some new ones.

How to use the React Developer Tools

Many of the same tools used to debug vanilla JavaScript apps work for React apps too. For example, it's common to log data to the console and use the Console tab in your browser's development tools to view that data.

However, React also provides the *React Developer Tools* browser extension, or *React DevTools* for short. This extension provides new tabs within a browser's developer tools that make it easier to view the hierarchy, state, props, hooks, and performance of React components.

Install the React Developer Tools

To install the React Developer Tools, you can start your browser and install its browser extension. For example, you can use the following procedure to add the React Developer Tools extension to the Chrome browser.

How to add the React Developer Tools to Chrome

1. Start Chrome.
2. Search for "react developer tools".
3. Click the link for the Chrome web store. This should display the page for the React Developer Tools.
4. Click the "Add to Chrome" button.

You can use a similar technique to add the React DevTools to most browsers.

View info for a component

Once you've added the React Developer Tools extension to your browser, you can access these tools by opening your browser's developer tools and selecting the Components tab as shown next.

The Components tab in Chrome

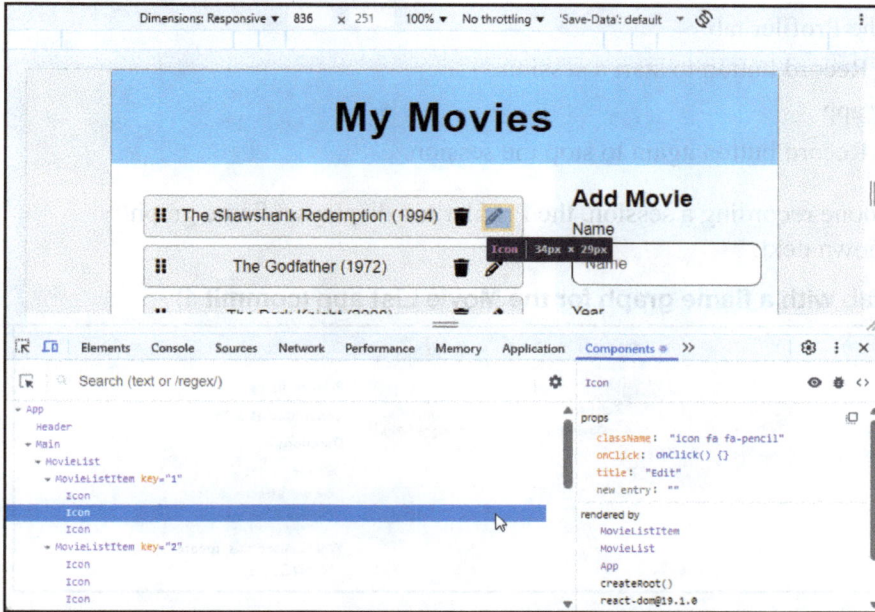

The Components tab displays a hierarchy of components in its left pane. To view the component that you're interested in, you can expand or collapse any node in the left pane.

If you hover over a component's node, the main browser window highlights the component. For example, in the previous screen, the mouse is hovering over the second Icon component in the first list item, so that's highlighted in the main browser window.

If you click on a component's node, the Components tab displays additional information about the component in the right pane. This includes information about props, which component rendered it, and where the source code for the component is located. For example, in the previous screen, the second Icon component is clicked, so the right pane displays information about its props and which components rendered it. This information can be extremely helpful in debugging React components.

Profile your components

The Profiler tab that's available from the React DevTools measures how your components render, including how long it takes each component to render. As a result, you can use it to identify bugs and performance issues in your React app.

To use the Profiler tab, you need to use the following steps to record a session where you test the parts of your app that you want to profile.

How to record a Profiler session

1. Display the Profiler tab.
2. Click the Record button to start a session.
3. Test your app.
4. Click the Record button again to stop the session.

When you're done recording a session, the Profiler tab displays a flame graph like the one shown next.

The Profiler tab with a flame graph for the Movie List app (commit 1)

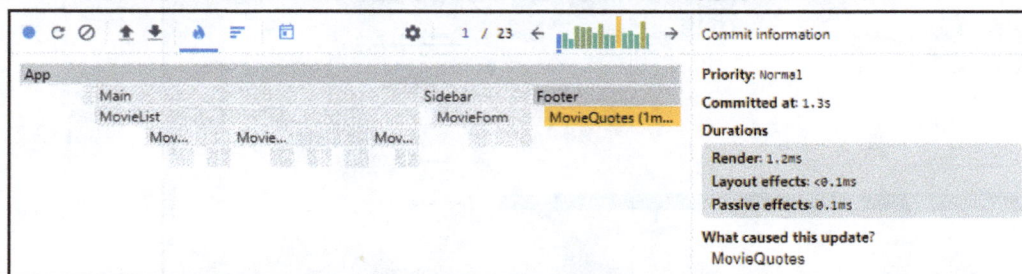

This flame graph provides a visual representation of how your components are rendering with wide components taking longer to render than narrow ones. In addition, it uses the following color coding.

Flame graph color coding

Color	Description
Green	Fast render time
Yellow	Moderate render time
Orange	Slower render time
Red	Slowest render time
Gray	Did not render

These colors show that the MovieQuotes component is the only component that rendered in the previous flame graph. That's what you want. If rendering the MovieQuotes component caused other components to render, that would be a bug that you would want to fix.

When you first display a flame graph, the right pane displays some general information about the commit. In the previous screen, this information shows that the MovieQuotes component caused the update. That makes sense because the MovieQuotes component uses a timer to update itself every 5 seconds.

If you want to get more information about a particular component, you can click on it. For example, you can click on the MovieQuotes component to display more details in the right pane such as how long it's taking to render.

The toolbar at the top of the Profiler tab displays the number of commits for the session and shows which commit you're viewing. In the previous screen, the fraction shows that you're viewing the first of 23 commits.

To view the next commit in the session, you can click the right arrow button in the toolbar. When you do, the Profiler tab displays a flame graph for that commit as shown next.

The Profiler tab with a flame graph for the Movie List app (commit 2)

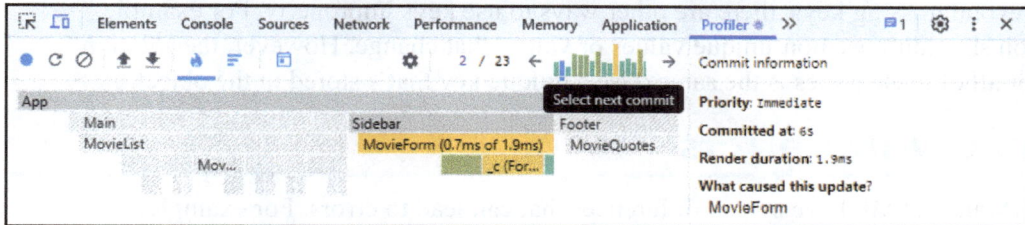

This flame graph shows that the MovieForm component caused the update, and that this updated caused all three of its child components to re-render.

Profiling an app can sometimes help you identify bugs and other performance issues. For example, the Profiler tab might show that a component is re-rendering when its parent state changes even though its props didn't change. In that case, you could investigate the code for the component and fix it so it only renders when its props change as explained in chapter 11.

Common JSX and rendering issues

Chapter 3 has already presented many of the most common issues React developers encounter with JSX and rendering. The following headings review some of these issues and explain some other issues.

Improper key usage in lists

React uses keys to track which items in a list have changed and need to be re-rendered. This allows React to re-render only the affected items. As a result, a missing key like the one shown next can cause rendering problems.

Improper key usage due to a missing key

```
{todos.map(todo => (
    <TodoItem todo={todo} /> // No key prop!
))}
```

When you don't set the key prop, it can cause problems like state sticking to positions instead of data when items are reordered, unnecessary DOM manipulations when items are removed or inserted, and focus or animation issues during list changes. The following code fixes this issue by using keys properly.

Proper key usage that specifies a unique key for each item

```
{todos.map(todo => (
    <TodoItem key={todo.id} todo={todo} />
))}
```

This code uses the unique id property of the todo object to specify the key. Beyond missing keys, there are other ways to use keys improperly. For example, you shouldn't use non-unique values or values that change. However, the solution for all of these issues is the same. Use a unique key that's stored in the object.

JSX syntax errors

JSX and HTML have syntax differences that can lead to errors. For example, JSX uses the className attribute while HTML uses the class attribute. Similarly, the JSX style attribute must be set to a JavaScript object while the HTML style attribute must be set to a string.

In addition, you must close all tags in JSX while HTML doesn't require this. For example, the following tag is allowed in HTML but causes a syntax error in JSX.

JSX that doesn't close a tag correctly

```
<img src={user.avatar}>
```

To fix this error, you can use the shorthand syntax for closing tags as shown next.

JSX that correctly closes a tag

```
<img src={user.avatar} />
```

Conditional rendering bugs

Conditional rendering bugs often occur when React attempts to render data that doesn't exist. To fix that issue, you can add conditional statements to your JSX to fix the way React renders the component.

For instance, in the following example, React renders an empty <h1> component if user.name is null, undefined, or an empty string, and that's probably not what you want.

JSX that renders an empty <h1> element when data doesn't exist

```
<h1>{user.name}</h1>
```

To fix this, you can use the nullish coalescing operator (??) to provide an alternative string to render as shown next.

JSX that renders 'Anonymous User' when data doesn't exist

```
<h1>{user.name ?? 'Anonymous User'}</h1>
```

In this case, if the user.name is null or undefined, React renders "Anonymous User" instead of "undefined". However, if you want React to render "Anonymous User" for an empty string too, you could use the OR operator (||) instead of the nullish coalescing operator.

Event handling issues

Small syntax errors can lead to unexpected issues with event handlers. For instance, in the following example, React calls the event handler when it renders the button instead of waiting for the user to click the button.

JSX that calls the event handler at the wrong time

```
<button onClick={handleClick(item.id)}>
```

That's because this code doesn't pass a function to the onClick attribute. Instead, it calls the handleClick() function and passes it the item id. To fix this, you can create an arrow function that calls the handleClick event as shown next.

JSX that calls the event handler at the right time

```
<button onClick={() => handleClick(item.id)}>
```

When you pass this function to the onClick attribute, it isn't executed until the user clicks the button.

State and prop issues

Chapters 2 through 4 have already presented many of the most common issues React developers encounter with state and props. The following headings review some of these issues and explain some other ones.

State fails to update correctly

In React, state updates are asynchronous and may be batched. As a result, when you use a setter function to set a state variable, the update doesn't happen immediately. Instead, React schedules the update to happen later and multiple state updates may be grouped together into a single re-render. The most common way to make sure state updates correctly is to pass a pure function to the code that sets the state variable as described in chapter 4.

If you don't treat state updates as asynchronous, you might get an outdated value if you read the state variable from within the setter function. This issue is known as *stale state*. Again, the most common way to make sure you don't use stale state is to pass a pure function to the state setter function that accesses the most current version of the state as described in chapter 4.

Components don't re-render

If you find that React isn't re-rendering a component when you want it to, it might be because you are directly modifying a state object or array. Although direct mutation changes the underlying data, React uses reference equality to determine if state has changed.

As a result, when you mutate an object directly as shown next, React thinks nothing has changed and doesn't re-render the component.

A bug caused by treating state as mutable

```
const [user, setUser] = useState({ name: 'John', age: 30 });
user.age = 31;
setUser(user);    // This won't trigger a re-render!
```

Instead, you should always create new objects or arrays when updating state as shown next.

Code that treats state as immutable

```
const [user, setUser] = useState({ name: 'John', age: 30 });
setUser((prevUser) => ({ ...prevUser, age: 31}));
```

This code creates a new user object using the spread operator (…) instead of mutating the existing state directly. Since this passes a new object reference to the state setter, it causes the component to re-render.

In the following example, the code directly mutates the object stored in the nested profile.bio property. Then, it passes that object to the setUser() function.

A bug caused by mutating a nested state object

```
user.profile.bio = 'New bio';   // Mutate nested object
setUser(user);                  // Component doesn't re-render
```

Even though this code changes the bio property, React doesn't re-render the component since the reference to the top-level user object remains the same.

To fix this bug, you can create new objects at every level of nesting that contains changes as shown next.

Code that fixes a bug by treating the nested state object as immutable

```
setUser(prevUser => ({ ...prevUser,
    profile: { ...prevUser.profile, bio: 'New bio' }
}));
```

This code uses the spread operator at both the user level and the profile level. This creates a new user object and a new profile object with the updated bio property. As a result, the code passes new object references to React, which triggers the re-renders.

Component lifecycle and hook issues

When working with React, it's common to come across bugs related to the useEffect hook. Typically, these bugs involve infinite re-render loops, memory leaks, and improper hook usage. Each of these issues can cause major problems as described in the following headings.

Infinite re-render loops

Infinite re-render loops often occur when the useEffect hook triggers state updates that cause a component to re-render. When the re-render happens, this triggers the effect again, which creates an infinite loop.

One common cause of an infinite re-render loop is forgetting to set the dependency array as shown next.

Code that causes an infinite loop

```
const UserProfile = ({ userId }) => {
    const [user, setUser] = useState(null);

    useEffect(() => {
        setUser(fetchUser(userId));
    }); // Missing dependency array - effect runs after every render
};
```

Since the useEffect() function doesn't include a dependency array, the effect gets called on every render, which creates an infinite loop.

To fix this, you can specify a dependency array to control when the effect runs as shown next.

Code that prevents an infinite loop

```
...
    useEffect(() => {
        setUser(fetchUser(userId));
    }, [userId]); // Dependency array controls when effect runs
};
```

In this case, the dependency array specifies the userId prop. As a result, the effect only runs on mount and when the userId prop changes.

Memory leaks from missing cleanup

You can use the useEffect hook to set up subscriptions, timers, or event listeners. When you create these types of objects, you should clean them up when the component unmounts or before the effect runs again. If you forget, you create a memory leak that can cause errors when the cleanup code tries to update unmounted components.

The following example presents code that causes a memory leak.

Code for a timer that causes a memory leak

```
useEffect(() => {
    setInterval(
        () => setSeconds((prev) => prev + 1), 1000
    );
    // Missing cleanup - interval never gets cleared
}, []);
```

To fix this code, you can add a cleanup function to clear the interval when the component unmounts as shown next.

Code for a timer that prevents a memory leak

```
useEffect(() => {
    const intervalId = setInterval(  // Get interval id needed for cleanup
        () => setSeconds((prev) => prev + 1), 1000
    );

    // Cleanup function runs when the component unmounts
    return () => clearInterval(intervalId);
}, []);
```

This version of the useEffect() function returns a cleanup function that React runs when the component unmounts. This provides a way for React to properly stop the timer and prevent the memory leak. So, make sure to return a cleanup function if your effect creates something that persists after the component lifecycle such as a subscription, timer, or event listener.

Detecting memory leaks can be tricky since JavaScript provides a garbage collector that periodically frees unreferenced memory. Because of this, the Memory tab in the browser development tools often shows memory rising and falling over time, even when the page isn't changing and the user isn't taking any further actions.

Improper hook usage

React relies heavily on consistent hook call order to maintain state. As a result, breaking the Rules of Hooks described in chapter 5 can cause React to lose track of hook state between renders. This can lead to bugs and can cause your app to crash.

Here's an example of improper hook usage.

Improper calling of a hook from within a conditional statement

```
const UserProfile = ({ showEmail }) => {
    const [name, setName] = useState('John');
    // Wrong - hook called conditionally
    if (showEmail) {
        const [email, setEmail] = useState('john@example.com');
    }

    return <div>{email}</div>;
}
```

This code violates the hook rules because it calls useState inside a conditional statement. When the condition is true, React calls two hooks. But when the condition is false, React only calls one. This breaks React's internal hook tracking system which relies on hooks being called in the same order every render. This causes React to throw an error or lose track of the state, which can cause bugs or crash your app.

To fix this issue, you can move the conditional statement into the JSX as shown next.

Proper hook usage with the condition moved into the JSX

```
const UserProfile = ({ showEmail }) => {
    const [name, setName] = useState('John');
    const [email, setEmail] = useState('john@example.com');

    return <div>{showEmail ? email : ''}</div>;
}
```

This code follows the Rules of Hooks by always calling both hooks at the top level of the component in the same order every render. If your app encounters an error in hook usage, React often logs the error to the Console tab. In addition, improper hook usage often causes your app to crash. So, if your app crashes when you test it, it often makes sense to start your debugging by making sure your code follows the Rules of Hooks.

Perspective

This chapter presented some important skills for debugging React apps and reviewed many issues that often arise when developing React apps. This should give you a solid foundation for fixing the bugs that you encounter when you're developing React apps.

Although it isn't shown in this chapter, AI can often help you debug an app. For example, if you encounter a bug in your app, you can often use Copilot (or another other AI assistant) to find and fix the bug that you're encountering. When you do this, it's important to make sure Copilot has all the context it needs to understand the problem. As a result, it's often helpful to provide Copilot with your code files, any error messages you're getting, and a brief description of the bug. If you do that, Copilot can often find the bug, suggest a fix, and save you a lot of time.

Terms

React Developer Tools

React DevTools

stale state

Exercise 7-1: Review and debug an app

Fix a bug

1. Use VS Code to open the my-playlist project in the ex_starts/ch07 folder.
2. Start the development server and run the app in a browser.
3. Open the developer tools and display the Console tab. It should display an error that says that every child in a list should have a unique key prop. Make a note of the component that's causing the error.
4. Use VS Code to open the component that's causing the error. Add a unique key prop to the list. Save this change.
5. Switch back to the browser and refresh. The error message should disappear.

Review the app in the React DevTools

6. If you haven't yet installed the React DevTools as described in this chapter, do it now.
7. In the browser, view the Components tab. It should display the App component and its Header, Playlist, and Footer child components.
8. Click on the App component to view details about it. In the hooks section, expand the first state hook to view the list of songs currently stored in state.
9. Click on the other components and inspect their details.
10. In the main browser window, click the Add Song button. This should display the form for adding a song, and it should add the SongForm component and its child Input components to the Components tab.
11. In the Components tab, click on each component to inspect its details.

Fix the Delete button issue

12. In the main browser window, click the Delete button for one song in the list. This shouldn't appear to do anything.
13. If the Add Song form is still open, click the Cancel button. Otherwise, click the Add Song button. This should update the playlist to remove the song you

attempted to delete in the previous step. This indicates that clicking a Delete button changes the state but doesn't trigger a re-render.

14. Open the Profiler tab, and start a profiling session. Click the Delete button for another song in the list, and stop the profiling session. This should display a message that no profiling data was recorded. That's because there was no re-render.

15. For comparison, start a new profiling session. If the Add Song form is open, click Cancel. Otherwise, click Add Song. Then, stop the profiling session. This time, the profiler displays correctly because clicking the button triggered a re-render.

16. Open the App.jsx file and review the handleDeleteSong() function. Note that it mutates the playlist state variable directly. Change this function to use a pure function to update state.

17. Switch to the browser, refresh, and run steps 12 and 14 again. Both the Delete button and the profiler should work correctly now.

Introduce an event handler bug

18. Open the Playlist.jsx file and find the JSX code that assigns the onClick event handler for the Delete button.

19. Change the code for the onClick attribute to remove the parentheses and arrow operator. Save this change.

20. Switch to the browser and note that the app doesn't display the playlist.

21. Display the Console tab and note that it displays an error message that indicates that you can't update the state in App while rendering Playlist.

22. Restore the parentheses and the arrow operator in the code for the onClick attribute. Save this change.

23. Switch to the browser and refresh it. This time, the app should work correctly with no errors.

Section 2

More skills as you need them

Section 1 presented the skills you need to get started with React. Now, this section presents more React skills that you can learn whenever you need them. To make that possible, each chapter in this section has been written as an independent module. As a result, you can read these chapters in whatever sequence you prefer.

Chapter 8

Create a single-page app with React Router

Single-page applications (SPAs) have transformed how developers build and interact with web applications. This approach creates fluid, app-like experiences that feel more responsive and engaging. This chapter guides you through the essential concepts of SPA development, from understanding the differences between MPAs and SPAs to implementing advanced routing patterns.

Introduction to single-page apps

To understand how a single-page app (SPA) works, it's helpful to compare an SPA to a traditional multi-page app (MPA).

How an MPA works

A traditional *multi-page application (MPA)* follows a request-response cycle where each user action triggers a complete page load. When you click a link or submit a form, the browser sends a request to the server, which returns a response that contains an entire new page. This process involves downloading new HTML, CSS, and JavaScript files, often causing a noticeable delay as the page loads.

How an SPA works

By contrast, a *single-page application (SPA)* operates on a client-side rendering model where JavaScript handles most of the application logic. When a user first visits an SPA, the browser downloads the HTML, CSS, and JavaScript needed by the app. The JavaScript files and libraries are known as the *JavaScript bundle*.

After downloading all of these files, the JavaScript takes control of the page and manages navigation, renders content, and communicates with web servers through API calls. This is known as *client-side routing*.

To do this, JavaScript receives navigation events and updates the page content accordingly. Typically, JavaScript doesn't need to update the entire page. Instead, it only needs to update the parts of the page that changed. This improves performance and user experience.

To implement client-side routing, JavaScript uses the browser's History API to change the URL without triggering a page reload. This lets SPAs maintain the expected browser behavior, such as forward and back buttons, while keeping the app responsive.

When a web page needs new data, an SPA typically uses JavaScript to make an asynchronous request to a web API. Then, it typically uses JavaScript to process the JSON in the response and convert it into HTML that can be used to update the page. This separation of data and presentation allows for more flexible and efficient apps.

Benefits and drawbacks of using an SPA

As described previously, an SPA offers some major advantages in user experience and performance over an MPA.

Another major advantage is the reduced server load. After the initial request, the server only needs to provide data through APIs rather than rendering complete HTML pages. This allows your apps to not request as much data from the server, potentially saving money.

An SPA can also enable better caching strategies. Since the application code is separated from the data, browsers can cache the static assets (HTML, CSS, and JavaScript) more effectively.

Developers also benefit from cleaner separation of concerns with frontend and backend teams able to work more independently by using well-defined API endpoints to communicate.

In summary, SPAs provide the following benefits.

Benefits of using SPAs

- Smoother navigation experience
- Reduced load times and server costs
- Better caching
- Cleaner separation of concerns

However, SPAs do have some drawbacks. The initial load time can be significantly longer because the browser must download the JavaScript bundle for the app before users can interact with it. This is particularly problematic for users with slower connections or less powerful devices.

Search engine optimization (SEO) presents another challenge. Traditional search engines expect a web page that's mostly HTML that has been rendered on the server. However, SPAs initially load with minimal HTML and rely on JavaScript to display the data for the page. While most search engines have improved at indexing JavaScript-heavy sites, SPAs still have some SEO disadvantages compared to MPAs.

In summary, SPAs have the following drawbacks.

Drawbacks of using SPAs

- Longer initial load time
- Potential SEO problems

A simple SPA

To understand how an SPA works, it's helpful to look at a simple example. For instance, the user interface for the following SPA provides a header and a navigation bar that provides links for navigating between three pages. When this app loads, it displays the Home page as shown next.

The Home page

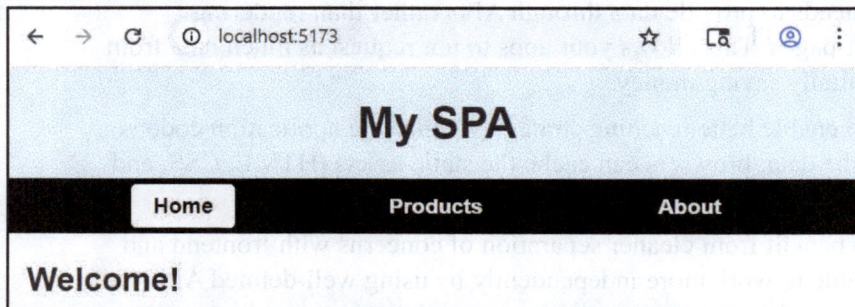

If you click on the Products link, the browser displays the Products page as shown next.

The Products page

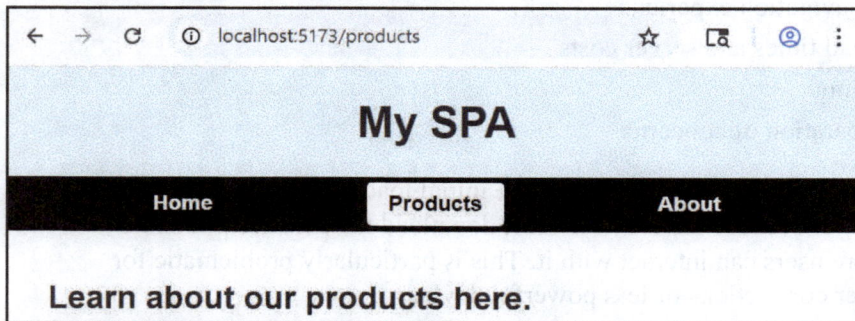

Although this looks like an MPA, it's an SPA because of how the navigation works. Instead of requesting new files from the server for each page, the JavaScript for the app intercepts the navigation request and updates only the URL, navigation bar, and content area.

In other words, if you click on the Products link, JavaScript intercepts that request, updates the URL to /products, and updates the parts of the page that changed. As a result, after the app loads for the first time, the pages load very quickly when the user clicks a link to navigate to another page.

When creating an SPA, it's a common pattern to store the JSX files that render the content for the pages of the app in a directory named pages as shown next.

The directory structure

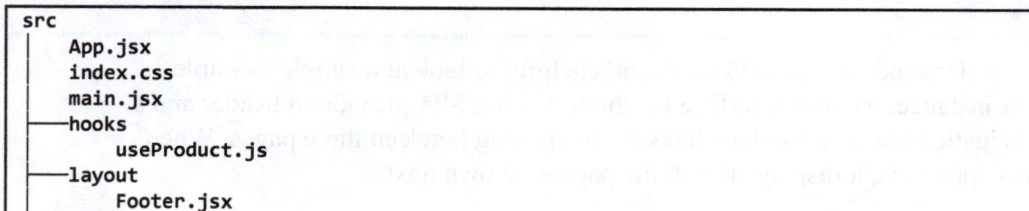

```
src
    App.jsx
    index.css
    main.jsx
  ─hooks
        useProduct.js
  ─layout
        Footer.jsx
```

```
        Header.jsx
        Navbar.css
        Navbar.jsx
    pages
        About.jsx
        Home.jsx
        Products.jsx
```

Here, the app stores the JSX files that define the layout that's used by multiple pages in a directory named layout.

The following table shows the URLs for each of the pages in this app.

The pages and their URLs

Page	URL
Home	/
Products	/products
About	/about

These clean, descriptive URLs are standard for modern web apps, whether they're SPAs or MPAs. However, in an SPA, JavaScript handles the URL changes on the client side. Meanwhile, an MPA uses the URL to request a page from the server.

How to get started with routing

Client-side routing makes SPAs possible because it provides a way to change the URL and the content of a page dynamically. When creating an SPA, you can choose from several client-side routers, but this chapter shows how to use React Router, the official client-side routing library for React.

Enable client-side routing for an app

Before you can start using React Router, you need to use the following command to install it.

The command to install React Router

```
npm install react-router-dom
```

After you install React Router, you can use it to implement client-side routing by adding the BrowserRouter component.

The BrowserRouter component

Component	Description
`<BrowserRouter>`	Processes URL navigation requests without reloading the page. It uses the HTML5 History API to modify the web browser address.

Typically you wrap the entire app with the BrowserRouter component so routing is available everywhere. For example, the following main.jsx file embeds the App component within BrowserRouter. This enables routing throughout the app.

A main.jsx file that enables client-side routing for an app

```
import { StrictMode } from 'react';
import { createRoot } from 'react-dom/client';
import { BrowserRouter } from "react-router-dom";
import App from './App.jsx';
import './index.css';

createRoot(document.getElementById("root")).render(
  <StrictMode>
    <BrowserRouter>
      <App />
    </BrowserRouter>
  </StrictMode>
);
```

Specify the routes for an app

After you enable client-side routing, you can define the routes for your app. To do that, you typically use the following components.

The Route and Routes components

Component	Description
`<Route path element />`	Maps a path prop for a URL to the specified element prop for a page.
`<Routes>`	A container that wraps all Route components.

For example, the following App component defines the routes for the three pages in the app.

An App component that defines three routes

```
import { Routes, Route } from 'react-router-dom';

import Header from './layout/Header';
import Navbar from './layout/Navbar';
import Footer from './layout/Footer';

import Home from './pages/Home';
import Products from './pages/Products';
import About from './pages/About';

const App = () => (
  <>
    <Header />
    <Navbar />
    <Routes>
      <Route path="/" element={<Home />} />
```

```
            <Route path="/products" element={<Products />} />
            <Route path="/about" element={<About />} />
        </Routes>
        <Footer />
    </>
);

export default App;
```

Here, the code for the App component starts by importing the Routes and Route components from the react-router-dom library. Then, it imports the components from the layout and pages directories that it needs. Finally, it uses JSX to define a Routes component that contains three Route components.

Each Route component specifies a path that accesses the content for a page. For example, the first route renders the Home component when the user navigates to the root path (/), the second route renders the Products component when the user navigates to the /products path, and the third route renders the About component when the user navigates to the /about path.

Code links for the routes

Route components don't define links that users can click. To create these links, you can use the two components described next.

Two components for navigation

Component	Description
`<Link to />`	Creates a general link. The to prop sets the path for the URL.
`<NavLink to end />`	Creates a navigation link that automatically gets the active class when current. The to prop sets the path for the URL, and the optional end prop makes sure the route matches exactly.

For example, to create links within a navigation bar, you can use a NavLink component within a Navbar component as shown next.

The Navbar component

```
import { NavLink } from 'react-router-dom';
import './Navbar.css';

const Navbar = () => (
    <nav className="navbar">
        <div className="nav-menu">
            <NavLink to="/" end>Home</NavLink>
            <NavLink to="/products">Products</NavLink>
            <NavLink to="/about">About</NavLink>
        </div>
    </nav>
);

export default Navbar;
```

Here, each NavLink component uses the to prop to specify a path that was defined in a Route component. That way, clicking the link uses the URL defined by the Route component to display the page for the route.

The NavLink for the Home link uses the end prop to use URL matching to control when a link is considered active. If this NavLink component didn't include the end prop, partial matching would be allowed. As a result, the specified path of / would also match the paths of /products and /about, and every link would get the active CSS class.

The other two NavLink components don't include the end prop. As a result, they allow partial matching. For example, the NavLink for the Products page matches /products as well as /products/1 and /products/2, so it gets the active attribute for any of these paths. This is probably what you want.

Store the routes in an array

As an app grows, it's common to have many Route objects, which can become difficult to manage. To help with this, you can store the props for your routes in a JSON object. Then, you can map the props to a Route component as shown next.

The updated routes in the App.jsx file

```
...
const routes = [
  { path: '/', element: <Home /> },
  { path: '/products, element: <Products /> },
  { path: '/about, element: <About /> },
];

const App = () => (
  <>
    <Header />
    <Navbar />
    <Routes>
      {routes.map(({ path, element }) => (
        <Route
          key={path}
          path={path}
          element={element}
        />
      ))}
    </Routes>
...
```

This code adds a key to each Route and uses the path as the key. The path makes a good key because each path is unique and directly related to the component.

Update the title for each route

When you store the route objects in an array, it's easy to add additional data such as a different title for the browser tab for each page as shown next.

The title in the browser tab for two routes

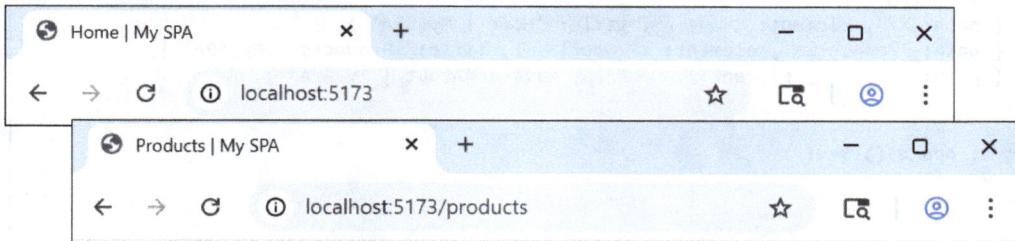

Here, the title for the first page is Home followed by the name of the app and the title for the second page is Products followed by the name of the app. Updating the title like this improves the user experience and SEO of the app.

To implement this change, you can use the TitleUpdater component shown next.

The TitleUdater component

```
import { useEffect } from 'react';

const TitleUpdater = ({ title, children }) => {
  useEffect(() => {
    if (title) document.title = title;
  }, [title]);

    // render children so this component can wrap page elements
    return children;
};

export default TitleUpdater;
```

This component uses an effect to update the title in the DOM after the TitleUpdater component mounts and whenever its title prop changes. Within the effect, it makes sure the title prop contains a value before updating the DOM.

Then, the component returns the children prop it receives. This renders any JSX between the opening and closing tags of the TitleUpdater component.

To use the TitleUpdater, you need to modify the route objects for your app so they define titles for each page. Then your App component can display the titles for each page as shown next.

The modified App component

```
import { Routes, Route } from 'react-router-dom';
import TitleUpdater from './layout/TitleUpdater';
...

// add a title for each route
const routes = [
  { path: '/', element: <Home />, title: 'Home | My SPA' },
  { path: '/products', element: <Products />, title: 'Products | My SPA' },
  { path: '/about', element: <About />, title: 'About | My SPA' },
];

const App = () => (
  <>
    <Header />
    <Navbar />
    <Routes>
      {routes.map(({ path, element, title }) => (  // pass title to each route
        <Route
          key={path}
          path={path}
          element={
            <TitleUpdater title={title} />   // use TitleUpdater
              {element}
            </TitleUpdater>
          } />
      ))}
    </Routes>
...
```

In this code, each route object has a title property. Then, the JSX maps the title prop to each Route and uses the TitleUpdater component to set the title for the page and render the element between its opening and closing tags.

Redirect a URL to a page

Sometimes, you may need to redirect users from one URL to another. For example, if you change the URL structure for your app, you may need to provide multiple URLs to the same content. Or, you may need to handle legacy URLs.

With React Router, you can use the Navigate component summarized next to redirect a request to another URL.

The Navigate component

Component	Description
`<Navigate to replace />`	Redirects a request to a new route. The to prop sets the path, and the replace prop prevents the redirected URL from being added to the browser's history.

For example, to redirect a request from the /home path to the root path, you can use the following code.

A route that redirects from /home to /

```
{ path: '/home', element: <Navigate to="/" replace /> }
```

Here, the Navigate component doesn't render any content, it just performs the redirect. In addition, this route doesn't set a title. That's because this route doesn't render a page. Instead, it redirects to another page that sets the title.

When redirecting, the replace prop makes sure that the browser's back button works correctly. If you include the replace prop, clicking the back button returns to the previous page, which is usually what you want. Otherwise, clicking the back button returns to the previous URL, which redirects back to the current page, which is not usually what you want.

Navigate to a route

Sometimes, you may need to programmatically navigate between routes in an app. For example, if the user submits a form or clicks a button, you may need to navigate to an appropriate page. To do that, you can use the useNavigate hook shown next.

The useNavigate hook

Hook	Description
useNavigate	Returns a function that you can call to navigate to different URLs.

For example, the following example shows how to redirect to the Home page after submitting a form.

An event handler that navigates to a route

```
import { useNavigate } from 'react-router-dom';   // import hook
...
const MyForm = ({ onAdd }) => {
    const navigate = useNavigate();                 // get navigate() function
    ...
    const handleSubmit = (e) => {
        // code that handles the form submit
        navigate("/");                              // navigate to Home page
    };
...
```

Here, the code imports the hook and uses it to create a function named navigate(). Then, it uses that function to navigate to the path for the Home page. In many cases, that's all you need to do to navigate to the route you want. However, you can also use the navigate() function to navigate through the browser's history as shown next.

Three more ways to navigate to a route

```
navigate(-1);                                    // Go back one page in history
navigate(1);                                     // Go forward one page in history
navigate("/products", { replace: true });        // Navigate to URL and replace the
                                                 // current entry in history
```

How to work with dynamic routes

So far, this chapter has shown how to work with *static routes*, which are hard-coded URL paths like /products and /about. Now, you'll learn how to work with *dynamic routes*, which are URL patterns that use *route parameters* like /products/:id where :id can be any value. This allows a single Route component to handle multiple related pages.

A dynamic route often uses the following patterns to work with URL segments.

Two patterns for URL segments

Pattern	Description
/:id	The colon (:) creates a named parameter that captures a dynamic value from the URL and makes it available to components.
/*	The asterisk (*) creates a wildcard that matches any remaining path segments in the current route.

Using the colon (:) to create a named parameter is essential for data-driven applications where you need to display specific items like product details or user profiles. In addition, using the asterisk (*) to match any remaining paths is useful for adding error pages.

Use a URL segment as a parameter

To work with named parameters, you can use the useParams hook summarized next.

The useParams hook

Hook	Description
useParams()	Extracts dynamic route parameters from the current URL and returns them as a JSON object with parameter names as keys.

For example, the following Products component displays links a user can click to request data for an individual product by its id.

The Products component

```
import { Link } from 'react-router-dom';

const Products = () => (
    <main className="content">
        <h2>Learn about our products here.</h2>
        <p><Link to="/products/1">Duct Tape</Link></p>
        <p><Link to="/products/2">Chewing Gum</Link></p>
    </main>
);

export default Products;
```

To do that, this page uses Link components to provide URLs like /products/1 and /products/2. When this page displays in a browser, it allows the user to display a product by clicking on a link as shown next.

The Products page

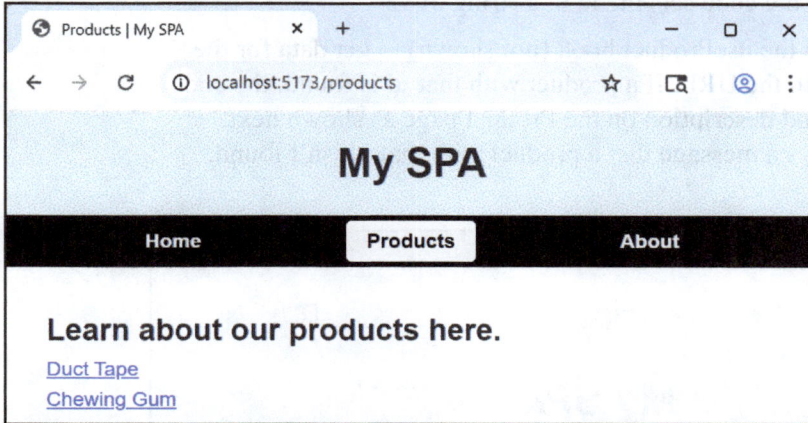

Since the links in the Products component match the /products/:id URL pattern, you need to add the following route object to the routes array for that pattern.

Route object for the dynamic route to display a product

```
{ path: '/products/:id', element: <Product />, title: 'Product | My SPA' }
```

Then, the following Product component can display a different page for each product.

The Product component

```jsx
import { useParams } from "react-router-dom";
import { useProduct } from "../hooks/useProduct.js"; // hook to get product data

const Product = () => {
    // use URL id parameter to retrieve product info
    const { id } = useParams();
    const product = useProduct(id);

    return (
        <>
            {product ? (
                <>
                    <h2>{product.name}</h2>
                    <p>{product.description}</p>
                </>
            ) : (
                <h2>Product {id} not found</h2>
            )}
        </>
    );
};

export default Product;
```

Here, the useParams() function extracts the dynamic parameters from the URL and returns them as an object. Then, this code uses destructuring to extract the parameter named id. In this example, when a user clicks on the link for /products/1, this code sets the id to a string of "1". And when a user clicks the link for /products/2, the code sets the id to a string of "2".

Then, this code uses the useProduct hook (not shown) to get data for the product with the id in the URL. If a product with that id is found, the code displays the name and description on the Product page as shown next. Otherwise, it displays a message that a product with that id isn't found.

A Product page

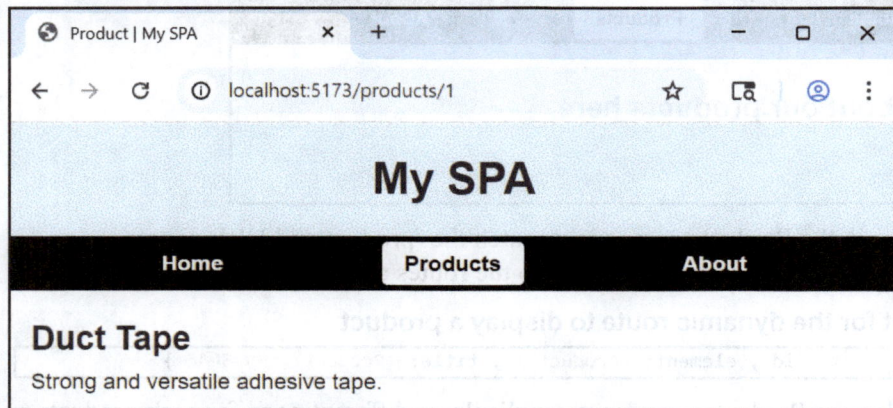

Here, the URL of /products/1 sets the Products link as the active class, which causes it to be highlighted in the navigation bar. That's because the NavLink component for the Products link specifies the /products URL and doesn't include the end prop. As a result, this link remains active even for URLs such as /products/1, products/2, and so on.

Add a dynamic title for a dynamic route

In the preceding example, the title for the dynamic product page is hard-coded as 'Product' followed by the app name. As a result, that's the title that displays for every product. However, it's common to display dynamic data such as the product name in the title for the page.

One way to do that is to move the code that updates the title to the component that gets the parameter from the URL and uses it to retrieve data. For instance, here's how you could update the Product component to display a dynamic title.

The updated Product component that displays a dynamic title

```
import { useParams } from 'react-router-dom';
import { useProduct } from '../hooks/useProduct.js';
import TitleUpdater from '../components/TitleUpdater.jsx';
```

```
const Product = ({ titleTemplate = "" }) => {
    // use URL id parameter to retrieve product info
    const { id } = useParams();
    const product = useProduct(id);

    // get dynamic title for selected product
    const name = product ? product.name : 'Product Not Found';
    const title = titleTemplate.replace(':placeholder', name);

    return (
        <TitleUpdater title={title}>
            {product ? (
                <>
                    <h2>{product.name}</h2>
                    <p>{product.description}</p>
                </>
            ) : (
                <h2>Product {id} not found</h2>
            )}
        </TitleUpdater>
    );
};

export default Product;
```

Here, the Product component imports the TitleUpdater component. Then, it uses the titleTemplate prop to create a title to pass to TitleUpdater. Finally, it embeds the JSX that displays the product data within TitleUpdater.

Since Product handles setting the title, App no longer needs to. Instead, App needs to pass the template Product needs to create the dynamic title. Here's the updated App component.

The updated App component for the dynamic Product title

```
...
// configure routes
const routeData = [
  { path: '/', element: <Home />, title: 'Home | My SPA' },
  { path: '/home', element: <Navigate to="/" replace /> },
  { path: '/products', element: <Products />, title: 'Products | My SPA' },
  { path: '/products/:id',
      element: <Product titleTemplate='Products | :placeholder | My SPA' />
  }, // no title property since Product handles dynamic title
  { path: '/about', element: <About />, title: 'About | My SPA' }
];

const App = () => {
    return (
        <>
            <Header />
            <Navbar />
            <main className="content">
                <Routes>
                    {routeData.map(({ path, element, title }) => (
                        <Route
                            key={path}
```

```
                                path={path}
                                element={
                                    <TitleUpdater title={title}>
                                        {element}
                                    </TitleUpdater>
                                }
                            />
                        ))}
                    </Routes>
                </main>
                <Footer />
            </>
        );
    }

export default App;
```

Here, the route object for the dynamic product route passes a title string that contains a placeholder for the project name to the titleTemplate prop of the Product component. Then, since Product handles the title, the route object for the dynamic product route doesn't include a title property.

This code wraps the element for every route in a TitleUpdater component. Since the Product component also wraps its JSX in a TitleUpdater component, the dynamic product route renders TitleUpdater twice, once in App and once in Product. That's OK, though, because TitleUpdater only updates the DOM if its title prop has a value.

The product page with a dynamic title

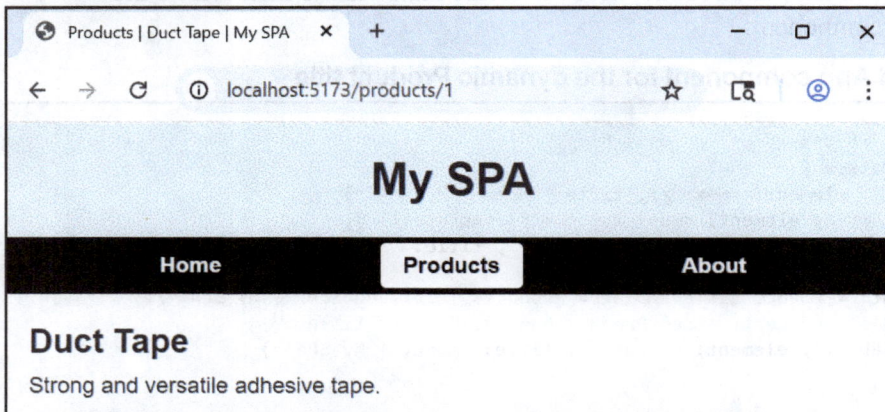

Add an error page

As described earlier, you can use an asterisk to define a wildcard route that matches any path. Because routes are evaluated in order, adding a wildcard path to the end of your routes is a common way to display an error page as shown next.

The routes with a wildcard route at the end

```
const routes = [
  { path: '/', element: <Home />, title: 'Home | My SPA' },
  { path: '/home', element: <Navigate to="/" replace /> },
  { path: '/products', element: <Products />, title: 'Products | My SPA' },
  { path: '/products/:id',
      element: <Product titleTemplate='Products | :placeholder | My SPA' />
  },
  { path: '/about', element: <About />, title: 'About | My SPA' },
  { path: '/*', element: <NotFound />, title: '404 Not Found | My SPA' }
];
```

In this routes array, the route for the NotFound component must be the last route. Otherwise, it won't be possible to reach any route that comes after the wildcard route.

The next example shows the code for the NotFound component that displays when a page isn't found.

The NotFound component

```
const NotFound = () => (
    <main className="content">
        <h2>404 - Page Not Found</h2>
    </main>
);

export default NotFound;
```

This component displays the page shown next anytime a user navigates to a route that doesn't exist in the app.

The 404 Not Found page

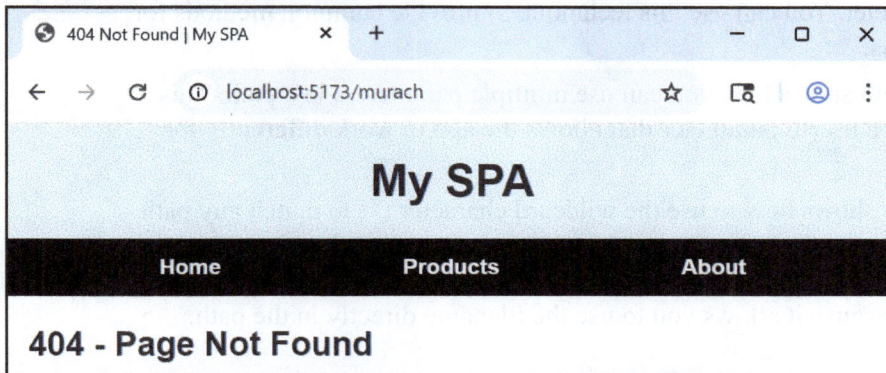

In the browser, the URL of /products/murach doesn't set any of the NavLink components as the active class. As a result, none of the links are selected in the navigation bar.

Other ways to create a dynamic route

Using parameters to create dynamic routes is a powerful feature, and there are many ways you can use route parameters and wildcards. The next table shows some example routes that demonstrate how you might combine or use these features in a more complex app.

Examples of dynamic routes

Path	Description
/products/:id	Parameters can be placed at the end of a URL.
/products/:id?	Adding a ? to the end of a parameter makes the parameter optional.
/products/:id/delete	Parameters can be placed between static items.
/user/:userId/products/:id?	Multiple parameters can be used in a path.
/files/*	Wildcards can be used to match all segments after a static endpoint.

Here, the first path shows how to include a parameter at the end of the URL to access a specific item.

The second path shows how to create an optional parameter. This path matches both /products and /products/:id. As a result, you can use it to replace the two product paths currently in the app with a single path. However, this makes it more difficult to set the title for each page.

The third path shows how you can include static segments after using a parameter. In particular, this path includes a static segment of "delete" after the :id parameter. You can use this technique to provide common methods for dynamic items.

The fourth path shows how you can use multiple parameters in a path. This path includes a userId parameter that allows the app to work differently for each user.

The fifth path shows how to use the wildcard character (*) to match any path after an existing path. In particular, this path matches all paths after /file. You can use this technique to display the files that have been uploaded to the app. This works because it allows you to use the filename directly in the path.

The Future Value app

So far, this chapter has presented some important skills for routing. Now, it shows how these skills can be used within a complete app. In particular, it shows how these skills can be used in an SPA version of the Future Value app that was presented in chapter 1. This shows how to implement client-side routing and create reusable navigation components.

The user interface

The following screen shows the Home page of the Future Value app after the user enters valid values and clicks the Calculate button.

The Home page

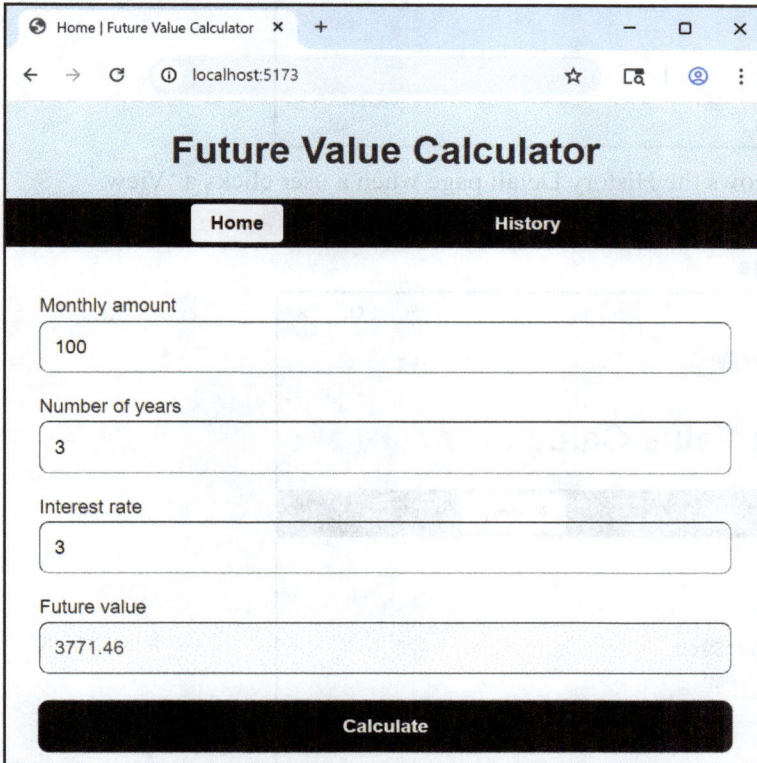

The following screen shows the History page for the Future Value Calculator app for two calculations.

The History page

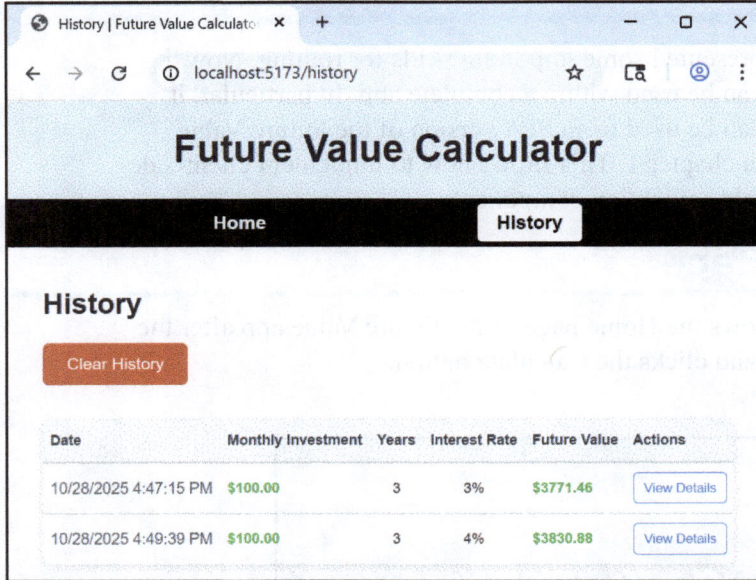

The following screen shows the History Detail page when a user clicks a 'View Details' button for a calculation on the History page.

The History Detail page

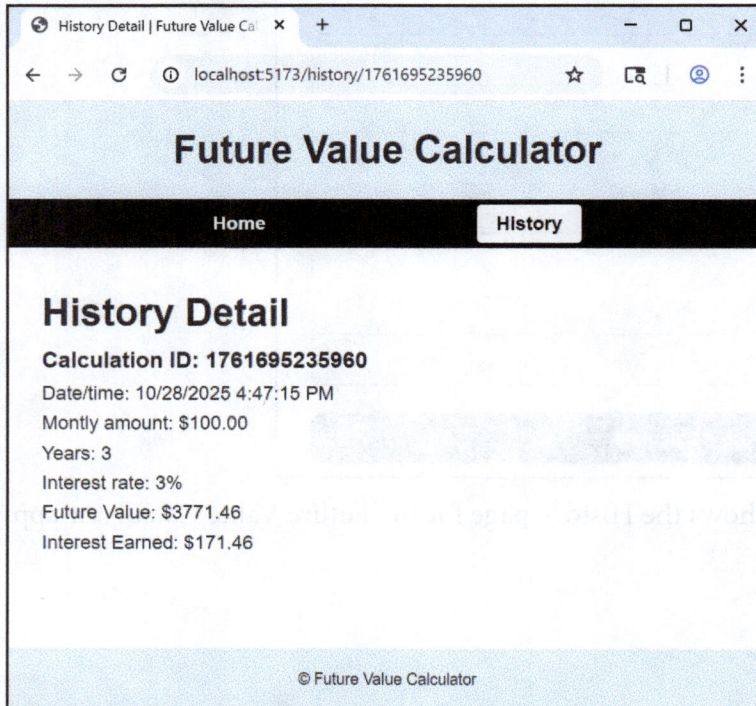

The directory structure

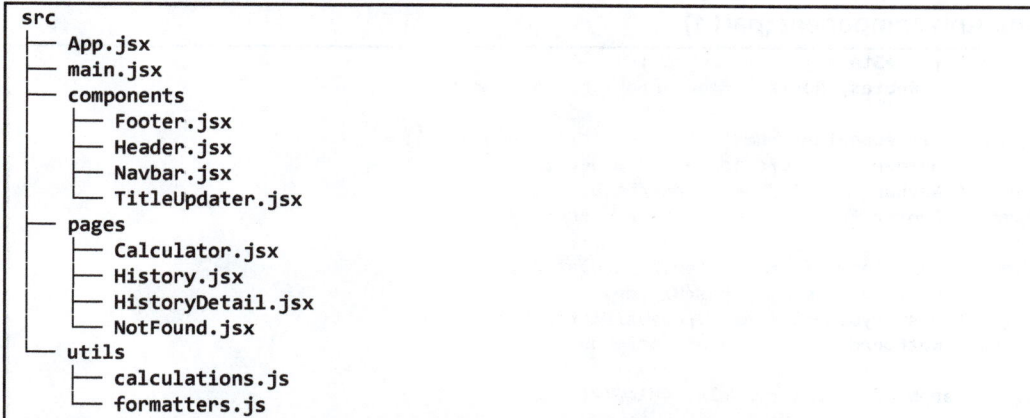

Here's the directory structure for the Future Value app. To save space, co-located CSS files aren't shown.

The directory structure

```
src
├── App.jsx
├── main.jsx
├── components
│   ├── Footer.jsx
│   ├── Header.jsx
│   ├── Navbar.jsx
│   └── TitleUpdater.jsx
├── pages
│   ├── Calculator.jsx
│   ├── History.jsx
│   ├── HistoryDetail.jsx
│   └── NotFound.jsx
└── utils
    ├── calculations.js
    └── formatters.js
```

In this structure, the components directory contains four components that the App component uses on every page. This includes the Header, Navbar, and Footer components that display the header, navigation bar, and footer for every page. In addition, it includes the TitleUpdater component that updates the title for each page as described earlier in this chapter.

The pages directory contains the components that define the content for the four pages of the app. This includes a Calculator component that lets you make future value calculations, a History component that views a list of calculations, a HistoryDetail component that views the details for a specific calculation, and a NotFound component that displays if a page is not found at a specified URL. The following table shows how these components map to the URLs.

The components and their URLs

Component	URL
Calculator	/
History	/history
HistoryDetail	/history/:id
NotFound	/*

Finally, the utils directory contains files with utility functions that are used by the page components. The calculations.js file contains functions to calculate future value and interest, and the formatters.js file contains functions to format currency and dates. To save space, the utility functions aren't shown in this chapter, but you can view them in the download for this book.

The App component

The App component uses state to store the calculations, and client-side routing to navigate between the pages. It starts by importing the hooks and components it needs. Then, it defines a constant that holds the name of the app.

The App component (part 1)

```
import { useState } from 'react';
import { Routes, Route } from 'react-router-dom';

import TitleUpdater from './components/TitleUpdater';
import Header from './components/Header';
import Navbar from './components/Navbar';
import Footer from './components/Footer';

import Calculator from './pages/Calculator';
import History from './pages/History';
import HistoryDetail from './pages/HistoryDetail';
import NotFound from './pages/NotFound';

const appName = 'Future Value Calculator';

const App = () => {
    const [calculations, setCalculations] = useState([]);

    const handleAddToHistory = (amount, years, rate, futureValue) => {
        const calc = {
            id: Date.now(), // simple ID using timestamp
            amount: parseFloat(amount),
            years: parseInt(years),
            rate: parseFloat(rate),
            futureValue: futureValue,
            date: new Date().toISOString()
        };
        setCalculations([...calculations, calc]);
    };

    const handleClearHistory = () => {
        setCalculations([]);
    };
```

The function for the component starts by defining the state for calculations. Then, it defines the event handlers to manage that state.

The event handler that adds to history creates a calculation object and adds it to the state array, while the event handler that clears the history sets the state array to an empty array. Note that the id property of the object created in the add function stores the number of milliseconds elapsed since January 1, 1970. For this app, this is a convenient way to uniquely identify each calculation. However, this technique for generating ids wouldn't be optimal for a multi-user app where two users might make a calculation at exactly the same time.

The App component (part 2)

```
const routeData = [
    { path: '/',
        navText: 'Home',
        element: <Calculator onAddToHistory={handleAddToHistory} />,
        title: 'Home | ' + appName },
    { path: '/history',
        navText: 'History',
        element: <History data={calculations}
                          onClearHistory={handleClearHistory} />,
        title: 'History | ' + appName },
    { path: '/history/:id',
        element: <HistoryDetail data={calculations} />,
        title: 'History Detail | ' + appName },
    { path: '/*',
        element: <NotFound />,
        title: '404 Not Found | ' + appName }
];

// extract the nav link data from the route data
const navData = routeData
    .filter(route => route.navText) // keep only those with navText
    .map(({ path, navText }) => ({ path, navText }));
```

To map the page components to their URLs, App uses an array to store the routes as objects. This array is defined within App because the page components have props that use the state variables and event handlers.

To make sure that each page displays the correct app name, this code appends the constant that stores the name of the app to the end of the title.

In addition, some of the route objects contain a navText property. Then, App uses this property to extract the data for the navigation links. To do that, App passes this data to the Navbar component that's shown later in this chapter, which uses it to define the NavLink components. This reduces code duplication.

Using the routes array to create the navigation links may seem like overkill in an app like this that only has two links in the navbar. However, if you code it this way, the navbar always stays in sync with the routes of the app. For instance, if you add a Contact Us route and include a navText property in the route object, the Navbar component automatically displays the new link. This makes your app easier to maintain.

The App component (part 3)

```
return (
    <>
        <Header />
        <Navbar navData={navData} />
        <Routes>
            {routeData.map(({ path, element, title }) => (
                <Route
                    key={path}
                    path={path}
```

```
                        element={
                            <TitleUpdater title={title}>
                                {element}
                            </TitleUpdater>
                        }
                    />
                ))}
            </Routes>
            <Footer />
        </>
    );
};

export default App;
```

The JSX for App renders the Header, Navbar, Routes, and Footer components, passing the navData array to Navbar. Within Routes, it maps each object in the routes array to a Route component. Within each Route, it uses the TitleUpdater component to set the title for each page.

The Navbar component

The Navbar component defines a navigation bar that collapses on small screens and expands on larger screens. It uses the navData prop to create the NavLink components for the navbar.

```
import { useState } from 'react';
import { NavLink } from 'react-router-dom';
import './Navbar.css';

const Navbar = ({ navData = [] }) => {
    // State variable to manage the menu state
    const [isExpanded, setIsExpanded] = useState(false);

    // event handler for menu button click
    const handleMenuClick = () => {
        // use the previous state to determine the new state
        setIsExpanded(prev => !prev);
    };

    // get the icon based on the menu state
    const icon = (isExpanded) ? "✖" : "☰";

    // get the CSS classes based on the menu state
    const menuClass = (isExpanded) ? 'nav-menu show' : 'nav-menu';

    // function to close the menu when a link is clicked
    const closeMenu = () => setIsExpanded(false)

    return (
        <nav className="navbar">
            <button className="menu-button" aria-label="Toggle menu"
                onClick={handleMenuClick}>{icon}</button>
            <div className={menuClass}>
                {navData.map(item => (
```

```
                    <NavLink
                        key={item.path}
                        to={item.path}
                        end={item.path === '/'}
                        onClick={closeMenu}
                    >
                        {item.navText}
                    </NavLink>
                ))}
            </div>
        </nav>
    );
};

export default Navbar;
```

This code uses NavLink components to display the links to the Home and History pages. When the path is the app root, it sets the end property to true. Otherwise, it sets the end property to false. This has the same effect as coding the end property for the Home link and omitting it for the other links.

The Calculator component

The Calculator component contains code that calculates a future value based on a series of monthly investments at a specified interest rate. To do this, it imports the calculateFutureValue() utility function. Calculator also uses the event handler prop it receives from App to save these calculations to state.

The Calculator component

```
import { useState } from 'react';
import { calculateFutureValue } from '../utils/calculations';
import './Calculator.css';

const Calculator = ({ onAddToHistory }) => {
    const [amount, setAmount] = useState('');
    const [years, setYears] = useState('');
    const [rate, setRate] = useState('');
    const [futureValue, setFutureValue] = useState('');

    const handleSubmit = (e) => {
        e.preventDefault();

        // validate user input
        if (
            isNaN(amount) || isNaN(years) || isNaN(rate) ||
            amount < 0 || years < 0 || rate < 0
        ) {
            setFutureValue("Please enter valid non-negative numbers.");
            return;
        }

        // calculate and display the future value
        const fv = calculateFutureValue(amount, years, rate);
        setFutureValue(fv.toFixed(2));
```

```
            // call the function passed via props to add calculation to history
        onAddToHistory(amount, years, rate, fv);
    };

    return (
        <div className="content">
            <form onSubmit={handleSubmit}>
                <div>
                    <label htmlFor="amount">Monthly amount</label>
                    <input type="number" id="amount" name="amount"
                        value={amount}
                        onChange={(e) => setAmount(+e.target.value)}
                        required autoFocus
                    />
                </div>
                <div>
                    <label htmlFor="years">Number of years</label>
                    <input type="number" id="years" name="years"
                        value={years}
                        onChange={(e) => setYears(+e.target.value)}
                        required
                    />
                </div>
                <div>
                    <label htmlFor="rate">Interest rate</label>
                    <input type="number" id="rate" name="rate"
                        value={rate}
                        onChange={(e) => setRate(+e.target.value)}
                        required
                    />
                </div>
                <div>
                    <label htmlFor="future-value">Future value</label>
                    <input type="text" id="future-value" name="future-value"
                        value={futureValue}
                        disabled
                    />
                </div>
                <div>
                    <button type="submit">Calculate</button>
                </div>
            </form>
        </div>
    );
};

export default Calculator;
```

The History component

The History page displays all of the saved calculations in a table, and clears
the history. To do that, the History component receives props from App that
contain the calculations in state and an event handler to clear the history. In
addition, it imports utility functions to format how the data displays.

The History component

```jsx
import { Link } from 'react-router-dom';
import { formatCurrency, formatDate } from '../utils/formatters';
import './History.css';

const History = ({ data, onClear }) => {
    const clearHistory = () => {
        if (window.confirm('Are you sure?')) {
            onClear();
        }
    };

    return (
        <div className="content">
            <div className="history-header">
                <h2>History</h2>
                <button onClick={clearHistory} className="clear-button">
                    Clear History
                </button>
            </div>

            <div className="table-container">
                <table className="calculations-table">
                    <thead>
                        <tr>
                            <th>Date</th>
                            <th>Monthly Investment</th>
                            <th>Years</th>
                            <th>Interest Rate</th>
                            <th>Future Value</th>
                            <th>Actions</th>
                        </tr>
                    </thead>
                    <tbody>
                        {data.map((calc) => (
                            <tr key={calc.id}>
                                <td>{formatDate(calc.date)}</td>
                                <td>{formatCurrency(calc.amount)}</td>
                                <td>{calc.years}</td>
                                <td>{calc.rate}%</td>
                                <td>{formatCurrency(calc.futureValue)}</td>
                                <td>
                                    <Link to={`/history/${calc.id}`}
                                        className="view-link">
                                        View Details
                                    </Link>
                                </td>
                            </tr>
                        ))}
                    </tbody>
                </table>
            </div>
        </div>
    );
};

export default History
```

This code begins by defining an event handler to clear the calculations from state. It uses the window.confirm() method to make sure the user wants to clear the calculations. If they do, it calls the onClearHistory() prop it received from App.

The JSX begins by displaying the heading for the page and the button to clear the calculations. Then, it displays the calculations in a table that includes the date and time of the calculation, each of the values supplied by the user, and the future value.

In addition, this table includes a Link component for each calculation that the user can click to view details. This component passes the id for the calculation to the route that displays the HistoryDetails component. For example, clicking a link with an id of 1761 requests a URL of /history/1761, which maps to the route for the HistoryDetail component.

The HistoryDetail component

The HistoryDetail page displays details about a specific calculation. To display this page, the HistoryDetail component uses the following code.

The HistoryDetail component

```
import { useParams } from 'react-router-dom';
import { formatCurrency, formatDate } from '../utils/formatters';
import { calculateInterest } from '../utils/calculations';
import './HistoryDetail.css';

const HistoryDetail = ({ data }) => {

    // get the ID from the URL parameters
    const { id } = useParams();

    // get the selected calculation from the data prop
    const calculation = data.find(calc => calc.id === parseInt(id));

    if (!calculation) {
        return (
            <div className="content">
                <h2>Calculation Not Found</h2>
            </div>
        );
    }

    const interestEarned = calculateInterest(
        calculation.amount, calculation.years, calculation.futureValue);

    return (
        <div className="content history-detail">
            <h2>History Detail</h2>
            <h3>Calculation ID: {calculation.id}</h3>
            <div>Date/time: {formatDate(calculation.date)}</div>
            <div>Montly amount: {formatCurrency(calculation.amount)}</div>
```

```
                <div>Years: {calculation.years}</div>
                <div>Interest rate: {calculation.rate}%</div>
                <div>Future Value: {formatCurrency(calculation.futureValue)}</div>
                <div>Interest Earned: {formatCurrency(interestEarned)}</div>
            </div>
        );
    };

    export default HistoryDetail;
```

This code calls the useParams() function to extract the id from the URL. Then, it uses the id to get the selected calculation from the data prop it receives from App.

If this code doesn't find a calculation with the specified id, it returns JSX that displays an appropriate error message. Otherwise, it uses the data from the calculation to calculate the amount of interest earned. Then, it returns JSX that displays all of the data for the calculation, including the interest earned. To do that, it uses the formatDate() and formatCurrency() utility functions that it imports.

Perspective

While SPAs aren't suitable for every project, they are commonly used in React and other web development frameworks. As a result, modern web developers should have a solid understanding of their capabilities and trade-offs. The patterns presented in this chapter provide a solid foundation for building scalable, professional single-page web apps. But, as you implement the routing concepts presented in this chapter, consider how each decision affects both user experience and app maintainability.

The last chapter in this book shows how to use a web development framework known as Next.js to create React apps. This framework provides a way to create SPAs with its own routing system. However, its file-based routing system works a little differently than React Router.

Terms

single-page application (SPA)

multi-page application (MPA)

JavaScript bundle

client-side routing

static route

dynamic route

route parameter

Exercise 8-1: Convert an app to an SPA

Rework the file structure

1. Open the my-playlist project in the ex_starts/ch08 folder.
2. Create a pages directory within the src directory.
3. Move the files for the SongForm and Playlist components into the pages directory and update the associated imports.

Add a Navbar component

4. Install react-router-dom for this project.
5. Open the main.jsx file and wrap the App component in a BrowserRouter component.
6. Open the Navbar.jsx file and examine the code.
7. Import the NavLink component and add two Navlink components to the <div> element in the navbar. The first should point to / and the second should point to /add. The onClick attribute for each link should be set to the closeMenu() function.
8. Open the App.jsx file and add the Navbar component under the Header component. Don't forget to import it.
9. In App.jsx, remove the onCancel attribute for the SongForm.
10. In App.jsx, replace the Add Song button with a <br> element.
11. Run the app and view it in a browser. Confirm that it displays the Navbar component. At this point, clicking the links should change the URL but not the page display.

Modify App to use routes

12. In App.jsx, import the Routes and Route components.
13. Delete the showForm state. Update or remove event handlers that use showForm state. Also remove the ternary operator in the JSX that uses it.
14. Modify the <main> element to contain a Routes object. This object should contain two Route objects. The first should route the Playlist component to a path of /. The second should route the SongForm component to a path of /add.
15. Refresh the app in your browser and confirm that clicking the Navbar links change the page display.

Modify SongForm

16. Open the SongForm component and remove its onCancel prop. Then, remove the Cancel button from the last <div> element.
17. Switch to the browser and add a song. Notice that nothing happens to indicate the add operation was successful.

18. In the SongForm component, import the useNavigate() hook. Then, use it to navigate back to the "/" page when the form is submitted.

Modify App to use a routes array

19. Open the App component and add a routeData array with objects that contain path and element properties for the routes.

20. Update the JSX to map the routeData array to create the Route components.

21. Run the app and make sure the navigation links work correctly.

22. Navigate to a path that doesn't exist, such as /murach. This should display a truncated page and an error in the console.

23. Add a NotFound component to the pages directory.

24. In App, import the NotFound component. Then, add a wildcard route to the end of the routeData array that routes to NotFound.

25. Run the app and navigate again to a path that doesn't exist. It should display the Not Found page.

Modify App to use a TitleUpdater component

26. Add a TitleUpdater component to the components directory. It should accept title and children props. Use an effect to set the document.title to the title property if it exists. Return the children prop so the component renders any JSX between its opening and closing tags.

27. In App, import TitleUpdater and add title properties to the routes array.

28. Update the JSX to extract the title property, pass it to TitleUpdater, and embed the element property within TitleUpdater.

29. Run the app and navigate to its routes, including the "not found" route. As you change pages, the app should display the title text in the browser tab.

Chapter 9

Style an app with CSS modules or Tailwind

So far, this book has shown how to use plain CSS to provide the styles that format a React app. Now, this chapter starts by introducing three more ways to provide the styles for an app. Then, it shows how to use the Tailwind CSS framework to style an app.

Four ways to style a React app

This chapter begins by summarizing four ways to style a React app. This includes a brief discussion of the pros and cons of each approach. To illustrate how each approach works, this chapter shows how to use each approach to style a Header component like the one shown next.

The Header component in a browser

Movie List

To display this Header component, an app can use the following code.

The code that displays the Header component

```
<Header text="Movie List" />
```

Plain CSS

To use plain CSS to style this header, you can create the following CSS file in the same directory as the Header.jsx file.

The Header.css file

```css
.header {
    background-color: lightblue;
    border-bottom: 1px solid darkblue;
    padding: .5em;
    h1 {
        font-size: 2.5rem;
        font-weight: bold;
    }
}
```

This CSS defines the styles needed to format the Header component. In particular, it defines a CSS class named header that formats the header and any <h1> elements within the header.

Then, in the JSX file for the component, you can import this CSS file and apply its styles as shown next.

A Header.jsx file that uses plain CSS

```jsx
import './Header.css';

const Header = ({ text }) => (
    <header className="header">
        <h1>{text}</h1>
    </header>
```

```
);

export default Header;
```

Using plain CSS is the simplest and most classic way to style a React app, and it has several advantages.

Advantages of plain CSS

- Uses the familiar CSS syntax
- Co-locates styles with their components
- Doesn't have any build dependencies

When you use plain CSS, all class names exist in a global namespace. This makes it easy for styles to accidentally override each other as your app grows. To solve this issue, many developers use CSS modules.

CSS modules

CSS modules address the global namespace issue by automatically generating unique class names to make sure your styles remain scoped to the component that uses them.

To convert a CSS file to a module, you add ".module" between the file name and extension. For example, to convert the Header.css file shown earlier to a module, you rename it to Header.module.css. However, you don't need to change any of the CSS within the file.

The Header.module.css file

```
Same CSS as the Header.css shown earlier
```

Before you can use a CSS module, you need to import it as shown next.

A Header.jsx file that uses a CSS module

```
import styles from './Header.module.css';

const Header = () => (
    <header className={styles.header}>
        <h1>Movie List</h1>
    </header>
);

export default Header;
```

When this code imports a CSS module, it specifies a name of styles for the module. Then, it uses that name to access the CSS class that's available from that module. For this to work, you need to make sure that you reference the style within curly braces rather than quotes.

When you convert a plain CSS file to a CSS module, global styles like CSS custom properties, element selectors, and ID selectors don't require any changes. However, class selectors automatically become locally scoped. As a result, CSS class names like .header and .navbar can only be accessed through the CSS module. This prevents naming conflicts between CSS classes while keeping your other CSS unchanged.

CSS modules provide the following advantages over traditional CSS.

Advantages of CSS modules over plain CSS

- Eliminates naming conflicts of CSS classes
- Built in to most React tooling

CSS-in-JS

CSS-in-JS also attempts to address the global namespace issue. To do that, it allows developers to write CSS directly in JavaScript, so they can take advantage of JavaScript to automatically scope CSS and to provide dynamic styles.

The next example shows how to use a CSS-in-JS library known as styled-components to style the Header component.

A Header.jsx file that uses CSS-in-JS

```
import styled from 'styled-components';

const StyledHeader = styled.header`
    background-color: lightblue;
    border-bottom: 1px solid darkblue;
    padding: .5em;
    h1 {
        font-size: 2.5rem;
        font-weight: bold;
    }
`;

const Header = ({ text }) => (
    <StyledHeader>
        <h1>{text}</h1>
    </StyledHeader>
);

export default Header;
```

This code begins by importing the styled-components library with a name of styled. Then, it defines the CSS for a component named StyledHeader. Finally, it uses the StyledHeader component to apply the styles to the Header component.

CSS-in-JS libraries such as styled-components were once popular but are now declining in popularity due to performance issues and compatibility issues with modern React features like Server Components. While CSS-in-JS libraries such as Emotion remain common in existing codebases and are still actively maintained, these days most developers building new React apps choose a traditional approach like CSS modules or a CSS framework like Tailwind.

Styling frameworks and libraries

Another option for styling your apps is to use a styling framework or library. A styling framework or library provides pre-written CSS classes or pre-written React components that have already been styled. When you use this approach, you don't need to write as much CSS, and it's often easier to create a consistent style for your whole app.

If you want to use a styling framework or library, there are dozens to choose from, but here are a few of the most popular ones.

Some popular styling frameworks and libraries for React

- Tailwind CSS
- Material UI (MUI)
- Bootstrap

Since the Tailwind CSS framework is currently the most popular of these options, the next example shows how to use Tailwind to create and style the Header component.

A Header.jsx component that uses Tailwind

```
const Header = ({ text }) => (
    <header className="bg-blue-200 p-4
                        border-b-2 border-blue-900»>
        <h1 className="text-4xl font-bold">{text}</h1>
    </header>
);

export default Header;
```

This code shows that Tailwind CSS provides low-level utility classes to build custom designs. Instead of writing custom CSS or using pre-built components, developers style an element by using small, single-purpose classes like bg-blue-200, p-4, or font-bold.

In most cases, Tailwind CSS eliminates the need for separate CSS files. This makes a component even more modular since the CSS is stored directly within the component's JSX. In addition, it prevents the common problem of unused styles accumulating in your code over time. Most importantly, Tailwind CSS makes it easy for developers to quickly create attractive and consistent designs.

Benefits of Tailwind CSS

- Makes it easier to quickly create attractive designs
- Makes it easier to create consistent designs
- Eliminates the need for CSS files
- Prevents the accumulation of unused CSS styles

How to get started with Tailwind CSS

Since the Tailwind CSS framework uses a different approach than plain CSS or CSS modules, and since it's a popular way to style React apps, this chapter now presents some basic skills for using it. If you're already familiar with CSS, you may find that using Tailwind seems familiar since many of its classes provide a shorthand way to set CSS properties.

Install and configure Tailwind

Before you can use Tailwind, you need to install it and configure it. To install it, you can open your Vite + React project and run the following command in the Terminal.

Install Tailwind CSS

```
npm install tailwindcss @tailwindcss/vite
```

This command installs Tailwind CSS and the Vite plugin that enables Tailwind to work seamlessly with your project.

After installing Tailwind CSS, you can configure it by opening the vite.config.js file and adding the highlighted code shown next.

Configure Vite in vite.config.js

```
import { defineConfig } from 'vite'
import react from '@vitejs/plugin-react'
import tailwindcss from '@tailwindcss/vite'

// https://vite.dev/config/
export default defineConfig({
  plugins: [react(), tailwindcss(),],
})
```

This adds the Tailwind CSS plugin to your Vite configuration so Vite can process Tailwind classes during the build process. As a result, you can use Tailwind classes in your components. But first, you need to use the index.css file to import Tailwind CSS as shown next.

Use the index.css file to import Tailwind CSS

```
@import "tailwindcss";
...
```

This imports all of Tailwind's classes, making them available throughout your React app.

Format text

Tailwind provides many classes for formatting text. These classes include the following classes for setting font size.

Classes for setting font size

Class	Description
text-xs	Extra small.
text-sm	Small.
text-base	Base or default size.
text-lg	Large.
text-xl	Extra large.
text-2xl	Larger than extra large, extends through 9xl.

To use these classes, you set the className prop just like you would with a CSS class that you wrote yourself as shown next.

JSX that sets font size

```
<h2 className="text-4xl">Heading</h2>
<p className="text-base">This is a paragraph that displays some content for the
page.</p>
<h3 className="text-2xl">Subheading</h3>
<p className="text-base">This is another paragraph that displays some content for the
page.</p>
<p className="text-sm">Copyright © XYZ Company</p>
```

The next example shows how these text sizes look when displayed in a browser.

The font sizes in a browser

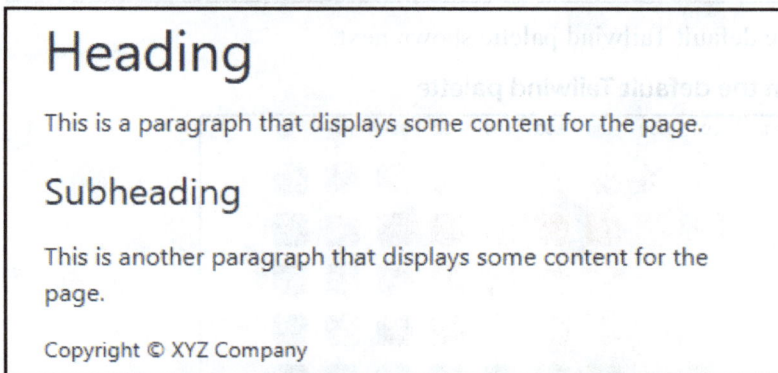

Heading

This is a paragraph that displays some content for the page.

Subheading

This is another paragraph that displays some content for the page.

Copyright © XYZ Company

Tailwind also provides classes to adjust how thick the font is, also known as the *font weight*. Some of these classes are presented next.

Classes for setting font weight

Class	Description
font-thin	Thin (weight 100).
font-light	Light (weight 300).
font-normal	Normal (weight 400).
font-medium	Medium (weight 500).
font-semibold	Semi-bold (weight 600).
font-bold	Bold (weight 700).
font-extrabold	Extra bold (weight 800).
font-black	Black (weight 900).

The following example shows how some of these weights look in the browser.

Some font weights in a browser

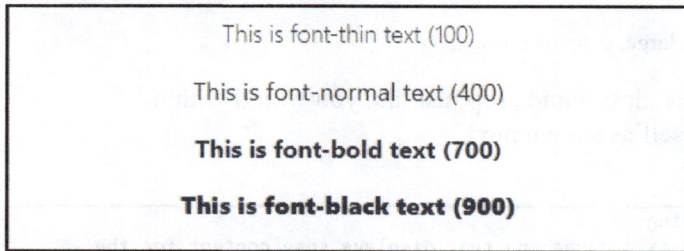

This is font-thin text (100)

This is font-normal text (400)

This is font-bold text (700)

This is font-black text (900)

Tailwind provides *color utilities* to set the color of text, backgrounds, borders, and more. To use these color utilities, you need to understand how Tailwind's color palette works. The first step in understanding this palette is to open the following link in a browser.

The URL for Tailwind's color palette

```
https://tailwindcss.com/docs/colors
```

This should display the default Tailwind palette shown next.

Some of the colors in the default Tailwind palette

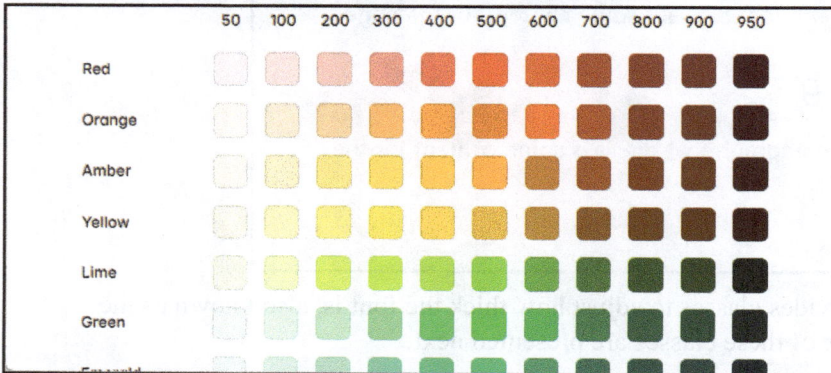

There are many more color options that the ones shown here, but this should give you an idea of what's available. Each color in the palette has 11 steps, with 50 being the lightest, and 950 being the darkest. To set a color and its step for text, you can use the following classes.

The text color utility

Class	Description
`text-{color}-{step}`	Specifies the text color and its step value. When you specify a color of black or white, you don't specify a step value.

When you specify a text color, you typically specify the color name and a step value such as 500 to modify how light or dark the color is. However, if you specify black or white as the color, you don't specify a step. For example, the following screen shows how some of these colors look when displayed in a browser.

Some text colors in a browser

This is text-black
This is text-blue-300
This is text-blue-500
This is text-blue-700
This is text-blue-950
This is text-red-500

Once you understand how to set color for text, you can use those skills to set colors for backgrounds, borders, and more as shown later in this chapter.

Tailwind provides the following classes to work with horizontal text alignment.

Classes for setting horizontal alignment

Class	Description
`text-left`	Left aligns text.
`text-center`	Centers text.
`text-right`	Right aligns text.
`text-justify`	Spreads text evenly across the line width.

When you use these classes, they may be inherited by child elements depending on the type of the child element. Inline elements such as <span> inherit the text alignment class from their parent element while block elements such as <div> do not. The next example shows how each of these classes aligns text in a browser.

The text alignment classes in a browser

```
                           text-left:
This text is left-aligned.


                          text-center:
                   This text is center-aligned.


                          text-right:
                                    This text is right-aligned.


                          text-justify:
This text is justified, which means the spacing between words is adjusted so that each
line (except the last) stretches from the left margin to the right margin. Notice how the
words are spaced to create even margins on both sides.
```

Tailwind provides the following classes to decorate text.

Classes for text decorations

Class	Description
underline	Adds an underline.
no-underline	Removes an existing underline.
italic	Italicizes text.
not-italic	Removes italics from text.

The next example shows how these classes look when displayed in a browser.

Text decoration classes in a browser

```
                           underline:
                  This text has an underline decoration

                          no-underline:
   This text explicitly has no underline (useful for removing default link underlines)

                            italic:
                    This text is italicized for emphasis

                          not-italic:
                 This text explicitly removes italic styling
```

Format backgrounds and borders

Formatting the backgrounds and borders of your elements can improve readability and help to visually separate the different components of your apps. Tailwind provides the following classes to work with backgrounds. This includes the background (bg) color utility and an *effect* that's used to set opacity.

Classes for setting background color and transparency

Class	Description
bg-{color}-{step}	Changes the background to the specified color and step value.
bg-transparent	Makes the background completely transparent.
opacity-{value}	Makes the background partially transparent based on the specified opacity value where 0 is completely transparent and 100 is completely opaque.

The bg-color utility provides a way to set the background to any color in the Tailwind color palette. By default, background colors are opaque, which means that they aren't transparent at all. However, you may occasionally use the bg-transparent class or the opacity effect to control how transparent your elements are.

The following screen shows how to work with background colors and opacity.

The background color classes in a browser

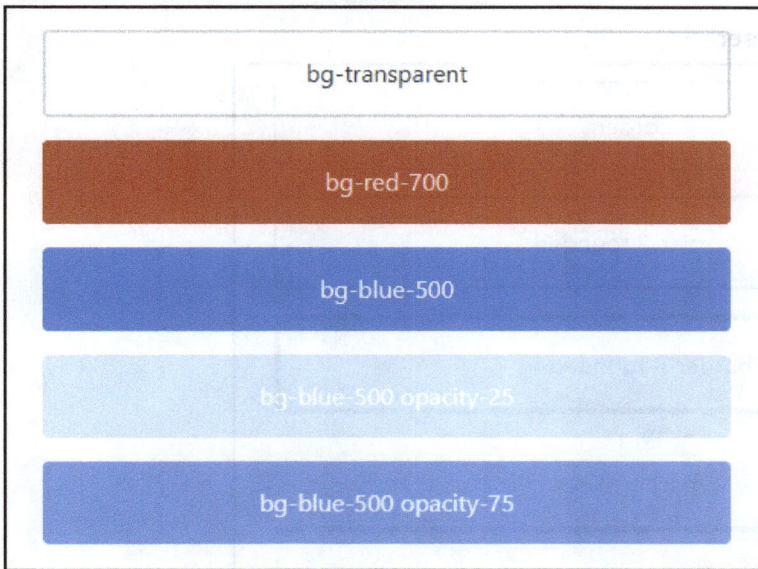

Here, the background of the first element is completely transparent. As a result, it looks white because that's the background color of the element behind it. The second and third elements set a background color, so they display that color. Finally, the fourth and fifth elements set a color but also set an opacity. For example, the fifth element sets opacity to 75. As a result, it's 75% opaque and 25% transparent.

Beyond backgrounds, you may want to use the following classes to set the border style of an element.

Classes for setting border style

Class	Description
border	Adds a border to the element.
border-{width}	Adds a border with the specified width in pixels.
border-{color}-{step}	Sets the color of the border and its step value.
border-{side}	Adds a border to a side. Valid values for side are t (top), b (bottom), r (right), l (left), x (left and right), and y (top and bottom).
rounded-{size}	Rounds the corners to the specified size. Valid values for size are xs (extra small), sm (small), md (medium), lg (large), xl (extra large), 2xl (even larger), and so on.
rounded-{side}-{size}	Rounds both corners on the specified side to the specified size.
rounded-{corner}-{size}	Rounds the specified corner to the specified size. Valid values for corners are tl (top left), tr (top right), bl (bottom left), and br (bottom right).

The next screen shows how to use these classes to create borders.

The borders in a browser

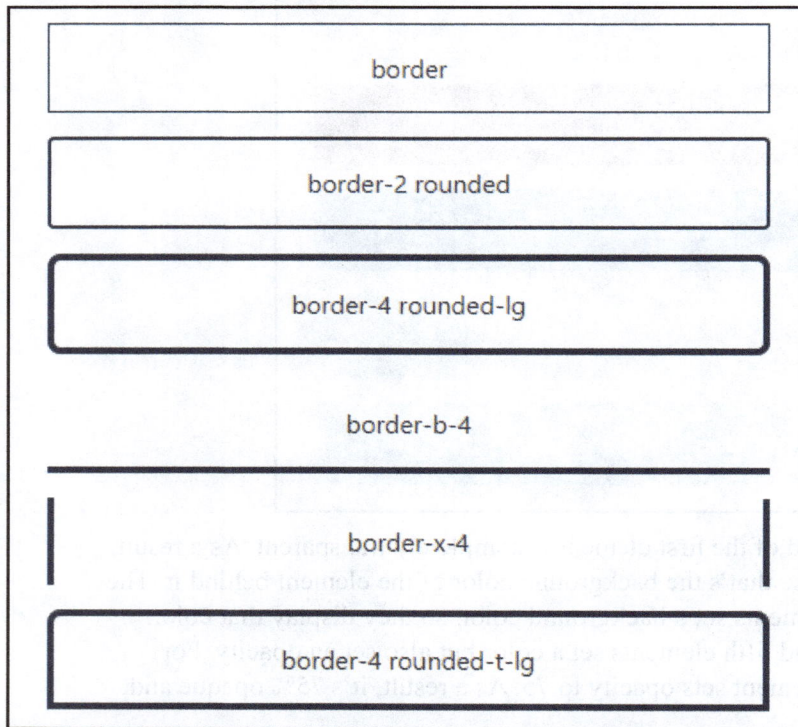

Here, the first three elements have borders on all four sides. The first element uses the border class to display a border with the default width of 1px and the default rectangular corners. The second element displays a border that's 2px wide with rounded corners. And the third example displays a 4px border with large rounded corners.

The next three elements show how to control which borders are displayed and rounded. The fourth example only displays a bottom border. The fifth example displays left and right borders. And the sixth example displays all four borders but only rounds the top borders.

Set width and height

Tailwind provides *number utilities* to set width, height, margins, padding, and more. By default, the Tailwind sizing numbers correspond to the following rem and pixel sizes.

Tailwind's default spacing scale

Number	Rem	Pixel
1	0.25rem	4px
2	0.5rem	8px
3	0.75rem	12px
4	1rem	16px
8	2rem	32px
...		

To use the Tailwind spacing scale, you can specify a number at the end of a class that works with sizing or spacing. For example, you can add it to the end of the w class for setting width that's shown next.

Classes for setting width

Class	Description
w-{number}	Sets width using Tailwind's spacing scale.
w-{fraction}	Sets width as a fraction of the parent container.
w-auto	Sets width to the element's automatic width behavior.
w-fit	Sets width to fit the width of the element's contents.
w-screen	Sets width to 100% of the viewport.
min-w-{number}	Sets the minimum width for the element.
max-w-{number}	Sets the maximum width for the element.

The next screen shows how you can use some of these classes to set width.

The width classes in the browser

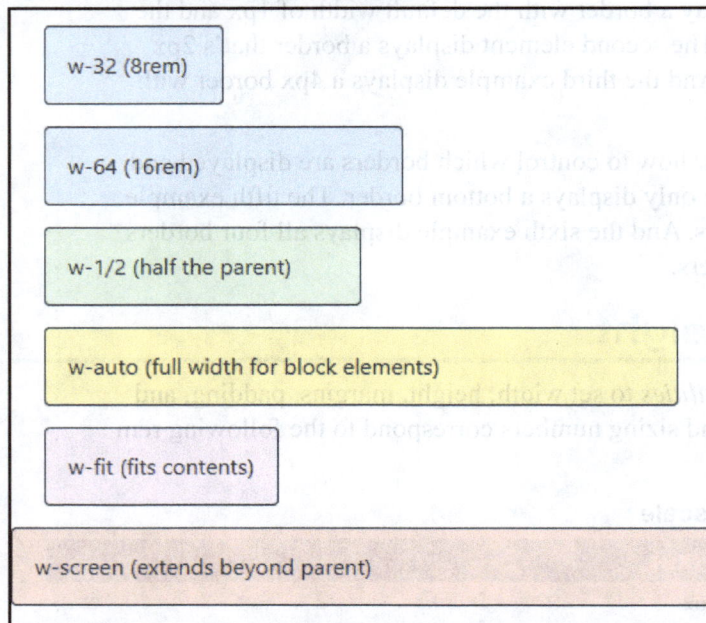

w-32 (8rem)

w-64 (16rem)

w-1/2 (half the parent)

w-auto (full width for block elements)

w-fit (fits contents)

w-screen (extends beyond parent)

In addition to the classes for working with width, Tailwind provides corresponding classes to work with height as summarized next.

Classes for setting height

Class	Description
h-{number}	Sets height using Tailwind's spacing scale.
h-{fraction}	Sets height as a fraction of the parent container.
h-auto	Sets height to the element's automatic height behavior.
h-fit	Sets height to fit the element's content.
h-screen	Sets height to 100% of the viewport.
min-h-{size}	Sets the minimum height for the element.
max-h-{size}	Sets the maximum height for the element.

These classes work like the classes for working with width. As a result, if you understand the classes for working with width, you should be able to understand the classes for working with height.

Set margins and padding

Tailwind provides spacing classes that control the margin outside of an element and the padding within an element. These classes use the same spacing scale as width and height where each unit represents 0.25rem (4px) by default. To set margins, you can use the following classes.

Classes for setting margins

Class	Description
m-{number}	Sets margin on all sides using the Tailwind spacing scale.
mx-{number}	Sets horizontal margins.
my-{number}	Sets vertical margins.
mt-{number}	Sets top margin.
mb-{number}	Sets bottom margin.
ml-{number}	Sets left margin.
mr-{number}	Sets right margin.
m-auto	Centers the element by setting the left and right margins to auto.

The next screen shows how to use some of the classes for setting margins.

Some margin classes in a browser

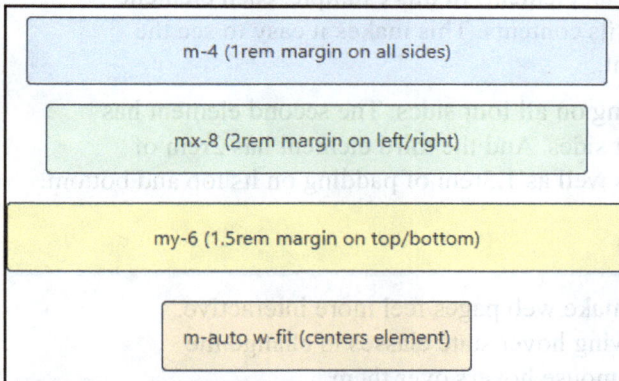

Here, the first element has a 1rem margin around all sides. The second element has a wider margin on its left and right sides, so it's a little narrower than the first element. The third element has a 1.5rem margin on its top and bottom but no margin at all on its left and right. And the fourth element uses m-auto to center the element, which is just wide enough to fit its contents.

To work with padding, you can use the following classes.

Classes for setting padding

Class	Description
p-{number}	Sets padding on all sides using Tailwind's spacing scale.
px-{number}	Sets the horizontal padding.
py-{number}	Sets the vertical padding.
pt-{number}	Sets the top padding.
pr-{number}	Sets the right padding.
pb-{number}	Sets the bottom padding.
pl-{number}	Sets the left padding.

The next screen shows how to use some of the classes to set padding.

The padding classes in a browser

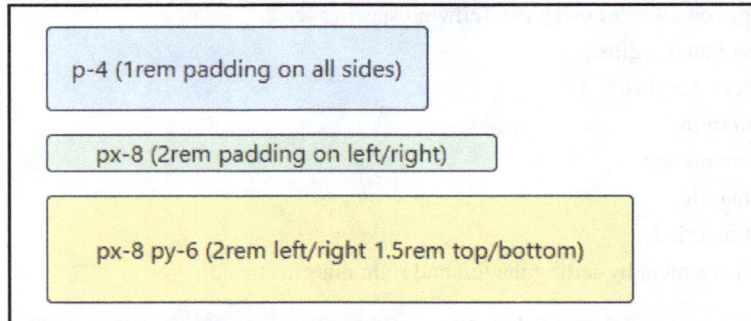

While setting the margin changes the spacing outside of an element, setting the padding changes the spacing within an element. In this example, each element uses the w-fit class so the width fits its contents. This makes it easy to see the padding that's added to each element.

The first element has 1rem of padding on all four sides. The second element has 2rem of padding on its left and right sides. And the third element has 2rem of padding on its left and right sides as well as 1.5rem of padding on its top and bottom.

Control interactivity

Tailwind provides many classes to make web pages feel more interactive. For example, you can use the following hover state classes to change the appearance of an element when the mouse hovers over them.

Classes for setting hover states

Class	Description
hover:bg-{color}-{step}	Changes background color on hover.
hover:text-{color}-{step}	Changes text color on hover.
hover:border-{color}-{step}	Changes border color on hover.

Similarly, you can use the following cursor classes to change the type of cursor that displays when the mouse hovers over an element.

Classes for setting cursor shapes

Class	Description
cursor-pointer	Shows a pointer cursor to indicate clickable elements.
cursor-wait	Shows a wait cursor.
cursor-move	Shows a move cursor.
cursor-not-allowed	Shows a not-allowed cursor for disabled elements.
cursor-default	Shows the default arrow cursor.

To illustrate hover states and cursor shapes, consider the following example.

A button that uses classes for hover states and mouse pointers

```
<button className="border rounded-md px-4 py-2 font-semibold
                   text-white bg-green-500
                   hover:bg-green-700 cursor-pointer">
    Add to Cart
</button>
```

This code changes the background color for the button to a darker shade of green when the user hovers the mouse over the button. Similarly, it changes the cursor from the default arrow to a finger pointer when the user hovers the mouse over the button as shown next.

The same button with and without the mouse cursor

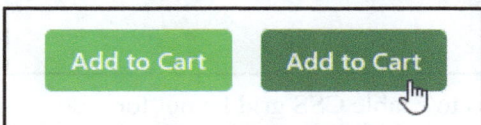

This provides immediate feedback that the button is interactive and clickable.

How to use Tailwind for page layout

In CSS, it's common to use grid and flexbox layouts to lay out the elements of a web page. Then, it's common to use media queries to adjust the layout based on the size of the screen. Now, this chapter shows how you can use Tailwind CSS to do the same.

Use grid layout

Tailwind provides the following classes to define and work with grid layouts.

The classes for defining a grid layout

Class	Description
grid	Creates a CSS container that lets you arrange child elements in rows and columns
grid-cols-{n}	Specifies the number of columns in the grid.
grid-rows-{n}	Specifies the number of rows in the grid.

Typically, you use these classes once in the root container of the document to define a grid layout for your whole app to use. However, you can also use them to define nested grids if needed.

Once you define a grid layout, you often want to use the following classes to add some space between each item in the grid.

The classes for spacing grid items

Class	Description
gap-{number}	Creates a gap on all sides between each grid item.
gap-x-{number}	Creates a gap on the left and right sides of each grid item.
gap-y-{number}	Creates a gap on the top and bottoms sides of each grid item.

For example, the following code creates a two-column grid with a .5rem gap between each item in the grid.

Code that creates a two-column grid

```
<div className="grid grid-cols-2 gap-2">
  <div className="bg-blue-100 p-4">Item 1</div>
  <div className="bg-blue-100 p-4">Item 2</div>
  <div className="bg-blue-100 p-4">Item 3</div>
  <div className="bg-blue-100 p-4">Item 4</div>
</div>
```

Here, the outer <div> element uses the grid class to enable CSS grid layout for the container, the grid-cols-2 class specifies that the grid has two columns, and the gap-2 class adds .5rem of spacing between all grid items.

This grid doesn't specify the number of rows. As a result, it automatically creates as many rows as needed to display its items.

When displayed in a browser, the four child elements automatically flow into the grid positions from left to right, top to bottom. This creates a grid where each item occupies one cell.

The two-column grid in a browser

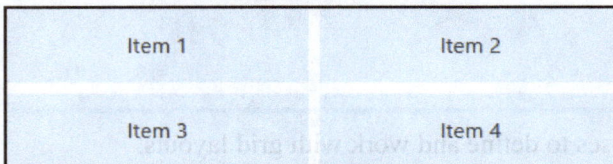

Item 1	Item 2
Item 3	Item 4

When creating grid layouts, you often want to create items that span multiple rows or columns. For example, headers and footers often span all of the columns so they display across the full width of the page. Similarly, some elements may span multiple rows. To achieve this, you can use the classes shown next.

The classes for placing items in a grid

Class	Description
col-span-{n}	Sets how many columns an element should span.
col-start-{n}	Sets which column an element should start in.
col-end-{n}	Sets which column an element should end in.
row-span-{n}	Sets how many rows an element should span.
row-start-{n}	Sets which row an element should start in.
row-end-{n}	Sets which row an element should end in.

For example, the following code creates a three-column grid that can be used for a simple web app like the Movie List app shown later in this chapter.

Code that creates a three-column layout

```
<div className="grid grid-cols-3 gap-2">
  <header className="bg-blue-100 p-4 col-span-3">Header</header>
  <main className="bg-blue-100 p-4 col-span-2 row-span-2">Main Content</main>
  <aside className="bg-blue-100 p-4">Sidebar 1</aside>
  <aside className="bg-blue-100 p-4">Sidebar 2</aside>
  <footer className="bg-blue-100 p-4 col-span-3">Footer</footer>
</div>
```

Here, the container element uses the grid, grid-cols-3, and gap-2 classes to define a grid layout that has three columns. Within the container, the <header> element uses the col-span-3 class to span the three columns. This causes it to stretch across the full length of the container.

The <main> element spans two columns, and the first <aside> element only spans one column. As a result, these elements span the three columns in the second row. In addition, the <main> element spans two rows. As a result, it also spans the first two columns of the third row, and the second <aside> element spans the third column of that row.

Finally, the <footer> element spans three columns. As a result, it stretches across the full length of the container just like the <header> component.

When displayed in a browser, these elements flow into the grid positions from left to right, top to bottom. However, it takes the col-span and row-span classes into account to produce the layout shown next.

The three-column grid in a browser

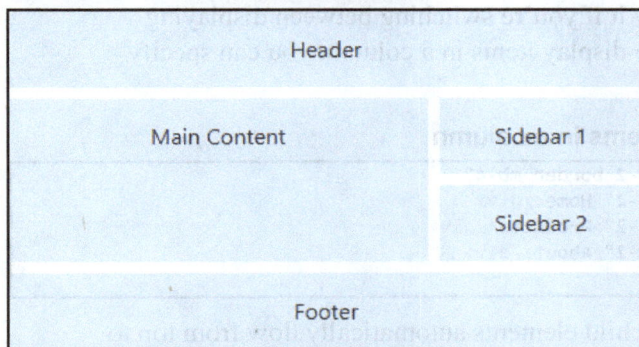

Because the elements in this grid were coded in a sequence that worked with the default way that elements flow into a grid (left to right, top to bottom), they didn't need to use the col-start-*, col-end-*, row-start-*, and row-end-* classes. However, if necessary, you can use these classes to adjust the way the elements flow into the grid.

Use flexbox layout

Tailwind provides the following classes to define and work with flexbox layouts.

The classes for defining a flexbox layout

Class	Description
flex	Creates a flexbox container.
flex-row	Displays items in a horizontal row (default).
flex-col	Displays items in a vertical column.

For example, the following code creates a three-column grid with a .5rem gap between each item in the row.

A flexbox layout that displays items in a row

```
<nav className="flex gap-2 border mb-4">
    <div className="bg-blue-100 p-2">Home</div>
    <div className="bg-blue-100 p-2">Products</div>
    <div className="bg-blue-100 p-2">About</div>
</nav>
```

Here, the <nav> element uses Tailwind classes to enable CSS flexbox layout for the container and to add .5rem of spacing between all grid items. When displayed in a browser, the child elements display in a row from left to right as shown next.

Items displayed in a row

Home	Products	About

Since the flex-row class is the default, you often don't need to specify it. However, you may need to specify it if you're switching between displaying items in a row and in a column. To display items in a column, you can specify the flex-col class as shown next.

A flexbox layout that displays items in a column

```
<nav className="flex flex-col gap-2 border mb-4">
    <div className="bg-blue-100 p-2">Home</div>
    <div className="bg-blue-100 p-2">Products</div>
    <div className="bg-blue-100 p-2">About</div>
</nav>
```

When displayed in a browser, the child elements automatically flow from top to bottom as shown next.

Items displayed in a column

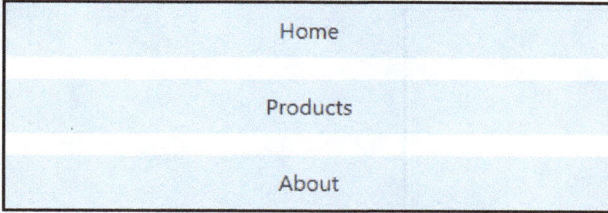

When displaying items in a row, you may often want to adjust the alignment or spacing of the items. To do that, you can use the following classes.

The classes for aligning items in a row

Class	Description
justify-start	Aligns items with the start of the container, which is usually the left side (default).
justify-center	Centers items horizontally in the container.
justify-between	Spaces the items evenly across the container.
justify-end	Aligns items with the end of the container, which is usually the right side.

For example, you can use the justify-center and justify-between classes to display the items in a row as follows.

The justify-center class

The justify-between class

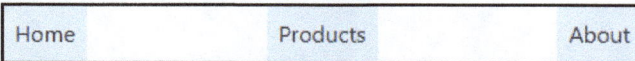

When displaying items in a column, you may also want to adjust the alignment or spacing of the items. To do that, you can use the following classes.

The classes for items in a column

Class	Description
items-center	Centers items horizontally (default).
items-start	Aligns items with the start of the container, which is usually the left side.
items-end	Aligns items with the end of the container, which is usually the right side.

For example, you can use the items-start class to display the items in a column as follows.

The items-start class

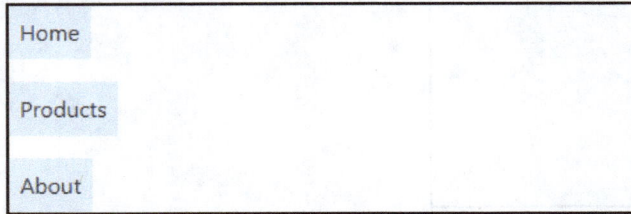

Home
Products
About

If necessary, you can nest one flexbox container within another. This can allow you to create complex layouts similar to the ones that you can create with the grid layout. However, the grid layout often works well for laying out the main structure for a web page, and flexbox layout often works well for other items such as menu items. That said, you can usually use either technique to lay out elements the way you want, and many of the classes for working with grid layout also apply to flexbox layout.

Create a responsive layout

Tailwind uses a *mobile-first* approach to responsive design. This means that Tailwind assumes that users are using a mobile device with a small screen. However, it provides the following classes to allow you to specify how to display components when they're displayed on larger screens.

The size classes for media queries

Class	Description
sm	640px and up (small tablets).
md	768px and up (tablets).
lg	1024px and up (laptops).
xl	1280px and up (desktops).
2xl	1536px and up (large desktops).

Consider the following code.

Code that uses the size classes to create a responsive design

```
<div className="grid grid-cols-3 gap-2">
  <header className="bg-blue-100 p-4 col-span-3">Header</header>
  <main className="bg-blue-100 p-4 col-span-3 md:col-span-2">Main Content</main>
  <aside className="bg-blue-100 p-4 col-span-3 md:col-span-1">Sidebar</aside>
  <footer className="bg-blue-100 p-4 col-span-3">Footer</footer>
</div>
```

Here, the code creates a responsive design for a 3-column layout by having the <main> and <aside> elements span all three rows for small screens. However, on medium screens that are 768 pixels or wider, the <main> element spans two columns, and the <aside> component spans one column. As a result, these components are displayed side by side with the <main> component using two thirds of the width and the <aside> component using one third of the width.

The responsive page on a small screen

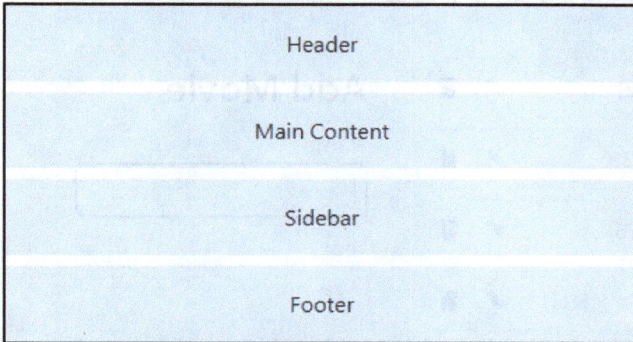

Header
Main Content
Sidebar
Footer

The responsive page on a medium or larger screen

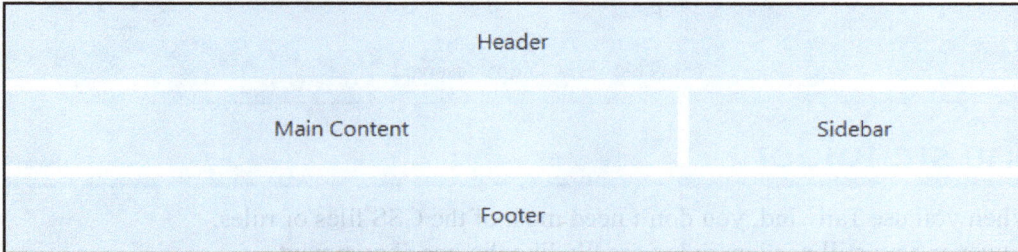

Header	
Main Content	Sidebar
Footer	

When working with responsive elements, you may find that some classes are overriding other ones. Tailwind uses the following rules to determine which class takes precedence when there are conflicting responsive classes.

The precedence rules for responsive classes

1. Media queries override regular classes.
2. Media queries for larger screens override media queries for smaller screens. The breakpoint size determines precedence, not the order of the classes in the className string.

The Movie List app

This chapter ends by showing how to modify the Movie List app presented in chapter 5 to use Tailwind instead of plain CSS. When displayed in a browser, the Tailwind version looks similar to the plain CSS version. However, the CSS is significantly different.

The Tailwind version of the Movie List app

My Movies

⠿	The Godfather (1972)	✏️ 🗑️
⠿	The Wizard of Oz (1939)	✏️ 🗑️
⠿	The Dark Knight (2008)	✏️ 🗑️
⠿	The Shawshank Redemption (1994)	✏️ 🗑️
⠿	Forrest Gump (1994)	✏️ 🗑️

Add Movie

Name

[Name]

Year

[Year]

[Add]

© My Movies. All rights reserved.

The src folder

When you use Tailwind, you don't need most of the CSS files or rules.
However, you still need an index.css file like the one shown next.

The index.css file

```
@import "tailwindcss";

body {
    width: 80%;
    margin: 0 auto;
    background-color: #f0f0f0;
}
```

This CSS file includes a directive that imports the Tailwind CSS library. That
way, you can use the Tailwind utility classes to style your components.

In addition, if you don't want to use the default styling for the <body> element,
you can specify any CSS for the <body> element that you want to apply. This
is consistent with Tailwind's guidance, which recommend using Tailwind
utility classes for component-level styles and plain CSS for global styles. Here,
the CSS in the index.css file sets the width of the body to 80% of the viewport,
centers the body in the viewport, and changes the background color.

Similarly, if you don't want to use the default reset selectors, you can specify
your own here. However, this isn't recommended since it can interfere with the
styles provided by Tailwind.

Once you setup the index.css file, you can use Tailwind's utility classes to format the main container defined by the App component as shown next.

The App.jsx file

```
...
    return (
        <div className="bg-white grid grid-cols-3 border-2 border-gray-400
                        rounded-lg">
            <Header text={appName} />
...
```

This <div> element uses several Tailwind classes to set up the outlined area that displays the main app content. The bg-white class sets the background of the main content area to white, which helps it stand out against the light gray background of the body that was set in the index.css file. The grid and grid-cols-3 classes define a grid layout for the app with three columns. The border-2, border-gray-400, and rounded-lg classes define a rounded 2px light gray border for the content area.

The layout folder

Since the App component uses Tailwind to define a grid, the components in the layout directory (Header, Footer, Main, and Sidebar) can use Tailwind to define the layout within that grid. In addition, they can use Tailwind to provide other types of style.

The Header component uses Tailwind classes to format the <header> and <h1> components.

The Header.jsx file

```
const Header = ({ text }) => (
    <header className="bg-blue-200 col-span-3 p-6 h-fit rounded-t-lg">
        <h1 className="text-5xl text-center font-bold">{text}</h1>
    </header>
);

export default Header;
```

The <header> element uses the className attribute to specify several classes that set the background color, number of columns, padding, and height. Here, the rounded-t-lg class rounds the corners at the top of the component to prevent the top corners of the blue background from extending beyond the rounded border established in the parent container.

The <h1> component also uses several Tailwind classes. The first displays the heading in extra-large text, the second centers the heading, and the third displays it in a bold font.

The Main component uses Tailwind classes to style the <main> element.

The Main.jsx file

```
const Main = ({ children }) => (
    <main className="h-auto col-span-3 md:col-span-2">
        {children}
    </main>
);

export default Main;
```

The classes for the <main> element start with h-auto which causes the height of the element to automatically scale with its content. The next two classes make the <main> element span three rows on small screens but only two rows on screens that are of a medium or larger size. That way, the Sidebar component shown next can be displayed in the third column on screens that are medium or larger.

The Sidebar.jsx file

```
const Sidebar = ({ children }) => (
    <aside className="bg-gray-100 h-auto p-3 col-span-3 md:col-span-1">
        {children}
    </aside>
);

export default Sidebar;
```

Within the Sidebar component, the first three classes set the background color to light gray, cause the height to scale automatically, and add .75rem of padding. Then, the last two classes control where the component displays within the grid. On small screens, the col-span-3 class causes Sidebar to span all three columns in the grid. As a result, it displays below Main on small screens. On medium or larger screens, the md:col-span-1 class causes the Sidebar to span only one column. As a result, it displays to the right of Main.

The Footer component works much like the Header component.

The Footer.jsx file

```
const Footer = ({ text, children }) => (
    <footer className="bg-blue-200 h-fit col-span-3 rounded-b-lg">
        { children }
        <p className="p-3  text-center">© {text}. All rights reserved.</p>
    </footer>
);

export default Footer;
```

To start, the classes of the <footer> element set the background color and container height and specify that the footer should be displayed across all three columns. Then, the last class rounds the bottom corners of the <footer> element to match it with the rounded border of the parent container.

Within the <footer> element, the classes of the <p> element set the styles for the copyright notice that's displayed in the footer. These styles add some padding to all sides and center the text.

The common folder

Like the components in the layout folder, the components in the common folder use Tailwind classes for styling instead of using plain CSS files. For example, the FormButtons component shown next uses Tailwind classes to style its <div> and <button> elements.

The FormButtons.jsx file

```jsx
const FormButtons = ({ isEditing, isDeleting, onCancel }) => (
    <div className="flex flex-col sm:flex-row gap-2 w-full mt-5">
        <button
            type="submit"
            className="border p-1 rounded-md bg-green-600 text-white
                       hover:bg-green-800 w-full w--1/2">
            {isDeleting ? 'Delete' : isEditing ? 'Update' : 'Add'}
        </button>
        {(isEditing || isDeleting) && (
            <button
                type="button"
                className="border p-1 bg-red-600 rounded-md text-white
                           hover:bg-red-800 w-full w--1/2"
                onClick={onCancel}>
                Cancel
            </button>
        )}
    </div>
);

export default FormButtons;
```

The Tailwind classes for the <div> element define it as a flexbox container that displays its buttons in rows for larger screens but in columns for small screens.

The classes for both <button> elements create buttons with rounded borders, .25rem of top and bottom padding, and white text. The first button has a green background, and the second has a red background.

Both buttons use the w-full and w-1/2 classes to specify their width. These classes might seem contradictory, but when combined with the flexbox behavior of the <div> element, they allow the buttons to use half of the available width when there are two buttons and all of the available width when there is one. For example, if there are two buttons and the screen is wide enough, they each take half of the width as shown next.

The two buttons displayed in a row

Edit Movie

Name

Forrest Gump

Year

1994

[Update] [Cancel]

The following FormInput component creates the labels and input fields for the form.

The FormInput.jsx file

```
const FormInput = ( {ref, label, name, value, onChange, ...props} ) => (
    <>
        <label className="block text-lg mt-2" htmlFor={name}>{label}</label>
        <input
            ref={ref}
            className="block w-full bg-white border border-gray-400 rounded-md
                       p-2"
            type="text"
...
```

The first Tailwind class for the <label> element makes it a block element so that it uses the full width of the container and starts on a new line. The next two set the font size to large and add a small top margin.

The classes for the <input> element start with block and w-full to make the inputs take up the full width of the parent container. Then, the bg-white class makes the background of the inputs white to help them stand out against the light gray background. And the last four classes create a border, set the color, round the corners of the border, and add .5rem of padding on all sides.

The Icon component doesn't use any Tailwind classes. That way, code that uses the Icon component can pass a className prop that uses Font Awesome classes to specify the correct icon. In addition, it can pass any Tailwind classes needed to style that icon.

The movies folder

Most of the components in the movies folder only need small padding and margin adjustments. As a result, their code isn't shown here. If you'd like to view this code, it's available from the download for the book. However, the MovieListItem component shown next requires significant styling adjustments.

The MovieListItem.jsx file (part 1)

```
import Icon from "../common/Icon";

const MovieListItem = ({ movie, onSelect, onDragStart, onDragOver,
                         onDragEnter, onDragEnd }) => (
    movie? (
        <li
            className="border border-gray-400 rounded-lg p-2 m-2
                       flex items-center justify-between
                       bg-gray-100 cursor-move»
            draggable="true"
            onDragStart={onDragStart} onDragOver={onDragOver}
            onDragEnter={onDragEnter} onDragEnd={onDragEnd}
        >
...
```

This component begins by applying many Tailwind classes to the <li> element. The first three classes set the border styles for the list item. Then, the next two set the padding and margins.

After setting the padding and margins, this code uses the flex class to use a flexbox layout to display all child elements such as the movie title and icons. The items-center class vertically centers the items within the list items and the justify-between class spreads the child elements horizontally while maximizing the space between the elements. As a result, if a list item contains three elements, the first is left aligned, the second is centered, and the third is right aligned.

After setting up the flexbox, this code uses one class to specify the background color. Then, it uses a class to change the cursor to a move pointer to indicate that the user can drag the item to move it to a new location.

For the flexbox layout to align a movie item correctly, each movie item is divided into three parts (left, middle, and right) as shown next.

The MovieListItem.jsx file (part 2)

```
...
            {/* Left side - Drag icon */}
            <Icon className="fa fa-grip-vertical mr-4"/>

            {/* Center - Movie info */}
            <span className="text-lg">
                {movie.name} ({movie.year})
            </span>

            {/* Right side - Action icons */}
            <div className="space-x-3">
                <Icon
                    className="icon fa fa-pencil ml-2"
                    title="Edit"
                    onClick={() => onSelect(movie, 'edit')} />
                <Icon
                    className="icon fa fa-trash ml-2"
```

```
                    title="Delete"
                    onClick={() => onSelect(movie, 'delete')} />
              </div>
          </li>
...
```

Each of these parts uses Tailwind classes to style their elements. The Icon components specify Font Awesome classes such as fa and fa-grip-vertical to display icons. In addition, they specify Tailwind classes to add margins to the right and left of the icons.

Perspective

This chapter has introduced several approaches to styling a React app. Since you've been using plain CSS throughout this book, and since CSS modules work much like plain CSS, you should be able to use either of these approaches now. In addition, this chapter has presented the basic skills for using Tailwind CSS. All three of these styling methods have their place in modern React development. As a result, understanding plain CSS, CSS modules, and Tailwind is important for React developers.

If you want to use Tailwind to style your app, the skills presented in this chapter provide a good foundation. However, Tailwind has many features and can provide just about any type of styling that's available from CSS. For example, Tailwind provides for color gradients, shadows, animations, and more. As a result, if you're using Tailwind and you want to use a CSS feature that isn't presented in this chapter, you can usually find out how to use that feature in Tailwind by searching the internet or asking AI.

Terms

font weight
color utilities
effect
number utilities
mobile-first development

Exercise 9-1: Use CSS modules

Review the starting code

1. Open the buttons project in the ex_starts/ch09 folder.
2. Install the dependencies and run the development server.
3. View the app in the browser and note that both the buttons are the same color.

4. Open the CancelButton.css and AcceptButton.css files and view the code. Note that the CSS states that the buttons should be different colors but that the buttons share the .button class name.

Convert the CSS files to CSS modules

5. Rename the AcceptButton.css file to AcceptButton.module.css.

6. Rename the CancelButton.css file to CancelButton.module.css

7. In the AcceptButton.jsx file, modify the import statement to import styles from the AcceptButton.module.css file.

8. Modify the className attribute for the <button> element to use the styles. button attribute.

9. In the CancelButton.jsx file, modify the import statement to import styles from the CancelButton.module.css file.

10. Modify the className attribute for the <button> element to use the styles. button attribute.

11. View the app in the browser again to confirm that the style collision has been resolved.

Exercise 9-2: Use Tailwind

This exercise shows how to modify the My Playlist app to use Tailwind CSS instead of plain CSS. When you're done, it should look something like the app shown next.

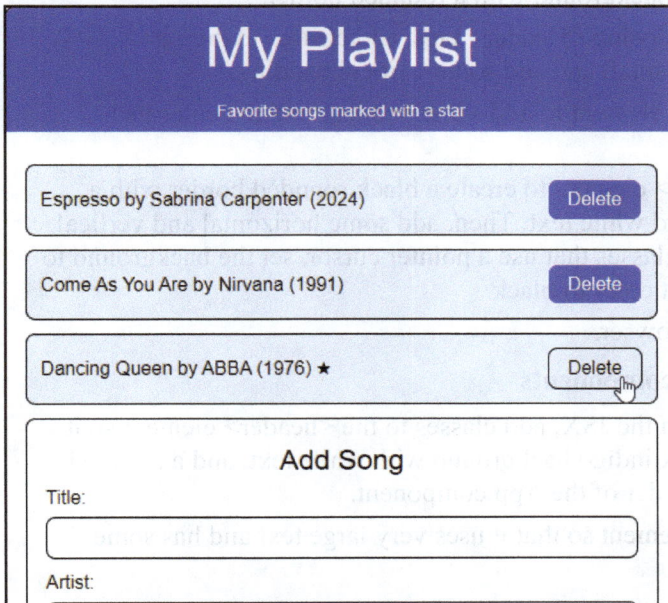

My Playlist
Favorite songs marked with a star

Espresso by Sabrina Carpenter (2024)   [Delete]

Come As You Are by Nirvana (1991)   [Delete]

Dancing Queen by ABBA (1976) ★   [Delete]

Add Song
Title:

Artist:

Review the starting code

1. Open the my-playlist project in the ex_starts/ch09 folder. Note that it doesn't contain any CSS files for its components.

2. Install the dependencies and run the development server.

3. View the app in a browser. Note that it hasn't been styled except for a few styles that have been applied to the body such as a light gray background. Click the Add Song button to display the form. Then, click the Cancel button to hide the form.

4. Open the App.jsx file. Note that it still contains some className attributes that point to old CSS classes. However, these classes don't provide any styling since the CSS files have been deleted and their import statements have been removed.

Install and configure Tailwind

5. Run the npm command to install the Tailwind CSS library.

6. Open the vite.config.js file, and configure Vite to work with the Tailwind plugin.

7. Open the index.css file and add an import statement for the Tailwind CSS library to the top of the file.

8. View the app in a browser. Note that Tailwind has changed the formatting for the components.

Style the App component

9. Open the App.jsx file. In the JSX, modify the top-level <div> element to add classes that create a white background with a rounded border.

10. Between the opening and closing <Header> tags, add classes to the <p> element that set the text to small and add some vertical padding.

11. Add classes to the <main> element to add some padding and to center its elements.

12. Add classes to the <button> element to create a black rounded border with a dark indigo background and white text. Then, add some horizontal and vertical padding. Next, add hover classes that use a pointer cursor, set the background to transparent, and set the text color to black.

13. View the changes in the browser.

Style the Header and Footer components

14. Open the Header.jsx file. In the JSX, add classes to the <header> element so it centers the text, uses a dark indigo background with white text, and a rounded top border to match the border of the App component.

15. Add classes to the <h1> element so that it uses very large text and has some vertical padding.

16. Open the Footer.jsx component. In the JSX, add classes to the <footer> element to set the background to dark indigo, the text to white, and the bottom border to match the rounded corners of the App component.

17. For the <p> element, set the text size to small, center the text, and add some padding.

Style the Playlist component

18. Open the Playlist.jsx file and view the JSX.

19. Add classes to the <li> element to give it a light indigo background, a rounded border, some padding, and a small vertical margin. To handle the spacing of the items in this element, use a flex row layout with the space set to justify between.

20. Add some padding to the <span> element that displays the star so it doesn't display too close to the text for the song.

21. Add classes to the <button> element. These should be the same classes used by the <button> element in the App component.

Add a Button component

22. In the components folder, add the JSX file for a Button component. This component should accept children and ...props arguments and define a <button> element that has the same classes as the <button> elements in App and Playlist. This works much like the Input component.

23. In the App and Playlist components, import the Button component and change the <button> elements to <Button> components. This reduces code duplication since the classes for styling the button are stored in the Button component.

Style the SongForm component

24. Open the SongForm.jsx file.

25. Modify the <form> element so it has a black border with large rounded corners.

26. Style the <h2> element so it uses large text and has some space above it.

27. Modify the <div> container for the <button> elements to use a flex row layout that adds some space between the two buttons and centers them. It should also add some space between the buttons and the bottom border of the container.

28. Import the Button component and change the <button> elements to <Button> components. This should apply styling to these buttons.

29. Open the Input.jsx file. Modify the top-level <div> element so it left aligns its elements and provides some horizontal padding.

30. Modify the <label> element so it uses block display and adds some top margin.

31. Modify the <input> element so it has a black border with large rounded corners, some padding, some vertical spacing, and is the width of the container.

32. View the app in the browser. It should look something like the one shown at the beginning of this exercise.

Chapter 10

Manage complex state

Until now, this book has shown how to use the useState hook to manage state in an app. Much of the time, that's all you need. However, issues can arise around managing and distributing state. To address these issues, you may need to use another approach to manage state.

In the past, many developers used a library known as Redux to manage complex state. However, recent years have seen a significant decline in the use of Redux. That's partly because recent releases of React have improved its built-in features for managing state. This chapter shows how to use two of these features, reducers and context, to manage complex state.

How to use a reducer to manage state

React's built-in useReducer hook helps you manage and centralize complex state logic. However, before you learn *how* to use a reducer, it's important to understand *when* to use one.

When to use a reducer

Much of the time, maybe even most of the time, the useState hook works well for creating and managing state. Sometimes, though, your state logic gets complex enough that managing it with useState might be cumbersome as described next.

Complex state that might be hard to manage with useState

- **The state variables are tightly related.** Example: a form with multiple fields and validation rules where changing one field effects another field.

- **Updating one state variable depends on another.** Example: a multi-step form where one step influences the next.

- **The number of state variables and event handlers is large.** Example: a component that supports view, edit, and delete modes with their own behaviors.

- **Several values must update together.** Example: a game or timer where multiple pieces of state change on the same event.

For example, the following App component has a large number of event handlers.

An App component with extensive state logic

```
import { useState } from 'react'

// import modules and define local variables - same as chapter 4

const App = () => {
    // set up two state variables, their setter functions, and initial values
    const [movies, setMovies] = useState(initialMovies);
    const [selectedMovie, setSelectedMovie] = useState(null);

    // add a new movie
    const handleAdd = (newMovie) => {
        setMovies((prev) => [...prev, newMovie]);
    };

    // select a movie and specify the mode (edit or delete)
    const handleSelect = (movie, mode) => {
        setSelectedMovie({...movie, mode});
    };

    // edit a movie
    const handleEdit = (updatedMovie) => {
        setMovies((prev) =>
            prev.map((movie) =>
                movie.id === updatedMovie.id ? updatedMovie : movie
```

```
            )
        );
        setSelectedMovie(null);
    };

    // delete a movie
    const handleDelete = (id) => {
        setMovies((prev) =>
            prev.filter((movie) =>
                movie.id !== id
            )
        );
        setSelectedMovie(null);
    };

    // cancel edit or delete
    const handleCancel = () => {
        setSelectedMovie(null);
    };

    // return JSX - same as chapter 4
};

export default App;
```

That's a lot of state logic, and it will only grow if you add features like sorting or filtering. Wouldn't it be great to be able to move that logic somewhere else where it can be organized? That's where reducers come in.

Create a reducer function

A *reducer* is a function that defines parameters for the current state and an *action object* and returns a new state based on those parameters. The action object often contains a *payload* such as data to be added, removed, or updated.

The following example presents a reducer function that manages a list of movies. It's stored in a file named movieReducer.js in a directory named reducers.

A reducer function

```
const movieReducer = (state, action) => {
    switch (action.type) {
        case 'ADD_MOVIE':
            return { ...state, movies: [...state.movies, action.payload] };
        case 'DELETE_MOVIE':
            return {
                ...state,
                movies: state.movies.filter(movie => movie.id !== action.payload),
            };
        default:
            return state;
    }
};

export { movieReducer };
```

Here, the switch statement uses the type property of the action object to determine the action to take. Each case starts by using the spread operator to make a copy of the state object. This is important because a reducer should return a new state object, not mutate the original state.

Each case also uses the payload property of the action object to get the value to add or delete. The ADD_MOVIE case adds the movie in the payload to the movies array, while the DELETE_MOVIE case removes the movie whose id matches the payload value.

You can call a reducer function directly, which makes it easy to test. However, its real power comes when you use it with React's useReducer hook. Then, React uses the reducer to manage state and automatically re-render when state changes.

Use the useReducer hook

Once you have a reducer function, you can use it with the useReducer hook. First, you import the hook from the React module.

An import statement for the useReducer hook

```
import { useReducer } from 'react';
```

Then, you call the useReducer() function.

The parameters of the useReducer() function

Parameters	Description
Reducer function	The function to manage state. Required.
Initial state	The initial value of the state. Required.
Initializer function	A function to transform the initial state. Optional.

When you call this function, you must pass it a reducer function and the initial value of the state as shown next.

Call the useReducer() function

```
const [state, dispatch] = useReducer(movieReducer, { movies:[] });
```

Here, this code passes the movieReducer() function presented earlier in this chapter as the reducer function. For the initial value for the state, this code passes an object with a movies property that's set to an empty array.

When you call useReducer(), it returns an array with two elements.

The elements in the array returned by useReducer()

Element	Description
State object	An object that contains the current state.
Dispatch function	A function you can call to change the state.

The *dispatch function* sends, or dispatches, an action object to React. Then, React runs the stored reducer with that action, changes the state, and re-renders with the new state.

A component that uses the dispatch() function

```
// import the useReducer hook from React
import { useReducer } from 'react'

// import the reducer function from the reducers directory
import { movieReducer } from './reducers/movieReducer';

const App = () => {
    const [state, dispatch] = useReducer(movieReducer, { movies:[] });

    // add a new movie
    const handleAdd = (newMovie) =>
        dispatch({ type: 'ADD_MOVIE', payload: newMovie });

    // delete a movie
    const handleDelete = (id) =>
        dispatch({ type: 'DELETE_MOVIE', payload: id });

    return (
        <div className="container">
            <MovieList movies={state.movies} />
            <MovieForm
                onAdd={handleAdd}
                onDelete={handleDelete}
            />
        </div>
    )
}

export default App;
```

The App component uses the state value returned by useReducer() to pass the movie data to MovieList. And it uses the dispatch() function returned by useReducer() to create event handlers for MovieForm. Both of these handlers call dispatch() and pass it an action object with a type and payload.

As a result, the App component still creates event handlers. However, it no longer needs to know the details of the state logic.

Use an initializer function

In React, it's a common pattern for the file that exports the reducer to also export an initial state value as shown next.

A reducer file that exports an initial state object

```
// default initial state object
const movieInitialState = {
    movies: []
};

// reducer function
const movieReducer = (state, action) => {
    switch (action.type) {
        ...
    }
};

// export initial state object and reducer function
export { movieInitialState, movieReducer };
```

This way, the reducer file provides a central definition of the shape of the state. For simple state, as in this example, it may not add much to have a central definition. But if your initial state is an object with many properties, or it will evolve over time, it can be useful to have a single source of truth.

If your reducer file exports an initial state object, you can import it and the reducer to use with useReducer().

A component that uses the imported reducer and initial state

```
import { useReducer } from 'react'
import { movieReducer, movieInitialState } from './reducers/movieReducer';

const App = () => {
    // pass the imported reducer function and initial state to useReducer()
    const [state, dispatch] = useReducer(movieReducer, movieInitialState);
    ...
};
```

Typically, the default data in the initial state provided by the reducer file is minimal. But sometimes you want to transform the initial data. For example, you may want to seed sample data for the page or for testing.

In React, the recommended way to transform initial state data is to pass an *initializer function* to useReducer() as the third argument. On mount, React passes the initial state in the second argument to the initializer function and stores the return value. On re-render, React ignores both the initial state and the initializer function. In other words, it only runs the initializer once, on mount, which avoids unnecessary processing on re-renders.

The following example presents a component that defines an initializer function and passes it as the third argument to useReducer().

Use an initializer function to transform initial state

```
import { useReducer } from 'react'
import { movieReducer, movieInitialState } from './reducers/movieReducer';

// define an initializer function that overrides the movies property
const initializer = (state) => {
    return {...state, movies: [ {id:1, name:'Wicked', year:2024} ]};
};


const App = () => {
    // pass the reducer function, initial state, and initializer function
    const [state, dispatch] = useReducer(movieReducer, movieInitialState,
                                         initializer);
    ...
}
```

Use action constants

So far, this chapter has shown how to hard-code strings like 'ADD_MOVIE' in the reducer function and in the component that uses the dispatch function. However, many developers consider hard-coding strings to be a poor practice because it's easy to introduce typos and therefore bugs.

A common way to address this is to define constants in the reducer file that components can import. That way, you won't have to worry about knowing the exact string to type, and most IDEs including VS Code can provide code completion to help you.

The following reducer file defines, uses, and exports action constants.

A reducer file that uses action constants

```
// action constants
const ACTIONS = {
    ADD: 'ADD_MOVIE',
    DELETE: 'DELETE_MOVIE'
};

// initial state
const movieInitialState = { movies: [] };

// reducer function
const movieReducer = (state, action) => {
    switch (action.type) {
        case ACTIONS.ADD:
            ...
        case ACTIONS.DELETE:
            ...
        default:
            return state;
    }
};

export { movieReducer, movieInitialState, ACTIONS };
```

And the following component imports and uses the action constants.

A component that uses the imported reducer, initial state, and action constants

```
import { useReducer } from 'react'

// import the reducer function, initial state, and action constants
import { movieReducer, movieInitialState, ACTIONS as M }
    from './reducers/movieReducer';

const App = () => {
    const [state, dispatch] = useReducer(movieReducer, movieInitialState);

    // add a new movie
    const handleAdd = (newMovie) =>
        dispatch({ type: M.ADD, payload: newMovie });

    // delete a movie
    const handleDelete = (id) =>
        dispatch({ type: M.DELETE, payload: id });
    ...
};
```

This component imports the ACTIONS object with an alias of a single letter (M). This helps keep the code short and also helps avoid conflicts with other reducers. For example, suppose your component uses reducers for movies and users, and both have action constant objects named ACTIONS. That can cause problems! Importing one as M and the other as U prevents those problems.

The Movie List app

The following headings present the Movie List app from chapter 4 after it has been updated to use a reducer.

The directory structure

The directory structure for the Movie List app is mostly the same as chapter 4. However, it adds a directory named reducers that contains a JavaScript file for the movie reducer.

The src directory structure

```
src
├── components (same as chapter 4)
├── reducers
│   └── movieReducer.js
└── (same as chapter 4)
```

The reducer file

The following JavaScript file exports a reducer function, an initial state object, and an action constants object.

The movieReducer.js file

```javascript
// action constants
const ACTIONS = {
    ADD: 'ADD_MOVIE',
    SELECT: 'SELECT_MOVIE',
    EDIT: 'EDIT_MOVIE',
    DELETE: 'DELETE_MOVIE',
    CANCEL: 'CANCEL',
};

// default initial state
const movieInitialState = {
    movies: [],
    selectedMovie: null,
};

// reducer function
const movieReducer = (state, action) => {
    switch (action.type) {
        case ACTIONS.ADD:
            return { ...state, movies: [...state.movies, action.payload] };
        case ACTIONS.SELECT:
            return {
                ...state,
                selectedMovie: { ...action.payload.movie,
                    mode: action.payload.mode }
            };
        case ACTIONS.EDIT:
            return {
                ...state,
                movies: state.movies.map(movie =>
                    movie.id === action.payload.id ? action.payload : movie
                ),
                selectedMovie: null,
            };
        case ACTIONS.DELETE:
            return {
                ...state,
                movies: state.movies.filter(movie => movie.id !== action.payload),
                selectedMovie: null,
            };
        case ACTIONS.CANCEL:
            return { ...state, selectedMovie: null };
        default:
            return state;
    }
};

// export action constants, initial state object, and reducer function
export { ACTIONS, movieInitialState, movieReducer };
```

Since this file stores all of the state logic for movies, it's easy to add more functionality such as filtering and sorting movies. Similarly, if your app becomes more complex and needs to work with movies in a multi-step form or access an external data store, you can store that code here and keep it out of your components.

The App component

The following App component has been updated to import and use the movie reducer.

The App.js file

```
// import from React and movieReducer.js
import { useReducer } from 'react'
import { movieReducer, movieInitialState, ACTIONS as M }
    from './reducers/movieReducer';

// import components and CSS, define local variables, same as chapter 4

// initializer function: override the movies property of the initial state object
const initializer = (state) => {
    return { ...state, movies: [
        { id: 1, name: "Wicked", year: 2024 },
        { id: 2, name: "The Matrix", year: 1999 },
    ]};
};

const App = () => {
    // pass reducer fn, initial state, and initializer fn to useReducer()
    const [state, dispatch] = useReducer(movieReducer, movieInitialState,
                                         initializer);

    // create event handlers
    const handleAdd = (newMovie) => dispatch({ type: M.ADD, payload: newMovie });

    const handleSelect = (movie, mode) =>
        dispatch({ type: M.SELECT, payload: { movie, mode } });

    const handleEdit = (updatedMovie) =>
        dispatch({ type: M.EDIT, payload: updatedMovie });

    const handleDelete = (id) => dispatch({ type: M.DELETE, payload: id });

    const handleCancel = () => dispatch({ type: M.CANCEL });

    return (
        <div className="container">
            <Header text={appName} />
            <Main>
                <MovieList
                    movies={state.movies}
                    onSelect={handleSelect}
                />
            </Main>
```

```
        <Sidebar>
            <MovieForm
                selectedMovie={state.selectedMovie}
                onAdd={handleAdd}
                onEdit={handleEdit}
                onDelete={handleDelete}
                onCancel={handleCancel}
            />
        </Sidebar>
        <Footer text={appName} />
    </div>
    )
}

export default App;
```

How to use context to distribute state

So far, this chapter has shown how a reducer can help when state becomes hard to manage. Sometimes, though, the challenge isn't managing state. Instead, the challenge is sharing it across multiple components. That's when using context can help.

When to use context

Most of the time, using props to pass state between components works well. Other times, it can cause the following issues.

Two possible issues with passing state via props

- **Deep prop drilling.** A state variable or event handler is passed from a parent through many intermediate components that don't need it to reach a descendent that does.

- **Cross-component propagation.** State is needed in so many components that you end up passing it to all or most of them.

In small apps, these issues aren't much of a problem. For instance, if prop drilling is only two or three levels deep, it's probably fine. Similarly, if all your components need some state, but you only have a handful of components, that's probably fine too.

But as your app grows, these issues can get messy. Deep prop drilling can make state hard to follow, which complicates debugging. If intermediate components are general purpose, you might end up adding domain-specific props that they shouldn't have, just to get state farther down the tree.

And if every component needs a piece of state and you have dozens (or hundreds) of components, prop-passing can become tedious and error prone.

Context can help solve these problems. However, it's not cost free. In some ways, using context is similar to using global variables. That is, it can make things easier, but it also creates hidden dependencies and makes your code harder to understand. So, before using context, make sure it's the best solution to your issue. Sometimes, you can avoid using context by reorganizing your components or co-locating state.

Use a context object for static values

There are several steps to using context, which can make it hard to understand at first. To start, consider the simplest use case, which is a context object that shares a static value. This isn't common because you usually need to be able to change the shared value. Still, it can be useful for things like configuration data that doesn't change.

To start, you need to import the createContext() function as shown next.

Import the createContext() function

```
import { createContext } from 'react';
```

Then, you can call the createContext() function summarized next.

The createContext() function

Function	Description
createContext(initValue)	Create a context object and specify an optional initial value for it. For static values, the initial value is the only way to set the value.

The following code shows how to call this function.

Call the createContext() function with a default value

```
const ThemeContext = createContext(
    { theme: "light" }
);
```

When this code runs, React creates a *context object* named ThemeContext. The argument you pass to createContext() provides the static value that React shares with components. However, the context object itself isn't the shared value. Rather, it's a special object that React uses behind the scenes.

To access the shared value, you need the useContext hook. To start, you import the useContext hook as shown next. In React19 and later, you can also use the use hook. For this purpose, the two hooks are interchangeable. In this chapter, the code uses useContext to make it clear that it's working with a context object.

Import the useContext hook

```
import { useContext } from 'react';
```

After importing this hook, you can call it and pass the context object to it as shown next.

Call the useContext() function to read the static value

```
const { theme } = useContext(ThemeContext);
```

To make it easy to work with a context, you can create a context file. This file exports the context object and a custom hook that returns the object returned by useContext(). This custom hook isn't required, but it makes it easy for a component to work with the context. For example, the following context file makes it easy to work with the context object that stores the value for the theme.

The ThemeContext.js file

```
// import the createContext() function and the useContext hook
import { createContext, useContext } from "react";

// context object with default value
const ThemeContext = createContext(
    { theme: "light" }
);

// custom hook to use the context
const useTheme = () => useContext(ThemeContext);

// export context and custom hook
export { ThemeContext, useTheme };
```

This file makes it easy for any component in the app to access the static value in the context as shown by the following App component.

An App component that accesses a static value

```
import { useTheme } from './contexts/ThemeContext';
// import other components and CSS

const App = () => {
    const { theme } = useTheme();
    const themeClass = (theme === 'dark') ? 'dark-theme' : '';
    return (
        <div className={`container ${themeClass}`}>
            <Main />
            <Sidebar />
        </div>
)};

export default App;
```

To start, this app imports the custom useTheme hook from the ThemeContext.js file that's in the contexts directory. Then, it calls the useTheme() function to get the value for the theme.

For static data, that's all you need to do. You can use the custom hook to access the context value from any component. However, static values have limited usefulness, because your components usually need dynamic data. For instance, what if you want users to be able to toggle between light and dark themes? To do that with context data, you need to add a provider component.

Use a provider component for dynamic values

In JSX, you can use the context object that's returned by createContext() to create a provider component. In React 19 and later, you can use the context object itself as shown next.

The JSX for a provider component (React 19 and later)

```
<ThemeContext value={value}>
    {children}
</ThemeContext>
```

In earlier versions of React, you need to use the Provider property of the context object as shown next.

The JSX for a provider component (React 18 and earlier)

```
<ThemeContext.Provider value={value}>
    {children}
</ThemeContext.Provider>
```

Both versions include the built-in children prop between their opening and closing tags. That's because a provider component wraps other components.

In addition, both versions provide a value attribute that can be updated dynamically. This value overrides the default value set by createContext(). As a result, any component that's wrapped by the provider can access the value in the value attribute via the useContext hook (or the custom hook you provide). By contrast, any component that's outside the provider can only access the default value via useContext (or the custom hook).

By itself, a provider component isn't stateful. That is, changing its value attribute doesn't trigger re-renders. However, provider components typically use state or a reducer internally to manage the value that's stored in context, and that's what makes the provider stateful.

For example, the following ThemeProvider component uses state to manage the current theme stored in context. This component is stored in a file named ThemeProvider.jsx in the contexts directory.

The ThemeProvider component

```
import { useState } from 'react'
import { ThemeContext } from './ThemeContext'   // import the context object

const ThemeProvider = ({ children }) => {
```

```
    // state to manage the current theme
    const [theme, setTheme] = useState('light');

    // function to toggle between light and dark themes
    const toggleTheme = () => {
        setTheme(prev => (prev === 'light' ? 'dark' : 'light'));
    };

    // object to assign to the value attribute
    const value = {
        theme,
        toggleTheme
    };

    // provider component JSX
    return (
        <ThemeContext value={value}>
            {children}
        </ThemeContext>
    );
};

// export provider
export { ThemeProvider };
```

This provider uses useState to store and update the current theme. This makes sure changing the theme triggers re-renders of components that use that theme. Then, the theme state variable and the function that calls the state setter are collected in an object that's assigned to the value attribute. Next, React stores that value in context. As a result, the value object is available to any component within the provider.

For example, the following code updates the main.jsx file to enclose the App component in the ThemeProvider component.

The main.jsx file with a ThemeProvider component

```
import { StrictMode } from 'react'
import { createRoot } from 'react-dom/client'
import { ThemeProvider } from './contexts/ThemeProvider'
import App from './App'
import './index.css'

createRoot(document.getElementById('root')).render(
    <StrictMode>
        <ThemeProvider>
            <App />
        </ThemeProvider>
    </StrictMode>
)
```

In this example, App and its descendants have access to the context value because App is coded within ThemeProvider. As a result, when App calls useTheme(), it retrieves the dynamic theme from state, not the static default theme. In addition, App and its descendants can call the toggleTheme() function to change the theme.

The following ToggleTheme component uses the custom hook to access the context provided by ThemeProvider.

The ToggleTheme component

```
import { useTheme } from "../contexts/ThemeContext";
import './ToggleTheme.css';

const ToggleTheme = () => {
    // get context provided by ThemeProvider
    const {theme, toggleTheme} = useTheme();

    return (
        <div className="toggle-theme">
            <p>Current theme: {theme}</p>
            <button onClick={toggleTheme}>Toggle Theme</button>
        </div>
    );
};

export default ToggleTheme;
```

The JSX for this component displays the current name of the theme as well as a button that changes the theme by calling the toggleTheme() function.

The following Sidebar component renders the ToggleTheme component.

The Sidebar component

```
import ToggleTheme from "./ToggleTheme";
import './Sidebar.css';

const Sidebar = () => (
    <div className="sidebar">
        <h2>Quick Links</h2>
        <nav>
            <ul>
                <li><a href="#">Home</a></li>
                ...
            </ul>
        </nav>

        <ToggleTheme />
    </div>
);

export default Sidebar;
```

Since Sidebar is a descendant of App, ToggleTheme can access the theme context. In addition, since ToggleTheme uses context, App doesn't need to pass any props to it through Sidebar.

Make sure context is used within a provider

As described earlier, if useContext() is called outside a provider, it passes its default value to the createContext() function. To prevent errors if the context is used outside a provider, you can use this default value as a fallback. For instance, the following example provides a fallback for the ThemeProvider.

A context object with a default fallback

```
const ThemeContext = createContext({
    theme: 'light',
    toggleTheme: () => {}
});
```

This provides a default theme. As a result, using this context outside a provider doesn't cause runtime errors. But, that might not be what you want. For instance, if you import toggleTheme() outside a provider, it doesn't throw errors, but it also doesn't do anything. Because of that, it might be difficult to determine why your code doesn't work.

To make sure your context is used within a provider, you can throw an error if it's used outside a provider. This way, your code fails right away, with a message that says exactly what the problem is. To do this, you can code a context with no default value and a custom hook that throws an error outside of a provider.

A context object that must be used within a provider

```
// context object with no default value
const ThemeContext = createContext();

// custom hook to consume the context; throw error if used outside provider
const useTheme = () => {
    const context = useContext(ThemeContext);    // undefined if outside provider
    if (!context) {
        throw new Error("useTheme must be used within a ThemeProvider");
    }
    return context;
};
```

Here, if the useTheme hook is called outside a provider, the call to useContext() returns the default value. Since no default value was set, this returns undefined. As a result, the hook throws an error with a message that describes the issue. Otherwise, it returns the result of calling useContext() with the context object.

This works well if the user calls the custom useTheme hook. But what happens if the calling code bypasses the custom hook by calling the useContext hook as shown next?

```
const { theme } = useContext(ThemeContext);
```

In this case, the code still causes an error to be thrown. However, the code throws a destructuring error because undefined has no theme property to extract. This might be a clue to what's wrong, but it's not as good as a message that says, "you can't do this outside a provider."

To prevent this, you can code your context object and provider component in the same file as shown next.

Context and provider in one file

```
import { createContext, useContext, useState } from 'react'

// context object with no default value
const ThemeContext = createContext();

// custom hook to consume the context; throw error if used outside provider
const useTheme = () => {
    const context = useContext(ThemeContext);
    if (!context) {
        throw new Error("useTheme must be used within a ThemeProvider");
    }
    return context;
};

// provider
const ThemeProvider = ({ children }) => {
    ...
    return (
        <ThemeContext value={value}>
            {children}
        </ThemeContext>
    );
};

// export provider and custom hook, but not the context object itself
export { ThemeProvider, useTheme };
```

Here, the code exports only the provider and the custom hook so any code that uses this module can't access the context object. As a result, context values can only be accessed via the custom hook. This guarantees helpful error messages and avoids silent failure.

Global scope vs feature scope

If a provider component wraps the App component, App and all its descendants can consume the context. In other words, the context has *global scope*.

Context with global scope has the benefit of being easy to access. However, it can also cause problems. If you use global context extensively, you can end up with one giant context that handles too many concerns. In turn, this can lead to excessive re-renders because every component that consumes the context re-renders when a state value in the context changes.

You can avoid these problems by using contexts with *feature* or *local scope* whenever possible. To do that, you place the provider around only the components in the tree that need it. This is similar to co-locating state and lifting it only when necessary. For example, the following App component uses MovieProvider and CartProvider contexts.

Providers with feature scope

```
const App = () => (
    <>
        <MovieProvider>
            <MovieList />
            <MovieForm />
        </MovieProvider>
        <CartProvider>
            <ShoppingCart />
        </CartProvider>
    </>
);
```

Here, the providers wrap only the components that need them. For instance, the MovieProvider component doesn't wrap the ShoppingCart component because ShoppingCart doesn't need access to the movie context.

Sometimes, you may find that you need to lift a provider to cover more components. For instance, you may need to lift the CartProvider to allow the MovieList component to add a movie to the cart.

However, lifting a provider may cause other problems. For instance, lifting CartProvider might cause ShoppingCart to re-render too often in response to movie changes. In that case, you can move CartProvider back down and move the functionality the movie components need into a smaller MovieCartProvider.

The idea is to keep your contexts as local and focused as you can. Then, like components, you can modify them to get the results you want.

The updated Movie List app

This chapter finishes by presenting a version of the Movie List app that uses a theme context with global scope and a movie context with feature scope. It's an updated version of the app presented earlier in this chapter, so it uses a reducer to manage its state. This provides a good example of an app that uses a reducer to manage state and a context to distribute it.

The user interface

The Movie List app works the same as the one from chapter 4. However, it includes a Toggle Theme button that toggles between a light and dark theme. To do that, this app uses the Toggle Theme component presented earlier.

The Movie List app with a dark theme

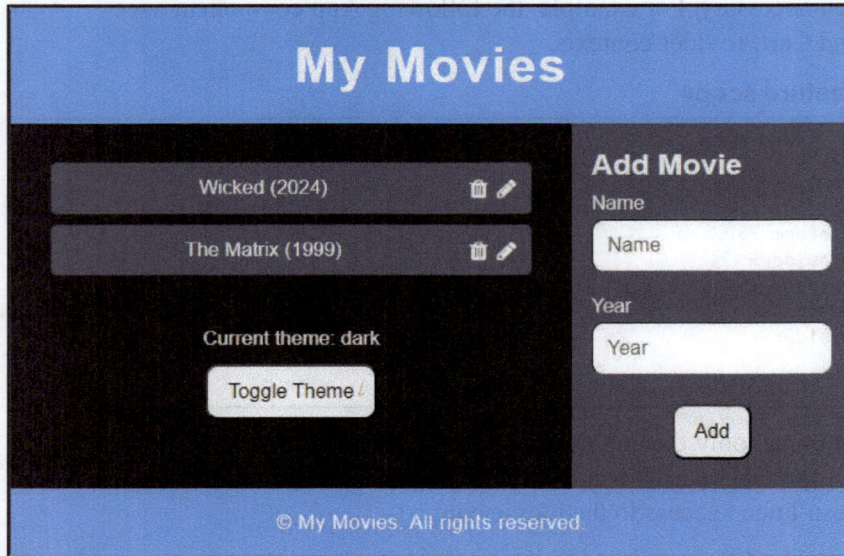

The directory structure

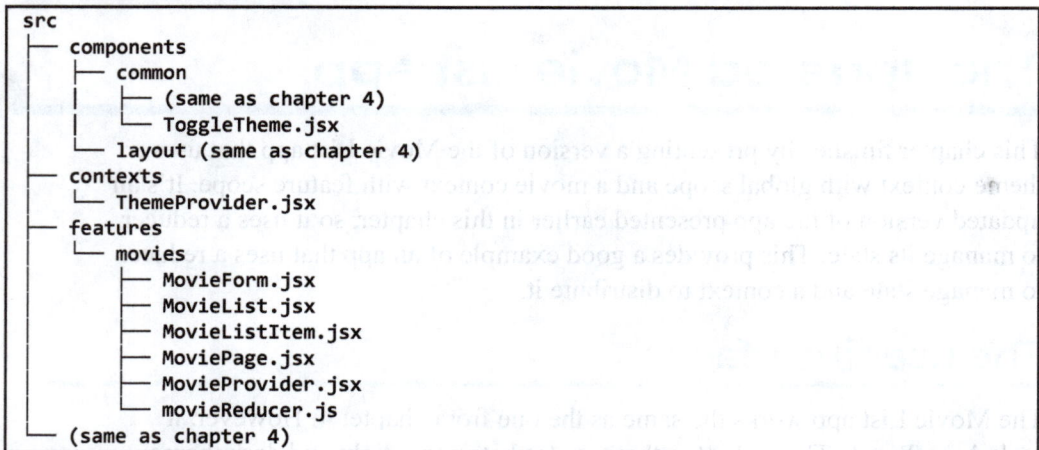

The directory structure for this app is organized by feature. This is a common way to group items that use a context with feature scope because it keeps all the files for a feature together. Typically, the subdirectory for a feature includes the context provider, the components that use the context, and any other files that are specific to that feature such as hooks, reducers, and so on.

The directory structure

```
src
├── components
│   ├── common
│   │   ├── (same as chapter 4)
│   │   └── ToggleTheme.jsx
│   └── layout (same as chapter 4)
├── contexts
│   └── ThemeProvider.jsx
├── features
│   └── movies
│       ├── MovieForm.jsx
│       ├── MovieList.jsx
│       ├── MovieListItem.jsx
│       ├── MoviePage.jsx
│       ├── MovieProvider.jsx
│       └── movieReducer.js
└── (same as chapter 4)
```

Here, the features directory has a movies subdirectory that contains the movie-specific components. To save space, the co-located CSS files aren't shown. This subdirectory also contains the movie context and the movie reducer.

Additionally, the features/movies directory contains a MoviePage component. This wrapper component sets up the movie context and renders the movie UI components. As a result, it keeps the context scoped to the components that need it, and it keeps App from having to concern itself with a lot of providers.

In this version of Movie List, the components directory only stores general-purpose components. This includes the ToggleTheme component. Similarly, the contexts folder only holds contexts with global scope such as the ThemeProvider component.

The theme context

The complete code for the theme context is shown next. Since all of this code has been presented earlier in the chapter, you should already understand how it works. In short, this module exports the ThemeProvider component and the custom useTheme hook.

The ThemeProvider component and its custom useTheme hook

```
import { createContext, useContext, useState } from 'react'

const ThemeContext = createContext();

const useTheme = () => {
    const context = useContext(ThemeContext);
    if (!context) {
        throw new Error("useTheme must be used within a ThemeProvider");
    }
    return context;
};

const ThemeProvider = ({ children }) => {
    const [theme, setTheme] = useState('light');

    const toggleTheme = () => {
        setTheme(prev => (prev === 'light' ? 'dark' : 'light'));
    };

    const value = {
        theme,
        toggleTheme
    };

    return (
        <ThemeContext value={value}>
            {children}
        </ThemeContext>
    );
};

export { ThemeProvider, useTheme };
```

The main.jsx file and App component

The main.jsx file imports the ThemeProvider component and applies it to the App component to give it global scope.

The main.jsx file

```
import { StrictMode } from 'react'
import { createRoot } from 'react-dom/client'
import { ThemeProvider } from './contexts/ThemeProvider'
import App from './App.jsx'
import './index.css'

createRoot(document.getElementById('root')).render(
    <StrictMode>
        <ThemeProvider>
            <App />
        </ThemeProvider>
    </StrictMode>,
)
```

The App component applies the current theme as shown next.

The App component

```
// import the theme context hook
import { useTheme } from './contexts/ThemeProvider';

// import the movie page
import MoviePage from './features/movies/MoviePage';

// import other components and CSS, define local variables

const App = () => {
    // get the theme from the context and use it to set the class
    const { theme } = useTheme();

    return (
        <div className={`container ${theme}`}>
            <Header text={appName} />
            <MoviePage />
            <Footer text={appName} />
        </div>
    )
};

export default App;
```

To start, App imports the custom useTheme hook and uses it to access the theme property. This property may contain a string of 'light' or 'dark'. Then, it uses this property to add the CSS class to the container.

App also imports the MoviePage component and displays it between the Header and Footer components. That way, the MoviePage component can apply the movie context to the MovieList and MovieForm components as shown later in this chapter. This gives these components feature scope.

Since this version of the Movie List app defines the movie event handlers in the movie context, this App component doesn't define any event handlers.

The movie context

The MovieProvider component uses the movie reducer presented earlier in this chapter to manage state.

The MovieProvider component

```
import { createContext, useContext, useReducer } from 'react';
import { movieInitialState, movieReducer, ACTIONS as M } from './movieReducer';

// create context with no default
const MovieContext = createContext();

// custom hook throws error if not used in provider
const useMovies = () => {
    const context = useContext(MovieContext);
    if (!context) {
        throw new Error('useMovies must be used within a MovieProvider');
    }
    return context;
};

const MovieProvider = ({ children, initialMovies = [] }) => {
    // initializer function for the reducer: inject initial movies
    const initializer = (state) => ({ ...state, movies: initialMovies });

    // create reducer to work with movies
    const [state, dispatch] = useReducer(movieReducer, movieInitialState,
                                         initializer);

    // event handlers to work with movies and selected movie
    const addMovie = (newMovie) =>
        dispatch({ type: M.ADD, payload: newMovie });

    const selectMovie = (movie, mode) =>
        dispatch({ type: M.SELECT, payload: { movie, mode } });

    const editMovie = (updatedMovie) =>
        dispatch({ type: M.EDIT, payload: updatedMovie });

    const deleteMovie = (id) =>
        dispatch({ type: M.DELETE, payload: id });

    const cancel = () =>
        dispatch({ type: M.CANCEL });

    // object to assign to value attribute
    const value = {
        movies: state.movies,
        selectedMovie: state.selectedMovie,
        onAdd: addMovie,
        onSelect: selectMovie,
        onEdit: editMovie,
```

```
            onDelete: deleteMovie,
            onCancel: cancel,
    };

    return (
        <MovieContext value={value}>
            {children}
        </MovieContext>
    );
}

// export provider and custom hook
export { MovieProvider, useMovies };
```

Here, the MovieProvider component defines two props. The children prop allows the context to wrap other components, and the initialMovies prop allows you to add initial movie data to the context.

The MoviePage component

The MoviePage component imports the MovieProvider component so its child components can access the movie context.

The MoviePage component

```
// import the movie provider
import { MovieProvider } from "./MovieProvider";

// import the subcomponents
import MovieList from "./MovieList";
import MovieForm from "./MovieForm";

// import the layout components
import Main from "../../components/layout/Main";
import Sidebar from "../../components/layout/Sidebar";

// import the theme toggle component
import ToggleTheme from "../../components/common/ToggleTheme";

// create some initial movies to pass to the provider
const initialMovies = [
    { id: 1, name: "Wicked", year: 2024 },
    { id: 2, name: "The Matrix", year: 1999 },
];

const MoviePage = () => (
    <MovieProvider initialMovies={initialMovies}>
        <Main>
            <MovieList />
            <ToggleTheme />
        </Main>
        <Sidebar>
            <MovieForm />
        </Sidebar>
    </MovieProvider>
);

export default MoviePage;
```

Because the components within MovieProvider have access to the state stored in the movie context, MoviePage doesn't need to pass any props to them. As a result, it only passes the initial movies array to MovieProvider.

The other movie components

The MovieList component uses the custom hook to access the movie context as shown next. As a result, it doesn't receive any props and doesn't pass as many props to the MovieListItem component. Instead, it uses the movie context to get the state it needs, which is the current list of movies.

The MovieList component

```
// import the custom hook to access the context
import { useMovies } from './MovieProvider';

// other imports - same as chapter 4

const MovieList = () => {
    // use the custom hook to access the shared context
    const { movies } = useMovies();

    return (
        <ul className="movie-list">
            {movies.length === 0 ? (
                <MovieListItem movie={null} />
            ) : (
                movies.map((movie) =>
                    <MovieListItem
                        key={movie.id}
                        movie={movie}
                    />
                )
            )}
        </ul>
    );
};

export default MovieList;
```

The MovieListItem component shown next also uses the custom hook to access the movie context. Then, it uses that context to get the state it needs, which is the event handler for the onSelect event.

The MovieListItem component

```
// import the custom hook to access the context
import { useMovies } from './MovieProvider';

// other imports - same as chapter 4

const MovieListItem = ({ movie }) => {
    // use the custom hook to access the shared context
    const { onSelect } = useMovies();

    return (
        // JSX and the rest of the component is the same as chapter 4
```

Similarly, the MovieForm component uses the custom hook to get the state it needs.

The MovieForm component

```
// import the custom hook to access the context
import { useMovies } from './MovieProvider';

// other imports - same as chapter 4

const MovieForm = () => {
    // use the custom hook to access the shared context
    const { selectedMovie, onAdd, onEdit, onDelete, onCancel } = useMovies();

    // state variables
    const [name, setName] = useState('');
    const [year, setYear] = useState('');

    // the rest of the code is the same as chapter 4
```

Here, the MovieForm component uses the custom hook to get the selected movie and the event handlers it needs to add, edit, and delete a movie. However, it manages its own local state for movie name and year. This shows that not all state for a feature belongs in context. Only state that's shared across components should go there.

Perspective

This chapter has shown how to use React to manage and distribute state. To do that, it presented some of the best practices for using reducers. In addition, it presented some of the best practices for working with context objects. If you understand how these features work, you have a solid set of skills for managing state.

Terms

reducer

action object

payload

dispatch function

initializer function

context object

global scope

feature scope

local scope

Exercise 10-1: Use a reducer

Review the starting code

1. Open the my-playlist1 app in the ex_starts/ch10 folder.
2. Note how the code provides event handlers for adding and deleting songs from the playlist.

Use a reducer to manage state

3. Create a reducers folder in the src folder.
4. Create a playlistReducer.js file.
5. Define ADD_SONG and DELETE_SONG constants and store them in an action object.
6. Create a playlistReducer() function that uses a switch statement to select the correct behavior based on the action type. Use the existing logic in the App component to help you.
7. Define a playlistInitialState object with a playlist property set to an empty array.
8. Export the action object, initial state, and reducer function.

Modify the app to use the reducer

9. Open the App.jsx file.
10. Import the useReducer hook.
11. Import the objects exported by the reducer file. Create an alias for the action object that's a single letter or a short word.
12. Create an initializer function that replaces the empty playlist array in the initial state with the initialSongs array.
13. Replace the code that uses the useState hook to track the playlist with code that calls the useReducer hook. Pass the reducer function, initial state, and initializer function to useReducer(). Note that you can still use the useState hook to track whether to show the Add Song form.
14. Update the event handlers for adding and deleting songs to use the dispatch() function returned by useReducer().
15. Update the JSX to use the playlist property of the state object.
16. Run the app and test it to make sure it works correctly.

Exercise 10-2: Use a context

1. Continue with the app from exercise 10-1, or open the my-playlist2 app in the ex_starts/ch10 folder.
2. Create a contexts folder in the src folder and add a PlaylistProvider.jsx file.
3. Import createContext, useContext, and useReducer from react.

4. Import the objects from the PlaylistReducer file. You can use the code in App.jsx as a guide.

5. Use the createContext() method to create a playlist context object with no default value.

6. Use the useContext hook to create a custom hook for the playlist context that must be used within a PlaylistProvider component.

7. Create a PlaylistProvider component that takes children as a prop and an initialSongs array as a prop.

8. Create an initializer function that uses the initialSongs prop to override the playlist property in the reducer initial state. You can use the code in App.jsx as a guide.

9. Create state and dispatch objects by calling the useReducer() function with the reducer function, initial state, and initializer as arguments.

10. Add a function named addSong(). This function should take a song as an argument and dispatch the ADD action constant with the song as the payload.

11. Add a function named deleteSong(). This function should take an id as an argument and dispatch the DELETE action constant with the id as the payload.

12. Create a value object that contains the playlist, addSong, and deleteSong items. Assign them to properties named songs, onAdd, and onDelete, respectively, so you don't need to change the JSX in the components.

13. Return a playlist context component with the value object as its value. It should wrap the children prop.

14. Export the PlaylistProvider component and the usePlaylist hook.

Modify the App component to use the context

15. Open the App.jsx file.

16. Add an import statement for the PlaylistProvider component.

17. Wrap the <main> element in the PlaylistProvider component. Pass the initial-Songs array to the initialSongs prop.

18. Remove the reducer code and event handlers for the playlist, but don't remove the event handlers for showing and hiding the form.

19. Remove the songs and onDelete attributes from the Playlist component and the onAdd attribute from the SongForm component.

Modify the Playlist component to use the context

20. Open the Playlist.jsx file and import the usePlaylist hook.

21. Remove the songs and onDelete props from the function's signature.

22. Use the usePlaylist hook to get the songs value and onDelete() function from the context.

Modify the SongForm component to use the context

23. Open the SongForm.jsx file and import the usePlaylist hook.
24. Remove the onAdd prop from the function's signature.
25. Use the usePlaylist hook to get the onAdd() function from the context.
26. Run the app and test it to make sure it works correctly.

Chapter 11

Improve performance with memoization

As described earlier in previous chapters, React re-renders a component whenever its state or props change. In other words, React re-runs the component function, generates new JSX, creates a new virtual DOM based on that JSX, compares the new virtual DOM to the previous one, and updates the browser DOM only where needed. And, it does the same for every descendent component. For large apps, that can be a lot of re-rendering!

Because React is designed to be fast, all this re-rendering is usually fine. Sometimes, though, excessive re-renders can cause performance issues. That's why this chapter presents some of the tools React provides to address these problems, as well as some guidance about when to use those tools.

An introduction to memoization

In programming, *memoization* means storing, or *caching*, a value so you don't have to compute or recreate it unnecessarily. The name memoization comes from the word "memo", as in "make a note of" or "remember" something.

What memoization is

When you memoize a value, that value can be the result of a computation or it can be a function such as an event handler. For instance, suppose your app performs an expensive calculation based on some props. On every re-render, that calculation runs again, even if the props haven't changed. With memoization, you can store the result of the calculation. Then, on subsequent re-renders, you can look up the stored value if the props haven't changed or recalculate the value if they have.

Benefits of memoization

- Avoids expensive calculations.
- Prevents repeated work when nothing has changed.
- Can improve performance for large apps.

Costs of memoization

- Cached values take up memory.
- Overhead of looking up a value can outweigh the cost of a simple calculation.
- Adds complexity to the code.

When and how to memoize in React

Most of the time, you don't need to use memoization in your React apps. That's because React is designed to be fast. Running component functions and diffing the virtual DOM is usually cheap, even if it happens repeatedly. As a result, memoization doesn't make an appreciable difference in most apps.

Because of that, you typically don't memoize components, values, or functions unless you encounter actual performance issues that memoization can help solve. In other words, it's a best practice to avoid memoization by default and only add it if you need to.

A possible exception to this best practice is when you're building components, hooks, or other items for a library. Libraries are typically used by others, so you might not be the one to assess performance. In that case, you may decide to memoize by default so your library items don't trigger unnecessary re-renders in the apps that use them.

If you decide to memoize, React provides three main features: the memo() function, the useMemo hook, and the useCallback hook.

Memoization functions provided by React

Function	Description
`memo(componentFn)`	Accepts a component function and caches it. The component only re-renders when its props change.
`useMemo(fn, deps)`	Accepts a function and a dependency array. Runs the function and caches the value it returns on mount and whenever a dependency changes.
`useCallback(fn, deps)`	Accepts a function and a dependency array. Caches the function on mount and whenever a dependency changes.

The memo() function works at the component level. As a result, it doesn't need to be a hook. On the other hand, the useMemo() and useCallback() functions work *inside* components and rely on React's render cycle and dependency tracking. As a result, they are hooks.

All of these functions perform a *shallow comparison* when checking if props or dependencies have changed. For objects, arrays, and functions, that means React only compares references, not the contents. This is called a *referential equality check*.

As you review the following examples, you should know that they are for demonstration purposes only, not examples of best practices. In other words, most of the examples presented in this chapter are too simple for memoization to actually be necessary! However, they illustrate principles that can be applied to more complex code to fix performance issues.

How to memoize components

React provides the memo() function to memoize a component. For example, you might memoize a component that receives props that rarely change but is contained within a component that re-renders frequently. Or, you might memoize a component that performs an expensive computation, such as a recursive mathematical calculation or an API call.

An app with components that aren't memoized

The following app presents a list of movies with the favorite movie marked with a star. The components in this app are normal, non-memoized components.

The My Movies app

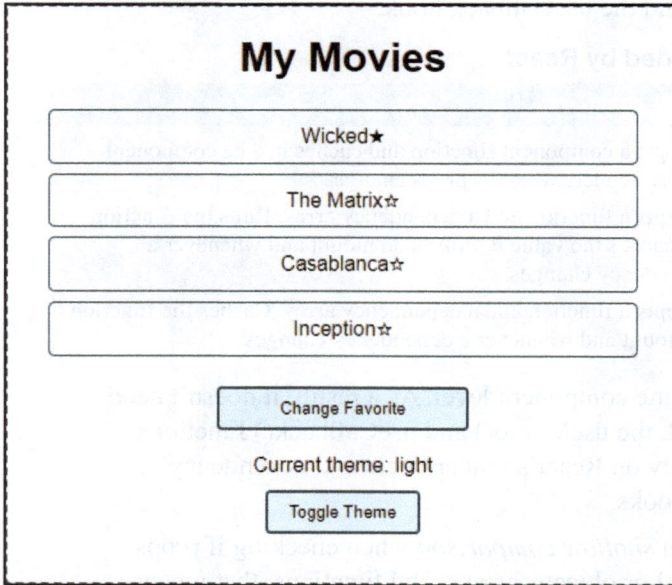

My Movies

Wicked★
The Matrix☆
Casablanca☆
Inception☆

Change Favorite

Current theme: light

Toggle Theme

In this app, clicking the Change Favorite button moves the star to the next movie in the list. And clicking the Toggle Theme button toggles the theme between light and dark. To do that, this app uses the ThemeProvider context and the ToggleTheme component described in chapter 10.

Clicking either button causes the App component to re-render, which in turn re-renders all the descendent components. As a result, changing the theme causes all the movie list components to re-render, even though the movie list itself doesn't change. However, that means React re-renders the movie list components in the virtual DOM, determines that nothing has changed, and doesn't change anything in the browser DOM. That's why you usually don't need to worry about re-renders.

The My Movies app uses the following components.

The App component

```
import { useState } from "react";
import { useTheme } from './contexts/ThemeProvider';
import MovieList from './components/MovieList';
import ChangeFavorite from './components/ChangeFavorite';
import ToggleTheme from './components/ToggleTheme';
import './App.css'

const App = () => {
    const { theme } = useTheme();

    const [movies, setMovies] = useState([
        { id: 1, title: "Wicked", isFavorite: true },
        { id: 2, title: "The Matrix", isFavorite: false },
```

```
            { id: 3, title: "Casablanca", isFavorite: false },
            { id: 4, title: "Inception", isFavorite: false },
        ]);

        // set next movie in list as favorite
        const changeFavorite = () => {
            setMovies((prev) => {
                const currentIndex = prev.findIndex((movie) => movie.isFavorite);
                const nextIndex = (currentIndex + 1) % prev.length;
                return prev.map((movie, i) => ({
                    ...movie,
                    isFavorite: i === nextIndex
                }));
            });
        };

        return (
            <div className={`container ${theme}`}>
                <h1>My Movies</h1>
                <MovieList movies={movies} />
                <ChangeFavorite onChangeFave={changeFavorite} />
                <ToggleTheme />
            </div>
    )};

export default App;
```

The MovieList component

```
import MovieListItem from "./MovieListItem";
import "./MovieList.css";

const MovieList = ({ movies }) => (
    <ul className="movie-list">
        {movies.map((movie) => (
            <MovieListItem
                key={movie.id}
                title={movie.title}
                isFavorite={movie.isFavorite}
            />
        ))}
    </ul>
);

export default MovieList;
```

The MovieListItem component

```
import "./MovieListItem.css";

const MovieListItem = ({ title, isFavorite }) => (
    <li className="movie-list-item">
        <span>{title}</span>
        <span>{isFavorite ? "★" : "☆"}</span>
    </li>
);

export default MovieListItem;
```

The ChangeFavorite component

```
import './ChangeFavorite.css';

const ChangeFavorite = ({ onChangeFave }) => (
    <button className="fave" onClick={onChangeFave}>
        Change Favorite
    </button>
);

export default ChangeFavorite;
```

The ToggleTheme component

```
import { useTheme } from './contexts/ThemeProvider';
import './ToggleTheme.css';

const ToggleTheme = () => {
    const {theme, toggleTheme} = useTheme();

    const handleClick = () => {
        toggleTheme();
    };

    return (
        <div className="toggle-theme">
            <p>Current theme: {theme}</p>
            <button onClick={handleClick}>Toggle Theme</button>
        </div>
    );
};

export default ToggleTheme;
```

To view how React renders these components for this app, you can use the Profiler tab of your browser's developer tools as described in chapter 7. For example, you can display the Profiler tab, start profiling, click the Change Favorite button, and click the Toggle Theme button. Then, you can review how React rendered the components after each button click.

After clicking the Change Favorite button, the profiler displays all components for the app as shown next.

After clicking the Change Favorite button

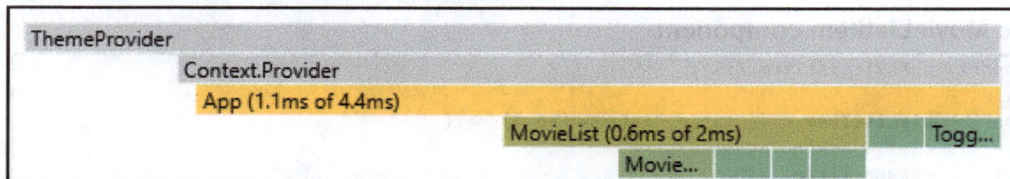

The gray coloring shows that React didn't re-render the ThemeProvider or the Context.Provider components. That makes sense as it would have rendered these components when the app loaded, and it doesn't need to re-render them to change the favorite. However, React re-renders the App component and all of its child components, even though some of these components didn't change.

After clicking the Toggle Theme button, the profiler displays all components for the app again as shown next.

After clicking the Toggle Theme button

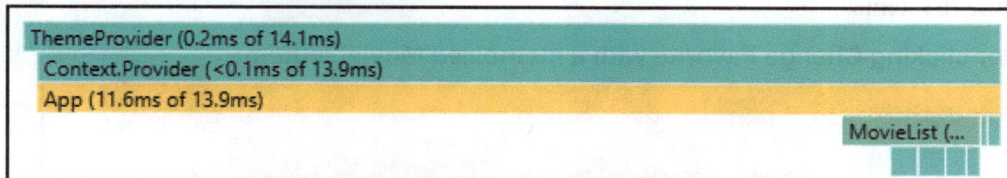

ThemeProvider (0.2ms of 14.1ms)
Context.Provider (<0.1ms of 13.9ms)
App (11.6ms of 13.9ms)
MovieList (...

This time, React re-renders every component. This is standard React behavior, and isn't usually a problem.

But what if you had thousands of MovieListItem components? Or what if each MovieListItem component made an expensive API call to get its data? If that slowed your app, you could memoize MovieListItem so it only re-renders when its props change.

Memoize a component

React provides a function named memo() that you can use to wrap and memoize a component. To use the memo() function, you begin by importing it from the React module.

Import the memo() function

```
import { memo } from 'react';
```

Then, you can memoize a component by passing its function to the memo() function. For example, you can pass the function for the MovieListItem component to the memo() function as part of the export statement as shown next.

Memoize MovieListItem

```
import { memo } from "react";
import "./MovieListItem.css";

const MovieListItem = ({ title, isFavorite }) => { ... };

// wrap with memo() to prevent unnecessary re-renders
export default memo(MovieListItem);
```

When you pass a component's function to memo(), you tell React to "make a note" of that component and its props. On subsequent renders, React checks whether any props have changed. If they haven't, React skips re-rendering the component and reuses its previous output.

In the previous example, the MovieListItem component that's passed to memo() only re-renders if its title prop or its isFavorite prop changes. To see how this works, you can reload the app in the browser, start the profiler again, click each button again, and view the rendering.

This time, clicking the Change Favorite button only re-renders two of the movie list items.

After clicking Change Favorite with a memoized MovieListItem

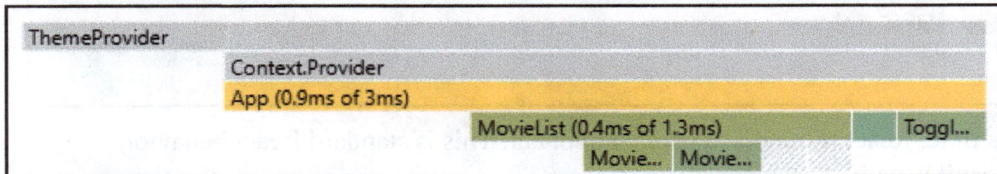

That makes sense because the isFavorite prop changed for the first two movie list items (the first changed to false and the second changed to true). As a result, React re-rendered them, and the profiler displayed them in color. By contrast, the isFavorite prop didn't change for the next two movie list items, so React didn't re-render them, and the profiler displayed them in gray.

Clicking the Toggle Theme button doesn't change any of the props of the MovieListItem component. As a result, React didn't re-render any of these components as shown next.

After clicking Toggle Theme with a memoized MovieListItem

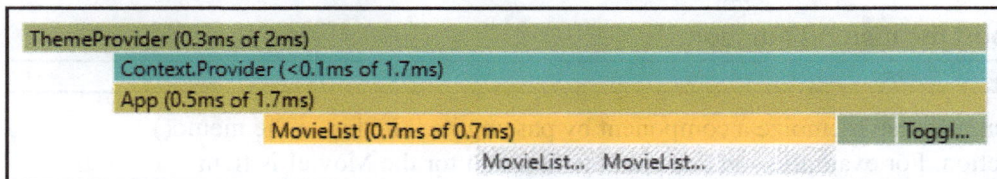

How to memoize a value

React provides the useMemo hook to memoize a value returned by a function. For example, you might want to memoize the result of an expensive calculation, such as a recursive mathematical calculation or an API call. Or, you might memoize an object or an array so React doesn't evaluate it as new when its contents haven't changed.

A memoized component with an object prop

To show how this works, the following example updates the memoized MovieListItem component from the previous example so it accepts a prop that's an object (movie) instead of individual values (title and isFavorite).

A MovieListItem component with a prop that's an object

```
import { memo } from "react";
import "./MovieListItem.css";

const MovieListItem = ({ movie }) => (
    <li className="movie-list-item">
        <span>{movie.title}</span>
        <span>{movie.isFavorite ? "★" : "☆"}</span>
    </li>
);

export default memo(MovieListItem);
```

Similarly, the following example updates the MovieList component so it passes a movie object to MovieListItem.

A MovieList component that passes the object to MovieListItem

```
import MovieListItem from "./MovieListItem";
import "./MovieList.css";

const MovieList = ({ movies }) => (
    <ul className="movie-list">
        {movies.map((movie) => {
            return (
                <MovieListItem
                    key={movie.id}
                    movie={movie}
                />
            );
        })}
    </ul>
);

export default MovieList;
```

If you profile the button clicks for the app again, the profiler should show that clicking the Change Favorites button now re-renders all movie list items, even though only two of them changed.

After clicking Change Favorite with a prop that's an object

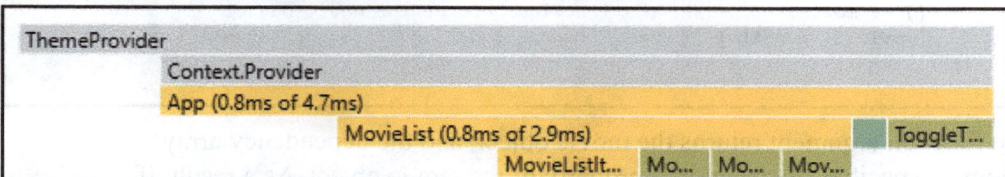

That's because the handler for Change Favorites updates the movie state like this:

```
prev.map((movie, i) => ({...movie, isFavorite: i === nextIndex}));
```

This creates a new movie object for every item in the array, even if the value of isFavorite didn't change. Since memo() does a shallow comparison of props, it evaluates every movie object as changed and re-renders all movie list items.

By contrast, clicking the Toggle Theme button doesn't affect movie state, so the movie objects in state remain the same references as before. As a result, memo() evaluates every movie object as unchanged and doesn't re-render the movie list items as shown next. In other words, toggling the theme still works as intended and doesn't re-render any movie list items.

To make Change Favorites work the same as before, you need to preserve the previous references for movies that don't change. One way to do that is with the useMemo hook.

Memoize a prop that's an object

To use the useMemo hook, you begin by importing it from the React module.

Import the useMemo hook

```
import { useMemo } from 'react';
```

Then, you call useMemo() and pass it a function that returns the value you want to cache and a dependency array that determines when React re-runs the function to cache a new value.

When useMemo() runs on mount, it executes the function and caches the value it returns. On subsequent re-renders, it checks if any dependencies changed. If so, it re-runs the function, updates the cached value, and returns this new value. Otherwise, it skips the function and returns the cached value.

For example, the following memoizeMovie() function defines a function that accepts a movie object and memoizes it with useMemo().

Call useMemo() to memoize a value

```
const memoizeMovie = (movie) => {
    return useMemo(
        () => movie,        // fn - function returns the movie object
        [movie.isFavorite] // deps - re-run function if fave changes
    );
};
```

The function argument returns the movie object, and the dependency array argument specifies the isFavorite property of the movie object. As a result, if the isFavorite value changes, the new movie object is cached and returned. Otherwise, the cached movie object is returned.

The following MovieList component is updated to use the memoizeMovie() function defined in the previous example to memoize the movie object.

Memoize movie object in MovieList

```
const MovieList = ({ movies }) => (
    <ul className="movie-list">
        {movies.map((movie) => {
            return (
                <MovieListItem
                    key={movie.id}
                    movie={memoizeMovie(movie)}  // pass memoized movie object
                />
            );
        })}
    </ul>
);

export default MovieList;
```

Here, the JSX for this component uses memoizeMovie() to pass the memoized movie object to MovieListItem. This makes the memoized MovieListItem work as before. As a result, if you profile clicking the Change Favorite button again, it should only render the necessary movie list items as shown next.

After clicking Change Favorite with a prop that's a memoized object

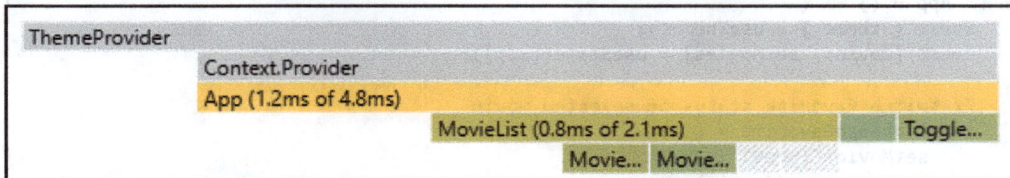

How to memoize a function

React provides the useCallback hook to memoize a function. Typically, you memoize a function when you don't want React to evaluate it as new when its logic hasn't changed.

A memoized component with a function prop

To show how this works, the following example updates the memoized MovieListItem component from the previous example to accept an event handler function.

MovieListItem with a prop that's a function

```
import { memo } from "react";
import "./MovieListItem.css";

const MovieListItem = ({ movie, onChangeFavorite }) => (
    <li className="movie-list-item"
        onClick={() => onChangeFavorite(movie.id)}
```

```
        >
            <span>{movie.title}</span>
            <span>{movie.isFavorite ? "★" : "☆"}</span>
        </li>
    );

    export default memo(MovieListItem);
```

This component uses the event handler to toggle the isFavorite value if the user clicks a movie. This way, a user can choose more than one favorite movie, and the Change Favorite button is no longer needed.

To make this work, the App component provides an event handler for changing the favorite as shown next.

App passes an event handler to MovieList

```
import { useState } from "react";
import { useTheme } from './contexts/ThemeProvider';
import MovieList from './components/MovieList';
import ToggleTheme from './components/ToggleTheme';
import './App.css'

const App = () => {
    const { theme } = useTheme();
    const [movies, setMovies] = useState([...]);

    // switch favorite status of selected movie
    const changeFavorite = (id) => {
        setMovies((prev) =>
            prev.map((movie) =>
                movie.id === id
                    ? { ...movie, isFavorite: !movie.isFavorite }
                    : movie
            )
        );
    };

    return (
        <div className={`container ${theme}`}>
            <h1>My Movies</h1>
            <MovieList movies={movies} onChangeFavorite={changeFavorite} />
            <ToggleTheme />
        </div>
)};

export default App;
```

The updated event handler now accepts an id value. If the id of the current element matches it, the code makes a copy of that element and toggles its isFavorite property. Otherwise, the code returns the existing element without making a copy.

This is significant because it preserves the object references for all the unchanged movies. Because of that, they don't look like new props when they're passed to MovieListItem. As a result, MovieList no longer needs to memoize them. This is a common way to preserve object references without memoizing.

MovieList passes handler and non-memoized movie object to MovieListItem

```
import MovieListItem from "./MovieListItem";
import "./MovieList.css";

const MovieList = ({ movies, onChangeFavorite }) => (
    <ul className="movie-list">
        {movies.map((movie) => {
            return (
                <MovieListItem
                    key={movie.id}
                    movie={movie}  // no longer memoized
                    onChangeFavorite={onChangeFavorite}
                />
            );
        })}
    </ul>
);

export default MovieList;
```

The new event handler eliminates the need for memoizing the movie object passed to MovieListItem, which is good. But, passing that event handler to MovieListItem causes all the components to re-render, even after Toggle Theme is clicked, which is bad.

For example, here's what the profiler displays after changing a favorite by clicking on the first movie list item.

After clicking on the first movie list item with a prop that's a function

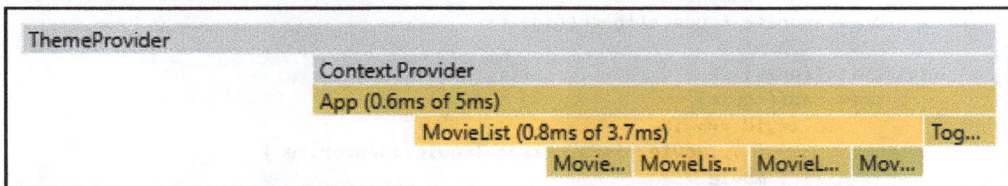

That's because App creates the event handler. So, whenever App re-renders, it creates a new event handler. Even though the handler's logic stays the same when it's passed to MovieListItem, memo() evaluates it as a new prop and re-renders. Since App re-renders when you click a movie or toggle the theme, both actions cause all the child components to re-render.

To fix this, you need to preserve the reference to the event handler between renders. Typically, you do that with the useCallback hook.

Memoize a prop that's a function

To use the useCallback hook, you begin by importing it from the React module as shown next.

Import the useCallback hook

```
import { useCallback } from 'react';
```

Then, you call useCallback(). When you do that, you pass it a function you want to cache and a dependency array that determines when React caches a new function.

Call useCallback()

```
const clearMovies = useCallback(() => setMovies([]), []);
```

When useCallback() runs on mount, it caches the function it receives. On subsequent re-renders, it checks if any dependencies changed. If so, it caches the new function and returns it. Otherwise, it returns the cached function. Here, the dependency array is an empty array, so React caches the function on mount and returns the cached function on all subsequent re-renders.

The following code shows the event handler in the App component after it has been updated so it's memoized.

The memoized event handler in App

```
import { useState, useCallback } from "react";
...

const App = () => {
    ...
    // switch favorite status of selected movie
    const changeFavorite = useCallback((id) => {

        setMovies((prev) =>
            prev.map((movie) =>
                movie.id === id
                    ? { ...movie, isFavorite: !movie.isFavorite }
                    : movie
            )
        );
    }, []);
    ...
}};

export default App;
```

In this code, the definition of the changeFavorite() event handler is wrapped in useCallback() and the dependency array is empty. As a result, React caches the function passed to useCallback() on mount.

On subsequent re-renders, useCallback() returns the cached function. Because of that, the reference stays the same across renders, and the memoized MovieListItem evaluates it as unchanged. As a result, a movie list item only re-renders when it has changed.

After clicking on the second movie list item with a memoized prop

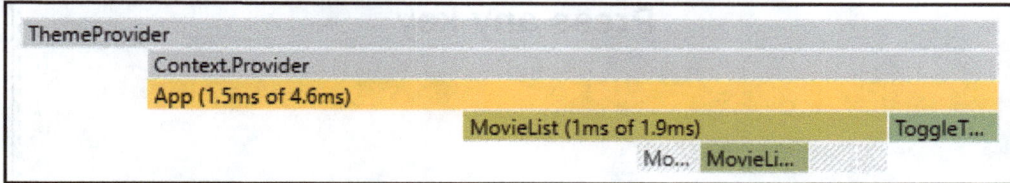

Memoization and dependency arrays

So far, this chapter has shown how the useMemo and useCallback hooks can be used to stabilize props passed to a memoized component. Those hooks can also be used to stabilize values in the dependency array passed to the useEffect hook.

Like useMemo and useCallback, useEffect performs a shallow comparison to check whether any value in the dependency array changed. As a result, if a dependency is a function, object, or array, React may evaluate it as changed even if its contents stay the same. This can lead to an effect running unnecessarily.

A component with a side effect

To show how to stabilize a dependency array, this chapter presents an app that captures and displays the key the user pressed. React can't add an event handler for the keydown event of the document object, so the app uses an effect to do that. This effect includes a cleanup function that removes the event handler.

The following screen shows how the user interface for the app looks after a user has pressed three keys to type out "fun".

The user interface

```
                        Key Logger

                     Press any key

                           fun

                          Reset
```

This app uses the KeyLogger component shown next.

The KeyLogger component

```javascript
import { useState, useEffect } from 'react';
import './KeyLogger.css';

const KeyLogger = () => {
    console.warn('KeyLogger rendered');
    const [keys, setKeys] = useState([]);

    // handler for keydown event
    const handleKeyDown = (e) => {
        console.log(`add '${e.key}' to state and re-render`);
        setKeys((keys) => [...keys, e.key]);
    };

    // handler for reset link
    const handleReset = (e) => {
        console.log('reset keys state and re-render');
        e.preventDefault(); // prevent navigation
        setKeys([]);
    };

    // side effect to add/remove event listener
    useEffect(() => {
        console.log('run effect - attach keydown handler');
        document.addEventListener('keydown', handleKeyDown);

        // cleanup function
        return () => {
            console.log('run cleanup - remove keydown handler');
            document.removeEventListener('keydown', handleKeyDown);
        };
    }, [handleKeyDown]); // handleKeyDown changes every render unless memoized

    return (
        <div>
            <h1>Key Logger</h1>
            <h2>Press any key</h2>
            <div className='keyDisplay'>{keys.join('')}</div>
```

```
                <a href="/" onClick={handleReset}>Reset</a>
        </div>
    );
};

export default KeyLogger;
```

This code logs messages to the console to show when it renders, when it updates state, and when it adds or removes the keydown event handler. The first statement in the component uses the warn() function rather than log(). As a result, it displays a red triangle and highlighting in the console. This makes it easy to see when this component renders.

The handleKeyDown() function is in the dependency array of the effect because it's used within the effect. However, since it isn't memoized, it's recreated on each re-render and React evaluates it as a changed dependency. As a result, React runs the cleanup function and effect on every re-render as shown next.

The console with log statements

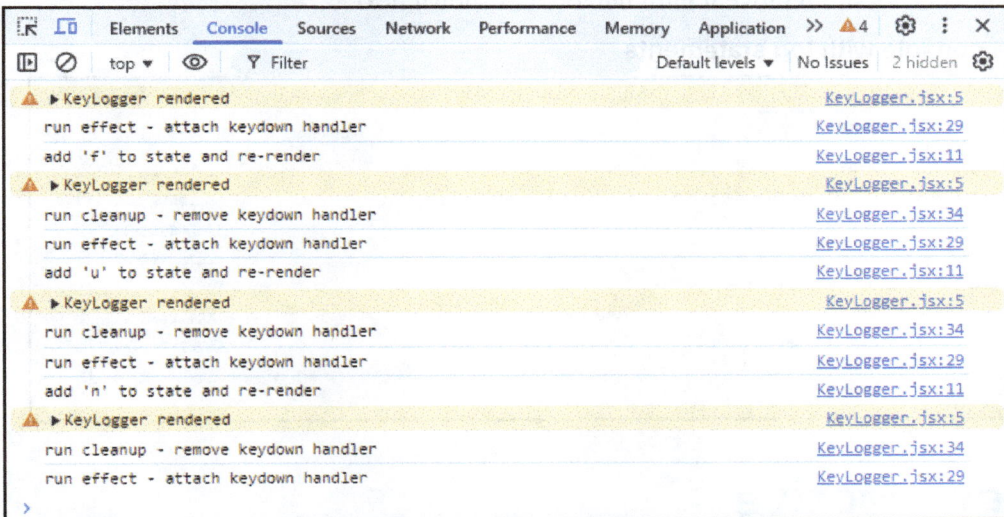

This shows that when the effect runs on every re-render, React removes the keydown event handler and then re-attaches it on every key press. To prevent this, you can use the useCallback hook to memoize the event handler before using it in the dependency array.

Memoize an event handler in the dependency array

Here's the event handler in KeyLogger, updated to memoize the event handler in the dependency array of the effect.

The KeyLogger component

```
import { useState, useEffect, useCallback } from 'react';
...
const KeyLogger = () => {
    ...
    // handler for keydown event
    const handleKeyDown = useCallback((e) => {
        console.log(`add '${e.key}' to state and re-render`);
        setKeys((keys) => [...keys, e.key]);
    }, []); // empty dep array - only run on mount
...
export default KeyLogger;
```

This code memoizes the handleKeyDown() function by wrapping it in useCallback() and passing an empty dependency array. As a result, the event handler is cached on mount

On subsequent re-renders, useCallback() returns the cached event handler. Because of that, the reference never changes, and React evaluates the dependency as unchanged. As a result, React attaches the event handler on mount and doesn't remove it until unmount as shown next.

The console with log statements

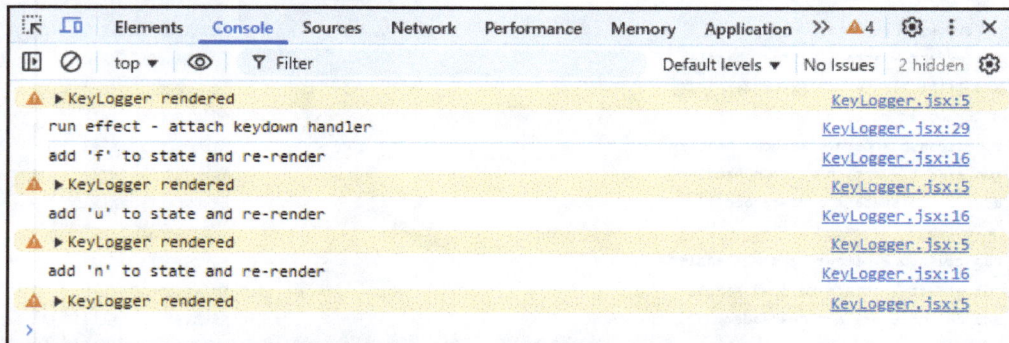

Perspective

This chapter shows how and when to memoize components, values, and functions in React. However, you might find yourself using these skills infrequently because React is so fast. For instance, it might seem like you'd obviously want to avoid adding and removing an event handler on every keypress. And yet, React processes this so quickly, it might not cause any performance issues.

In addition, sometimes you can preserve object references without memorizing. In this chapter, that was shown by the event handler that returned references to existing objects instead of creating new objects when the object's contents were unchanged. Still, memoization is a useful tool to have in your React skillset.

Terms

memoization

caching

shallow comparison

referential equality check

Exercise 11-1: Memoize a value

Review the starting code

1. Open the my-playlist project in the ex_starts/ch11 folder.

2. Review the code for the FeaturedSong component. Note that this component has an expensive operation that takes 3 seconds to complete and that it logs messages to the console at the start and end of this operation.

3. Run the app in the browser. It should display a featured song above the playlist, but it should take a long time for the page to load.

4. Open the browser console and review the log messages. This app isn't in Strict Mode, so the console should not display each message twice.

5. Click Delete for a song and then click Confirm. Note that there's a delay for each action and that the console messages indicate when the expensive operation runs.

6. Click Delete for a song and then click Cancel. Note that there's a delay for each action and that the console messages work the same as before.

7. Add a song. Note the delays and console messages.

Memoize a value

8. Open the FeaturedSong component and import the useMemo hook.

9. Find the code that calls the expensive function and memoize its return value with the useMemo hook.

   - For the first argument, pass an anonymous function that calls the expensive function and returns the song data object.

   - For the second argument, pass a dependency array that includes the song id.

10. Test the app again. The expensive operation should only run on initial load or if you delete the featured song.

Chapter 12

Validate data types with TypeScript

Using TypeScript can help you to catch errors earlier, improve autocomplete suggestions within your IDE, and help document your code. This chapter shows how to get started with TypeScript as well as some common TypeScript patterns used by professional developers.

How to get started with TypeScript

TypeScript only adds features to JavaScript. It doesn't change or remove any features. As a result, TypeScript is a *superset* of JavaScript. In other words, any valid JavaScript is also valid TypeScript, but valid TypeScript can use features that aren't supported by JavaScript.

TypeScript adds *static typing* to JavaScript. This means that it can specify the data types for variables, function parameters, object properties, and so on. Then, if you use invalid data, TypeScript can identify the error immediately, which makes it easier for you to fix the error. Without TypeScript, you often don't realize that you've used invalid data until later when you run your app and it crashes or doesn't work correctly. With TypeScript, an IDE such as VS Code can identify the error. In addition, TypeScript can help IDEs provide better autocomplete suggestions.

Using TypeScript in a React component clearly communicates the valid data types for each prop. This creates self-documenting code that helps other developers understand the code, which makes the code easier to maintain.

There are also some costs associated with TypeScript. First, since specifying types requires some additional code, TypeScript is more verbose than JavaScript. Second, there may be a learning curve for any developers who aren't familiar with TypeScript.

In summary, using TypeScript provides the following benefits and costs.

Benefits of TypeScript

- It catches errors earlier.
- It improves autocomplete suggestions.
- It creates self-documenting code.

Costs of TypeScript

- It's more verbose.
- Some developers might need time to learn it.

For larger projects, the benefits typically outweigh the costs. As a result, TypeScript has strong community support and is used by many large organizations.

Set up a React project to use TypeScript

To set up a React project to use TypeScript, you can run the "npm create" command shown in chapter 1 and select TypeScript instead of JavaScript. Or, you can use the command shown next to specify the react-ts template.

The command for creating a React project that uses TypeScript

```
npm create vite@latest my-react-app -- --template react-ts
```

A React project that uses TypeScript has several key differences from a plain React project. First, TypeScript files use the extensions of .ts and .tsx, not .js and .jsx. Second, using TypeScript adds several configuration files to a React project as summarized next.

TypeScript configuration files

File	Description
tsconfig.json	Main TypeScript configuration file for the project.
tsconfig.app.json	Specific TypeScript configuration for a React app.
tsconfig.node.json	Specific TypeScript configuration for build tools and Node.js.
vite-env.d.ts	Type definitions for Vite-specific features.

Of these files, this chapter shows how to work with the tsconfig.app.json file.

A function that specifies data types

A common way to use TypeScript is to add type annotations to the parameter list of a function. In the example that follows, TypeScript specifies that the getGreeting() function expects a name argument of the string type and an age argument of the number type.

A function with type annotations in the parameter list

```
export const getGreeting = (name: string, age: number) => {
    return `Hello ${name}! You are ${age} years old`;
};
```

Here, the parameter list of the function specifies the name and data type for each parameter. To do that, it separates the name and data type with a colon.

You can also add type annotations to specify the return value of a function, as shown next.

A function with a return type annotation

```
export const getGreeting = (name: string, age: number): string => {
    return `Hello ${name}! You are ${age} years old`;
};
```

Here, the parameter list is followed by the return type of the function, separated by a colon. If the function doesn't return a value, you annotate it with the void return type, as shown next.

A function that doesn't return a value

```
export const displayGreeting = (name: string, age: number): void => {
    console.log(`Hello ${name}! You are ${age} years old`);
};
```

Code that uses an incorrect data type

The following illustrates what happens if a component attempts to use the getGreeting() function but specifies the wrong type of data for the age parameter.

A component that passes the wrong data type to a function

```
import { getGreeting } from './utils/greeting';

const Greeting = () => {
  const name = 'John Doe';
  const age = 'ten';   // Error - should be a number

  return <h2>{getGreeting(name, age)}</h2>;
};

export default Greeting;
```

Without TypeScript, you might not notice this error until runtime, potentially causing the app to crash or the component to display incorrectly.

Use VS Code to view type errors

With TypeScript, VS Code displays a squiggly red line under type errors immediately as shown next.

Code in VS Code with a type error

```
return <h2>{getGreeting(name, age)}</h2>;
```

If you hover the mouse over the red line, VS Code displays the following error.

A type error displayed by VS Code

```
Argument of type 'string' is not assignable to parameter of type
'number'. ts(2345)

const age: "ten"
View Problem (Alt+F8)   Quick Fix... (Ctrl+.)   ✖ Fix (Ctrl+I)
```

Here, the error message shows that the code attempted to assign a string to a parameter that expects a number. Similarly, if the component doesn't pass the age parameter at all, VS Code displays an error like the one shown next.

Another type error displayed by VS Code

```
Expected 2 arguments, but got 1. ts(2554)

greeting.ts(5, 44): An argument for 'age' was not provided.

(alias) getGreeting(name: string, age: number): string
import getGreeting
View Problem (Alt+F8)   Quick Fix... (Ctrl+.)   ✖ Fix (Ctrl+I)
```

This early error detection becomes increasingly valuable as your app grows. When you have dozens of components passing data between each other, TypeScript makes sure that data flows correctly throughout your component tree and alerts you immediately if any data doesn't match the expected type.

Use the command line to check for type errors

If you want to manually check your project for type issues, you can run the following command.

A command that checks for type issues

```
npx tsc --noEmit -p tsconfig.app.json
```

Here, the "npx tsc" command calls the *TypeScript compiler*. This allows the compiler to check for type issues. However, the --noEmit flag specifies not to actually compile the files. That way, you can check if there are any type issues without compiling files for production use.

The last argument, "-p tsconfig.app.json", specifies the config file to use. You don't need to worry about what's in the config file for now since the default configuration works well. Just know that this file tells the compiler where to look for your code.

When you run this command and your project contains TypeScript errors, the Terminal displays those errors as shown next.

A type error displayed in the Terminal

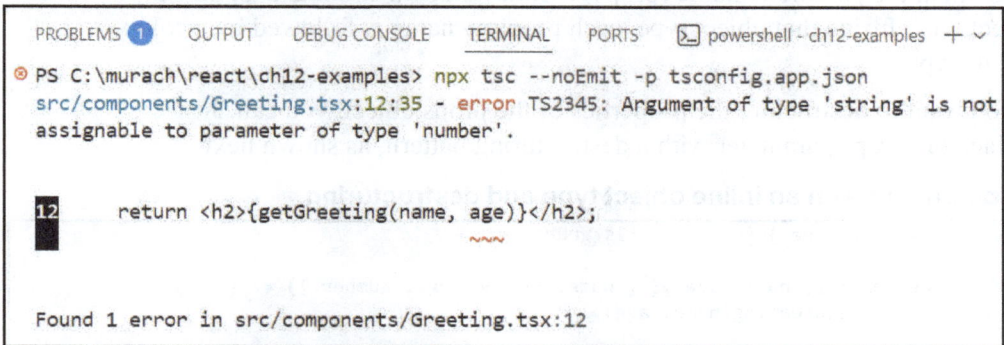

```
PROBLEMS 1    OUTPUT    DEBUG CONSOLE    TERMINAL    PORTS    powershell - ch12-examples  + ∨

⊘ PS C:\murach\react\ch12-examples> npx tsc --noEmit -p tsconfig.app.json
  src/components/Greeting.tsx:12:35 - error TS2345: Argument of type 'string' is not
  assignable to parameter of type 'number'.

  12      return <h2>{getGreeting(name, age)}</h2>;
                                        ~~~


  Found 1 error in src/components/Greeting.tsx:12
```

Since it's easy to view type errors in VS Code, you may think that there's no reason to use this command. That's often true. However, using the command line can be useful for larger projects because it provides a quick way to check all files in the project with a single command.

How to specify types in components

In a React app, you can use TypeScript to specify the correct types for your components. This helps you define exactly what type of data your components expect, what they return, and how they should be used.

Specify the prop type inline

A React component always receives a single props object, so you can't annotate primitive parameters directly like you saw in the previous example. Instead, you define an inline *object type* and add type annotations to its properties. Then, you use that object type as the type annotation of the props parameter.

For example, the following shows how to add inline type annotations for a Greeting component with name and age props.

A component with an inline object type for the props object

```
import { getGreeting } from './utils/greeting';

const Greeting = (props: { name: string, age: number }) => {
  return <h2>{getGreeting(props.name, props.age)}</h2>;
};

export default Greeting;
```

Here, the Greeting component specifies the type of the props object it receives. To do that, the parameter name (props) is followed by a colon and an inline object type. Inside that object type, each property name is followed by a colon and its type.

If you want to destructure the properties of the props object, you can. Just replace the props parameter with a destructuring pattern, as shown next.

A component with an inline object type and destructuring

```
import { getGreeting } from './utils/greeting';

const Greeting = ({ name, age }: { name: string, age: number }) => {
  return <h2>{getGreeting(name, age)}</h2>;
};

export default Greeting;
```

Here, the destructuring pattern extracts the name and age properties from the props object. The destructuring pattern is followed by a colon and the same object type used in the last example.

Specify the prop type with an interface

So far, you've only seen inline type annotations. However, if your component has more than one or two parameters, inline annotations can get messy fast. In addition, if you have the same parameters in multiple components, inline annotations lead to code duplication.

Luckily, TypeScript allows you to define an *interface* that specifies the name and type for each of the props of a component. When you define a props interface, you specify the types your component expects to receive. This makes your components more predictable and easier to use correctly. The following example presents a Greeting component that uses an interface.

A component with an interface

```
import { getGreeting } from "../utils/greeting";

interface GreetingProps {
    name: string;
    age: number;
    showAge: boolean;
}

const Greeting = ({ name, age, showAge }: GreetingProps) => {
    return <h2>{getGreeting(name, age, showAge)}</h2>;
};

export default Greeting;
```

Here, the code begins by defining an interface named GreetingProps that specifies the name and type for each of the props of the Greeting component. To do that, it separates the name and type with a colon. Then, the Greeting component uses a colon to specify that it expects its props to use the types specified by the GreetingProps interface.

This interface serves as a contract that defines the *shape* of data the component expects. In particular, it expects an object with a name prop of the string type, an age prop of the number type, and a showAge prop of the Boolean type. This shows how to specify the three most common primitive types in JavaScript: number, string, and boolean.

Specify the prop type with a type alias

In addition to an interface, you can also use the type keyword to create a *type alias*. For instance, here's GreetingsProp defined as a type alias.

The GreetingProps type

```
type GreetingProps = {
    name: string;
    age: number;
    showAge: boolean;
}
```

This syntax is similar to the syntax for an interface. However, type aliases can do more than interfaces. They can represent function types, union types, conditional types, and mapped types. While some of these types are beyond the scope of this book, this chapter shows how to use function types and union types a little later.

At this point, you may be wondering when to use inline type annotations, interfaces, and type aliases. Generally, you use inline typing for simple, one-off situations like a component with one parameter that doesn't need to be reused. You use interfaces for clear, well-defined objects, such as props objects. And you use type aliases for everything else.

Specify optional and union props

To this point, this chapter has presented interfaces and type aliases that require all specified props to have a valid value. In the real world, however, components often need more flexibility. For example, components may need to support optional props as shown in the next example.

An optional prop

```
age?: number;    // optional, defaults to undefined
```

Here, the code marks the age prop as being optional. To do that, it adds a question mark to the end of the prop name. When you mark a prop as optional, the value defaults to undefined if a value is not provided.

If you need to allow a prop to be one of multiple types, you can use the pipe symbol (|) to create a *union property* as shown in the next example.

A union prop

```
id: number | string;
```

This union property allows the variable to be either a string or a number. If a value other than a string or number is assigned to the variable, such as a Boolean, that causes a type error.

One common union property is the *string literal union*. A string literal union is a string type that must be one of the strings in the specified list. The following Button component shows how this works.

A Button component that allows three sizes

```
interface ButtonProps {
  size: 'small' | 'medium' | 'large';
  children: string;
}

const Button = ({ size, children }: ButtonProps) => (
  <button className={`btn-${size}`}>
    {children}
  </button>
);

export default Button;
```

This allows the size prop for a Button to be set to one of the three predefined values. For instance, in the following example, the first Button component specifies a valid value of "large" for the size prop. However, the second Button component specifies an invalid value of "tiny" for the size prop.

Valid and invalid Button components

```
<Button size="large">Click Me</Button> {/* valid */}
<Button size="tiny">Click Me</Button>  {/* invalid, not an allowed value */}
```

As a result, the second Button component causes a type error.

Specify union types

You just saw how to use the pipe symbol to create a union property. You can also use it to create a *union type*. This is a type alias that allows more than one possible shape.

For example, the following type alias allows an object to have one of two possible shapes. Then, the Greeting component uses this type alias to make sure its props object matches one of those shapes.

The Greeting component with a union type

```
// union type - props must be one of the specified object shapes
type GreetingProps =
    { mode: 'short', name: string } |                    // first shape
    { mode: 'long', firstName: string, lastName: string }; // second shape

const Greeting = (props: GreetingProps) => {
    if (props.mode === 'short') {     // first shape
        return <h2>Hello, {props.name}!</h2>;
    } else {                          // second shape
        return <h2>Hello, {props.firstName} {props.lastName}!</h2>;
    }
};

export default Greeting;
```

Here, the first allowed shape of the GreetingProps type has a mode property with a value of 'short' and a name property of the string type. If the props object matches this shape, the code in the if statement executes.

The second allowed shape of the GreetingProps type has a mode property with a value of 'long' and firstName and lastName properties of the string type. If the props object matches this shape, the code in the else statement executes.

With a union type, you know that if a conditional branch matches an allowed shape, you can safely use the props of that shape. By contrast, optional props don't provide the same guarantees because some, all, or none of the optional props could exist.

There are two main differences between union types and union properties. The first is where they're applied. A union type, sometimes called an *object-level union*, determines the overall shape of the object. A union property, by contrast, doesn't change the shape of the object. That is, the property key always exists, but the type of the value assigned to that key can vary.

The second difference is where they can be used. A union property can be used with both type aliases and interfaces. A union type, by contrast, can only be a type alias.

Specify a type for the children prop

For some components, you may want to specify the type for the children prop. For example, the string type works well enough for the Button component presented earlier. However, this only allows the component's children to be of the string type, not other types of content such as HTML elements. To allow a component to render other types of data, you can use the following React types.

Two types for working with children props

Type	Description
React.ReactNode	Any type of content that can be rendered by React. In other words, a single React element, multiple React elements, a string, a number, a null value, and so on.
React.ReactElement	One React element only. Not multiple React elements, a string, a number, or a null value.

In this table, a "React element" can be either an HTML element like <div> or a React component like <Header>. The most common and flexible way to specify a type for children is to use the ReactNode type as shown next.

A Card component that accepts any valid React content

```
interface CardProps {
  title: string;
  children: React.ReactNode;
}

const Card = ({ title, children }: CardProps) => (
```

```
  <div className="card">
    <h3>{title}</h3>
    {children}
  </div>
);

export default Card;
```

Since this code sets the type for the children prop to ReactNode, the Card component can wrap any valid React content as shown in the following examples.

The Card component with one child element

```
<Card title="User Information">
    <UserProfile user={user} showEmail onEdit={handleEdit} />
</Card>
```

The Card component with two child elements

```
<Card title="Quick Actions">
    <button>Edit Profile</button>
    <button>Delete User</button>
</Card>
```

The Card component with a child that's a string

```
<Card title="Hello!">Welcome to my app!</Card>
```

The Card component with zero child elements

```
<Card title="No Children" />
```

These examples show that the ReactNode type allows React to render whatever is passed to the child, a single element, multiple elements, a string, or a null value. Since this permissive and flexible approach works well for most situations, it's usually a good starting point for specifying a type for the children prop.

However, if you want to restrict the type for the children prop, you can use the ReactElement type. The following examples show several ways you can use it.

Restrict the content that's allowed for the children prop

```
// A single React element (not multiple elements, strings, numbers, null, etc)
children: React.ReactElement;

// Multiple React elements (not a single element, strings, numbers, null, etc)
children: React.ReactElement[];

// One or more React elements (not strings, numbers, null, etc)
children: React.ReactElement | React.ReactElement[];

// Zero or more React elements (not strings, numbers, etc)
children: null | React.ReactElement | React.ReactElement[];
```

By itself, the ReactElement type allows one and only one React element. However, you can add square brackets ([]) to the end of this type to allow an array that stores two or more elements, you can use the pipe symbol (|) to create a union type that combines multiple types, and you can use the null keyword to allow zero elements.

Specify a function type for a prop

Up until now, you've seen type annotations for primitive values and objects. However, you can also add type annotations for functions. These are called *function types*, and they describe the shape a function must have: the parameters it accepts and the value it returns.

In the next example, User and UserProfileProps interfaces specify the props for a UserProfile component. The UserProfileProps interface defines three props: a user prop of the User type, a showEmail prop of the boolean type, and an onEdit prop that's a function type.

The UserProfile component

```
interface User {
  id: number;
  name: string;
  email: string;
}

interface UserProfileProps {
  user: User;
  showEmail: boolean;
  onEdit: (user: User, showEmail: boolean) => void;
}

const UserProfile = ({ user, showEmail, onEdit }: UserProfileProps) => (
  <div className="user-profile">
    <h2>{user.name}</h2>
    {showEmail && <p>{user.email}</p>}
    <button onClick={() => (onEdit(user, showEmail))}>Edit Profile</button>
  </div>
);

export default UserProfile;
```

Here, the onEdit prop specifies a function that accepts two arguments and returns no value. To start, the code specifies the name for each argument, a colon, and the type for each argument. Then, it specifies void for the return type to indicate that the function has no return value.

The previous example presents an inline function type, but you can use an interface or a type alias, too, as shown next.

An interface for a function type

```
interface OnEditFn {
  (user: User, showEmail: boolean): void;
}
```

```
  }

interface UserProfileProps {
  user: User;
  showEmail: boolean;
  onEdit: OnEditFn;
}
```

A type alias for a function type

```
type OnEditFn = (user: User, showEmail: boolean) => void;

interface UserProfileProps {
  user: User;
  showEmail: boolean;
  onEdit: OnEditFn;
}
```

When you define a separate interface or type alias for a function type, you can reuse it in other components or functions that require the same signature.

You can use either an interface or a type alias for a function type, but most developers prefer type aliases. That's because the syntax of a type alias resembles the function it defines the type for.

More skills for using TypeScript

As you build React apps with TypeScript, there are some patterns that you can follow to help you write better code. These patterns help you address challenges you'll face as your apps grow.

Store a type in a separate file

As your React apps grow, organizing the types that you define with TypeScript becomes increasingly important. If only one component uses the type, it's common to define it locally in the same file as the component, as shown in the previous examples. However, if multiple components need to access a type, you can store that type in a separate .ts file that can be imported when needed.

For example, the following shows the GreetingProps interface stored in a separate file. Files like this are often stored in a directory named types.

The GreetingProps.ts file

```
export interface GreetingProps {
    name: string;
    age: number;
    showAge: boolean;
}
```

To use a type in a separate file, you import it with the type keyword, as shown next.

Import the GreetingProps interface

```
import type { GreetingProps } from "../types/GreetingProps";
```

It's important to note that you use the type keyword regardless of whether the type in the separate file is defined as an interface or a type alias.

Extend a type

You can create a new type that builds on an existing type. Then, the new type automatically includes all the properties of the existing one, so you only need to define properties that are new. This helps you avoid code duplication and keep your component types consistent.

To extend an interface, you use the extends keyword, as shown next.

Extend the GreetingProps interface

```
import { getGreeting } from "../utils/greeting";
import type { GreetingProps } from "../types/GreetingProps";

interface IntlGreetingProps extends GreetingProps {
    language: string;
}

const IntlGreeting = ({ name, age, showAge, language }: IntlGreetingProps) => {
    const greeting = getGreeting(name, age, showAge);
    if (language === 'fr') {
        const frenchGreeting = greeting.replace('Hello', 'Bonjour');
        return <h2>{frenchGreeting}</h2>;
    }
    return <h2>{greeting}</h2>;
};

export default IntlGreeting;
```

Here, the IntlGreeting component that imports the GreetingProp interface needs to add an additional language prop to it. To do that, it uses the extends keyword to build on the existing GreetingProps interface and add the new language property. Then, the IntlGreeting component uses the new IntlGreetingProps interface in its type annotation.

To extend a type alias, you use the *intersection operator* (&), as shown next.

Extend the GreetingsProp type alias

```
import { getGreeting } from "../utils/greeting";
import type { GreetingProps } from "../types/GreetingProps";

type IntlGreetingProps = GreetingProps & {
    language: string;
};

// IntlGreeting function is same as previous example
```

Here, the intersection operator (&) creates a new type alias that adds an additional property to an existing type. You can use the intersection operator with either type aliases or interfaces. For example, this code works whether GreetingProps is defined as a type alias or an interface.

By contrast, the extends keyword only works with interfaces. In other words, you can't use the extends keyword to extend a type alias.

Omit or pick props from a type

When you extend a type, the new type inherits all the properties of the existing type. However, you may only want a subset of those properties. TypeScript provides the Pick and Omit *utility types* shown next to help you do that.

Two utility types

Type	Description
`Omit<Type, Keys>`	Creates a new type by removing the specified props from a type.
`Pick<Type, Keys>`	Creates a new type by selecting only the specified props from a type.

The Omit utility type takes two parameters. The Type parameter specifies the original type that you want to modify and the Keys parameter specifies a string or a union of strings for the prop names to exclude. The next example shows how you can use Omit to remove two props from the User interface to create a new type named UserMin.

Omit two props from a type

```
// Original type
interface User {
  id: number;
  name: string;
  email: string;
  createdAt: string;
}

// New type (omit id and createdAt)
type UserMin = Omit<User, 'id' | 'createdAt'>;
```

This code omits two props from the User type. To do that, the Omit utility specifies the User type as its first argument and a union of prop names as the second argument.

When you use Omit, you should be aware of a few pitfalls. The first is that TypeScript doesn't provide warnings if you attempt to omit a non-existent prop. As a result, if you misspell a prop, you might not realize that until later. Consider the next example.

Code that fails to omit a prop

```
type UserMin = Omit<User, 'id' | 'createdat'>;  // error, should be createdAt
```

Here, the capitalization for the createdAt prop is incorrect, so TypeScript doesn't omit that prop, and it doesn't display a warning. As a result, the UserMin type still includes the createAt prop, which probably isn't what you intended.

Another pitfall is that the Omit utility is *shallow*. In other words, it doesn't work with nested props.

The Pick utility works like Omit in reverse. It creates a new type containing only the props that you pick. For example, you can create the same UserMin type created earlier with the Pick utility as shown next.

Pick two props from a type

```
type UserMin = Pick<User, 'name' | 'email'>;
```

Here, the Pick utility specifies the names of the props that you want to keep. Pick has some of the same pitfalls as Omit when it comes to nonexistent props. As a result, make sure to use proper spelling and capitalization when specifying prop names.

Since the Pick and Omit utilities work similarly, you can use whichever results in the shortest code. So, if you only need a few props from the base type, you should use Pick. Or, if you need most of the props from the base type, you should use Omit. If you need roughly half of the props, using Pick typically makes your code easier to read. In all cases, you can use Pick and Omit to modify an interface or a type alias, but the resulting type must be a type alias.

Specify a type for an event object

React also allows you to use TypeScript to specify a type for an event object in an event handler. To do that, you can use the following types.

Some types for event objects

Type	Event object for
React.ChangeEvent<element>	Change events such as the onChange event for input elements such as <input>, <textarea>, and <select>.
React.FormEvent<element>	Form events such as onSubmit.
React.MouseEvent<element>	Mouse events such as onClick, onMouseDown, and onMouseUp.
React.DragEvent<element>	Drag events such as onDragStart, onDragEnter, onDragOver, and onDragEnd.
React.KeyboardEvent<element>	Keyboard events such as onKeyDown and onKeyUp.

These types are known as *generic types* because they allow you to use the angle brackets to specify the type of HTML element they work with. As a result, these types can be made more specific for different elements.

Unlike Pick and Omit, which are built-in TypeScript utility types, the types in this table come from React's TypeScript type definitions. In other words, TypeScript defines Pick and Omit, while React defines the types shown here.

To get an idea of how these types work, consider the following code.

A form that uses two event object types

```
import { useState } from 'react';

const SimpleForm = () => {
  const [name, setName] = useState('');

  const handleNameChange = (e: React.ChangeEvent<HTMLInputElement>) => {
    setName(e.target.value);
  };

  const handleSubmit = (e: React.FormEvent<HTMLFormElement>) => {
    e.preventDefault();
    console.log('Submitted:', name);
  };

  return (
    <form onSubmit={handleSubmit}>
      <label>Name:</label>
      <input value={name} onChange={handleNameChange} />
      <button>Submit</button>
    </form>
  );
};

export default SimpleForm;
```

Here, the ChangeEvent<> type specifies that the event object named e is for the onChange event of an HMTL <input> element. The main benefit of specifying the type of the event object is that it helps to identify errors that occur if you attempt to use properties that don't exist for the event object. In this case, the code uses the e.target.value property, which exists. As a result, it doesn't cause a type error. However, if you attempted to enter an invalid property or method, a type error would occur, and you could fix it right away.

Similarly, the FormEvent<> type specifies that the event object named e is for the onSubmit event of an HTML <form> element. In this case, the code calls the e.preventDefault() method, which is valid for the form event. As a result, it doesn't cause a type error.

When specifying the type for an event object, you need to specify the HTML element for the event handler. To do that, you need to know how the HTML elements correspond to the DOM interfaces. The following table presents some common elements and their corresponding DOM interfaces.

How HTML elements compare to the DOM interfaces

Element	DOM interface
`<input>`	`HTMLInputElement`
`<textarea>`	`HTMLTextAreaElement`
`<select>`	`HTMLSelectElement`
`<form>`	`HTMLFormElement`
`<button>`	`HTMLButtonElement`
`<div>`	`HTMLDivElement`
`<img>`	`HTMLImageElement`
`<a>`	`HTMLAnchorElement`
`<p>`	`HTMLParagraphElement`
Any element	`HTMLElement`

The names of the DOM interfaces follow a pattern. As a result, you can usually guess the correct name of a DOM interface based on the name of the HTML element. However, there are a few exceptions such as the <a> element corresponding with the HTMLAnchorElement.

When specifying the ChangeEvent<> and KeyboardEvent<> types, you typically specify a DOM interface for the <input>, <textarea>, or <select> elements. Similarly, when specifying a FormEvent<> type, you typically specify the DOM interface for a <form> element.

When specifying the MouseEvent<> or DragEvent<> types, you can specify many different HTML elements, but the element should correspond with what you expect the user to interact with. For example, if you expect the user to interact with a <div> element, you can specify the DOM interface for that element. However, if you want to allow the user to interact with anything in the component, or if you're unsure of what you want the user to interact with, you can specify HTMLElement.

Specify a type for a built-in hook

React's built-in hooks like useState and useRef support generic types. As a result, you can use generics to specify the data type for these functions.

With the useState hook, you can specify the type for the state variable by enclosing the type in angle brackets (<>) just before the parentheses in the useState() function as shown next.

Use generics to specify a type for a state variable

```
// TypeScript can infer these types, so the generics aren't necessary
const [count, setCount] = useState<number>(0);        // initial number
const [name, setName] = useState<string>('');         // initial string
```

```
// TypeScript can't infer these types, so the generics are necessary
const [user, setUser] = useState<User | null>(null);   // initial null
const [movies, setMovies] = useState<Movies[]>([]);     // initial empty array
```

If possible, TypeScript infers the data type based on the initial value for the state variable. For instance, in the previous example, TypeScript can infer that the variable in the first statement is of the number type and the variable in the second statement is of the string type. As a result, it isn't necessary to use generics to specify these types, but you can if you want.

However, if you supply an initial value of null or an empty array, TypeScript can't infer the data type. In those cases, you can specify a type as shown in the third and fourth statements. For instance, the third statement specifies that the user variable must be null or of the User type, and the fourth statement specifies that the movies variable must be an array of Movie objects.

You can use a similar technique to specify the type for the useRef hook when the ref is used to store a value between renders. That is, TypeScript can infer the type from the initial value, or you can provide a generic if needed, as shown next.

Type a reference that stores a value between renders

```
const countRef = useRef(0);                // infer number type
const userRef = useRef<User | null>(null); // explicitly typed
```

However, when a ref points to a DOM element, you typically use one of the DOM interfaces to specify a type of HTML element, as shown next.

Type a reference that points to a DOM element

```
const inputRef = useRef<HTMLInputElement>(null);
```

Here, the constant named inputRef must be an <input> element. However, it's initialized with null because the DOM element doesn't exist until after the first render. The generic HTMLInputElement tells TypeScript that the ref will eventually point to an <input> element, which enables proper type checking when accessing that element's properties.

Use generic types in your own code

Besides using generic types when working with built-in hooks, you can also use generics for working with your own hooks and even functions. To do that, it's a common pattern to define a generic type named T. For example, the following function uses a generic type named T to allow the consumer of the function to specify the type of data that's returned by the function.

A function that has a generic type

```
async function fetchData<T>(url: string): Promise<T> {
  const response = await fetch(url);
  if (!response.ok) {
```

```
      throw new Error(`HTTP error! status: ${response.status}`);
  }
  return response.json();
}
```

As a result, the code that uses this function can specify the type of data that the function should return as shown next.

Use the function with two different types of data

```
const users = await fetchData<User[]>(baseURL + '/users');
const posts = await fetchData<Post[]>(baseURL + '/posts');
```

Here, the first statement specifies that the fetchData() function must return an array of User objects, and the second statement specifies that the fetchData() function must return an array of Post objects.

To keep things simple, the previous two examples just show how to work with a function, not a hook. However, you can apply the same concept to your own custom hooks or to your own components.

The Movie List app

So far, this chapter has presented a solid foundation in TypeScript skills. Now, it shows how you can apply these skills to a modified version of the Movie List app from chapter 6.

The directory structure for the app is mostly the same as the app from chapter 6. However, the TypeScript version adds a types directory as shown below.

The directory structure

```
src
    components (Same as chapter 6 but with .tsx extensions)
        common
        layout
        movies
    hooks (Same as chapter 6 but with .ts extensions)
    types
        DragAndDrop.ts
        Movie.ts
        Quote.ts
```

The types directory contains files that define Movie and Quote types, as well as a file that contains a function type for working with drag and drop events. In addition, since this is a TypeScript project, the files for components that contain TypeScript and JSX use an extension of .tsx, not .jsx. Similarly, files that only contain TypeScript use an extension of .ts, not .js.

The common folder

The common folder contains reusable UI components such as FormButtons, FormInput, and Icon. The FormButtons component uses an interface to define the types for its props as shown next.

The FormButtons component

```
...
interface FormButtonsProps {
    isEditing: boolean;
    isDeleting: boolean;
    onCancel: () => void;
}

const FormButtons = ({ isEditing, isDeleting, onCancel }: FormButtonsProps) => (
...
```

This code makes sure the isEditing and isDeleting properties are of the Boolean type, and it makes sure the onCancel property is a function that takes no parameters and returns nothing.

Similarly, the FormInput component uses an interface to specify types for its props as shown next.

The FormInput component

```
...
interface FormInputProps extends React.InputHTMLAttributes<HTMLInputElement> {
    label: string;
    name: string;
    value: string;
    onChange: (e: React.ChangeEvent<HTMLInputElement>) => void;
    ref?: React.Ref<HTMLInputElement>;
}

const FormInput =
    ({ label, name, value, onChange, ref, ...props } : FormInputProps) => (
...
```

Here, the props interface begins by extending an interface that specifies all attributes for the HTML <input> element. This makes it possible to check the types of the attributes that may be passed as part of the …props parameter.

Within the props interface, the first three props specify that the label, name, and value props should be of the string type. The fourth prop specifies that the onChange prop should be a function that handles the onChange event of an <input> element. And the fifth prop specifies that the ref prop is optional but should be a reference to an <input> element.

The Icon component also uses an interface to specify the types for its props.

The Icon component

```
...
interface IconProps extends React.HTMLAttributes<HTMLElement> {
    title: string;
    className: string;
    onClick?: React.MouseEventHandler<HTMLButtonElement>;
}

const Icon = ({ title, className, onClick, ...props }: IconProps) => {
...
```

This interface begins by extending an interface that provides attributes for any HTML element. This provides some type safety for its ...props attribute. It can't be more specific because this component returns a <button> element for clickable icons, and an <i> element for decorative icons.

Within the interface, the first two props specify that the title and className props must be of the string type. Then, the third prop specifies that each icon can optionally include an event handler for the onClick event of a clickable icon.

The layout folder

The layout folder contains the components for the layout of the app. These components define the header, footer, sidebar, and main content areas.

The Header component uses an inline type annotation to specify a single prop of the string type as shown next.

The Header component

```
...
const Header = ({ text }: { text: string }) => (
...
```

The Footer component could also use an inline type annotation, since it only has two props. However, to keep things readable, it uses an interface, as shown next.

The Footer component

```
...
interface FooterProps {
    text: string;
    children?: React.ReactNode;
}

const Footer = ({ text, children }: FooterProps) => (
...
```

Like the Header component, the interface for Footer specifies a prop of the string type. However, it also specifies the ReactNode type for the children prop.

This allows the Footer component to wrap any valid React content.

The Main and Sidebar components shown next each use an inline type annotation to specify a children prop that can represent any valid React content.

The Main component

```
...
const Main = ({ children }: { children: React.ReactNode }) => (
...
```

The Sidebar component

```
...
const Sidebar = ({ children }: { children: React.ReactNode }) => (
...
```

The types folder

The components in the common and layout folders use existing types. However, the components in the movies folder need some custom types. So, before reviewing those components, this section introduces the types they use, which are defined in files in the types folder.

The Movie.ts file uses an interface to define the Movie and SelectedMovie types and a type alias to define a function type, as shown next.

The Movie.ts file

```
// type that represents a movie
export interface Movie {
    id: number;
    name: string;
    year: number;
}

// type that represents a movie that's selected for an action
export interface SelectedMovie extends Movie {
    mode: 'edit' | 'delete';
}

// function type for when a movie is selected
export type OnMovieSelect = (movie: Movie, mode: 'edit' | 'delete') => void;
```

The Movie type specifies three props: an id of the number type, a name of the string type, and a year of the number type. The SelectedMovie type extends Movie and adds a mode property that's a string literal union property. This means it only accepts a string that's in the specified list.

The OnMovieSelect type specifies a function that accepts two parameters and has no return value. The first parameter is of the Movie type, and the second is the same string literal union property as SelectedMovie.

The Quote.ts file uses a type alias to build on the Movie type to define the Quote type for a quote about a movie. To do that, it imports the Movie type, as shown next.

The Quote.ts file

```
import type { Movie } from './Movie';

// use a property from Movie and add new ones
export type Quote = Pick<Movie, 'year'> & {
    movie: string;
    quote: string;
}
```

The Quote type uses the Pick utility to include the year property from the Movie type. Then, it uses the intersection operator to add two new properties, the movie name and the quote. Both new properties are of the string type.

In this example, it might not seem worth it to build on the Movie type, since only one property is used. However, this approach keeps the shared property in sync. For example, if the year property in Movie changes from the number type to a custom type, it will automatically change in Quote as well.

The Movie.ts and Quote.ts files contain types that represent specific *entities*, sometimes called *domain entities*. That is, Movie.ts contains types that represent movies, and Quote.ts contains a type that represents movie quotes.

By contrast, the DragAndDrop.ts file doesn't contain a type that represents an entity. Rather, it contains a generic function type used to handle drop events, as shown next.

The DragAndDrop.ts file

```
export type OnDrop<T> = (from: T, to: T) => void;
```

Here, OnDrop<T> represents a generic event handler, not a domain entity. That's why it's in its own file. By contrast, the OnMovieSelect event handler presented earlier is domain-specific. That is, it's tied to the Movie entity. That's why it belongs in the same file as the Movie type.

The movies folder

The movies folder contains the code that renders the main content of the app.

The MovieForm component demonstrates several important TypeScript techniques.

The MovieForm component

```
...
import type { FormEvent } from "react";
import type { Movie, SelectedMovie } from "../../types/Movie";
```

```
// function types for form handlers (optional - improves readability)
type OnMovieAddEdit = (movie: Movie) => void;
type OnMovieDelete = (id: number) => void;
type OnCancel = () => void;

interface MovieFormProps {
    selectedMovie: SelectedMovie | null;
    onAdd: OnMovieAddEdit;
    onEdit: OnMovieAddEdit;
    onDelete: OnMovieDelete;
    onCancel: OnCancel;
}

const MovieForm = ({ selectedMovie, onAdd, onEdit, onDelete,
                     onCancel }: MovieFormProps) => {
    // state variables
    const [name, setName] = useState('');          // infer string type
    const [year, setYear] = useState('');          // infer string type

    // useRef to manage focus on name field
    const nameRef = useRef<HTMLInputElement>(null);    // explicitly type
    ...
    const handleSubmit = (e: FormEvent<HTMLFormElement>) => {
...
```

To start, this component imports the FormEvent type from React. This is a TypeScript type provided by React that represents the object that's automatically passed to form event handlers like onSubmit or onChange. It's a generic type, so you can specify the HTML element that triggers the event. Then, it imports the Movie and SelectedMovie types from the Movies.ts file.

Next, the file defines three function types for form handlers. The OnMovieAddEdit type accepts an argument of the Movie type, the OnMovieDelete type accepts a movie id of the number type, and the OnCancel type has no arguments. All three function types have no return value.

These function types are used as type annotations in the MovieFormProps interface. Since they are only used in this interface, they could be defined inline. However, defining them separately improves readability. In addition, if another component later needs a function type with the same signature, it's easy to move the type to the types folder to be reused.

Within the MovieForm component, the types of the state variables are inferred from the initial values passed to the useState() function. By contrast, the ref is explicitly typed to refer to an HTMLInputElement.

Finally, the FormEvent<HTMLFormElement> type is used to type the event object passed to the handleSubmit() function. This makes sure TypeScript knows the event comes from a <form> element, which provides type-safe access to form-specific properties and methods like currentTarget and preventDefault().

The MovieList component shown next also imports and uses the Movie type. In addition, it imports the OnMovieSelect and OnDrop function types.

The MovieList component

```
...
import type { Movie, OnMovieSelect } from "../../types/Movie";
import type { OnDrop } from "../../types/DragAndDrop";

interface MovieListProps {
    movies: Movie[];
    onSelect: OnMovieSelect;
    onReorder: OnDrop<Movie>;
}

const MovieList = ({ movies, onSelect, onReorder }: MovieListProps) => {
    // pass onReorder to the useDragAndDrop hook and get the object it returns
    const dnd = useDragAndDrop<Movie>(onReorder);
...
```

Here, the props interface uses Movie[] to define a movies prop that can store a list of Movie objects. The onSelect prop specifics the OnMovieSelect type, which accepts a Movie object and a mode union property. Finally, the onReorder prop specifies the OnDrop<Movie> type. When you pass Movie as the type argument to the generic OnDrop type, you *specialize* the generic type to Movie objects. So, the OnDrop<Movie> type accepts two objects of the Movie type.

The MovieListItem component uses a props interface to set the types for its props as shown next.

The MovieListItem component

```
...
import type { DragEventHandler } from 'react';
import type { Movie, OnMovieSelect } from "../../types/Movie";

interface MovieListItemProps {
    movie: Movie | null;
    onSelect?: OnMovieSelect;
    onDragStart?: DragEventHandler<HTMLLIElement>;
    onDragOver?: DragEventHandler<HTMLLIElement>;
    onDragEnter?: DragEventHandler<HTMLLIElement>;
    onDragEnd?: DragEventHandler<HTMLLIElement>;
}

const MovieListItem = ({ movie, onSelect, onDragStart, onDragOver,
    onDragEnter, onDragEnd }: MovieListItemProps) => (
...
```

This props interface defines a movie prop that's null or of the Movie type. Then, it defines function types for the event handlers supported by the component. All of these event handlers are optional since they're not needed when the movie prop is null.

The onSelect prop specifies the OnMovieSelect type. Then, the drag event handlers use the DragEventHandler to specify a function type for working with an <li> element.

To make it easier to code these function types, this code imports the DragEventHandler from the React library. That way, you don't need to code React before DragEventHandler.

The MovieQuotes component imports the Quotes type and uses it to specify that the quotes prop should be an array of Quote objects.

The MovieQuotes component

```
...
import type { Quote } from '../../types/Quote';

const MovieQuotes = ({ quotes }: { quotes: Quote[] }) => {
...
```

The hooks folder

The hooks folder contains two custom hooks that can benefit from TypeScript. The useTimer hook specifies data types for both of its parameters.

The useTimer hook

```
export const useTimer = (
    onTick: () => void,
    tickInterval: number | null) => {
...
```

This code specifies that the onTick parameter must be a function that takes no arguments and returns nothing. Then, it specifies that the tickInterval parameter must be either a number or a null value.

The useDragAndDrop hook uses the generic type of T to allow it to work with any type of data while also providing type checking.

The useDragAndDrop.ts file

```
import { useRef } from "react";

import type { OnDrop } from "../types/DragAndDrop";

// Generic type parameter T for the item type being dragged
export const useDragAndDrop = <T>(onDrop: OnDrop<T>) => {

    const dragItem = useRef<T | null>(null);
    const dragOverItem = useRef<T | null>(null);

    const handleDragStart = (item: T) => {
        dragItem.current = item;
    };

    const handleDragEnter = (item: T) => {
```

```
        dragOverItem.current = item;
    };

    const handleDragOver = (e: React.DragEvent) => {
        e.preventDefault();
    };
...
```

To start, this hook imports the generic OnDrop type, which takes two items of the generic type T and returns nothing. Then it uses that type to specify that the onDrop event handler required by this hook takes two items of the same type and returns nothing.

Within the function for the useDragAndDrop hook, the useRef hook specifies that the two refs can store either an item of type T or null. The handlers for the dragstart and dragend events specify that they accept items of type T. And the handler for the dragover event uses TypeScript to specify that it accepts an object of the DragEvent type.

Since the useDragAndDrop hook uses generic types, code that calls the hook needs to specify the type. For example, the MovieList component that calls the useDragAndDrop hook specifies the Movie type. To do that, it uses angle brackets as shown next.

Code in MovieList that calls useDragAndDrop()

```
const dnd = useDragAndDrop<Movie>(onReorder);
```

This replaces all instances of T with Movie. As a result, TypeScript can check to make sure that the hook doesn't have any type errors.

The App component

The App component uses the Movie and SelectedMovie types, so it includes an import statement for them at the top of the file.

The import statement for the Movie and SelectedMovie types

```
import type { Movie, SelectedMovie } from './components/movies/Movie';
```

Within the App component, the state variables use generics to specify that the movies variable can store an array of Movie objects and the selectedMovie variable must be a SelectedMovie object or a null value.

The state variables

```
const App = () => {
    const [movies, setMovies] = useState<Movie[]>(moviesData);
    const [selectedMovie, setSelectedMovie] =
                        useState<SelectedMovie | null>(null);
```

Beyond that, the event handlers specify the types for their arguments. To start, the handleReorder() function takes two Movie objects as arguments.

The handleReorder() function

```
const handleReorder = (fromMovie: Movie, toMovie: Movie) => {
...
```

The handleAdd() function takes a Movie object as an argument.

The handleAdd() function

```
const handleAdd = (newMovie: Movie) => {
...
```

The handleSelect() function takes a Movie object and a string value of "edit" or "delete" as its arguments.

The handleSelect() function

```
const handleSelect = (movie: Movie, mode: 'edit' | 'delete') => {
...
```

The handleDelete() function takes a numeric id as an argument.

The handleDelete() function

```
const handleDelete = (id: number) => {
...
```

The handleEdit() function takes a Movie object as its argument.

The handleEdit() function

```
const handleEdit = (updatedMovie: Movie) => {
...
```

Perspective

This chapter has shown how to use TypeScript to add static typing to your React apps. The skills presented in this chapter can make development easier by helping you catch errors earlier, by improving autocomplete suggestions in your IDE, and by encouraging you to write code that's self-documenting. Because of these advantages, the use of TypeScript has been growing in recent years, especially for large projects. However, for smaller projects, many developers still prefer the simplicity of plain old JavaScript.

Terms

superset
static typing
TypeScript compiler
object type
interface

shape of data

type alias

union property

string literal union

union type

object-level union

function type

intersection operator

utility type

shallow

generic type

entity

domain entity

specialize a generic

Exercise 12-1: Add TypeScript to an app

Review the starting code

1. Open the my-playlist project in the ex_starts/ch12 folder. Note that it contains the TypeScript configuration files and that it uses the .tsx extension for files that define components that use JSX.

2. Install the dependencies for the app and run it to make sure it works correctly.

3. Open several of the .tsx files and note that their props have red squiggles. This is because they don't use TypeScript to specify types. Hover your mouse over a red squiggle and review the error message.

4. Use the command line to check for type errors. Note that the project contains many type errors.

Add types to the Header, Footer, and Input components

5. In the components folder, open the Footer.tsx file. Then, use an inline object type to specify the type for the prop. This should remove the error that's displayed.

6. Open the Header.tsx file and define a type alias named HeaderProps for its props. Then, specify that the props for the Header component should be of the HeaderProps type.

7. Open the Input.tsx file and provide types for its props. Make sure to provide for ...props by extending the InputHTMLAttributes type for an HTML <input> element.

Create the Song and SongForAdd types

8. In the src folder, create a folder named types.

9. Within the types folder, create a file named Song.ts.

10. Within the Song.ts file, create a Song type that specifies all of the properties that this app uses for a song.

11. Create a SongForAdd type. This type should have most of the properties of the Song type, but it should omit the id property.

Add types to the Playlist component

12. Open the Playlist.tsx file.

13. Import the Song type from the Song.ts file.

14. Provide types for the Playlist props. The songs prop should specify that it stores multiple objects of the Song type. The onDelete prop should specify that it accepts a function that accepts an id parameter and doesn't return any data.

15. Modify the code that maps each song so it uses a variable of the Song type.

Add types to the SongForm component

16. Open the SongForm.tsx file.

17. Import the SongForAdd type from the Song.ts file.

18. Provide types for the SongForm props so the onAdd and onCancel props specify the correct signatures for the event handlers. The onAdd property should have a parameter of the SongForAdd type. The onCancel property should not have any parameters. Neither event handler should return any data.

19. Note that the year variable for the state uses the string type, even though the year prop for a song uses the number type. To account for that, find the onAdd() event handler and modify the code so it converts the year variable to a number before setting it in the song object.

20. For the event object of the submit event for the form, specify the FormEvent type for an HTML <form> element.

Add types to the App component

21. Open the App.tsx file.

22. Import the SongForAdd type from the Song.ts file.

23. Modify the handleAddSong() function so it specifies the SongForAdd type for its parameter.

24. Modify the handleDeleteSong() function so it specifies the number type for its parameter.

25. Use the command line to check for type errors. At this point, the project shouldn't contain any type errors. If it does, use the skills presented in this chapter to fix them.

Chapter 13

Unit test with Jest

Unit testing is an essential part of modern web development because it makes sure your code works as expected and continues to work as expected as your app changes. This chapter shows how to create automated unit tests for a React app using Jest and the React Testing Library.

An introduction to unit testing

Unit testing tests the individual units of a program. In React, this typically means testing functions, methods, and components to make sure they behave as expected. Unit tests are automated, which makes it easy to run them repeatedly. That way, you can run the tests after every significant code change to make sure the code still works as expected.

Some benefits of unit testing

Unit testing provides the following benefits. These benefits become increasingly important as your app grows.

Some benefits of unit testing

- **Improved code quality.** That's because unit tests encourage developers to create modular code that performs data validation and handles edge cases and errors.
- **Early bug detection.** Unit tests make it easier to find bugs early, before they can affect other parts of the codebase.
- **Easier modification and refactoring.** That's because unit tests provide a way to quickly make sure your changes don't break existing functionality or introduce bugs.
- **Easier debugging.** That's because a failing test gives you info about the bug that you can use to find and fix the bug.
- **Enhanced documentation.** That's because the descriptive names for the unit tests document the expected behavior of the code.
- **Enhanced collaboration.** When working on a team, unit tests help new developers understand how existing code works.

Jest and the React Testing Library

This chapter shows how to use Jest as your *testing framework* and it shows how to use the React Testing Library for rendering and interacting with components.

Two tools for unit testing a React app

Tool	Description
Jest	Provides a framework for base JavaScript testing functionality.
React Testing Library	Provides a library for additional testing functionality for React components.

Jest is a comprehensive JavaScript testing framework that was developed by Meta (previously Facebook). It serves as the foundation for JavaScript testing by providing the test runner, assertion library, mocking capabilities, and code coverage reporting.

The React Testing Library is designed for testing React components in a way that simulates how users interact with React apps. It also provides functions and objects that make it possible to test how your components render in a browser.

The Future Value app

To show how to work with unit testing, this chapter adds some unit tests to the Future Value app presented in chapter 1. The Future Value app presented in this chapter has the same user interface as the app presented in chapter 1.

The user interface

However, it exports the helper function named calcFutureValue() as shown next.

The calcFutureValue() function in the App.jsx file

```
...
export const calcFutureValue = (monthlyAmount, years, interestRate) => {
    let futureValue = 0;
    const months = years * 12;
    const monthlyRate = interestRate / 12 / 100;
    for (let i = 0; i < months; i++) {
        futureValue = (futureValue + monthlyAmount) * (1 + monthlyRate);
    }
    return futureValue;
}
...
```

This makes it possible to import the calcFutureValue() function into a unit test with an import statement like the one shown next.

An import statement for the calcFutureValue() function

```
import { calcFutureValue } from './App';
```

After you import this function into a unit test, you can use Jest to test it as its own unit, which is the whole point of unit testing. Then, after you're sure the calcFutureValue() function is working correctly, you can test the other units of the app such as the Header, Display, CalculatorForm, and App components.

How to get started with unit testing

Even though Jest was designed for testing plain JavaScript, it also works well for testing the behavior of React components when it's used with the React Testing Library. The following headings show how to set up unit testing with Jest and the React Testing Library.

Install the packages

Before you can start working with Jest and the React Testing Library, you need to run the following npm command to install the required packages.

The npm command for installing all necessary packages

```
npm install --save-dev jest jest-environment-jsdom @babel/preset-env
@babel/preset-react identity-obj-proxy @testing-library/react @testing-
library/jest-dom @testing-library/user-event
```

Here, the --save-dev parameter identifies the packages as *development dependencies*, which are libraries the app depends on only for development, not for production. The advantage of this approach is that you don't need to include these libraries with a production app.

When you run the previous install command, you may get warnings that some packages have been deprecated. In most cases, you can ignore those warnings, and the Jest and the React Testing Library will still work. That's because you may not even need to use the deprecated packages. However, if you need to use a deprecated package, you can attempt to install a later version.

Although the previous install command is hard to read, it installs the following packages.

The installed packages

Package	Description
jest	Provides the core Jest testing framework including the test runner, assertion library, and basic functionality.
jest-environment-jsdom	Provides a browser-like DOM environment rather than a Node.js environment.
@babel/preset-env	Allows Jest to understand modern JavaScript (ES6+).
@babel/preset-react	Allows Jest to understand JSX syntax.
identity-obj-proxy	Prevents errors when components import CSS files.
@testing-library/react	Provides the core functionality for the React Testing Library.
@testing-library/jest-dom	Extends Jest so it can test elements in the DOM.

These packages work together to create a testing environment for React apps built with Vite.

The @testing-library/react package provides the core functionality for testing React components. It includes the render() function for rendering components in a test environment, the screen object for querying elements, and the fireEvent object for simulating user interactions.

Since this list of packages is long, you may forget to install a package, or you may find that one didn't install correctly. In that case, you can execute the npm command again for a single package as shown next.

The npm command for installing a single package

```
npm install --save-dev @testing-library/react
```

Create and edit the config files

After you install the necessary packages for using Jest with the React Testing Library, you need to create several config files in the root directory of your app. In addition, you need to edit the packages.json file, which is also in the root directory.

To get Babel to work correctly, you need to create a config file named babel.config.js as shown next.

Create the babel.config.js file in the root directory

```
export default {
  presets: [
    '@babel/preset-env',
    ['@babel/preset-react', { runtime: 'automatic' }],
  ],
};
```

This file specifies the presets that Babel should use to transform the code. In this case, preset-env transforms the JavaScript and preset-react transforms the JSX.

You also need to create a jest.config.js file like the one shown next.

Create the jest.config.js file in the root directory

```
export default {
  // Use jsdom for environment to simulate a browser DOM
  testEnvironment: 'jsdom',

  // Set the transform property to use babel-jest for .js and .jsx files
  transform: { '^.+\\.[jt]sx?$': 'babel-jest', },

  // Setup file for @testing-library/jest-dom extensions
  setupFilesAfterEnv: ['<rootDir>/setupTests.js'],

  // Tell Jest how to handle module imports (like CSS)
  moduleNameMapper: { '\\.(css|less|scss|sass)$': 'identity-obj-proxy', },
};
```

This config file controls how Jest runs your tests. You don't need to understand the details of this file, but if you're interested it's described next.

The testEnvironment property is set to jsdom which simulates a browser DOM environment. The transform property uses a regular expression to tell Babel to process .js, .jsx, .ts, and .tsx files. The setupFilesAfterEnv property points to a setup file that runs after the test framework is installed, which allows you to configure additional testing utilities. And the moduleNameMapper property handles non-JavaScript imports like CSS files by mocking them with identity-obj-proxy, preventing errors when your components import stylesheets.

The jest.config.js file specifies that you must create a setupTests.js file in the root directory like the one shown next.

Create the setupTests.js file

```
import '@testing-library/jest-dom';
```

This setup file imports the @testing-library/jest-dom package. By importing this file once in your Jest configuration, all of your test files gain access to it without needing to import them individually.

After adding these configuration files, you should edit the package.json file for your app to add the "test" script as shown next.

The package.json file after the "test" script has been added

```
"scripts": {
  "dev": "vite",
  "build": "vite build",
  "lint": "eslint .",
  "preview": "vite preview",
  "test": "jest"
},
```

Adding the "test" script to your package.json allows you to enter "npm test" on the command line to run Jest and execute all test files in your project. This is a common convention that provides a consistent way for developers to run tests. It's also commonly used by automated *CI/CD (Continuous Integration / Continuous Deployment)* pipelines that need a consistent command to verify code quality before deployment. As a result, it's a good practice to add this script to your package.

Create two tests

Before you can create a test, you need to create a file to store the tests. To create the test file, you just add ".test" before the suffix for the file. For example, you can create a file named App.test.jsx to test the App.jsx file.

But where should you store this file? One popular approach is to store the test file in the same folder as the file it's testing. In other words, you can co-locate the test file for a component in much the same way that you co-locate its CSS file.

Another approach is to create a tests folder that contains all of the test files for an app. However, this book shows how to co-locate the test files because it provides the following advantages.

Advantages of co-locating the test file

- Makes it easy to find the tests for a component
- Encourages you to develop tests as you develop components
- Provides a clear one-to-one relationship between a component and its tests
- Shortens the paths for importing the component into the tests

The next example shows the start of an App.test.jsx file that tests the code in the the Future Value app.

The App.test.jsx file

```
import App from './App';
import { render, screen } from '@testing-library/react';
import { calcFutureValue } from './App';

test('App renders correctly', () => {
    render(<App />);
    expect(screen.queryByText("Calculate")).toBeInTheDocument();
});

test('calcFutureValue calculates correctly', () => {
    const result = calcFutureValue(100, 3, 3);
    expect(result).toBeCloseTo(3771.46, 2);
});
```

This file starts by importing the App component. Since the test file is in the same folder, this import statement is short and sweet. Then, it imports the render() function and screen object from the React Testing Library, and it imports the calcFutureValue() function from the App component.

After the import statements, this code uses the test() function to create two tests. You don't need to import the test() function or the expect() function because Jest provides them as global testing functions.

The first test checks whether App renders correctly. To do that, it uses the render() function to render App. Then, it uses the expect() function to test whether the result of the test matches the expected value. This is known as an *assertion*. In this case, the queryByText() method of the screen object asserts that an element with text of "Calculate" is in the DOM for the rendered App component. In this case, the assertion is true because App contains a button that displays text of "Calculate". As a result, the test passes.

The second test checks whether the calcFutureValue() function calculates correctly. To do that, it creates an assertion that says that a monthly payment of 100 for 3 years with an annual interest rate of 3% should be close to 3771.46. This assertion is also true. As a result, this test passes.

To thoroughly test whether App renders correctly and whether the calcFutureValue() function calculates correctly, you need to add more tests with more assertions as shown later in this chapter. However, these two tests are a good starting point for understanding how unit tests work.

Run the tests and view the results

If you've configured your test command as described earlier, you should be able to run all tests in your project with the following command.

The command for running all tests

```
npm test
```

This should run all of the tests in each file that has ".test" in its filename. Then, it should display the results of the tests as shown next.

The results for two tests that pass

```
PASS  src/App.test.jsx
  √ App renders correctly (84 ms)
  √ calcFutureValue calculates correctly (1 ms)

Test Suites: 1 passed, 1 total
Tests:       2 passed, 2 total
Snapshots:   0 total
Time:        2.431 s
Ran all test suites.
```

Here, the PASS indicator shows that all of the tests passed. The checkmark in front of the message for each test shows that each test passed. In Jest, a *test suite* is a file that contains tests. As a result, in this example, Jest runs one test suite (App.test.jsx) that contains two tests.

Debug a failing test

When a test fails, Jest provides detailed information to help you find and fix the problem. To start, Jest displays a message that identifies the test that failed as shown next.

The results for a test that fails (part 1)

```
FAIL  src/App.test.jsx
  × App renders correctly (74 ms)
  √ calcFutureValue calculates correctly (2 ms)
...
```

Here, the FAIL indicator shows that some of the tests failed, and the x in front of the "App renders correctly" message indicates that this test failed. A message like this one is typically followed by many more error messages. These error messages usually include an attempt to identify the code that that caused the test to fail as shown next.

The results for a test that fails (part 2)

```
...
    5 |  test('App renders correctly', () => {
    6 |      render(<App />);
  > 7 |      expect(screen.queryByText("Calculator")).toBeInTheDocument();
      |                                               ^
    8 |  });
...
```

This indicates that the toBeInDocument() method that's called on line 7 of the test threw an error. So, the problem is either that the test is making an assertion that isn't true or that App doesn't pass the test.

In this case, the problem is that the test is making an assertion that isn't true. That's because no element in the DOM for the App component should contain text of "Calculator". The App component has a <header> element with text of "Future Value Calculator" and a <button> element with text of "Calculate", but it doesn't contain a component with text of "Calculator". As a result, you need to fix the test so it checks for something that should be true.

How to work with Jest

Now that you know how to create and run a couple unit tests, you're ready to learn more details for using Jest.

Check for equality

To create an assertion that checks expected results against the actual results, you typically use the expect() function to specify the actual result, and you chain a call to a *matcher method*, or *matcher*, to specify the expected result as shown in the following syntax.

The syntax for calling a matcher method

```
expect(actualResult).matcher(expectedResult)
```

For example, the following example uses the matcher method named toBe() to check whether a simple calculation works correctly.

Check a calculation for equality

```
expect(2 + 2).toBe(4);      // pass
```

This works because the expect() function returns an object that contains matcher methods for checking many different conditions. For example, you can use the matcher methods in the next table to check for equality between the expected and actual results.

Matchers for working with equality

Matcher	Checks for...
toBe(val)	Strict equality (===). Use for primitive types.
toBeCloseTo(val, prec)	Approximate equality. Use for floating-point values. Optionally, specify the precision of the comparison.
toEqual(val)	Deep equality. Use with objects and arrays.

Consider the following examples.

Check values for equality

```
// primitive types
expect(2 + 3).toBe(5);                    // pass
expect('5').toBe(5);                       // fail (different data types)
expect('hello').toBe('hello');            // pass
expect(true).toBe(true);                  // pass
expect(0.1 + 0.2).toBe (0.3);             // fail (rounding error)

// floating-point numbers
expect(0.1 + 0.2).toBeCloseTo(0.3);       // pass (avoid rounding error)
expect(9.99 / 3).toBeCloseTo(3.33);       // pass (avoid rounding error)
expect(3.145).toBeCloseTo(3.14, 2);       // pass (2 decimal places)

// objects and arrays
expect({ name: 'Alice', age: 30 }).toEqual({ name: 'Alice', age: 30 });  // pass
expect({ name: 'Bob', age: 25 }).toEqual({ age: 25, name: 'Bob' });      // pass
expect([1, 2, 3]).toEqual([1, 2, 3]);                                    // pass
```

Here, the toBe() method checks for strict equality between two primitive types, which means the value and the data type must be the same. As a result, a string of "5" doesn't match an int value of 5 since their data types don't match.

The toBeCloseTo() method checks for approximate equality. This method provides a way to avoid rounding errors that are common with floating-point numbers. It also provides a second parameter that allows you to specify the number of decimal places that you want to check.

The toEqual() method checks for deep equality. In other words, it compares the contents and structure of objects and arrays rather than just checking if they refer to the same location in memory.

If you want the opposite result for a matcher, you can call the matcher from the not object that's available from the expect() method as shown by the following syntax.

The syntax for negating a matcher

```
expect(value).not.matcher(expectedValue)
```

This reverses, or negates, the value that's returned by the matcher. For example, the following code makes sure the calculation is not equal to -1.

An example that negates a matcher

```
expect(2 + 3).not.toBe(-1);
```

Although this example shows how to use the not object with the toBe() matcher, the not object works with all matchers.

Compare numbers

Jest provides some specialized matchers for comparing numbers.

Matchers for comparing numbers

Matcher	Checks if number is...
toBeGreaterThan(val)	Greater than the expected value.
toBeGreaterThanOrEqual(val)	Greater than or equal to the expected value.
toBeLessThan(val)	Less than the expected value.
toBeLessThanOrEqual(val)	Less than or equal to the expected value.

These matchers let you to verify numeric relationships. They're particularly useful for testing any code that processes numerical data where you need to assert relationships between values rather than exact equality. Consider the following examples.

Compare numeric values

```
expect(5.5).toBeGreaterThan(5.4);
expect(2.3).toBeLessThan(2.4);
expect(2+2).toBeGreaterThanOrEqual(4);
expect(1.99).toBeLessThanOrEqual(2.0);
```

All of these assertions evaluate to true. As a result, they all pass.

Check Boolean, null, and undefined values

The next table shows the matchers for working with Boolean, null, and undefined values.

Matchers for Boolean, null, and undefined values

Matcher	Checks if a value...
toBeTruthy()	Evaluates to true in a Boolean context.
toBeFalsy()	Evaluates to false in a Boolean context.
toBeNull()	Is null.
toBeUndefined()	Is undefined.
toBeDefined()	Is *not* undefined.

For example, the following assertions check if a value is truthy or falsy. A *truthy* value is any value that's evaluated as true in a Boolean context, such as an if statement. This includes non-zero numbers, non-empty strings, objects, arrays, and true. A *falsy* value is one that's evaluated as false in a Boolean context. This includes zero, empty strings, null, undefined, NaN, and false.

Check whether a value is truthy or falsy

```
// truthy
expect(true).toBeTruthy();       // pass
expect(42).toBeTruthy();         // pass - non-zero numbers are truthy
expect('hello').toBeTruthy();    // pass - non-empty strings are truthy
expect(' ').toBeTruthy();        // pass - even a single space is truthy

// falsy
expect(false).toBeFalsy();       // pass
expect(0).toBeFalsy();           // pass - 0 is falsy
expect('').toBeFalsy();          // pass - empty string is falsy
expect(null).toBeFalsy();        // pass - null is falsy
expect(undefined).toBeFalsy();   // pass - undefined is falsy
```

This shows that you can use the toBeTruthy() and toBeFalsy() methods to check whether a value (Boolean, string, number, null, or undefined) evaluates to true or false.

Similarly, the following assertions check if a value is null or undefined.

Check if a value is null or undefined

```
const getUser = () => null;
const person = { name: 'Alice', age: null };

expect(getUser()).toBeNull();          // pass - getUser returns null
expect(person.email).toBeUndefined();  // pass - email is not defined
expect(person.name).toBeDefined();     // pass - name is defined
expect(person.age).toBeDefined();      // pass - age is null, not undefined
```

Here the first assertion checks whether the getUser() function returns a null value. Then, the next three assertions check whether various properties of the person object are defined. This shows that the email property is not defined, the name property is defined, and the age property is defined even though it has been set to null.

Check strings, arrays, and objects

The next table shows matchers that can be used to work with strings, arrays, and objects.

Matchers for working with strings, arrays, and objects

Matcher	Checks if...
toMatch(x)	A string matches the specified string or regular expression.
toContain(x)	A string contains the specified string, or an array contains the specified value.
toHaveLength(num)	A string or array has the specified length.
toHaveProperty(name, val)	An object has the specified property and optionally the specified value.

The following example shows how to use the first three of these matchers with strings.

Check strings

```
const message = 'Unit testing fun';

expect(message).toMatch('Unit testing fun');  // pass - string literal
expect(message).toMatch(/^Unit/);             // pass - regex start
expect(message).toMatch(/test/);              // pass - regex substring
expect(message).toMatch(/TEST/i);             // pass - regex case-insensitive
expect(message).toMatch(/fun$/);              // pass - regex end

expect(message).toContain('Unit');            // pass
expect(message).toContain('test');            // pass

expect(message).toHaveLength(16);             // pass
```

Here, the first statement defines a string. Then, five assertions use the toMatch()

method to check if the string matches a string literal or a regular expression. Here the first regular expression checks if the string starts with "Unit", the second checks if the string contains "test" anywhere in the string, the third performs a case-insensitive check if the string contains "test" anywhere in the string, and the fourth checks if the string ends with "fun".

The next two assertions use the toContain() method to check if the string contains "Unit" or "test" anywhere in the string. And the last assertion checks if the string has 16 characters.

The next example shows how to work with the matchers for arrays and object.

Check arrays and objects

```
const fruits = ['apple', 'banana', 'orange']
expect(fruits).toContain('banana');        // pass
expect(fruits).toHaveLength(3);            // pass

const person = { name: 'Alice', address: { city: 'Wonderland' }};
expect(person).toHaveProperty('name');              // pass
expect(person).toHaveProperty('name', 'Alice');     // pass
expect(person).toHaveProperty('address.city');      // pass
```

This shows that you can use the toContain() and toHaveLength() methods to check whether an array contains an element or has a specified length.

It also shows that you can use the toHaveProperty() method to check whether an object has the specified property. Optionally, you can check whether the specified property has the specified value. In addition, you can check nested properties by using the dot operator (.) to the specify the nested property.

Tests for the calcFutureValue() function

The next example shows the start of an App.test.jsx file for the Future Value app. This file imports the calcFutureValue() function from the App component. In addition, it uses the Jest describe() function to create one group of tests for the calcFutureValue() function and another group of tests for the App component.

The App.test.jsx file with two describe() functions

```
import App from './App';
import { calcFutureValue } from './App';
import { render, screen } from '@testing-library/react';

describe('calcFutureValue', () => {
    test('calculates correct value for $100/month, 1 year, 12% rate', () => {
        const result = calcFutureValue(100, 1, 12);
        expect(result).toBeCloseTo(1280.93, 2);
    });

    test('calculates correct value for $100/month, 3 years, 3% rate', () => {
        const result = calcFutureValue(100, 3, 3);
```

```
            expect(result).toBeCloseTo(3771.46, 2);
    });

    test('calculates correct value when interest rate is 0', () => {
        const result = calcFutureValue(100, 2, 0);
        expect(result).toBe(2400); // 100 * 24 months
    });

    test('returns 0 when monthly amount is 0', () => {
        const result = calcFutureValue(0, 5, 6);
        expect(result).toBe(0);
    });

    test('returns 0 when years is 0', () => {
        const result = calcFutureValue(100, 0, 6);
        expect(result).toBe(0);
    });

    test('handles floating point input values', () => {
        const result = calcFutureValue(50.5, 1.5, 5.5);
        expect(result).toBeGreaterThan(50.5 * 1.5);
    });

    test('returns Infinity for extremely large input', () => {
        const result = calcFutureValue(10000, 10000, 12);
        expect(result).toBe(Infinity);
    });
});

describe('App component', () => {
    test('renders with Calculate button', () => {
        render(<App />);
        expect(screen.queryByText("Calculate")).toBeInTheDocument();
    });
});
```

The first two tests check if the calcFutureValue() function works correctly for
valid inputs. They test the *happy path* where everything goes right. In this case,
the calling code passes valid data to the function and the calculation works as
expected.

The next five tests check *edge cases* where the user enters data that's not
expected. The first three of these tests check that the calculation works if the
monthly amount is zero, the number of years is zero, or the interest rate is zero.
The fourth checks that the function can handle floating-point inputs. And the
fifth checks that the function returns Infinity for extremely large values.

These edge case tests verify that the function handles unusual but valid inputs
correctly. By testing these cases, you can be confident that your function
behaves predictably across the full range of possible inputs.

When you run these tests, the describe() function groups the results as shown
next.

The results grouped by the describe() functions

```
PASS  src/App.test.jsx
  calcFutureValue
    √ calculates correct value for $100/month, 1 year, 12% rate (5 ms)
    √ calculates correct value for $100/month, 3 years, 3% rate (1 ms)
    √ calculates correct value when interest rate is 0 (2 ms)
    √ returns 0 when monthly amount is 0 (1 ms)
    √ returns 0 when years is 0 (2 ms)
    √ handles floating point input values (1 ms)
    √ returns Infinity for extremely large input (2 ms)
  App component
    √ renders with Calculate button (68 ms)


Test Suites: 1 passed, 1 total
Tests:       8 passed, 8 total
```

This code doesn't test the edge case of negative inputs, null inputs, or undefined inputs. That's because the Future Value app checks to make sure that the user enters positive numbers before calling the calcFutureValue() function. However, more thorough tests would make sure that the calcFutureValue() function behaved correctly for these types of inputs anyway.

How to work with the React Testing Library

While Jest provides the testing framework, it doesn't know how to interact with React components or simulate user behavior in a browser environment. The React Testing Library fills this gap by providing tools to render React components in a test environment and to simulate user actions.

Test a child component

When creating tests for a React app, it's often a good strategy to start with the smallest and simplest components. This can help you build confidence and momentum. For example, the Header component in the Future Value app only displays a <header> element with an <h1> element that displays the name of the app. As a result, you can test it by creating a Header.test.jsx file like the one that follows.

The Header.test.jsx file

```
import Header from './Header';
import { render, screen } from '@testing-library/react';

describe('Header component', () => {
    test('renders header', () => {
        render(<Header />);
```

```
        const header = screen.getByRole('banner');
        expect(header).toBeInTheDocument();
    });

    test('contains a heading with the correct text', () => {
        render(<Header />);

        const heading = screen.getByRole('heading', { name: /Future Value/i });
        expect(heading).toBeInTheDocument();
    });
});
```

This file begins by importing the Header component. Then, it imports the render() function and the screen object from the React Testing Library. Next, it performs two tests on the Header component of the Future Value app.

The first test begins by using the render() function to render the Header component. This creates a virtual DOM for the Header component that's used by the rest of the test. If a test isn't able to render a component, the test fails, and Jest displays error messages that can help you identify the problem. If a test renders a component successfully, you can use the screen object to get and check the elements that were rendered.

The first test continues by using the screen object to get the element with a role of "banner". Typically, this is the <header> element. Then, it uses a matcher method to make sure the element is in the document (the DOM). As a result, if the Header component renders and contains a <header> element, the test passes.

The second test also begins by rendering the Header component. Then, it uses a regular expression to get a heading that has the text of "Future Value" in it. Next, it uses a matcher method to check if this heading is in the document. As a result, if the Header component renders and contains a heading element such as an <h1> element that displays the name of the app, the test passes.

If you have multiple test files and you run them all, Jest displays a quick summary of the results as shown next.

The results when you run all tests

```
PASS    src/components/Header.test.jsx
PASS    src/App.test.jsx

Test Suites: 2 passed, 2 total
Tests:       8 passed, 8 total
```

This shows that Jest considers each file to be a test suite. If want to see the details for a specific test suite, you can specify the name of the file after the test command as shown next.

Run a single test file

```
npm test src/components/Header.test.js
```

This command tells Jest to run the tests for a specific test file rather than all test files in your project. Then, Jest provides more details about the test as shown next.

The results when you run a single test

```
PASS  src/components/Header.test.jsx
  Header component
    √ renders header (62 ms)
    √ contains a heading with the correct text (12 ms)

Test Suites: 1 passed, 1 total
Tests:          2 passed, 2 total
```

Although these tests are simple, they make sure the Header component is working as expected. Then, when you test the App component later, you don't need to test the Header component in as much detail. Instead, you can focus on how the child components of the App component work together.

Get and check elements

When you use the screen object to search for an element, it automatically searches within the entire rendered component tree. To get elements, you typically use the methods of the screen object as shown next.

Methods of the screen object

Method	Description
getByRole(role, options)	Gets an element by accessibility role. If necessary, you can specify an options object.
getByAllRole(role)	Gets multiple elements by accessibility role.
getByLabelText(text)	Get an element by its label's text.
getByText(text)	Gets an element by its text content. If not found, throws error.
queryByText(text)	Get an element by its text content. If not found, returns null.

The getByRole() method gets elements by their accessibility role. This is a good practice since it helps to make sure that your React app follows HTML accessibility standards. The next table shows some of the most common roles that you can use with this method.

Roles for the getByRole() method

Role	Description
banner	Header elements such as <header>.
navigation	Navigate menus, breadcrumbs, and other nav elements.
link	Navigation links.
main	The <main> element.
heading	Heading elements such as <h1> and <h2>.
form	A <form> element.
button	Buttons.

The following examples show how you can use the screen object to get elements.

Get elements from the screen

```
const main = screen.getByRole('main');
const form = screen.getByRole('form', { name: /Calculator/i });
const h1 = screen.getByRole('heading', { name: /Future Value/i, level: 1 });
const buttons = screen.getByAllRole('button');
const input = screen.getByLabelText(/Monthly amount/i);
const div1 = screen.getByText(/Future Value:/i));
const div2 = screen.queryByText(/Future Value:/i));
const div3 = screen.queryByText(/\$15,592.93/));
```

The first three statements show how to use the getByRole() method. Of these statements, the second one specifies an optional options object that uses a regular expression to get the <form> element with a name that contains "Calculator" or "calculator". To make it possible for this to work, the <form> element must have an aria-label attribute like the one shown next.

The aria label for the <form> element

```
<form onSubmit={handleSubmit} aria-label="Calculator Form">
```

The third statement also specifies an optional options object. This object uses a case-insensitive regular expression to find a level-1 heading that contains text of "Future Value". To do that, it specifies a lowercase i (for insensitive) at the end of the regular expression for the name property, and it specifies a value of 1 for the heading property.

The getByText() and queryByText() methods both get an element by searching for text or a regular expression. However, the getByText() method throws an error if it doesn't find the text while the queryByText() method returns a null value. As a result, if you want to make sure an element is in the document, you can use the getByText() method since it fails if it doesn't find the element. However, if you want to make sure an element is *not* in the document, you need to use the queryByText() method as shown next.

An assertion that checks if an element is not in the document

```
expect(screen.queryByText(/error/i)).not.toBeInTheDocument();
```

Although you can use the methods of the screen object to get most elements, you may occasionally want to use the following methods of the document object that's automatically available to your tests.

Methods of the document object

Method	Description
querySelector(cssSelector)	Gets first found element by CSS selector.
querySelectorAll(cssSelector)	Gets all found elements by CSS selector.

The benefit of using these methods is that they work the same as the standard JavaScript methods for getting elements from the DOM. As a result, you can use the same CSS selectors that you are already familiar with to select elements as shown next.

Use CSS query selectors to get elements

```
const div = document.querySelector('.display');
const inputs = document.querySelectorAll('input');
```

Here, the first statement selects an element that has a class of "display", and the second statement selects all <input> elements in the document.

Once you've selected an element or elements from the DOM, you can use matcher methods to work with them. The next table summarizes a few of the most common matcher methods, and you can find a complete list by searching online.

Some matchers for working with elements

Matcher	Checks if an element...
toBeInTheDocument()	Is in the document.
toBeVisible()	Is visible to users (not hidden by CSS).
toBeEmptyDOMElement()	Is in the document but empty.
toHaveTextContent(x)	Has the specified text content.
toHaveValue(val)	Has the specified value.
toHaveClass(class)	Has the specified CSS class.

The following examples show how you can use these matchers to test elements.

Check elements

```
expect(heading).toBeInTheDocument();
expect(heading).toBeVisible();
expect(div).toBeEmptyDOMElement();
expect(button).toHaveTextContent(/calculate/i);
expect(input).toHaveValue(100);
expect(main).toHaveClass('container');
```

Test another child component

To better understand how to get and check elements, consider the following code. It tests another child component of the Future Value app, the Display component. This component displays the calculated future value or an error message, depending on whether it receives a value prop or an error prop.

The Display.test.jsx file

```
import Display from './Display';
import { render, screen } from '@testing-library/react';

describe('Display component', () => {
    test('renders empty display when no props provided', () => {
        render(<Display />);

        const displayDiv = document.querySelector('.display');
        expect(displayDiv).toBeInTheDocument();
        expect(displayDiv).toBeEmptyDOMElement();
    });

    test('renders future value when value prop is provided', () => {
        render(<Display value={1234.56} />);

        const valueDiv = screen.getByText(/Future Value:/i);
        expect(valueDiv).toBeInTheDocument();
        expect(valueDiv).toHaveTextContent(/\$1,234.56/);
    });

    test('renders error message when errorMsg prop is provided', () => {
        const errorMsg = 'Invalid input';
        render(<Display errorMsg={errorMsg} />);

        const errorDiv = screen.getByText(errorMsg);
        expect(errorDiv).toBeInTheDocument();
        expect(errorDiv).toHaveClass('error');
    });

    // other tests omitted for brevity
});
```

Here, the first test checks that this component renders correctly if it doesn't receive any props. To do that, the code checks to make sure that it displays an element with a class of "display" that's empty.

The second test checks whether this component renders correctly if it receives a value prop. To do that, it uses the getByText() method to get the <div> element that contains text of "Future Value:". Then, it checks to make sure this element is in the document and that it displays the future value with the correct format. To check this, the code uses a regular expression that includes a dollar sign (\$) and a comma.

The third test checks whether the component renders correctly if it receives an error prop. To do that, it uses the getByText() method to make sure the error message is in the document and has a class of "error".

Now that this chapter has shown some tests for two components in a React app, you might be asking yourself, what are some of the best practices for creating these types of tests?

Best practices for testing React apps

- **Test what users see.** Check for visible text, not implementation details
- **Keep it simple.** Don't test every single element, just key indicators
- **Use accessible queries.** Prefer the getByRole(), queryByText(), and getByLabelText() matcher methods.
- **Test one concept per test.** Each test should verify one thing.
- **Make your test names descriptive.** Each name should clearly document the goal of the test.

Most of the tests for the Display component follow these practices. However, the first test doesn't test what users see. Instead, it tests whether an element with a class of "display" is in the document and is empty. That's an implementation detail. Testing this implementation detail means that the component won't pass this test if a developer changes the name of the class. As a result, you should only test this implementation detail if you're sure that it won't change.

When creating tests, it's important to balance thoroughness with flexibility. The first test is thorough because it makes sure that the DOM only contains an empty element when the Display component doesn't receive any props. However, it isn't flexible because it tests the implement details of the component, which limits the ways in which a developer can change the component. In the end, finding the right balance often depends on the type of app being developed.

Test user actions

The React Testing Library provides a way to simulate user actions with your app such as clicking on an element, submitting a form, changing an input field, or pressing a key. To do that, you can use the fireEvent object to trigger DOM events on elements. But first, you need to import this object from the React Testing Library as shown next.

Import the object for firing DOM events

```
import { fireEvent } from '@testing-library/react';
```

Once you import the fireEvent object, you can use it to test a workflow for the CalculatorForm component in the Future Value app. To do that, you can start by making sure the component updates the value of an <input> element as the user types as shown next.

A simple test that uses the fireEvent object

```
import CalculatorForm from './CalculatorForm';
import { render, screen, fireEvent } from '@testing-library/react';

describe('CalculatorForm component', () => {
    test('updates input value as user types', () => {
        render(<CalculatorForm />);

        const amountInput = screen.getByLabelText(/Monthly amount/i);
        fireEvent.change(amountInput, { target: { value: '100' } });
        expect(amountInput).toHaveValue(100);
    });
});
```

This test begins by rendering the CalculatorForm component, which displays three <input> elements. Then, it gets the first <input> element by its label. Next, it uses the fireEvent object to fire the change event for the <input> element and change its value to '100'. To do that, it sets a value for the target property of the event object. Finally, it checks whether the value of the <input> element is 100.

For brevity, this test only checks one <input> element. However, to thoroughly test this form, the code should be expanded to test all three input elements.

To test the click event of a button, you can use the jest object that's available globally to get a mock function object that's designed for working with unit tests. To do that, you just call the fn() method of the jest object as shown next.

The CalculatorForm.test.jsx file

```
import CalculatorForm from './CalculatorForm';
import { render, screen, fireEvent } from '@testing-library/react';

describe('CalculatorForm component', () => {
    test('renders form with labeled inputs and button', () => {
        // not shown here for brevity
    });

    test('updates input values as user types', () => {
        // not shown here for brevity
    });

    test('calls handleSubmit with numeric values when form is submitted', () => {
        const handleSubmit = jest.fn();
        render(<CalculatorForm onSubmit={handleSubmit} />);

        const amountInput = screen.getByLabelText(/Monthly amount/i);
        const yearsInput = screen.getByLabelText(/Number of years/i);
        const rateInput = screen.getByLabelText(/Interest rate/i);
        const buttonInput = screen.getByRole('button', { name: /Calculate/i });

        fireEvent.change(amountInput, { target: { value: '100' } });
        fireEvent.change(yearsInput, { target: { value: '1' } });
        fireEvent.change(rateInput, { target: { value: '0' } });
        fireEvent.click(button);
```

```
            expect(handleSubmit).toHaveBeenCalledTimes(1);
            expect(handleSubmit).toHaveBeenCalledWith(100, 1, 0);
        });
    });
```

Here, the third test begins by using the fn() method of the jest object to get
a mock function named handleSubmit that can be used for testing. Then, it
renders the CalculatorForm component and passes the handleSubmit function
to the onSubmit prop.

After rendering the component, this test gets the three <input> elements and
a button, fires the change event to change the values stored in the <input>
elements, and fires the click event for the button. Next, it checks to make sure
the function has been called the correct number of times (once) and that it
has been called with the correct values. This is possible because the function
returned by the fn() method provides matcher methods.

Since CalculatorForm doesn't display the result of the calculation, it tests that
the form works correctly, not that the calculation is correct. To test whether the
calculation is correct, you need to test the App component.

Perform integration tests

Verifying that multiple parts of your app work together correctly is known as
integration testing. In a React app, you can perform integration testing in the
App component, after you have thoroughly tested all of the child components.
Then, your tests can focus on how these components work together. For
example, the tests for the App component can start by testing the initial render
as shown next.

The App.test.jsx file (part 1 – test initial render)

```
import App from './App';
import { render, screen, fireEvent } from '@testing-library/react';
import { calcFutureValue } from './App';

describe('calcFutureValue', () => {
    // same as the tests shown earlier in this chapter
});

describe('App component', () => {
    test('renders main UI elements', () => {
        render(<App />);
        expect(screen.getByRole('banner')).toBeInTheDocument();
        expect(screen.getByRole('heading', { level: 1 })).toBeInTheDocument();
        expect(screen.getByRole('main')).toHaveClass('container');

        const form = screen.getByRole('form', { name: /Calculator/i });
        expect(form).toBeInTheDocument();
        expect(form.querySelectorAll('input')).toHaveLength(3);
        expect(screen.getByRole('button')).toBeInTheDocument();
    });
```

```
test('initial render shows no future value or error', () => {
    render(<App />);
    expect(screen.queryByText(/Future Value:/i)).not.toBeInTheDocument();
    expect(screen.queryByText(/valid/i)).not.toBeInTheDocument();
});
...
```

Here, the first test checks to make sure all of the main UI elements of the App component render. It confirms that the App component displays <header>, <h1>, <main>, and <form> elements with the correct CSS class applied to the <main> element. In addition, it checks to make sure the form contains three <input> elements and a <button> element. By using getByRole(), this test verifies not only that these structural elements exist but also that they're coded correctly for accessibility.

The second test verifies that the initial render doesn't display the future value or any error messages. The assertions within this test use queryByText() instead of getByText() because they expect the elements to *not* be present. That's because getByText() would throw an error if it didn't find the text, and the code wouldn't be able to use the not object to make sure the text was not present.

The tests for the App component continue by testing valid input for the happy path where everything should work as expected.

The App.test.jsx file (part 2 – test valid input)

```
test('calculates and displays future value for valid input', () => {
    render(<App />);
    const monthlyInput = screen.getByLabelText(/Monthly amount/i);
    const yearsInput = screen.getByLabelText(/Number of years/i);
    const rateInput = screen.getByLabelText(/Interest rate/i);
    const button = screen.getByRole('button', { name: /Calculate/i });

    fireEvent.change(monthlyInput, { target: { value: '100' } });
    fireEvent.change(yearsInput, { target: { value: '3' } });
    fireEvent.change(rateInput, { target: { value: '3' } });
    fireEvent.click(button);

    expect(screen.queryByText(/\$3,771.46/)).toBeInTheDocument();
});
```

This test simulates the workflow for the Future Value app. It starts by rendering App and getting all the elements from the form using accessible queries.

After getting all elements from the form, this test uses the fireEvent object to simulate a user typing values into each <input> element. Then, it uses the fireEvent object to simulate the user clicking the Calculate button.

After simulating this user input, the test verifies that the App component displays the correct future value on the screen. To do that, it uses a regular expression to check for the correct formatted future value.

You can also use the fireEvent object to verify that your apps perform as expected when a workflow fails. For instance, the next two tests for App check if it behaves as expected with a negative value or empty fields.

The App.test.jsx file (part 3 – test invalid input)

```
test('shows error and hides future value for invalid input', () => {
    render(<App />);
    const monthlyInput = screen.getByLabelText(/Monthly amount/);
    const yearsInput = screen.getByLabelText(/Number of years/);
    const rateInput = screen.getByLabelText(/Interest rate/);
    const button = screen.getByRole('button', { name: /Calculate/i });

    fireEvent.change(monthlyInput, { target: { value: '-100' } });
    fireEvent.change(yearsInput, { target: { value: '10' } });
    fireEvent.change(rateInput, { target: { value: '5' } });
    fireEvent.click(button);

    expect(screen.queryByText(/enter valid/i)).toBeInTheDocument();
    expect(screen.queryByText(/Future Value:/)).not.toBeInTheDocument();
});

test('does not submit or show future value if fields are empty', () => {
    render(<App />);
    const button = screen.getByRole('button', { name: /Calculate/i });
    fireEvent.click(button);
    expect(screen.queryByText(/Future Value:/)).not.toBeInTheDocument();
});
});
```

Here, the first test checks if App handles the invalid input of a negative number correctly. After simulating the form submission with this invalid data, the test verifies that App displays an error message and that it doesn't display a future value calculation.

The second test verifies the behavior of the HTML5 form validation. Since the <input> elements have the required attribute, the browser should prevent form submission if the user doesn't enter any input. The test starts by simulating the user clicking the Calculate button without entering any data. Then, it verifies that App doesn't display the future value. This confirms that the browser's built-in validation is working as expected.

More skills for unit testing

As a test suite grows larger, you may need more control over how you run and analyze your tests. In addition, you may want to measure how thoroughly your tests cover your codebase. Finally, you may want to use a VS Code extension to automatically run your tests.

Organize tests into groups

So far, this chapter has only used one level of describe() functions to group tests. However, you can also nest describe() functions to organize your tests as shown next.

How to group the tests by purpose

```
describe('App component', () => {
    describe('initial render', () => {
        test('renders main UI elements', () => {});
        test('initial render shows no future value or error', () => {});
    });
    describe('workflows', () => {
        test('calculates and displays future value for valid input', () => {});
        test('shows error and hides future value for invalid input', () => {});
        test('does not submit if fields are empty', () => {});
    });
});
```

Here, the outer describe() function groups all tests for the App component while the two inner describe() functions create another level of grouping. The first inner function groups tests that verify the initial render of the component, and the second inner function groups tests that simulate user workflows. Grouping tests like this makes it easier to find the test you're looking for and allows you to run each group separately.

Run a group of tests

When working with a test suite that has multiple groups, you may want to run only a specific group of tests rather than the entire suite. This can save time and help you focus on the tests you're working on. To run a specific group of tests, you can use Jest's -t parameter followed by the text that matches any part of the description for the group that you want to run.

The command for running only specified tests

```
jest src/App.test.jsx -- -t "Workflow"
```

When you use this command, Jest performs a case-insensitive search and matches any part of the description for a group or test. So, the text "Workflow" shown here is a match for the "workflows" group shown previously. In addition, you need to make sure to use the jest command, not the "npm test" command.

When you use the -t parameter, Jest still displays all of the tests in the test suite. However, it marks the tests that it doesn't run as "skipped" as shown next.

The results for the command shown above

```
...
App component
    initial render
        o skipped renders main UI elements
        o skipped initial render shows no future value or error
    workflows
        √ calculates and displays future value for valid input (136 ms)
        √ shows error and hides future value for invalid input (25 ms)
        √ does not submit or show future value if fields are empty (10 ms)
```

Here, Jest doesn't run either test in the "initial render" group. As a result, it displays a circle and "skipped" before them. However, it runs all three tests in the "workflows" group. Since these tests all pass, Jest displays a checkmark before each one.

Check code coverage of your tests

Test coverage measures how much of your code is tested by your tests. It's expressed as percentages across four metrics: statements (lines of code executed), branches (if/else paths tested), functions (functions called), and lines (executable lines covered). Coverage helps identify untested parts of your code.

To check the test coverage for your app, you can use the following command.

The command for checking test coverage

```
jest -- --coverage
```

When you run this command, Jest displays a table that provides information about the coverage for the components of your app. For this example, if you remove all tests in the workflow group from the App.test.jsx file, Jest should display the following table.

The coverage for the Future Value app

File	% Stmts	% Branch	% Funcs	% Lines	Uncovered Line #s
All files	86.48	38.46	90.9	86.11	
src	72.22	0	66.66	70.58	
App.jsx	72.22	0	66.66	70.58	28-36
...ponents	100	100	100	100	
...rm.jsx	100	100	100	100	
...ay.jsx	100	100	100	100	
...er.jsx	100	100	100	100	

This table shows that the tests cover most of the app. The Uncovered Lines #s column in the table attempts to indicate where your tests are missing coverage. As a result, you can look at these lines and determine if you need to add tests to cover them.

While 100% coverage might seem ideal, it's often not practical or necessary. A good target for most projects is 80% overall coverage, with critical business logic aiming for 90% or higher. Remember that high coverage doesn't guarantee bug-free code. It only confirms that the code was executed during tests, not that it was tested meaningfully. As a result, you should focus on writing quality tests for important functionality rather than raising coverage numbers. Some code, like simple UI components or configuration files, may not need extensive testing.

Use VS Code's Jest extension

Instead of using the command line to run Jest, you can add the Jest extension to VS Code. Then, it automatically runs tests as you create them and displays them in a Testing window. To install the Jest extension, you can use the following procedure.

How to install the Jest extension

1. Start VS Code.
2. Click the Extensions icon that's on the left side of the window.
3. Type "jest" in the search box at the top of the Extensions window. This window should display several options.
4. Choose the Jest extension by Orta.
5. Click Install.

Once you install the Jest extension, VS Code should display a Testing (beaker) icon that you can click to open the Testing window. However, sometimes VS Code doesn't display the Testing (beaker) icon. If that happens, you can restart VS Code.

When the Testing icon is displayed, you can click it to display a Testing window like the one shown next.

The Testing window with one failing test

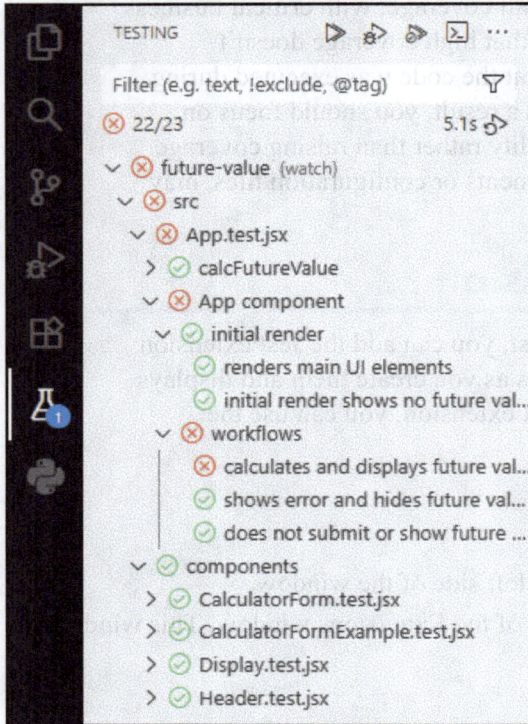

```
TESTING                    ▷  ▷  ▷  >_  …

Filter (e.g. text, !exclude, @tag)        ▽
⊗ 22/23                            5.1s ↻
∨ ⊗ future-value (watch)
  ∨ ⊗ src
    ∨ ⊗ App.test.jsx
      > ⊘ calcFutureValue
      ∨ ⊗ App component
        ∨ ⊘ initial render
          ⊘ renders main UI elements
          ⊘ initial render shows no future val...
        ∨ ⊗ workflows
          ⊗ calculates and displays future val...
          ⊘ shows error and hides future val...
          ⊘ does not submit or show future ...
    ∨ ⊘ components
      > ⊘ CalculatorForm.test.jsx
      > ⊘ CalculatorFormExample.test.jsx
      > ⊘ Display.test.jsx
      > ⊘ Header.test.jsx
```

By default, the Jest extension sets Jest in watch mode, as indicated by the (watch) designation after the program name. In watch mode, Jest automatically discovers and runs the tests whenever you save a file in your project.

The Testing window displays all of the tests for the app in a hierarchy that includes their groups. If you want to expand or collapse a group, you can do that by clicking on it.

The Testing window marks tests that pass with a green check and tests that don't pass with a red X. In this example, the app contains one test that fails, the first test in the "workflows" group. As a result, you can view that test and fix it. When you save your changes, the Jest extension should automatically update the Testing window accordingly.

Perspective

This chapter has shown how to get started with Jest and the React Testing Library to create automated unit tests for React apps. However, there's always more to learn. For example, this chapter doesn't show how to test external dependencies such as web APIs. It also doesn't explain how to use test-driven development (TDD). For more information on those topics, you can search the internet or ask AI.

Terms

unit testing

testing framework

development dependencies

CI/CD (Continuous Integration / Continuous Deployment)

assertion

test suite

matcher method

matcher

truthy

falsy

happy path

edge cases

integration testing

Exercise 13-1: Add unit tests to an app

Review the starting code

1. Open the my-playlist project in the ex_starts/ch13 folder.
2. Open the package.json file and review its code. Note that the development dependencies include Jest and the React Testing Library.
3. Review the files in the root folder and note that the babel.config.js, jest.config.js, and setupTests.js files exist.
4. Open the App.jsx file and review its code.
5. Run the app and add a new song to the playlist to understand how it works.
6. Run the "npm test" command and note that there aren't any tests yet.

Add tests for the Header component

7. In the components folder, open the Header.jsx file and review its code.
8. Create a Header.test.jsx file.
9. In the Header.test.jsx file, import the render() function and the screen object from the React Testing Library. Also, import the Header component that's being tested.
10. Add a describe() function that describes the component that's being tested.
11. Within the describe() function, add a test that checks if the Header component renders and has a component with the banner role.
12. Run the test and make sure it passes.

13. Add another test that checks if the Header component contains a heading that displays the app name that's passed to the appName attribute of the component.

14. Run the tests to make sure they're both working correctly.

Add tests for the SongForm component

15. In the components folder, open the SongForm.jsx file and review its code.

16. Add a SongForm.test.jsx file.

17. In the SongForm.test.jsx file, import the SongForm component, the render() function, the screen object, and the fireEvent object.

18. Add a describe() function that describes the component.

19. Within the describe() function, add a test that checks whether the form initially renders the <input> elements associated with the "Title", "Artist", "Year", and "Favorite" labels.

20. Run the tests for all components. Note how this doesn't display the description for each component or its tests.

21. Run the test for the SongForm component. Note how this displays the description for the component and its test.

22. Add a test that checks whether the form initially renders the Add and Cancel buttons.

23. Add a test that checks whether the change event works correctly for the first three the <input> elements in the form.

24. Add a test that checks whether the click event works correctly for the fourth <input> element in the form.

25. Add a test that checks whether clicking the Add button calls the event handler that's passed to the onAdd attribute with values from <input> elements that were updated after their change or click events occurred.

26. Run the tests for the SongForm component to make sure they're all working correctly.

Add tests for the App component

27. In the src folder, open the App.jsx file and review its code.

28. Add a file named App.test.jsx file.

29. In the App.test.jsx file, import the App component, the render() function, the screen object, and the fireEvent object.

30. Add a describe() function that describes the component.

31. Within the describe() function, add a test that checks whether the initial render of the App component displays the correct elements. This initial render should display the Add Song button, but not the Add Song form. One way to check whether the form is visible is to check if the screen displays the Cancel button.

32. Add a test that checks whether clicking the Add Song button displays the Add Song form.

33. Add a test that simulates adding a song to the playlist. To start, add code that simulates the user clicking on the Add Song button, typing "Don't Let Me Down", "The Beatles", and "1969" into the first three <input> elements in the form, and clicking the Add button. Then, add code that checks whether the correct text is displayed on the screen.

34. Run the tests for the App component to make sure they're all working correctly.

35. Run the tests for all components to make sure they're all working correctly.

Chapter 14

Render on the server with Next.js

Server-side rendering (SSR) changes how React apps deliver content by allowing them to render some or all of the HTML for a page on the server before sending it to the browser. Next.js makes it easy for React developers to implement SSR because it handles the setup automatically, allowing the developer to focus on building features.

This chapter shows how to use Next.js to implement server-side rendering. In addition, it shows how to use the router that comes with Next.js to create a single-page app (SPA) instead of using the React Router as shown in chapter 8.

An introduction to server-side rendering

Before React, most web apps rendered HTML on the server and returned pages that contained a lot of HTML with some JavaScript to make the page interactive. This is known as *server-side rendering (SSR)*.

React changed how developers build user interfaces by returning pages that contained little more than a <div> element for the root of the web page and a *JavaScript bundle* to render the rest of the HTML. This approach, which moved most of the HTML rendering to the browser, is known as *client-side rendering (CSR)*.

While client-side rendering enables more interactive experiences, it also creates some challenges. Users can face blank screens while waiting for the first page of the app to download the JavaScript bundle and run it. Search engines can struggle to index content that only exists after the JavaScript runs. And as an app grows, the JavaScript bundle typically gets larger, which makes it take longer to load the first page of the app.

Server-side rendering can mitigate these challenges by moving some of the initial rendering back to the server. Instead of sending little more than a <div> element to the browser, the server can send more HTML and content to the browser. That way, the browser can display this HTML immediately while React works in the background to make it interactive.

When you use server-side rendering, React waits for the initial HTML to load. Then, it attaches JavaScript to the initial HTML to add event listeners and make the HTML interactive. This process is known as *hydration*.

Static site generation (SSG) is a different but related approach that pre-renders pages at build time rather than on each request. This creates static HTML files that can be served instantly from a *content delivery network (CDN)*. This is a common approach, but it isn't covered in this book.

The benefits of SSR

SSR offers many benefits. Here's a list of some of them.

The benefits of SSR

- Faster initial page load
- Improved SEO
- Secure server-side data access
- Better social media sharing
- Improved accessibility

The most immediate benefit is improved performance for the initial load of the page. With CSR, the app sometimes displays a blank screen while the JavaScript downloads and runs. With SSR, the app displays meaningful content instantaneously.

Improved search engine optimization (SEO) is another advantage. Search engines can immediately read and understand your content because it exists in the HTML. While modern search engines like Google can run JavaScript, they still prefer content that's readily available in the initial HTML. This preference can impact how well your pages rank in search results.

Server-side rendering makes it possible to fetch data from databases, use API keys, and access server-only resources without exposing credentials to the browser. This provides a way to keep your server-side data secure while still personalizing content.

Social media sharing also benefits from server-side rendering. When someone shares your page on most social media sites, these platforms look for titles, descriptions, and images in the HTML. Client-side rendered pages often don't provide this information quickly enough which results in missing previews.

There are accessibility improvements too. Since the initial page is rendered on the server, users who have JavaScript disabled in their browsers can still access that page. Similarly, it can improve access for users who have devices with limited processing power that struggle to perform the client-side rendering. This approach makes sure your app works for everyone, not just users with the latest browsers and fastest connections.

How Next.js handles SSR

Next.js is a framework that provides server-side rendering for React apps. It also provides other features that you can use for routing, creating a web API, and static site generation. However, this chapter focuses on how you can use Next.js to provide server-side rendering for your React apps.

In a web app, a *router* maps URLs to specific UI components. For example, chapter 8 shows how to use the React Router, the official client-side routing library for React. However, Next.js includes a built-in router named App Router.

Because App Router is based on the directory structure of the app, it isn't as flexible as React Router. However, when you use App Router to display a page, Next.js uses server-side rendering for that page by default.

When Next.js processes a request for a page, the following steps happen behind the scenes.

How Next.js processes a request for a page

1. The browser requests a page from the Next.js server.
2. The server renders the HTML for the page. This includes fetching data that's needed by the page.
3. The server sends the HTML to the browser.
4. The browser displays the HTML.
5. The browser downloads the JavaScript bundle.
6. React hydrates the page by attaching the event listeners that make the HTML interactive.

To use server-side rendering in Next.js, you don't need to configure your app. It's the default behavior as long as you're using the App Router.

How to get started with Next.js

Now that you have a general idea of how Next.js handles SSR, you're ready to create your first app with Next.js.

Create and configure a project

To get started, you can create a project based on a template for a Next.js app by using the npx command to run the create-next-app package as shown next.

Create and configure a Next.js project

```
> npx create-next-app@latest movie-list
Need to install the following packages:
create-next-app@16.0.3
Ok to proceed? (y) y

√ Would you like to use the recommended Next.js defaults? » No, customize settings
√ Would you like to use TypeScript? ... No / Yes
√ Which linter would you like to use? » ESLint
√ Would you like to use React Compiler? ... No / Yes
√ Would you like to use Tailwind CSS? ... No / Yes
√ Would you like your code inside a `src/` directory? ... No / Yes
√ Would you like to use App Router? (recommended) ... No / Yes
√ Would you like to customize the import alias (`@/*` by default)? ... No / Yes
Creating a new Next.js app in C:\Users\...
```

This npx command creates the directory that you specify. For instance, the command shown here creates the movie-list directory. So, be sure to run it where you want to create that directory.

When you run this npx command, it may ask if it's OK to install the create-next-app package. You can type 'y' and press Enter to install this package.

In addition, it asks a series of configuration questions for your project. In most cases, you can press Enter to select the default answer. However, you can also use the arrow keys to select a different answer before pressing Enter.

The previous example underlines the answers used to set up the projects for this chapter. To keep things simple, these prompts don't install TypeScript or Tailwind. However, if you want to use these features in your project, you can answer yes to these prompts.

To run the Next.js app, navigate to the directory you created and enter the same "npm run dev" command that you use to run a Vite app. By default, Next.js uses port 3000 for the development web server. As a result, after you start this server, you can display the app that's generated by using your browser to navigate to localhost:3000 as shown next.

The generated app in a browser

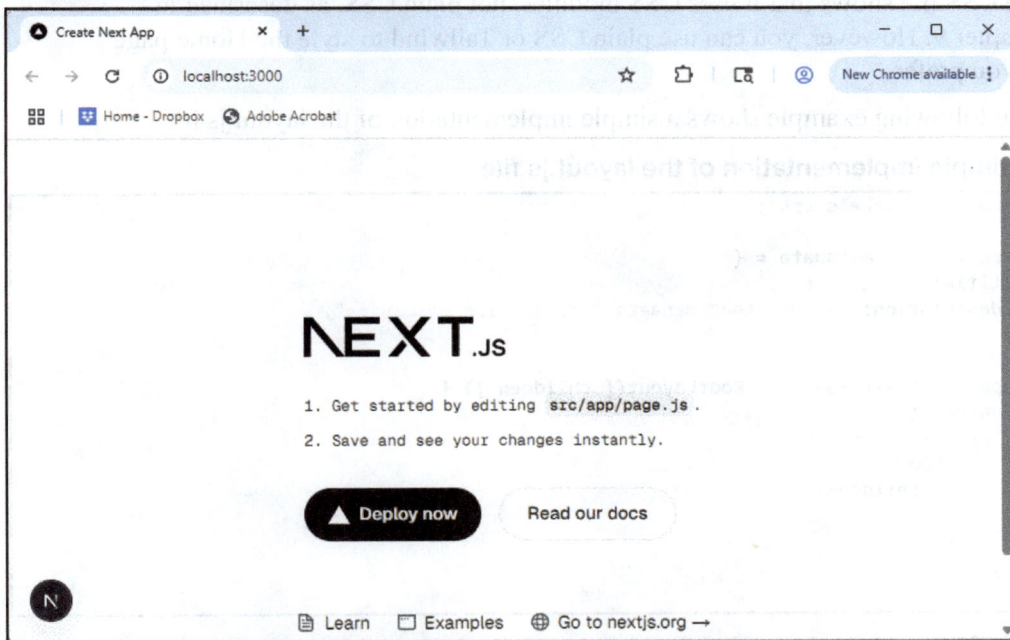

Review the initial files

By default, the App Router that's provided by Next.js looks for the starting code for the app in the src/app directory. If you use the settings shown previously, the src/app directory should contain the following files.

The default files in the src/app directory

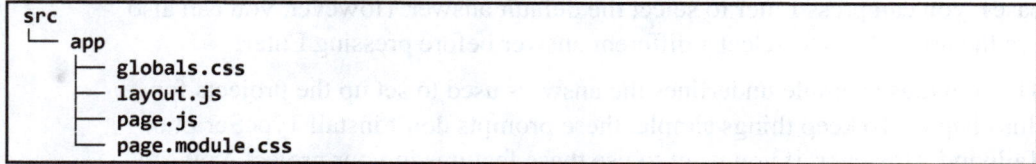

```
src
└── app
    ├── globals.css
    ├── layout.js
    ├── page.js
    └── page.module.css
```

Here, the globals.css file contains the CSS that's applied to all pages in the app. Similarly, the layout.js page contains the JavaScript and JSX that defines the shared layout for all pages in the app. This file has an extension of .js even though it contains JSX because Next.js automatically treats .js files as .jsx files if they contain JSX.

The page.js file contains the JavaScript and JSX for the Home page of the app, and the page.module.css file stores the CSS for this page. The name for the CSS file shows that it uses CSS modules, not plain CSS, as described in chapter 9. However, you can use plain CSS or Tailwind to style the Home page if you prefer.

The following example shows a simple implementation of the layout.js file.

A simple implementation of the layout.js file

```
import "./globals.css";

export const metadata = {
  title: "Movie List",
  description: "An app that manages a collection of movies",
};

export default function RootLayout({ children }) {
  return (
    <html lang="en">
      <body>
        {children}
      </body>
    </html>
  );
}
```

This file begins by importing the globals.css file that provides the styles that apply to all pages in the app. Then, it defines and exports a metadata object that applies to all of the pages in the app.

After specifying the metadata for the app, this file defines and exports a function for a component named RootLayout. This component provides the layout for all pages in the app. This simple implementation of the RootLayout component only provides <html> and <body> elements. However, if you want, you can modify this file to provide other HTML elements such as <header>, <nav>, and <footer> or React components such as <Header>, <Navbar>, and <Footer>.

To define a function for the component, the Next.js template doesn't use an arrow function. Instead, it uses the function keyword to declare a function. Similarly, it doesn't use a separate export statement. Instead, it adds the export default keywords to the beginning of the function declaration.

So far, this book has been using arrow functions and separate export statements to define components. However, since the starting code for the Next.js template uses function declarations and inline exports, this chapter uses that approach too. Either way, you create a component by defining a function, and you make the function the default export so it's available to other components. So, the syntax is different, but the result is the same.

How to work with Next.js components

Next.js provides two ways to implement server-side rendering. *Server Components* run only on the server. As a result, if they render HTML, they render it on the server. By contrast, *Client Components* run on both the server and the client. With a Client Component, Next.js starts by rendering as much HTML as possible on the server. Then, it renders the rest of the HTML on the client. This allows the client to provide interactivity that isn't possible with just a Server Component.

Create a Server Component

By default, App Router uses Server Components. Fetching data via a Server Component allows your apps to render complete HTML for a static web page as shown next.

A page.js file for a Server Component that fetches data

```
export default async function MovieList() {
  // asynchronously fetch data from external API (see chapter 6)
  const response = await fetch('http://localhost:2000/movies',
    { cache: 'no-store' } // Always fetch fresh data
  );
  const movies = await response.json();

  // return static HTML with data
  return (
    <main>
        <h1>Movies</h1>
          <ul>
            {movies.map(movie => (
              <li key={movie.id}>{movie.name} ({movie.year})</li>
            ))}
          </ul>
    </main>
  );
}
```

For this code to work, the Movies API described in chapter 6 needs to be running. To run that API, start a second instance of VS Code, open the apps/ch06/movies-api folder, open the Terminal window, and install the dependencies. Then, enter the "node app.mjs" command.

The Server Component shown here asynchronously fetches movie data during the rendering process on the server. This is possible because you can use the async keyword when you define the function for the Server Component. Then, you can call async functions such as fetch() from within the Server Component and use the await keyword to wait for the response from the server. Being able to run code asynchronously makes Server Components optimal for performing any server-side processing for your app.

Here, the code waits for the data to be retrieved from a web API. Then, it wraps that data in the HTML for the page and sends it to the client. As a result, when the page loads, it displays all of this data immediately as shown next with no loading states or blank screens.

The page displayed in a browser

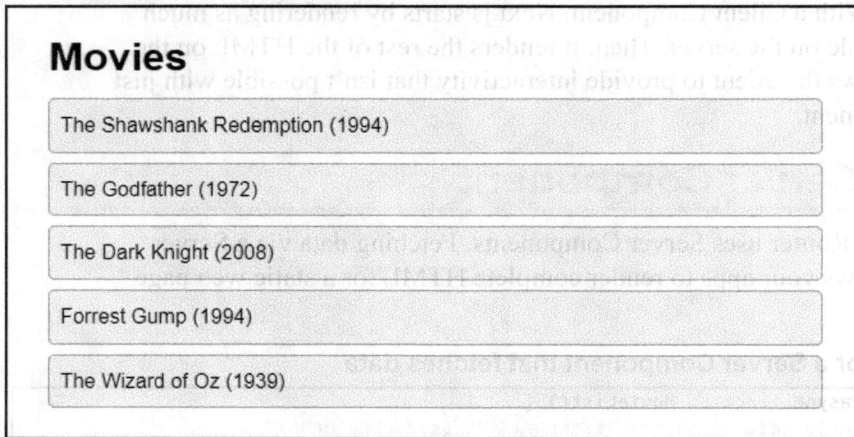

Movies

| The Shawshank Redemption (1994) |
| The Godfather (1972) |
| The Dark Knight (2008) |
| Forrest Gump (1994) |
| The Wizard of Oz (1939) |

When you call the fetch() method in a Server Component, it caches the data that's returned by default. That way, it can use that data again later if necessary. This works well for static data that doesn't change. However, if you don't want to cache the data, you can pass an object to the fetch() method that controls how it caches data. In the previous example, the code passes an object that always fetches fresh data. Alternately, you can pass an object that specifies the number of seconds that Next.js should refresh the cache. The objects for all three of these options are shown next.

Three ways to control caching for the fetch() method

```
{ cache: 'force-cache' }      // The default - Cache data
{ cache: 'no-store' }         // Always fetch fresh data
{ next: {revalidate: 3600} } // Revalidate every hour
```

Provide a loading page

When you use a Server Component for a page, Next.js provides an easy way to display a message while the page is loading. To do that, you just put a loading.js file in the same directory as the page.js file. For example, if you put the following loading.js file in the same directory as the page.js file for the Server Component shown above, it displays a "Loading Movies…" message while the page is loading.

A loading.js file with a loading message

```
export default function LoadingMovies() {
  return (
    <main>
        <h1>Loading Movies...</h1>
    </main>
  );
}
```

Although this loading page is simple, its page layout matches the layout of the page that's being loaded, so it has a smooth transition between the two pages. If you wanted to provide better *user experience (UX)*, the loading page could use CSS to display a spinner. Better yet, the loading page could use a *skeleton screen* to provide a placeholder UI that mimics the layout of your actual content as shown next.

A loading.js file for a skeleton screen

```
export default function LoadingMovies() {
  return (
    <main>
      <h1>Movies</h1>
      <ul>
        {[1, 2, 3].map(n => (
          <li key={n} className="pulse">Loading...</li>
        ))}
      </ul>
    </main>
  );
}
```

This code also uses the same layout as the page, but it provides three placeholder list items that say "Loading…" and has a CSS class that provides an animation that makes them pulse as shown next.

A skeleton screen that displays while the page is rendering

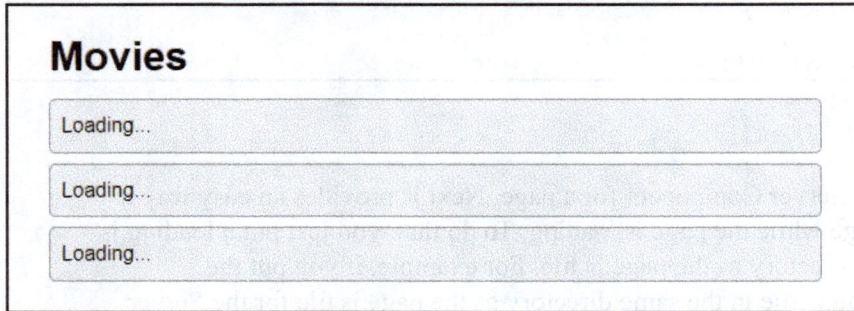

> ## Movies
>
> Loading...
>
> Loading...
>
> Loading...

Provide an error page

Next.js also provides an easy way to provide a message when an error occurs during server-side rendering. To do that, you just put an error.js file in the same directory as the page.js file, or in a parent directory. If multiple error.js files exist, the one in the same directory as page.js overrides any error.js file in a parent directory.

For example, the following error.js file displays a message that says, "Something went wrong!" along with the error message.

An error.js file

```
'use client';

export default function error({ error }) (
    <main>
        <h1>Something went wrong!</h1>
        <p>Error message: {error.message}</p>
    </main>
}
```

This error page works much like the loading page described earlier. In addition, it accepts a prop named error that provides access to the error object.

However, unlike a loading page, an error page must be a Client Component, which is why this file starts with the 'use client' directive. This allows an error page like this one to catch and display errors that occur in a Server Component.

In general, you should use Server Components to fetch data for initial page loads and static content. The following list summarizes some of the benefits of using Server Components.

Advantages of Server Components

- They make it easy to run asynchronous code on the server
- They don't send their code to the browser
- The loading.js and error.js files provide an easy way to display loading and error messages

Since Server Components make it easy to run asynchronous code on the server, they're ideal for performing server-side tasks like directly accessing databases, reading files, and so on. And since they don't send their code to the browser, they're more secure than Client Components. For example, you can use them to send credentials to a web API.

However, Server Components have some limitations too, as summarized next.

The limitations of Server Components

- You can't use React hooks such as useState and useEffect
- You can't access browser APIs such as localStorage

Because Server Components can't use React hooks, you can't use them to create interactive components. To do that, you need to create a Client Component.

Create a Client Component

To create a Client Component, you can add the 'use-client' directive to the top of the component file as shown next.

A Client Component that fetches data

```
'use client';
import { useState, useEffect } from 'react';

export default function MovieList() {
    const [movies, setMovies] = useState([]);
    const [error, setError] = useState(null);
    const [loadingAdd, setLoadingAdd] = useState(false); // for add button

    // use effect to asynchronously fetch data on component mount
    useEffect(() => {
        const fetchMovies = async () => {
            try {
                setError(null);

                const response = await fetch('http://localhost:2000/movies');
                if (!response.ok) {
                    throw new Error(`HTTP error! status: ${response.status}`);
                }

                const movies = await response.json();
                setMovies(movies);
            } catch (err) {
                setError(err.message || 'Something went wrong');
            }
        };

        fetchMovies();
    }, []);

    // event handler to add a new movie
    const addMovie = async () => {
```

```
        setError(null);
        setLoadingAdd(true);
        try {
            setMovies((prev) => [...prev, {
                id: prev.length + 1, name: 'Wicked', year: '2024'}]);
        } catch (err) {
            setError(err.message || 'Failed to add movie');
        } finally {
            setLoadingAdd(false);
        }
    }

    return (
        <main>
            <h1>Movies</h1>
            {/* Show error if there is one */}
            {error && <p className='error'>Error: {error}</p>}

            <ul>
                {/* Show loading message */}
                {!movies.length && !error &&
                    <li className='pulse'>Loading movies...</li>}

                {movies.map(movie => (
                    <li key={movie.id}>{movie.name} ({movie.year})</li>
                ))}
            </ul>

            {/* Show Add button after load complete
                Disable Add button during add action */}
            {movies.length > 0 && (
                <button onClick={addMovie} disabled={loadingAdd}>
                    {loadingAdd ? 'Adding...' : 'Add Movie'}
                </button>
            )}
        </main>
    );
}
```

This Client Component begins by importing two React hooks, useState and useEffect. Then, within the function for the component, the code sets up state for the movies variable, an error variable, and a loading variable for the Add Movie button.

The last two state variables are necessary because a Client Component can't use an error.js file or loading.js file like a Server Component can. Instead, it must handle its own errors and loading state. You could also add a state variable to determine whether the initial load has completed, but this code checks the length of the movies variable to determine that the initial load is complete.

Within the useEffect() function, the code fetches data from a web API. To do that, it defines and calls an asynchronous function named fetchMovies(). This is necessary because a Client Component can't call an asynchronous function from within an effect unless it defines that asynchronous function first.

To demonstrate interactivity, this Client Component defines an addMovie() event handler and an Add Movie button that you can use to add a movie to the list. Clicking this button updates the movies variable in state, which causes React to re-render the page on the client.

Finally, the JSX uses the state variables to conditionally render loading and error messages. Again, this is necessary because a Client Component must handle its own loading and error states.

As mentioned earlier, Client Components render as much HTML as possible on the server. In this case, Next.js renders all of the HTML for the page except the <li> elements and the button that depend on the movies and error state. As a result, the server returns the initial HTML for the following page.

The initial HTML for the page rendered by the server

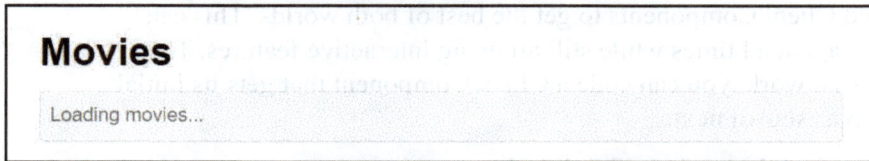

Movies

Loading movies...

After this page mounts, Next.js makes the page interactive by downloading the JavaScript bundle, running its code, and attaching its event handlers. In other words, it hydrates the page.

For this page, Next.js runs the effect that fetches the data for the movies and sets it in state. This change of state causes React to re-render the page so it displays the movies. In addition, Next.js attaches the event handler for the page. When it's done, the app displays the movies and the Add Movie button as shown next.

The page after it's hydrated on the client

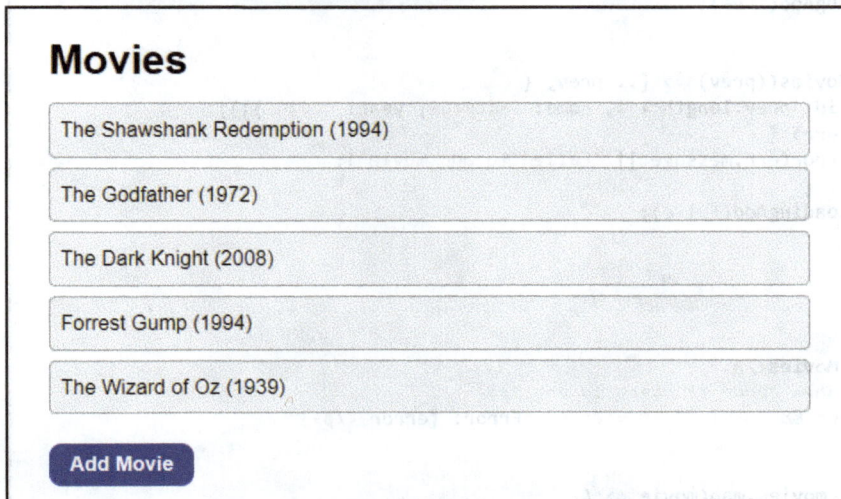

Movies

The Shawshank Redemption (1994)

The Godfather (1972)

The Dark Knight (2008)

Forrest Gump (1994)

The Wizard of Oz (1939)

Add Movie

Once Next.js hydrates a page, the user can click buttons, submit forms, and use all other interactive features.

If you want to view a page before it's hydrated, you can disable JavaScript in your browser. Then, Next.js still sends the initial HMTL to the browser. However, the browser can't run the JavaScript bundle. Because of that, the interactive features don't work and the client can't load any data. Then, when you want to hydrate the page, you can enable JavaScript in the browser and refresh the page. When you do, the interactive features should work and the browser can load data.

Use a hybrid approach

When working with Next.js, it's a common pattern to combine Server Components and Client Components to get the best of both worlds. This can optimize initial page load times while still allowing interactive features. To make this approach work, you can code a Client Component that gets its initial data from a prop as shown next.

A Client Component that gets initial data from a prop

```
'use client';
import { useState } from 'react';

export default function MovieListClient({ initialMovies }) {
    const [movies, setMovies] = useState(initialMovies);  // initialize with prop
    const [error, setError] = useState(null);
    const [loadingAdd, setLoadingAdd] = useState(false);  // for add button

    // event handler to add a new movie
    const addMovie = async() => {
        setError(null);
        setLoadingAdd(true);

        try {
            setMovies((prev) => [...prev, {
                id: prev.length + 1, name: 'Wicked', year: '2024'}]);
        } catch(err) {
            setError(err.message || 'Failed to add movie');
        } finally {
            setLoadingAdd(false);
        }
    }

    return (
        <main>
            <h1>Movies</h1>
            {/* Show error if there is one */}
            {error && <p className='error'>Error: {error}</p>}

            <ul>
                {movies.map(movie => (
                    <li key={movie.id}>{movie.name} ({movie.year})</li>
```

```
            ))}
        </ul>

        {/* Disable add button during add action */}
        <button onClick={addMovie} disabled={loadingAdd}>
            {loadingAdd ? 'Adding...' : 'Add Movie'}
        </button>
    </main>
    );
}
```

This creates a component named MovieListClient that works like the Client
Component shown previously. However, this component doesn't need to use an
effect to fetch data after it mounts. Instead, it gets that data from a prop. This
also means that it no longer needs to provide a loading message for the initial
load, or hide the Add Movie button while the page loads. However, it still uses
state to provide interactivity and to handle the loading and error states of that
interactivity.

To provide the initial data, you can code a Server Component that fetches the
data and passes it to the Client Component as shown next.

A Server Component that passes data to a Client Component

```
import MovieListClient from './MovieListClient';

export default async function MovieListServer() {
  // asynchronously fetch data from external API
  const response = await fetch('http://localhost:2000/movies',
    { cache: 'no-store' } // Always fetch fresh data
  );
  const movies = await response.json();

  // pass initial data to Client Component as prop
  return (
    <MovieListClient initialMovies={movies} />
  );
}
```

This component gets data like the Server Component shown previously. Then,
it passes that data to the MovieListClient component as a prop.

In this hybrid approach, Next.js uses the loading.js file to display loading
messages while it's rendering the initial HTML on the server. And, it uses the
error.js file to display messages for any errors that occur on initial load. Then, it
displays the complete page for the movie list.

After the initial load, the Client Component provides interactivity that lets the
user add a movie without requiring a page refresh. And, it handles the error and
loading states for when a movie is added.

This hybrid approach separates concerns more clearly. The Server Component
performs the asynchronous processing on the server, while the Client
Component provides the state and event handlers that make the app interactive.

Handle browser APIs

As mentioned earlier, Client Components render on the server and then on the client. This can cause issues because the server doesn't have access to browser APIs such as localStorage. For example, the following Client Component fails during server-side rendering because the localStorage object is only available on the client, not on the server.

A Client Component that fails during server-side rendering

```
'use client';
import { useState, useEffect } from 'react';

export default function Message() {
    // localStorage is not available on the server
    const storedMessage = localStorage.getItem('message');
    const [message, setMessage] = useState(storedMessage);
...
```

To fix this, you can use an effect to make sure that the code that accesses the localStorage object only runs on the client as shown in the next example.

A Client Component that renders on the server and the client

```
'use client';
import { useState, useEffect } from 'react';

export default function Message() {
    const [message, setMessage] = useState([]);

    useEffect(() => {
        // localStorage is available after mount
        const storedMessage = localStorage.getItem('message');
        setMessage(storedMessage)
    }, []);

    const sayHello = () => {
        // event handlers are attached after mount too
        localStorage.setItem('message', 'Hello!');
        setMessage('Hello!');
    }

    const clearMessage = () => {
        localStorage.setItem('message', '');
        setMessage('');
    }

    return (
        <main>
            <h2>{message || 'Message not found'}</h2>
            <button onClick={sayHello}>Say Hello</button>
            <button onClick={clearMessage}>Clear Message</button>
        </main>
    );
}
```

Here, the effect runs after the component has mounted. As a result, it can use the localStorage object. In this case, it gets a message from local storage and sets it in state.

Similarly, both event handlers are attached after the component has mounted. As a result, they can also use the localStorage object. In this case, they set a message in local storage and in state.

The Movie List app

To show how these skills work within the context of a larger app, the following headings show how to convert the Movie List app from chapter 6 to work with Next.js.

To users, the Next.js version looks a lot like the Vite version. However, the Next.js version uses server-side rendering to pass movie data to the app. As a result, it provides the user experience and SEO benefits of server-side rendering.

The directory structure for this app is shown next.

The directory structure

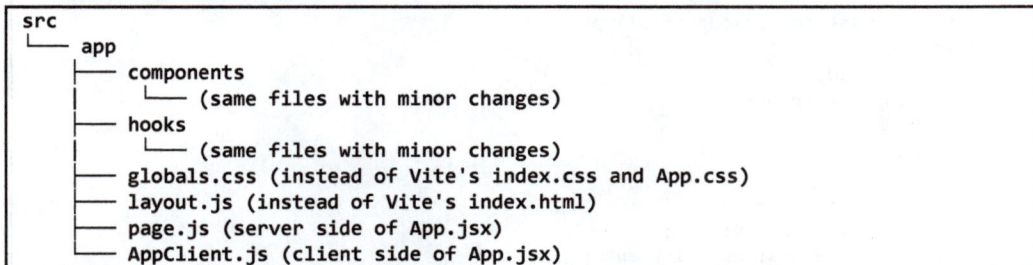

```
src
└── app
    ├── components
    │       └── (same files with minor changes)
    ├── hooks
    │       └── (same files with minor changes)
    ├── globals.css (instead of Vite's index.css and App.css)
    ├── layout.js (instead of Vite's index.html)
    ├── page.js (server side of App.jsx)
    └── AppClient.js (client side of App.jsx)
```

To create this directory structure, you can run the create-next-app package shown at the beginning of this chapter to create an app that includes standard Next.js files such as globals.css, layout.js, and page.js. Then, you can copy the components and hooks directories from the Movie List app from chapter 6 to the src/app directory. Next, you can add an AppClient.js file to the src/app directory. Finally, you can cut and paste code from the Vite app into the Next.js app as described later.

The global.css and layout.js files

The globals.css file provides the styles that apply to every page in the app. This centralized approach prevents multiple imports of the same resource and makes sure you use consistent styles across the app. This is especially important for apps that provide multiple pages as described later in this chapter.

For the Next.js version of the app, the global.css file starts by importing a URL that provides access to the Font Awesome icons that are used by the Vite version. Then, it imports styles from the index.css and App.css files used by the Vite version as shown next.

The globals.css file

```
/***************************
Import CSS URL from index.html (Vite)
***************************/
@import url(
'https://cdnjs.cloudflare.com/ajax/libs/font-awesome/6.4.0/css/all.min.css');

/***************************
Styles from index.css (Vite)
***************************/
/* reset styles */
* {
    margin: 0;
    padding: 0;
    box-sizing: border-box;
}
...

/***************************
Styles from App.css (Vite)
***************************/
/* custom classes for layout of all pages */
.container {
    display: grid;
    grid-template-areas:
        "header"
        "main"
        "aside"
        "footer";
    grid-template-columns: 1fr;
    grid-template-rows: auto 1fr auto;

    text-align: center;
    border: 1px solid var(--border-color);
    border-radius: 4px;
}
...
```

Although a Next.js app consolidates the CSS that's applied to all pages of the app, it still allows developers to provide CSS files for each component.

To convert the Vite app to a Next.js app, you need to convert the index.html and App.jsx files to layout.js and page.js files. To start, you can create a layout.js file like the one shown next.

The layout.js file

```javascript
import './globals.css';

import { join } from 'path';
import { readFile } from 'fs/promises';

import Header from './components/layout/Header';
import Footer from './components/layout/Footer';
import MovieQuotes from './components/movies/MovieQuotes';

export const metadata = {
  title: 'Movie List',
  description: 'An app that manages a collection of movies',
};

async function readMovieQuotes() {
  // read movie quotes from file in public directory
  let quotes = [];
  try {
    const file = join(process.cwd(), 'public', 'movie_quotes.json');
    const text = await readFile(file, 'utf8');
    quotes = JSON.parse(text);
  } catch (e) {
    quotes = [];
  }
  return quotes;
}

export default async function RootLayout({ children }) {
  const quotes = await readMovieQuotes();

  return (
    <html lang="en">
      <body>
        <div className="container">
          <Header text={metadata.title} />
          {children}
          <Footer text={metadata.title}>
            <MovieQuotes quotes={quotes} initialIndex={0} />
          </Footer>
        </div>
      </body>
    </html>
  );
}
```

This code provides the layout for all pages in the app. In this case, the Movie List app only provides one page. However, if your app provided multiple pages, the layout.js file would apply to all of them.

The layout component begins by importing the globals.css file. This makes the global styles available throughout the app, and it's the only place where global CSS can be imported in Next.js. In addition, the layout component imports other components that it needs such as the Header, Footer, and MovieQuotes components.

After the imports, the layout component creates a metadata object that sets the title and description for the app. Then, it defines an asynchronous function that reads an array of movie quotes from a file. This gets the movie quotes that are displayed within the Footer component. It's possible to use an asynchronous function here because the layout component is a Server Component.

After getting the array of movie quotes, the layout uses the Header and Footer components to set up the layout for the app. In addition, it displays the MovieQuotes component and passes the movies quotes to that component as a prop.

Because the MovieQuotes component uses state to store the index of the quote to display, it must be a Client Component as shown next. Otherwise, it works the same as the MovieQuotes component in the Vite app.

The MovieQuotes component

```
'use client';

import { useState } from 'react';
import { useTimer } from '../../hooks/useTimer';
import './MovieQuotes.css';

const MovieQuotes = ({ quotes }) => {
  const [index, setIndex] = useState(0);
...
```

The AppServer and AppClient components

The page.js file defines a Server Component that performs some server-side rendering before displaying the first and only page of the app. More specifically, this code defines a component named AppServer that fetches an array of movie objects from a web API.

The page.js file for the AppServer component

```
import AppClient from './AppClient';

// base URL for Movies API presented in chapter 6
const API_URL = 'http://localhost:2000';

export default async function AppServer() {
    let movies = [];
    const response = await fetch(`${API_URL}/movies`,
        { cache: 'no-store' });
    if (!response.ok) {
        throw new Error(`Failed to fetch movies: ${response.status}`);
    }
    movies = await response.json();

    // pass initial data to client component
    return (
        <AppClient initialMovies={movies} apiUrl={API_URL} />
    );
}
```

After fetching the movies data, the AppServer component passes this data as a prop to the AppClient component shown next.

The AppClient component (part 1)

```
'use client';

import { useState } from 'react';
import { useFetch } from '../../hooks/useFetch';

import Main from '../layout/Main';
import Sidebar from '../layout/Sidebar';
import MovieList from './MovieList';
import MovieForm from './MovieForm';

const AppClient = ({ initialMovies = [], apiUrl }) => {
  const [movies, setMovies] = useState(initialMovies);
  const [selectedMovie, setSelectedMovie] = useState(null);

  const { fetchData, createOptions, loading, error } = useFetch();

  // allow client to reload movies from the API if needed
  const loadMovies = async () => {
    const data = await fetchData(`${apiUrl}/movies`);
    if (data) setMovies(data);
  };

  // other event handlers
...
```

Since the AppClient component uses React's useState hook and the custom useFetch hook, it must be a Client Component. This allows the component to manage the state for movies, loading indicators, and error conditions using the same React hooks and patterns as the Vite app.

In summary, the Movie List app uses a Server Component to provide the movies for the initial page load, but it uses a Client Component to work with the movies after the initial page load. To make this work, the Server Component uses a loading.js page to display a loading indicator for the initial page load, and an error.js file to handle errors on initial page load.

After the initial page load, the Client Component displays the movies in the prop immediately and only shows the loading indicator if the Client Component fetches the data again. To do that, it uses the movies and loading state variables as shown next.

The AppClient component (part 2)

```
  return (
    <>
      <Main>
        {error && (
          <div className="error-message">
            {error} <button onClick={loadMovies}>Reload</button>
          </div>
```

```
    )}
    {/*
        Show movies fetched by server immediately.
        Show loading indicator for client fetch only.
    */}
    {loading && (!movies || movies.length === 0) ? (
      <p>Loading movies...</p>
    ) : (
      <MovieList
        movies={movies ?? []}
        onSelect={handleSelect}
        onReorder={handleReorder}
      />
    )}
  </Main>
  <Sidebar>
    <MovieForm
      selectedMovie={selectedMovie}
      onAdd={handleAdd}
      onEdit={handleEdit}
      onDelete={handleDelete}
      onCancel={handleCancel}
    />
  </Sidebar>
  </>
  );
};

export default AppClient;
```

Similarly, if the Server Component throws an error while fetching the data, Next.js handles the error by displaying the error.js page. However, if the Client Component throws an error, it uses the error state variable to handle the error.

Other Client Components and hooks

The rest of the components and hooks work the same as they do for the Vite version of the app. However, it's a good practice to mark any of the components or hooks that use React hooks with the 'use client' directive.

This isn't required for most of these components and hooks because they automatically become part of the client bundle when a Client Component imports them. As a result, MovieList, MovieForm, and useFetch become part of the client bundle when the AppClient component imports them. However, it's still a good practice to add the 'use client' directive to these components and hooks as shown next because it's more explicit and self-documenting.

The MovieForm component

```
'use client';
import { useState, useEffect, useRef } from 'react';
...
const MovieForm = ({ selectedMovie, onAdd, onEdit, onDelete, onCancel }) => {
    const [name, setName] = useState('');
...
```

Here, the MovieForm component must be a Client Component because it uses three React hooks. The 'use client' directive clearly indicates that this component is a Client Component.

The useDragAndDrop hook

```
'use client';
import { useRef } from "react";

export const useDragAndDrop = (onDrop) => {
...
```

In this example, the useDragAndDrop hook must be used within a Client Component because it uses the useRef hook. Again, the 'use client' directive clearly indicates that this hook can only be used in a Client Component.

How to create a single-page app

A *single-page app (SPA)* loads a single HTML page and uses JavaScript to dynamically update its content when the user clicks a link to navigate to another page. By contrast, a *multi-page app (MPA)* loads an entirely new page from the server each time the user navigates to another page. To make an SPA work, JavaScript takes control of the page and manages navigation. This is known as *client-side routing*, and it makes the user experience feel faster and more like an app.

If you want to use Next.js to create a single-page app (SPA), you can use App Router to do that. This chapter finishes by showing how to create a Next.js version of the demonstration My SPA app that was presented in chapter 8.

The My SPA app

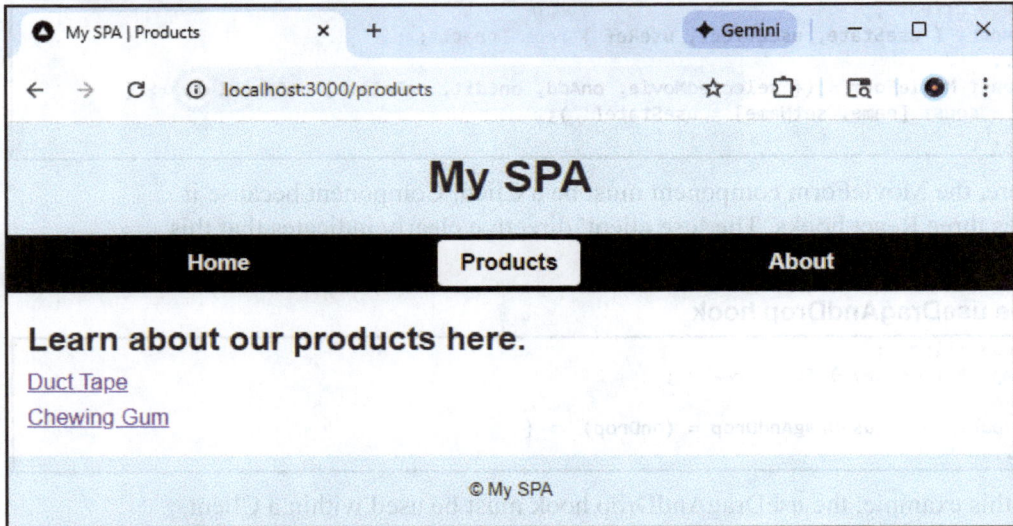

If you haven't already read chapter 8, here's a brief description of how this app works. To start, it uses the same layout for several pages. To navigate between these pages, it provides a navigation bar (navbar) that's displayed across the top of the app. When the app navigates from one page to another, the router updates the URL that's displayed in the browser. Here, the URL path has been updated to /products for the Products page. In addition, the app updates the title that's displayed in the browser tab. Here, the tab has been updated to "My SPA | Products".

Set up routing for pages

Since App Router uses file-based routing, you can add a page and its routing just by adding a directory with a page.js file. For example, you could use the following directory structure to add an About page that maps to the /about path and a Products page that maps to the /products path.

The directory structure for an SPA with three pages

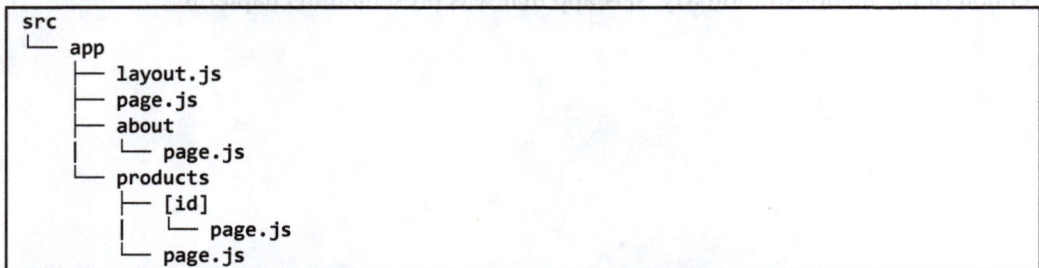

```
src
└── app
    ├── layout.js
    ├── page.js
    ├── about
    │   └── page.js
    └── products
        ├── [id]
        │   └── page.js
        └── page.js
```

In addition, you can put square brackets around a directory name to create a dynamic route. For instance, in the example above, the [id] directory allows the URL to pass an id parameter to a page as shown in the following table.

How URL paths map to page.js files

URL path	File
/	app/page.js
/about	app/about/page.js
/products	app/products/page.js
/products/1	app/products/[id]/page.js
/products/2	app/products/[id]/page.js

Here, /about and /products are *static routes* because they don't accept parameters. However, products/[id] is a *dynamic route* because it accepts a parameter. In this case, /products/1 and products/2 pass a parameter to the page in the /products/[id] directory. As a result, this page can get the id parameter from the URL as shown next.

A dynamic page that gets an id parameter

```
import { useProduct } from '../../hooks/useProduct.js';

// Next.js App Router passes dynamic segments via the params prop.
// In some versions, params can be a Promise, so await it.
export default async function Product({ params }) {
    const { id } = await params;
    const product = useProduct(id);

    return (
        <>
            {product ? (
                <>
                    <h2>{product.name}</h2>
                    <p>{product.description}</p>
                </>
            ) : (
                <h2>Product {id} not found</h2>
            )}
        </>
    );
};
```

Here, the Product page accepts a prop named params that contains all of the parameters that are in the URL. In this case, there's only one parameter, and it has a name of id. As a result, the code gets the id parameter from the params prop. To do that, it uses the await keyword to wait for the id. That's because some versions of App Router pass the params prop as a Promise.

After the page gets the id parameter, it uses that parameter to get the product object from the data store. Then, it displays that product, or it displays a message that indicates that the product wasn't found.

Set up specialized routes

Since each directory represents a route to a page, you can only have one page.js file per directory. However, you can include the following special files in the same directory as a page.js file.

Special files for routing in Next.js

File	Displays if...
loading.js	The page is still loading.
error.js	The page encounters a JavaScript error.
not-found.js	The page isn't found (instead of default 404 page).

Of these files, this chapter has already shown examples of the loading.js and error.js files. However, when you use these files in a SPA, their place in the routing system matters.

To apply a specialized file to a specific page, you can put it in the directory for that page. Then, Next.js applies the specialized file to that page and all pages in subdirectories of that page. For example, if you want to display a loading page for the Products page, you can put a loading.js file in the app/products directory. Then, Next.js displays that loading page for the Products and Product pages, but not for the Home or About pages.

Typically, you want the not-found.js page to apply to all pages. To do that, you can put it in the src/app directory. The following example shows a simple NotFound page.

A not-found.js file in the src/app directory

```
export default function NotFound() {
  return (
    <main>
        <h1>Page Not Found</h1>
        <p>Please check the URL and try again.</p>
    </main>
  )
}
```

Add a navbar to the app

To navigate between the pages in a SPA, it's common for an app to provide a navigation bar. Next.js provides a Link component and a usePathname hook that you can use to create a Navbar component like the one shown next.

A Navbar component

```
'use client';
import Link from 'next/link';
import { usePathname } from 'next/navigation';
import './Navbar.css';

const Navbar = () => {
    const pathname = usePathname();

    const isActive = (href, exact = false) => {
        if (exact && pathname === href)
            return 'active';
        if (pathname === href || pathname.startsWith(href + '/') )
            return 'active';
        return '';
    };

    return (
        <nav className="navbar">
            <div className="nav-menu">
                <Link href="/" className={isActive('/', true)}>
                    Home
                </Link>
                <Link href="/products" className={isActive('/products')} >
                    Products
                </Link>
                <Link href="/about" className={isActive('/about')} >
                    About
                </Link>
            </div>
        </nav>
    );
};

export default Navbar;
```

Here, the Link component provides a way to code links that use App Router to navigate to the different pages in the app. For example, the first Link component uses App Router to navigate to the Home page. This changes the content that's displayed on the page and the URL that's displayed in the browser.

The usePathname hook gets the current path from the URL and it automatically updates that path if the URL changes. This path doesn't include any query parameters or other data appended to the URL. Since usePathname is a hook, the component that uses it must be a Client Component.

Once you have the current path, you can use it to determine whether a link is active and set a CSS class for it. In this code, the isActive() function checks the current path. Then, if that path matches the href attribute of the Link component, the isActive() function returns a CSS class named active. Otherwise, it returns an empty string.

To make this work, the link for the Home page sets the exact parameter to true. As a result, this link only becomes active if the current path and the href attribute match exactly. In other words, this link only becomes active if they are both /. By contrast, the link for the Products page becomes active for /products as well as child paths such as /products/1 and /products/2.

Update the title for each route

When you use Next.js to create an SPA, you often want to improve SEO by setting the title for each page to reflect the content on the page. To do that for a static route, you can update the metadata for the page by editing its page.js file as shown next.

Update the title for a static route

```
export const metadata = {
    title: 'My SPA | Home'
};

export default function Home() {
    return (
        <h2>Welcome!</h2>
    );
}
```

Here, the code updates the title for the Home page by exporting a metadata object that has a new title that overrides the title in the metadata object from the layout.js file.

If a page uses a dynamic route, you can use the generateMetadata() function to override the metadata for the layout.js file. For example, to update the title in the metadata for the Product component presented earlier in this chapter, you can add the following function to its page.js file.

Update the title for a dynamic route

```
export async function generateMetadata({ params }) {
    const { id } = await params;
    const product = useProduct(id);

    // get name for selected product
    const name = product ? product.name : 'Product Not Found';

    return { title: 'My SPA | Products | ' + name };
}
```

This works because Next.js passes the parameters in the URL to the generateMetadata() function. As a result, the code can get the product object based on the id parameter. Then, it can set the title accordingly.

Perspective

This chapter has shown how to use Next.js to provide server-side rendering. This can help you build SEO-friendly apps that have excellent user experience (UX) on the initial page load. In addition, this chapter has shown how to get started with using Next.js for creating a single-page app (SPA).

These skills provide a solid foundation for getting started with Next.js. However, there's always more to learn. For example, you can use Next.js to create a web API like the Movies API presented in chapter 6.

Terms

server-side rendering (SSR)

client-side rendering (CSR)

JavaScript bundle

hydration

static site generation (SSG)

content delivery network (CDN)

router

Server Component

Client Component

user experience (UX)

skeleton screen

single-page app (SPA)

multi-page app (MPA)

client-side routing

static route

dynamic route

Exercise 14-1: Render on the server

Open an existing Vite app

1. Open the my-playlist folder in the ex_starts/ch14 folder.
2. Open the App.jsx file and review its code. Note that it contains code that simulates a network delay for loading the initial songs and displays a loading message while that's happening.
3. Run the app to see how it works. Refresh the page in the browser to review how the loading message works.

Start a new Next.js app

4. Start a second instance of VS Code.

5. Open the ex_solutions/ch14 folder and use the npx command to create a Next.js app named my-playlist.

6. Change the current directory to the my-playlist directory, start the development server, and use a browser to view the generated page for the app.

7. In the src/app folder, review the initial files for the app focusing on the globals.css, layout.js, and page.js files.

Convert the Vite app to a Next.js app

8. Copy the components folder from the Vite version to the Next.js version.

9. Delete the page.module.css file.

10. Open the globals.css file and delete all of the CSS that it contains.

11. Copy the CSS that's in the index.css file of the Vite version into the blank globals.css file.

12. At the top of the globals.css file, add code that imports the CSS library that's needed for the app to work with Font Awesome icons as shown in this chapter.

13. Copy the App.jsx and App.css files from the Vite version to the src/app folder in the Next.js version.

14. Rename App.jsx to AppClient.js, add a 'use client' directive to the top of the file, and update the component name and export statement.

15. Move any code that defines the overall layout of the page such as code that displays the Header and Footer components from the AppClient.js file to the layout.js file. Make sure to keep the <html> and <body> elements and the children prop in the layout.js file but delete any extra constants that aren't needed.

16. In the layout.js file, modify the metadata object to set an appropriate title and description.

17. Modify the page.js file so it uses an asynchronous function to define a component named AppServer. Then, delete all import statements and JSX for this file.

18. Move any code that should run on the server, such as the code that gets the initial data for the songs, from the AppClient component to the AppServer component. When you move this code, keep the code that simulates the network delay.

19. Modify the AppClient component to make it accept the initial song data as a prop. Then, use that prop to set the initial state of the playlist variable.

20. Modify the AppServer component so it imports the AppClient component and passes the initial songs as a prop.

21. In the src/app folder, add a file named loading.js. Then, move the code that displays the loading message from AppClient to the loading.js file.

22. In AppClient, make sure to delete all code that gets data and tracks the initial loading state. This should make the AppClient component shorter and simpler. Don't delete the loading state variable, though.

23. Run the app and test it to make sure it works correctly. When data is loading, it should display the "Loading" message that's defined in the loading.js page. When it's done loading, it should render all of the movies on the server and return HTML for the page to the browser.

Improve the loading page by providing a skeleton screen

24. Modify the loading.js file so it displays a <ul> element that's a placeholder for the playlist and four <li> elements that are placeholders for the songs.

25. Add CSS to the global.css file that styles the <ul> and <li> placeholder elements so they transition smoothly into the Playlist component. Use the songlist and song classes from the Playlist.css file as a guide.

26. Apply the CSS class named pulse that's in the global.css file to the <li> elements that are placeholders for the songs. This should provide a CSS animation that makes these elements pulse.

Add a loading message to the Client Component

27. In AppClient, change the initial value of the loading variable to false.

28. In handleAddSong(), add code that sets loading to true. This should be at the start of the function, before any other code.

29. Simulate a network delay of two seconds. For that to work, make handleAddSong() asynchronous.

30. Set loading back to false after the song is added.

31. In the JSX, add a <p> element that displays an 'Adding Song…' message while loading is true. Apply the pulse CSS class to the <p> element.

Index

DELETE method, 141, 145
dependency array, 116
   memoization, 289-292
describe(), 340-342, 353
destructuring, 46-47, 65
development dependencies, 330
DevTools (React), 164-167
diffing algorithm, 11
dispatch function, 248-249
DOM (virtual), 11
DOM interface
   compared to HTML, 312
domain entity, 318
DragEvent<> type, 310
dynamic route
   React, 190-192, 196
   Next.js, 385

E

eager initialization, 115
ECMAScript module, 47
edge case, 341
effect (opacity), 221
embed JavaScript in JSX, 62
endpoint, 140
entity, 318
error (type), 298-299
error page, 194-195
error.js file (Next.js), 370, 386
ES6 module, 47
event handler, 80-81
   issues, 169
event object types, 310
expect(), 336
export module, 47-48
extend a type, 308

F

feature scope, 262-263
Fetch API, 141
fetch() method, 141
   caching, 369
filter an array, 44-45
filter() function, 42
fireEvent object, 348-349
first-class citizen, 35
flame graph (DevTools), 167
flex classes (Tailwind), 230
font classes (Tailwind), 218
font weight, 217

FormEvent<> type, 310
fragment, 56
fulfilled state (Promise), 142
function initializer, 114-115
function type, 306-307
functional programming, 34-37

G

gap classes (Tailwind), 228
generateMetadata(), 387
generic type, 310
   custom, 313-314
GET method, 141-143
getByAllRole(), 334-345
getByLabelText(), 334
getByRole(), 334-345
getByText(), 334
global scope, 262
global.css (Next.js), 366
grid classes (Tailwind), 227

H

h classes (Tailwind), 224
happy path, 341
History API (browser), 180
hook, 80, 110-113
   conventions, 123
   custom, 122-126
   rules, 111-112
hover classes (Tailwind), 226
HTML
   compared to DOM interface, 312
HTML attributes
   compared to JSX attributes, 60
HTTP methods, 141
hybrid approach (Next.js), 374
hybrid component, 87
hydration, 362

I

identity-obj-proxy, 331
immutable methods, 42-43
immutable parameter, 39
imperative code, 6
import module, 47-48
improper
   hook usage, 172-173
   key usage, 167-168
infinite re-render loop, 171

no-italic class (Tailwind), 220
not-found.js (Next.js), 386
no-underline class (Tailwind), 220
npm, 13
    create, 15
    install, 16
    list, 15
    run dev, 16
    test, 334
    test (group), 353
    test (single), 344
npx, 364
    tsc, 299
number utilities (Tailwind), 223

O

object
    destructuring, 65
    property syntax, 40
    type, 300
    update, 39-40
object-level union, 304
Omit utility type, 309
opacity class (Tailwind), 221
open-ended prop, 67-69
optional prop, 66, 302
override props, 68

P

p classes (Tailwind), 225
page.js file (Next.js), 367
payload (reducer), 247
pending state (Promise), 142
Pick utility type, 309-310
pipe symbol, 302
plain CSS, 212
plain JavaScript app, 4
POST method, 141, 144-145
presentational component, 87
Profiler tab (DevTools), 167
Promise object, 142
prop, 28, 46, 65-69
    drilling, 99
prop type,
    alias, 301-302
    interface, 301
property name syntax, 40
pure function, 36-38, 115
PUT method, 141, 145, 146

Q

queryByText(), 334
querySelector(), 346
querySelectorAll(), 346

R

React component, 5
React Developer Tools, 164-167
React DevTools, 164-167
React fragment, 56
React Router, 183-186
React Testing Library, 328, 342-351
ReactElement, 304
ReactNode, 304
react-router-dom, 183
react-ts template, 297
reduce an array, 45-46
reduce() function, 42
reducer (state), 247-252
reducer function (useReducer), 248
ref attribute, 120
reference type, 39
referential equality check, 277
rejected state (Promise), 142
rendering cycle, 110
representational state transfer, 140
responsive design (Tailwind), 232
REST, 140
rest operator, 67
RESTful API, 140
role (element), 345
rounded classes (Tailwind), 222
Route component, 184
route parameter, 190
route title, 186
router, 363
routes array, 186
Routes component, 184
row classes (Tailwind), 228
Rules of Hooks, 111-112
run development web server, 16

S

save-dev parameter, 330
scaffold an app, 15
separation of concerns, 5
Server Component (Next.js), 367
server-side rendering, 362-364
setupTests.js, 332
shallow, 310

V

vanilla JavaScript app, 4
virtual DOM, 11
Visual Studio Code, *see VS Code*
Vite, 15
    starter app, 17-19
vite-env.d.json, 297
VS Code
    install, 12
    Jest extension, 355
    start second instance, 147

WXYZ

w classes (Tailwind), 223
web API, 140-142
wildcard route, 195
xl class (Tailwind), 232
YAGNI principle, 59

Murach also has books on these subjects:

AI-assisted programming
AI-Assisted Programming with Copilot

Web development
HTML and CSS
Modern JavaScript
JavaScript and jQuery
PHP and MySQL
ASP.NET Core MVC

Programming languages
Python
Java
C#
C++

Databases
MySQL
SQL Server
Oracle

Data science
Python for Data Science
R for Data Analysis

For more on Murach Books,
please visit us at www.murach.com.

100% Guarantee

When you order directly from us, you must be satisfied. Try our books for 30 days or our eBooks for 14 days. They must work better than any other programming training you've ever used, or you can return them for a prompt refund. No questions asked!

Mike Murach, Publisher

Ben Murach, President

We want to hear from you

Do you have any comments, questions, or compliments to pass on to us? It would be great to hear from you! Please share your feedback in whatever way works best.

Email: murachbooks@murach.com

Phone: 1-800-221-5528 (Weekdays, 8 am to 4 pm Pacific Time)

Facebook: facebook.com/murachbooks

Instagram: instagram.com/murachbooks

LinkedIn: linkedin.com/company/mike-murach-&-associates

What software you need for this book

- **VS Code.** This book shows how to use VS Code to develop React apps because it's an excellent IDE that you can use to write the HTML, CSS, and JavaScript that's needed by React apps. In addition, VS Code provides an integrated terminal that provides access to the command line.
- **Node.js.** This book shows how to use Node.js to install most of the packages required for React development. In addition, it shows how to use Node.js to run a web API that provides the data for a React app.

This software can all be downloaded from the internet for free.

How to download the files for this book

1. Go to www.murach.com.
2. Navigate to the page for *React*.
3. Scroll down to the "FREE downloads" tab and click it.
4. Click the Download Now button for the zip file. This should download a zip file.
5. Double-click the zip file to extract the files for this book into a folder named react.

For more details, please see chapter 1.

What the download includes

- The apps presented in this book
- The starting points for the exercises at the end of each chapter
- The solutions to those exercises